WAR CRIMES LAW COMES OF AGE

War Crimes Law
Comes of Age

Essays

THEODOR MERON
Charles L. Denison Professor of Law,
New York University

OXFORD
UNIVERSITY PRESS

OXFORD

UNIVERSITY PRESS

Great Clarendon Street, Oxford OX2 6DP

Oxford University Press is a department of the University of Oxford.
It furthers the University's objective of excellence in research, scholarship,
and education by publishing worldwide in

Oxford New York

Athens Auckland Bangkok Bogotá Buenos Aires Calcutta
Cape Town Chennai Dar es Salaam Delhi Florence Hong Kong Istanbul
Karachi Kuala Lumpur Madrid Melbourne Mexico City Mumbai
Nairobi Paris São Paulo Singapore Taipei Tokyo Toronto Warsaw

and associated companies in Berlin Ibadan

Oxford is a registered trade mark of Oxford University Press
in the UK and in certain other countries

Published in the United States
by Oxford University Press Inc., New York

British Library Cataloguing in Publication Data

Data available

Library of Congress Cataloging in Publication Data
Meron, Theodor, 1930–
War crimes law comes of age: essays/Theodor Meron.
p. cm.
Includes bibliographical references.
K5301.M47 1998
341.6'9–dc21 98—42948
ISBN 0–19–826856–4

3 5 7 9 10 8 6 4 2

Printed in Great Britain
on acid-free paper by
Biddles Ltd., Guildford and King's Lynn

To my sons,
Dan and Amos

Contents

Preface

Developing international humanitarian law and enhancing its effectiveness by promoting individual criminal responsibility for people who commit serious violations of its norms have been at the focus of my concerns for a number of years. This volume reprints, in largely unedited form, several of my essays from various publications, as well as two chapters from my Clarendon books: 'Medieval and Renaissance Ordinances of War: Codifying Discipline and Humanity' is taken from *Henry's Wars and Shakespeare's Laws* (1993); 'Geneva Conventions as Customary Law' draws on *Human Rights and Humanitarian Norms as Customary Law* (1989).

A collection of essays inevitably lacks the unity and the coherence of a monograph. However, a picture of the historical evolution of international humanitarian and criminal law, slow at first, but dramatic since the beginning of the atrocities in the former Yugoslavia and Rwanda, somewhat compensates for this failure.

I greatefully acknowledge the permission extended by the following publishers to reprint essays from the indicated publications:

American Journal of International Law: *Shakespeare's Henry the Fifth and the Law of War; Common Rights of Mankind in Gentili, Grotius and Suàrez; Rape as a Crime Under International Humanitarian Law; The Time has Come for the United States to Ratify Geneva Protocol I; International Criminalization of Internal Atrocities; The Continuing Role of Custom in the Formation of International Humanitarian Law; Crimes and Accountability in Shakespeare; Classification of Armed Conflict in the Former Yugoslavia: Nicaragua's Fallout; War Crimes Law Comes of Age.*

Columbia Journal of Transnational Law: *Francis Lieber's Code and Principles of Humanity.*

Foreign Affairs: *The Case for War Crimes Trials in Yugoslavia*, reprinted by permission of FOREIGN AFFAIRS, Vol. 72, No. 3, 1993. Copyright 1993 by the Council on Foreign Relations, Inc.; *Answering for War Crimes: Lessons from the Balkans*, reprinted by permission of FOREIGN AFFAIRS, Vol. 76, No. 1, 1997. Copyright 1997 by the Council on Foreign Relations, Inc.

Military Law Review: *From Nuremberg to the Hague*, reprinted by permission of the Military Law Review, from Department of the Army Pamphlet 27–100–149, Summer 1995, at 107.

Israel Yearbook on Human Rights: *The Normative Impact on International Law of the International Tribunal for Former Yugoslavia.*

Asbjørn Eide and Scandinavian University Press: *Deportation of Civilians as a War Crime Under Customary Law*; reprinted from Broadening the Frontiers of Human Rights: Essays in Honour of Asbjørn Eide 201 (Donna Gomien ed. 1993).

I

Medieval and Renaissance Ordinances of War: Codifying Discipline and Humanity

Medieval ordinances of war were issued either by kings for the campaigns in which they happened to be engaged, or by commanders-in-chief in accordance with the authority granted to them in their commissions from their kings. The ordinances were not promulgated in a void. On many questions they restated the customary *jus armorum*, as transmitted orally between heralds and other experts, as described by such writers as Honoré Bouvet, Giovanni da Legnano, and Christine de Pisan, and as applied by the courts. Several of the ordinances, as I shall show, mentioned customary law as a residuary source to be applied in cases for which explicit provision was not made.

Offenders were judged in the court of the Lord High Constable and the Lord Marshal, in lower courts of constables and marshals, and, in much later periods, in courts martial. In cases of great importance, prominent defenders were tried before the Parliament.[1]

This essay explores in greater detail the development, from the beginning of the thirteenth century until the death of Hugo Grotius (1645), of those provisions of some ordinances of war which went beyond purely disciplinary or tactical matters, or such matters as the division of ransom and spoils of war. Of course, such disciplinary orders as were directly relevant to the protection of the population and the treatment of prisoners will be considered. I shall focus on the protective provisions of the ordinances, norms that articulated principles of humanity, and other rules that shaped the evolving law of war, leaving aside jurisdictional provisions. Not surprisingly, in later ordinances the balance shifted in some measure from discipline to humanity.

Prior to the nineteenth century, law of war matters were governed by either national ordinances or bilateral treaties. Indeed, national ordinances were the principal means for developing and codifying the law of war. The first multilateral agreement was the (first) Geneva Convention

---

[1] Francis Grose, *Military Antiquities* 52–7 (vol ii, 1788).

for the Amelioration of the Condition of the Wounded in Armies in the Field of 22 August 1864.[2]

John's 'Constitutions to be Made in the Army of our Lord the King' (1214) ordered marshals to ensure that the army paid the full value of supplies found in churches and church yards, where in time of war peasants found shelter for themselves, their belongings, and cattle. Peasants and their families would thus benefit from the immunity of the Church: 'if it should be found necessary to take any thing from the churches or church yards, for the wants of the army, the superintendants of the churches shall remain there, in order that those things which the army may want, shall be exposed to sale, and that before they are removed they may be paid its value.'[3]

Of greater importance were the Ordinances of War made by Richard II at Durham (1385).[4] These ordinances prohibited robbery and pillage,[5] especially from the Church, as well as the killing or capture of unarmed persons belonging to the Church and of unarmed women. The touching of the pyx was prohibited and capital punishment imposed on the offender. The Ordinances proscribed the rape of women and stipulated that offenders were to be punished by hanging.[6]

Although Henry V's Ordinances of War[7] (Mantes, July 1419) were issued four years after Harfleur and Agincourt, these were not the first ordinances that Henry promulgated after landing in France. Henry's Mantes Ordinances drew on those of Richard II, especially in the provisions protecting women from rape, and unarmed women and unarmed persons belonging to the Church from capture. The killing of persons belonging to the Church and pillage of churches were prohibited.[8]

Addressing the approaching execution of a soldier for having robbed a church, Shakespeare's Henry declared: 'We would have all such offenders so cut off, and we here give express charge that in our marches through the country there be nothing compelled from the villages,

---

[2] 22 Stat. 940, 1 Bevans 7, 22 Stat. 940, 55 BFSP 43 (1864–5). See generally Howard S. Levie, *Documents on Prisoners of War*, Naval War College, International Law Studies, 60 (1979), 5–44.

[3] Grose, *supra* note 1, at 57–8.

[4] The French text of these Ordinances is given in *The Black Book of Admiralty*, repr. in Travers Twiss (ed.), Monumenta Juridica, i (1871), 453. I shall cite the English translation by Francis Grose: Grose, *supra* note 1, at 60.

[5] 'VII. Item, that no one be so hardy as to rob or pillage another of money, victuals, provisions, forage or any other thing, on pain of losing his head; nor shall any one take any victuals, merchandise, or any other thing whatsoever, brought for the refreshment of the army, under the same penalty.' Grose, *supra* note 1, at 61.

[6] 'III. Item, that none be so hardy as to rob and pillage the church, nor to destroy any man belonging to holy church, religious or otherwise, nor any woman, nor to take them prisoners, if not bearing arms; nor to force any woman, upon pain of being hanged.' Ibid., 60.

[7] *Black Book of Admiralty, supra* note 4, at 459. See also Samuel Bentley (ed.), *Excerpta Historica* (1831), 30; Grose, *supra* note 1, at 66.

[8] *Black Book of Admiralty, supra* note 4, at sec. 3.

nothing taken but paid for, none of the French upbraided or abused in disdainful language' (*Henry V*, iii. vi. 108–12). Consistent with Henry's reaction to the stealing of the pyx, an explicit provision prohibited the touching of the box in which the sacrament was kept.[9] Following Richard's example, Henry prohibited robbing merchants of their goods, and particularly to secure provisions for the army.[10]

In several respects, however, Henry's Mantes Ordinances were more protective of the population than Richard's Durham Ordinances. The ordinances prohibited entering a place where a woman was lying in, as well as robbing her.[11] Peasants involved in the cultivation of the soil and their work animals were protected from capture or harassment.[12] Importantly, burning or torching property – a practice extensively employed by Henry and other military commanders – without king's orders was prohibited.[13] The typical penalty for violation was death.

Another rule proscribed the capture of children below the age of 14, with the exception of the children of lords, captains or other persons of rank.[14] While the prohibitory portion of this provision had obvious humanitarian aspects, the exception was grounded in the expectation that handsome ransoms would be paid for the children's liberation.

That Henry was both sincere in attempting to enforce fully his ordinances and aware that his soldiers breached them is demonstrated by the orders he issued on 25 April 1421 to the captain of Rouen (similar orders were issued to other captains). Those orders stated or restated certain restrictions, and imposed severe punishments for violations.[15] In issuing these orders, it is likely that Henry was moved not only by the desire to maintain order and discipline, and to pacify the population of occupied Normandy, but also by the humanitarian consideration of protecting the peaceful population. The preamble explained the need for the measure:

> Whereas many captains of towns, and fortresses, and their lieutenants in the dutchy [*sic*] of Normandy, usurp greater powers than the king has invested them with, or than is proper, oppressing and plundering his subjects, both of money and provisions, and committing divers enormities and excesses, and permitting the same to their soldiers.[16]

One of the new provisions prohibited the captains from exacting any grain or cattle from the inhabitants.[17] To address the possibility that the captains and soldiers 'in future plead ignorance of these matters [the king ordered that] certain inclosed articles ... be publicly proclaimed [and that the captains and lieutenants] do not, by any means, usurp or

---

[9] Ibid., sec. 2.   [10] Ibid., sec. 8.   [11] Ibid., sec. 29.   [12] Ibid., sec. 33.
[13] Ibid., sec. 37.   [14] Ibid., sec. 28.   [15] Grose, *supra* note 1, at 79.
[16] Ibid. 79–80.   [17] Ibid. 80.

encroach on the ordinary jurisdiction belonging to his bayliffs and other justices.'[18]

Henry did not take it for granted that his officers and soldiers would abide by these orders any more than those he had issued in the past. Determined to persevere in his attempts to enforce discipline and the protective rules which it encompassed, on 5 May 1421 Henry issued a commission of enquiry to Sir John Radcliff, instructing him to visit towns, castles, and fortresses to investigate 'the discipline and government [of Henry's officers] relative to ... the safe keeping and wholesome government of the towns ... assigned to them'.[19] Radcliff was instructed to learn, in particular, how the officers and soldiers 'behave ... to the ... people'.[20]

Given the failure of his earlier attempts, Henry's scepticism about the prospects for compliance was mirrored in the language of his mandate to Radcliff

> particularly to enquire respecting extortions, pillagings, robberies, impositions, appaticisements [money paid by the inhabitants to obtain the protection of their towns from the ravages of war], and other undue actions, by them as it is said, done, and perpetrated; and whether the said captains, *etc. etc.* have done, or attempted any thing, contrary to the king's admonitions, prohibitions, ordonnances, and mandates, so *repeatedly directed to them*; and also, many times proclaimed by the bailiffs.[21]

By the time Henry died on 31 August 1422 at the age of 35, a tired warrior, whose health suffered irreparable damage through the hardship of his campaigns (especially the siege of Meaux), his daunting task of establishing discipline and through it a modicum of protection for the inhabitants remained largely unaccomplished. His sincerity of purpose should not be questioned, however. Only Charles VII – among all contemporary princes – took steps to limit the excesses of soldiery comparable to Henry's efforts.

During the reign of Henry VI, John Talbot, Earl of Shrewsbury promulgated ordinances (*c.*1425) designed to govern the conduct of the army under his command.[22] The ordinances prohibited pillage and the taking of prisoners in pacified territories ('countre appatised'),[23] as well as destruction of fruit trees and vineyards.[24] They also extended particular protection to the Church.[25]

Perhaps the most comprehensive and impressive royal ordinance aimed at preventing the abuses of the soldiery and protecting the population was that issued by Charles VII at Orléans on 2 November 1439, to

---

[18] Grose, *supra* note 1, at 81.   [19] Ibid.   [20] Ibid. 81–2.
[21] Ibid. 82 (emphasis added).   [22] *Excerpta Historica, supra* note 7, at 28, 40.
[23] Ibid. 40.   [24] Ibid. 41.   [25] Ibid. 42.

Prevent Pillage and Abuses by Soldiers ('Lettres de Charles VII, pour obvier aux pilleries & vexations des Gens de guerre').[26] Charles's goal was to abolish the free companies and establish the core of a regular army. As the editors' preface emphasized, most of the companies – raised by their captains without the permission of the king – 'were not so much concerned with the defence of France as with its devastation'.[27] Charles ordered the abolition of the companies and directed that in the future only he would appoint captains and that only those captains would be able to raise a certain number of men-at-arms and archers, for whom they would be accountable. Both raising and leading of soldiers without Charles's written authorization were forbidden. Lords who had soldiers in their castles were to be accountable for them and obliged to pay for their upkeep. These lords were not, however, permitted to use this as a 'pretext'[28] to impose exactions on their lands or to appropriate a part of the taxes levied by Charles on his subjects with the consent of the three estates to finance the war.[29]

The goal of the ordinance, as defined in the preamble, was to prevent the 'great abuses and the pillage committed by soldiers [which Charles had no intention of tolerating any longer and which resulted] in poverty, oppression, and destruction suffered by his people'.[30] Invoking the threat of the supreme penalty of *lèse-majesté*, Charles prohibited plundering, imprisoning, or ransoming people in their homes or on the highways.[31] The seizure of merchants' and farmers' animals, carts, and tools was prohibited, as was molesting merchants and peasants.[32] Farmers, craftsmen, and others were to be allowed to work in peace; neither they nor their tools could be captured or ransomed.[33] Cattle were not to be seized

---

[26] *Ordonnances des rois de France de la troisième race*, ed. Louis Guillaume de Vilevault and Louis G. O. F. de Bréquigny (1782), xiii. 306.

[27] Ibid., Preface, p. xxvii (my own translation).

[28] Ibid.   [29] Ibid.   [30] Ibid., Preamble.

[31] '6. *Item*. The King orders captains, soldiers and all others, subject to the penalties attached to the crime of *lèse-majesté* – i.e. loss of all honours and public offices and of all rights, primarily those pertaining to nobility, for the offender himself and his descendants, and confiscation of his property – not to plunder or rob nor permit anyone to plunder or rob in any way churchmen, noblemen, merchants, farmers, or others on the highways or roads, in their dwellings or elsewhere, nor to take them away, imprison them, or ransom them, but instead, subject to the said penalty, to let them go and pass and stay in their houses and dwellings and elsewhere safely and securely.' Ibid.

[32] '7. *Item*. The King orders all captains and soldiers not to take nor stop any merchants, farmers, oxen or horses, or other animals used for drawing a plough or a carriage, or any carriage or cart drivers or their carriages or the goods they carry, nor to ransom them in any way, but to let them plough and drive and carry their goods peacefully and safely, without asking them anything and without stopping or disturbing them.' Ibid.

[33] '15. *Item*. The King orders all captains and soldiers to let farmers plough and craftsmen and other people work, whatever their trade, without disturbing them in any way and without capturing and ransoming them or their tools or ordering or allowing anyone to do so.' Ibid.

or ransomed.[34] Destruction of corn, wine, and food supplies and the breaking of the vessels in which they were stored was prohibited.[35] The ordinance further barred cutting corn, destroying cornfields, vines, or fruit-trees, or extorting ransom for corn, grapes, and fruit, either before or after the harvest.[36] Burning tools, appliances, winepresses and other property was proscribed, as were burning or destroying of houses.[37] This provision was of obvious importance because burning and destruction of property was frequently used by soldiers to extort payments from a reluctant population.

Aware of the difficulties inevitably facing enforcement of such provisions, especially when the offenders were powerful and the King's justice weak, Charles included in the ordinance elaborate jurisdictional and penal provisions.[38] Not only were persons who robbed travellers or attacked people in their houses to be severely punished, but all law enforcement officers and all noblemen were ordered to fight the offenders as if they were enemies, capture them, and bring them to justice. The ordinance established incentives as well as punishments: the offenders' horses and any other belongings with them at the time of capture would thus become the property of the captor. The latter would not be held responsible for the death of any offenders killed during capture.[39]

---

[34] *Ordonnances des rois de France, supra* note 26, Item 8.
[35] Ibid., Item 9.
[36] Ibid., Items 10–12.
[37] Ibid., Items 13–14.
[38] '20. *Item.* The King orders that the present and future members of his Parliament, his accountants, treasurers, bailiffs, *sénéchaux*, judges, provosts, lawyers, prosecutors, investigators, and all other law officers of his Kingdom, implement and enforce this Law and Ordinance and ensure its strict implementation by punishing the offenders without fail, according to this Law and Ordinance.

21. Item. Furthermore, he orders that they investigate all abuses and offences committed by soldiers in … areas under their jurisdiction, in violation of this Law and Ordinance, and punish the offenders; if, however, they cannot carry out the punishment because the offenders are so powerful, owing to the lords' support or otherwise, they should proceed expeditiously with the adjournments, trials, sentences, judgments and statements against the offenders as reasonably required, and bring them immediately before the King or the Parliament Court to stand trial as reasonably required, and the King shall promptly ensure the enforcement of the said awards, judgments and statements, as required. …

25. Moreover, since the above mentioned robberies, pillage, ransoming, and other misdeeds are often committed in places or on roads where it is impossible to get prompt judicial assistance or to call on captains for help, the King wishes and orders that the wounded be able to turn to justice and otherwise mobilize men-at-arms against the offenders in order to forcibly take them and bring them to justice; and if any such offender is killed, the King shall pardon the man who has done the killing and orders that no questions be asked from him, that the law officers of his kingdom do not allow any lawsuit to be initiated against him and that he should be deemed to have acted well.' Ibid.

[39] '16. … the King orders all *sénéchaux*, bailiffs, provosts and other law enforcement officers of his Kingdom and all noblemen and others, as soon as they know that such robbers,

The ordinance established the principle that a captain was responsible for offences committed by his subordinates. Offences were to be attributed to a captain if he did not bring the offender to justice.[40] Soldiers and others present during the commission of offences who did not prevent or resist abuses, such as robberies, or denounce them to the judicial authorities 'shall be held responsible for the offence as accessories to it and shall be punished in the same manner as the offenders'.[41]

The Statutes and Custom of the Marches (frontier) in Time of War (Statutis and Use of Merchis in Tym of Were),[42] adopted during the reign of James II of Scotland by Earl William of Douglas (1448) dealt primarily with tactical questions, with rights to prisoners and to ransom. More significantly, the statutes relied on custom as a source of law and as a rule of decision. The statutes were adopted after an assembly of lords and freeholders testified about the statutes, ordinances, and customs that had been used on the Marches in the days of Archibald the Grim, the third Earl of Douglas.[43] Not only did several articles of the statute explicitly mention the custom of the Marches as a basis of a particular rule, but the ultimate article reco͏ gͫ͏zeͫ' custom as a residuary source supplying the warden and his advisers with a rule of decision for cases not explicitly addressed:

> Item. It is ordained th.... all other things that are not now put in writing which are matters of war used before in time of warfare shall be ruled by the warden and his council and by the eldest and most worthy borderers that best know of the old custom of the Marches, in all times to come.

The Statutes and Ordinances for the Warre issued by Henry VIII (1544)[44] were more detailed than those of Henry V, but drew heavily on Henry's

---

looters and highwaymen are in the country, to fight them with a group of men-at-arms or otherwise, as they would fight enemies, and capture them and bring them to justice; and the King shall give to those who capture them their horses, harnesses, and other things they may carry with them and all their spoils; the King wishes and orders that, if any of these offenders is killed during the fight or during his capture, the person who did the killing should not be blamed but instead praised for his action and should not be prosecuted in any way.' Ibid.

[40] '18. *Item*. The King orders that each captain or lieutenant be held responsible for the abuses, ills, and offences committed by members of his company, and that as soon as he receives any complaint concerning any such misdeed or abuse, he bring the offender to justice so that the said offender be punished in a manner commensurate with his offence, according to these Ordinances. If he fails to do so or covers up the misdeed or delays taking action, or if, because of his negligence or otherwise, the offender escapes and thus evades punishment, the captain shall be deemed responsible for the offence as if he had committed it himself and shall be punished in the same way as the offender would have been.' Ibid.

[41] Ibid., Item 19.

[42] 1 Acts of the Parliaments of Scotland 350 (App. IV) (1844). I am grateful to Mr C. C. Kidd of All Souls College for translating for me the text of these statutes from Scottish.

[43] Ranald Nicholson, *Scotland: The Later Middle Ages* (1974), 346. See also the preamble to the Statute, *supra* note 42.

[44] Grose, *supra* note 1, at 85.

Mantes text with regard to several matters important to the development of rules of war. The desecration of the sacrament or the pyx, and the seizure of provisions and other goods from any person having proper papers, without the agreement of senior officers, were both prohibited.[45] An important provision ordered officers to pay soldiers' wages regularly.[46] Because non-payment of wages often triggered pillage and other abuses, this order took on added significance.

Robbery of merchants bringing provisions for the troops was again proscribed.[47] The burning, without an order issued by the King or his 'head officer', of towns or houses was forbidden, 'except the king's ennemies be within it, and cannot be otherwise taken'.[48] Except when authorized by senior officers, the taking of horses or oxen from peasants was forbidden, and the death penalty was to be imposed on offenders.[49] In a territory which freely surrendered to the King's obedience or otherwise came under his authority, robbery, pillage and capture of prisoners was proscribed 'upon peyne of death'.[50] Following the Mantes text, special protection was extended to women lying in and their belongings,[51] and the capture of children below the age of 14 was prohibited (again with the exception of children of lords, captains, and rich men).[52]

The 1639 Lawes and Ordinances of Warre, for the Better Government of his Majesties Army Royall, in the Present Expedition for the Northern Parts, and Safety of the Kingdome, under the Conduct of ... Thomas Earl of Arundel and Surrey[53] restated several of the provisions contained in earlier ordinances of war, such as the prohibition of rape, burning of houses,[54] or pillage of merchants and others.[55] A particularly clear and categorical provision was designed to protect the population of a territory under the King's obedience.[56] In the absence of explicit articles relevant to cases that might arise in the future, and until additional written orders were issued by the Lord General, this ordinance stipulated that resort should be made to the residuary source of 'ancient course of marshall discipline'.[57]

The laws and ordinances of war issued by the Earl of Northumberland for the army of Charles I in 1640, Lawes and Ordinances of Warre

---

[45] Grose, *supra* note 1, at 86, art. II.   [46] Ibid. 88, art. VII.   [47] Ibid. 92, art. XVI.
[48] Ibid. 97, art. XXXI.   [49] Ibid. 98, art. XXXIV.   [50] Ibid. 98, art. XXXV.
[51] Ibid. 105, art. LII.   [52] Ibid. 105, art. LIII.
[53] Charles M. Clode, *The Military Forces of the Crown* (1869), 429.
[54] Ibid. 431.   [55] Ibid. 436.
[56] Ibid. 434: 'No companies of souldiers, either of horse or foot, in their marching, retreating or enquartering in or thorow any townes or countries within the allegiance of the King, shall doe hurt, spoile, or injurie unto the persons or goods of the inhabitants, upon pain of death, or other such grievous punishment as the qualitie of the offence shall have demerited.'
[57] Ibid. 439.

Established for the Better Conduct of the Service in the Northern Parts',[58] reiterated a number of provisions that appeared in earlier codes but, importantly, added several new rules. The first category included the prohibitions of desecrating churches and religious objects, of rape, robbery, and murder, and of injuring farmers or seizing their horses, cattle, or goods. Soldiers were forbidden to cut down trees, burn – without orders – houses and barns, or destroy ships, boats, and carriages which might be useful for the army, even 'in the enemies countrey'.[59] They were ordered to pay the normal value of requisitioned food.

The most important innovation was the explicit guarantee of the right to quarter: 'None shall kill an enemy who yeelds and throws down his arms, upon pain of death.'[60] Although the right to be granted quarter was recognized by the customary *jus armorum*, and by some scholars, it was not stated in English ordinances of war at the time of Agincourt. Northumberland recognized and declared the principle in a written ordinance of war, and prescribed the death penalty for violations. Finally, the ordinance recognized the role of customary law as a residuary source for punishing matters not mentioned in the ordinances: '[a]ll other faults, disorders and offences, not mentioned in these articles, shall be punished according to the general customes and laws of warre.'[61]

In 1643, a very important ordinance was issued highlighting the rights of the population: Articles and Ordinances of War for the Present Expedition of the Army of the Kingdom of Scotland, by the Committee of Estates [and] the Lord General of the Army.[62] The ordinance provided for its wide publication, so '[t]hat no man pretend ignorance, and that every one may know the duty of his place, that he may do it.'[63] In addition to restating in categorical language the prohibitions of rape,[64] destruction, and pillage, and the obligation to pay the value of requisitioned food,[65] the ordinance contained a statement of the prohibition of murder in time of war as enlightened as those that can be found in the best Nuernberg judgments: '[m]urder is no less unlawful and intollerable in the time of war, than in time of peace, and is to be punished with death.'[66] Another significant provision was the order not to kill an enemy who has surrendered (right to quarter): '[i]f it shall come to pass, that the enemy shall force us to battle, and the lord shall give us victory, none shall kill a

---

[58] Grose, *supra* note 1, at 107.   [59] Ibid. 118.   [60] Ibid.
[61] Ibid. 126. Cf. ibid. 156, art. LXIV '[a]ll other faults, misdemeanours and disorders not mentioned in these articles, shall be punished according to the laws and customs of war, and discretion of the court-martial.' English Military Discipline: Of Councils of War or Courts Martial (issued 1686 during the reign of James II), ibid. 137.
[62] Grose, *supra* note 1, at 127.   [63] Ibid.   [64] Ibid. 132, art. VIII.
[65] Ibid. 134, art. X.   [66] Ibid. 132, art. VIII.

yielding enemy.[67] The ordinance concluded with an eloquent provision establishing not only custom but also the law of nature as a residuary source, thus enhancing the principle of humanity which is inherent in the law of nature:

> Matters, that are clear by the light and law of nature, are presupposed; things unnecessary are passed over in silence; and other things may be judged by the common customs and constitutions of war; or may upon new emergents, be expressed afterward.[68]

This provision is an important antecedent of the Martens clause, whose object was to substitute principles of humanity for the unlimited discretion of the military commander.[69]

---

[67] Grose, *supra* note 1, at 136, art. XV. Also prohibited were 'ransoming of persons, spoiling [and] pillaging', ibid.

[68] Ibid. 137.

[69] The Martens clause reads as follows: 'Until a more complete code of the laws of war has been issued, the High Contracting Parties deem it expedient to declare that, in cases not included in the Regulations adopted by them, the inhabitants and the belligerents remain under the protection and the rule of the principles of the law of nations, as they result from the usages established among civilized peoples, from the laws of humanity, and the dictates of the public conscience.' This clause appears in the preamble to (Hague) Convention (No. IV) Respecting the Laws and Customs of War on Land, with Annex of Regulations, 18 Oct. 1907, 36 Stat. 2277, TS 539, 1 Bevans 631 (a similar clause appears in the preamble to the parallel convention of 29 July 1899). See also Theodor Meron, *Human Rights and Humanitarian Norms as Customary Law* (1989), 46 and n. 127; Helmut Strebel, Martens' Clause, in [Instalment 3] Rudolf Bernhardt (ed.), *Encyclopedia of Public International Law* (1982), 252.

II

Shakespeare's Henry the Fifth and the Law of War*

I INTRODUCTION

William Shakespeare wrote during the Elizabethan Renaissance, a period of revived and intense interest in history.[1] *The Life of Henry the Fifth*, written in 1599,[2] one of Shakespeare's histories, is a patriotic, epic portrayal of a phase in the bloody Hundred Years' War (1337–1453) between England and France. It describes a medieval campaign led by a chivalrous and virtuous king, who could perhaps do wrong but not a great deal of wrong, and in which the few acting in a just cause defeat the many. In this play, Shakespeare relives past glories.

King Henry V (1387–1422) succeeded to the throne of Henry IV in 1413 and two years later invaded France. The play telescopes the phase of the Hundred Years' War that started in 1415 with the landing of Henry's army near Harfleur and its victory at Agincourt and ended in 1420 with the conclusion of the Treaty of Troyes, which pronounced Henry the heir to the French throne and seemed to mark the ascendancy of England – until Joan of Arc's rallying of the French in 1429 sparked a turning point eventually leading to the defeat of England. The play is an ideal vehicle for consideration of the late medieval practice and rules of warfare: first, because it narrates a wide range of relevant events, including assertion of the just cause of the war, issuance of an ultimatum or declaration of war, episodes showing the conduct of the war and negotiation of the treaty of

* I acknowledge with thanks the helpful comments made on early drafts of this essay by Luigi Condorelli, Gerald Harriss, Graham Hughes, Peter Lewis, Andreas Lowenfeld, David Norbrook, Ashley Roach, Linda Silberman, Donna Sullivan and Malcolm Vale. In addition, for their important help, I thank Philip Uninsky and my research assistants David Berg and Maria Chedid. I am particularly grateful to Maurice Keen and Peter Haggenmacher for their invaluable advice and guidance. I also wish to express my appreciation to the Filomen D'Agostino and Max E. Greenberg Research Fund of New York University Law School, the Fellows and the staff of All Souls College, Oxford, where, as a Visiting Fellow, I completed this essay, and the Graduate Institute of International Studies, Geneva, for their support.

[1] L. Campbell, Shakespeare's "Histories": Mirrors of Elizabethan Policy 18–20 (1947).

[2] The Complete Works of Shakespeare 835 (G. Kittredge ed. 1971) [hereinafter Kittredge]. This essay will cite *Henry V* with annotations from the Yale Shakespeare (R. Dorius ed. 1955).

peace; and second, because it is not an imaginary tale but, on the whole, a rather close reflection of the sixteenth-century chronicles that were its principal sources, those of Raphael Holinshed[3] (1498–ca.1580) and Edward Hall[4] (or Halle) (ca. 1498–1547).

My purposes in this essay are to provide an international lawyer's commentary on the play by examining how Shakespeare used international law for his dramatic ends; to compare his version with its principal sources,[5] the chronicles of Holinshed and Hall, and occasionally with other historians' views as to what transpired during the reign of Henry V; to assess Shakespeare's text in the light of fifteenth- and sixteenth-century norms of *jus gentium*, primarily as reflected in the writings of

---

[3] Hosley, *Introduction* to R. HOLINSHED: AN EDITION OF HOLINSHED'S CHRONICLES, at xvii (R. Hosley ed. 1968) (2d ed. 1587) [hereinafter Hosley].

More than any other source, the second edition of Holinshed's *Chronicles* guided and inspired Shakespeare. L. CAMPBELL, *supra* note 1, at 72. This edition will therefore be referred to in this essay. R. HOLINSHED, HOLINSHED'S CHRONICLES (Clarendon Press, eds. R. Wallace & A. Hansen, 1923) (2d ed. 1587), *reprinted by* Greenwood Press (1978). Holinshed's work, however, should not be regarded as the effort of a single historian. It was rather a "group project [of which in 1573] Holinshed became ... the co-ordinator." L. CAMPBELL, *supra*, at 72.

[4] Richard Grafton posthumously published Hall's *Chronicle* in 1548. L. CAMPBELL, *supra* note 1, at 67. The 1809 edition, which collates the editions of 1548 and 1550, is the version I shall cite. HALL'S CHRONICLE; CONTAINING THE HISTORY OF ENGLAND, DURING THE REIGN OF HENRY THE FOURTH, AND THE SUCCEEDING MONARCHS, TO THE END OF THE REIGN OF HENRY THE EIGHTH (1809), *reprinted by* AMS Press (1965) [hereinafter E. HALL]. The original title (1548) was "The Union of the Two Noble and Illustre Famelies of Lancastre & Yorke."

The playwright's close attention to these chroniclers gives his play a solid historical basis, but it also means that Shakespeare probably did not know about some of the events they did not mention. Consequently, at times, events of great dramatic potential were overlooked; for example, the real Henry's challenge to the Dauphin, after the conquest of Harfleur, to decide the conflict by single combat (a similar opportunity, the trial by combat between Mowbray and Bolingbroke in *Richard II*, act 1, scene 3, was provided by Holinshed's account of that monarch's reign).

[5] For a comprehensive discussion of the sources Shakespeare used in writing *Henry V*, see 4 NARRATIVE AND DRAMATIC SOURCES OF SHAKESPEARE 347–75 (G. Bullough ed. 1962). Shakespeare may have been somewhat influenced by an anonymous play, *The Famous Victories of Henry the Fifth. Id.* at 348, 299.

Shakespeare's histories actually "reproduc[e] thousands upon thousands of [Holinshed's] words." Hosley, *supra* note 3, at xviii. Richard Posner observes that the notion of plagiarism in the Renaissance was limited: "the imitator was free to borrow as long as he added to what he borrowed." R. POSNER, LAW AND LITERATURE 346 (1988); *see also* Meron, *Common Rights of Mankind in Gentili, Grotius and Suárez*, 85 AJIL 110, 112 n. 18 (1991). Plagiarism was also common among medieval writers. The important author and compiler of the laws of war and customs of chivalry, Christine de Pisan, vigorously defended liberal use of others' writings. C. DE PISAN, THE BOOK OF FAYTTES OF ARMES AND OF CHYVALRYE 190 (W. Caxton trans. 1489, A. Byles ed. 1932) (written 1408–09).

Both Holinshed and Hall were writing "to show the significance of the facts and to establish by them general moral and more especially general political laws." L. CAMPBELL, *supra* note 1, at 75. As a result, Holinshed's account emphasizes the morals of the Tudor era (*id.* at 74) rather than those of the Middle Ages, and Hall's work has even been described as a work of propaganda (*id.* at 68, citing W. Gordon Zeeveld). Holinshed and Hall wrote some 100 years after the real events, describing them often in the light of sixteenth-century attitudes and assumptions that were not always quite those of Henry's own time.

contemporary jurists and earlier medieval jurists; and, now and then, to show how attitudes toward the law of war have changed since Shakespeare's times, and thus to illustrate the law's evolution.

My tasks were made easier by the works of modern writers on medieval and Renaissance law such as Maurice Keen, on whom I often draw.

II THE LEGAL ENVIRONMENT

Medieval Kings of England, including Henry V, occasionally promulgated ordinances governing the conduct of war and severely punishing violators. Through Holinshed's *Chronicles*, Shakespeare learned about Henry V's proclamations of rules of war. Holinshed explicitly mentions these proclamations and they are reflected in the play. Thus, when told about the likely execution of a soldier for having robbed a church, Shakespeare's Henry declares: "We would have all such offenders so cut off. And we give express charge that in our marches through the country there be nothing compell'd from the villages, nothing taken but paid for, none of the French upbraided or abused in disdainful language" (3, 6, 111–15).

This proclamation, which anticipated the modern law of war, is explained by Shakespeare on grounds of effectiveness rather than abstract humanity, in much the same way as is taught by modern academies of military law: "For when lenity and cruelty play for a kingdom, the gentler gamester is the soonest winner" (*id.*, 116–17).

A glance at the titles of the principal works of jurists of Henry's time – such as *Tractatus de bello, de represaliis et de duello* by Giovanni da Legnano (completed in 1360 and first published in 1477), *The Tree of Battles* (published ca. 1387) by Honoré Bonet (or Bouvet, as he is now known) and *Book of Fayttes of Armes and of Chyvalrye* by Christine de Pisan (written in 1408–1409)–suffices to demonstrate that at the time of Henry V, the bulk of *jus gentium* was the law relating to war, i.e., the law of arms or *jus armorum*, though there were also rules of canon and civil law pertaining to soldiers.[6] The customary rules of *jus armorum*, or *jus militare*, regulated the conduct of soldiers within Christendom,[7] but not between Christians and Muslims or other non-Christians. *Jus armorum* was not, it must be stressed, a body of law governing the relations between contending nations, but a body of norms governing the conduct

---

[6] On the nature of the medieval law of war, see Haggenmacher, *La Place de Francisco de Vitoria parmi les fondateurs du Droit International*, in ACTUALITÉ DE LA PENSÉE JURIDIQUE DE FRANCISCO DE VITORIA 27, 77–80 (1988); P. HAGGENMACHER, GROTIUS ET LA DOCTRINE DE LA GUERRE JUSTE 626 (1983).

[7] M. KEEN, THE LAWS OF WAR IN THE LATE MIDDLE AGES 17 (1965).

of warring men.[8] The law of arms was in fact the law of chivalry applicable to knights and to nobility, that is, to those who had the right to bear arms and to make war,[9] regardless of their nationality.

The law of chivalry could be enforced by courts of chivalry, which routinely handled disputes between knights of different nationality, the *curia militaris* or the court of knights (e.g., the courts held by such *magistri militum* as the Constable and the Marshal in England, the courts of the Constable and the Marshal of France, and, with broader jurisdiction, the French Parlement de Paris). The most effective sanction ensuring compliance with the rules of *jus armorum* was the knight's fear of dishonor and public reprobation, feelings associated with the reversal (placing upside down) of a knight's coat of arms (*subversio armorum*), a measure frequently imposed for breach of promise to pay ransom.[10] Holinshed's *Chronicles* of the reigns of medieval English monarchs – which informed Shakespeare's histories – contain many references to such chivalric practices as trial by combat and letters of defiance (a medieval form of declarations of war) and they are occasionally reflected in those histories. On the basis of Holinshed, Shakespeare's French King Charles VI commands his herald, Montjoy, to "greet England with our sharp defiance" (3, 5, 37) and Montjoy accordingly tells Henry: "Thus says my King: ... To this add defiance, and tell [Henry], for conclusion, he hath betrayed his followers, whose condemnation is pronounc'd" (3, 6, 123–41).

In *Henry V*, Shakespeare wrote of a late medieval war fought between Catholic kings who were committed, at least in principle, to the medieval chivalric law of arms. Despite those constraints, which had called for a modicum of humane conduct, this war was both cruel and bloody.

In contrast to the dramatist's familiarity with Holinshed and Hall, "[i]t cannot be maintained that Shakespeare even knew of the works"[11] of the various contemporary writers on *jus gentium*.[12] These include the Spanish Dominican Francisco de Vitoria (1480–1546), who in 1532 delivered his

---

[8] *Id.* at 133. Haggenmacher, *Grotius and Gentili: A Reassessment of Thomas E. Holland's Inaugural Lecture*, in Hugo Grotius and International Relations 133, 159 (H. Bull, B. Kingsbury & A. Roberts eds. 1990).

[9] M. Keen, *supra* note 7, at 19. Keen points out that a peasant could not claim rights to ransom in an enemy prisoner under the law of arms, because that law did not apply to him. *Id.*

[10] *Id.* at 20. Regarding the Ordinances of War attributed to Henry V, see *infra* note 89. Regarding courts of chivalry, see M. Keen, *supra* note 7, at 23–59; G. Squibb, The High Court of Chivalry 1–28 (1959); P.-C. Timbal, La Guerre de cent ans vue à travers les registres du Parlement (1337–69); C. Allmand & C. Armstrong, English Suits before the Parlement of Paris 1420–1436 (1982); Rogers, *Hoton v. Shakell: A Ransom Case in the Court of Chivalry, 1390–5*, 6 Nottingham Medieval Studs. 74 (L. Thorpe ed. 1962). For an illustration of a contested case of *subversio armorum*, see P.-C. Timbal, *supra*, at 307–13.

[11] G. Keeton, Shakespeare's Legal and Political Background 82 (1967).

[12] Because of the dates when the works of Gentili and Suárez were completed, finding much of an echo of their work in either Holinshed or Hall seems nearly impossible. That is not

famous lectures *De Indis et de jure belli hispanorum in barbaros*; Alberico Gentili (1552–1608), Shakespeare's contemporary in England;[13] and Francisco Suárez (1548–1617), the Spanish Jesuit scholar.[14] The best-known Renaissance writer on international law, the Dutchman Hugo Grotius (1583–1645), wrote somewhat later (his magisterial *De jure belli ac pacis* of 1625[15] appeared after Shakespeare's death). There is no evidence that the sixteenth-century writers on *jus gentium* influenced Shakespeare the dramatist either directly or indirectly. However, their work, and sometimes that of earlier, medieval writers, demonstrates the legal environment of the era.

The fact that Shakespeare preceded the birth of modern international law does not mean that no broadly recognized rules applied, at least in principle, to nations' conduct of war. Indeed, much as in the Middle Ages, most rules of *jus gentium* formed part of the law of war and there was hardly any discrete law of peace.[16] The law of peace was largely limited to rules dealing with the termination of war and the conclusion of peace. For the most part, however, as in the medieval period, the sixteenth-century law of warfare "was not international but municipal and military."[17] Sixteenth-century treaties on the law of war failed, on the whole, to distinguish among strategy, military discipline and legal rules governing warfare.[18] Not surprisingly, the lack of clarity regarding these distinctions also characterizes Shakespeare's histories.[19]

necessarily true of Vitoria, but his special interest in the law concerning colonization and wars with "barbarians" was one the English were not yet encountering to a marked degree.

[13] G. KEETON, *supra* note 11, at 80. *See generally* Meron, *supra* note 5. Gentili, an Italian Protestant, took refuge in England and in 1587 became the Regius Professor of Civil Law in Oxford (the Regius Chair was first established in 1546). Gentili's Oxford lectures appeared in book form in 1588 under the title *Prima commentatio de jure belli* and were republished, in considerably expanded form, in 1598 as *De jure belli libri tres*.

[14] Suárez's *De legibus, ac deo legislatore* (Treatise on Law and God the Legislator) was published in 1612. The law of war was the subject of *De triplici virtute theologica, fide, spe, et charitate* (The Three Theological Virtues, Faith, Hope and Charity), published posthumously in 1621.

[15] The principal work on Grotius is P. HAGGENMACHER, *supra* note 6.

[16] Haggenmacher, *supra* note 8, at 157.

[17] A. NUSSBAUM, A CONCISE HISTORY OF THE LAW OF NATIONS 69 (1954).

[18] G. KEETON, SHAKESPEARE AND HIS LEGAL PROBLEMS 59 (1930). Consider, e.g., the title of Balthazar Ayala's work, "Three Books on the Law of War and on the Duties Connected with War and on Military Discipline" (1582).

[19] Shakespeare tends to refer to the law of arms, disciplines of war, etc. In *Henry V*, Captain Fluellen regards the law of war sometimes as a purely military discipline and sometimes as normative. His plea for silence in the proximity of the enemy ("I warrant you, that there is no tiddle-taddle nor pibble-pabble in Pompey's camp") relies on "the true and aunchient prerogatifes and laws of the wars" as a military discipline (4, 1, 67–71). But the law of arms is invoked by Fluellen in the strictly normative sense in his famous condemnation of the French attack on the English encampment (see section VII *infra*). Shakespeare also refers to the normative significance of the laws of war in *Henry VIII*: "Nay ladies, fear not./By all the laws of war y'are privileg'd' (1, 4, 51–52). Kittredge, *supra* note 2.

III JUST WAR: *JUS AD BELLUM AND JUS IN BELLO*

In invading France in 1415, Henry hoped not only to recover lost territory but, far more importantly, to reactivate the English claim to the French crown that had been asserted – though never pursued in such earnestness – since the beginning of the Hundred Years' War. That claim derived from Isabel, the mother of his great-grandfather Edward III (Isabel was the daughter of French King Philip IV and the wife of Edward II). In the play, Henry is anxious to have the Archbishop of Canterbury reassure him that the Salic law,[20] which disqualified women and the female line from succession to the crown of France, does not bar his claim. He commands the Archbishop to give him an objective and balanced opinion:

> *King.* Why the law Salic that they have in France
> Or should or should not bar us in our claim.
> And God forbid, my dear and faithful lord,
> That you should fashion, wrest, or bow your reading ....
>
> [1, 2, 11–14]

The Archbishop reassures the King that his claim to the throne of France is just.[21]

---

[20] White writes:

> The code of laws known as the *salic law* is a collection of the popular laws of the Salic or Salian Franks, committed to writing in barbarous Latin, in the 5' century. Several texts of this code are in existence, but because of the dark ages in which it had its origin, more or less mystery surrounds it. The code relates principally to the definition and punishment of crimes, but there is a chapter ... relating to the succession of salic lands, which was probably inserted in the law, at a later date. *Salic lands*, or *terra salica*, came to mean inherited land as distinguished from property otherwise acquired, but even in the 15' century ... there was but little known as to the origin or exact meaning of this law. It was by a very doubtful construction that the salic law in the 14' century was held to exclude the succession of females to the throne of France, but on the accession of Phillip the Long, it was given this interpretation, and the fact that Edward III rested his claim to the throne on female succession no doubt led the French to place this meaning on the law ....

E. WHITE, COMMENTARIES ON THE LAW IN SHAKESPEARE 283–84 (1913) (footnotes omitted). On Salic law and just war, see also J. O'MALLEY, JUSTICE IN SHAKESPEARE: THREE ENGLISH KINGS IN THE LIGHT OF THOMISTIC THOUGHT 42–45 (1964); G. KEETON, *supra* note 18, at 64.

[21]
> There is no bar
> To make against your highness' claim to France
> But this which they produce from Pharamond:
> *In terram Salicam mulieres ne succedant–*
> "No woman shall succeed in Salic land."
> Which Salic land the French unjustly gloze
> To be the realm of France, and Pharamond
> The founder of this law and female bar.
> Yet their own authors faithfully affirm
> That the land Salic is in Germany,

The modern reader cannot but marvel at the craftsmanship and time-lessness of Canterbury's legal arguments: Territorially, Salic land does not mean France but a specific area in Germany. The law was wrongly inter-preted as applying to France. Since the Salic lands became a French possession under the reign of Charles the Great, 421 years after the death of the supposed author of the Salic law – the Frankish King Phar-amond – its continued vitality is in doubt. French kings themselves have succeeded to the crown, in Shakespeare's words, through "the right and title of the female." They are therefore precluded from invoking the law against Henry.[22] Finally, Henry's claim is bolstered by the Old Testament,

> Between the floods of Sala and of Elbe ....
> Then doth it well appear the Salic law
> Was not devised for the realm of France,
> Nor did the French possess the Salic land
> Until four hundred one and twenty years
> After defunction of King Pharamond,
> Idly suppos'd the founder of this law ....
> So that, as clear as is the summer's sun,
> King Pepin's title and Hugh Capet's claim,
> King Lewis his satisfaction, all appear
> To hold in right and title of the female.
> So do the kings of France unto this day,
> Howbeit they would hold up this Salic law
> To bar your highness claiming from the female ....
>   *King.* May I with right and conscience make this claim?
>   *Canterbury.* The sin upon my head, dread sovereign!
> For in the Book of Numbers is it writ:
> When the man dies, let the inheritance
> Descend unto the daughter.

[1, 2, 35–100]

[22] *See* P. Saccio, Shakespeare's English Kings 75–77, 79 (1977). It is not clear that, in the period from Hugh Capet to Philip the Tall, anyone thought the Salic law was relevant to the French royal succession, or knew of its implications. P. S. Lewis observes that while the question of succession was complicated by the English claim to the throne of France, "[t]he exclusion of women derived, not from the Salic Law (which was first invoked in its aid in the reign of Jean II [1350–1364]), but from custom ..." P. Lewis, Later Medieval France 94–95 (1968). C. Wood, Joan of Arc and Richard III, at 12–14 (1988), explains the exclusion of women from rights of succession in France by reference to the adulteries of the daughters of Philip the Fair, which were discovered in 1314. He emphasizes that doubts about legitimacy played an important role in changing the anticipated royal succession and the accession of Philip V, and he concludes that, "[a]lthough these theories were not to reach full flower until Charles V – or even Charles VII – France was well on its way to inventing the Salic law." *Id.* at 26.

First invoked and applied in 1317, as a categorical but unexplained customary rule, to the Valois succession, the Salic law was later "rationalized" by theological and philosophical arguments, in which antifeminism and nationalism played an important role, and eventually matured into a constitutional principle. The Salic law was first mentioned in terms in 1358 by Richard Lescot and first invoked against the English claims by Jean de Montreuil between 1408 and 1413. Contamine, *"Le Royaume de France ne Peut Tomber en Fille": Fondement, Formulation et Implication d'une Théorie Politique à la Fin du Moyen Age*, 13 Perspectives Médiévales 67 (1987). The ancient Frankish legend of the Salic law, which resembles Hall's-Holinshed's-Shakespeare's version, first appeared in an anonymous work in 1464 which explicitly commands that "[i]f a man die, and have no son, then ye shall cause his inheritance to pass unto his daughter."[23] The biblical argument should not necessarily be viewed as exclusively theological; it may have been presented under the law of nature, or *jus naturale*,[24] which so prominently figures later in the play in Exeter's ultimatum to the King of France (see section IV below).

Shakespeare's account of the exchange between the Archbishop and the King very closely follows Archbishop Chichele's prepared statement ("prepared tale" in Holinshed's words; "prepared purpose" in Hall's), as reported by Holinshed in his *Chronicles*.[25] The striking legal craftsmanship of Shakespeare's Henry therefore cannot be credited to the dramatist alone. Shakespeare the dramatist must share the credit either with the person who actually voiced these arguments in the court of Henry V in *anno regni* 2 (1414) or with the chroniclers.[26]

In addition to assuring himself of the legitimacy of his claim, Henry needed to be satisfied that the war that might be necessary to secure that

under the title *La Loy salicque, premiere loy des françois*. Potter, *The Development and Significance of the Salic Law of the French*, 52 ENG. HIST. REV. 235, 249–51 (1937). On the different view in England of legitimacy and succession, see C. WOOD, *supra*, at 14–18.

[23]   *Numbers* 27:8.

[24]   *See generally* G. KEETON, *supra* note 11, at 78.

[25]   R. HOLINSHED, *supra* note 3, at 9–11. *See also* E. HALL, *supra* note 4, at 49–52. Hall clearly set out the temporal element: Pharamond, the supposed author of the Salic law, could not have created it for a land he neither possessed nor knew of at the time it was issued. The biblical argument, by invoking God's authority, was intended to put to rest any doubts that may have survived the secular reasoning. *Id.* at 50–51.

[26]   Henry Chichele, Archbishop of Canterbury at the time of Agincourt, is perhaps best remembered by international lawyers for the (Oxford) Chichele Chair of Public International Law and for having cofounded in 1438 with Henry VI the All Souls College (the College of All Souls of the Faithful Departed) at Oxford, in memory of those fallen in the wars in France, of which Henry V's campaign was but one segment. *See* J. SIMMONS, ALL SOULS COLLEGE: A CONCISE ACCOUNT 1 (1988); J. SIMMONS, ALL SOULS COLLEGE, THE CODRINGTON LIBRARY AND THE LAW 1 (1986). Thus, the person to whom Hall (followed by Holinshed) attributed the justification for starting the campaign later founded the memorial to the souls of those who died in it. It is doubtful, however, whether this attribution was appropriate. P. SACCIO, *supra* note 22, at 79, asserts that "Archbishop Chichele almost certainly never made the speech on the Salic law that is assigned to him." The anonymous early sixteenth-century work, THE FIRST ENGLISH LIFE OF KING HENRY THE FIFTH 24–25 (C. Kingsford ed. 1911) (1513) does not mention Canterbury's participation in the deliberations of the King's Council, and refers to him as having delivered the King's answer to the French ambassadors. It was Henry's Chancellor, Bishop Beaufort, who appears to have had a leading role in the discussions in Henry's court and with the envoys of France. *See also* 1 J. WYLIE, THE REIGN OF HENRY THE FIFTH 491 (1914); E. JACOB, HENRY V AND THE INVASION OF FRANCE 73 (1947) [hereinafter HENRY V]; 3 W. STUBBS, A CONSTITUTIONAL HISTORY OF ENGLAND 89–90 (1880); 1 E. JACOB, THE REGISTER OF HENRY CHICHELE, at xxxiv–xxxv (1943); C. KINGSFORD, HENRY V, at 109–10 (1901). The critical role of Beaufort in advocating resort to arms to uphold Henry's just cause is made clear by G. HARRISS, CARDINAL BEAUFORT 71–73, 84–86 (1988).

In his "Aphotegms New and Old," written about a quarter of a century after *Henry V*, Francis Bacon demonstrated England's skepticism regarding the very existence of the Salic law. FRANCIS LORD. VERULAM VISCOUNT ST ALBAN, APHOTEGM NO. 184 (32), at 150 (1625).

claim (should France refuse to yield) was grounded in a just cause.[27] The question was important for spiritual reasons (the immortality of his soul) and for such secular reasons as the validity of the title that he and his troops would acquire over the spoils of war; their enjoyment of combatant privileges; their protection by the laws of war; and, in consequence of these considerations, his ability to raise troops and to sustain their morale. Although, as a matter of realpolitik, a victorious prince faced few difficulties in maintaining that his war was just, this could have posed a real problem to a knight whose right to ransom or to other spoils of war was contested before a court of chivalry applying the customary *jus armorum*. The discussion that follows suggests that there was ample reason in contemporary legal doctrine for Shakespeare's Henry to follow a prudent course by attempting to establish as just a cause as possible for the invasion of France.

A just cause was essential to avoid responsibility for causing death. In requesting Canterbury's opinion on the justness of his cause, Shakespeare's Henry emphasizes that "God doth know how many now in health/Shall drop their blood in approbation/Of what your reverence shall incite us to" (1, 2, 18–20). That spiritual responsibility was critical to Henry is demonstrated by his deathbed speech, as reported by Holinshed in his *Chronicles*,[28] and by the following conversation between Shakespeare's Henry and one of his soldiers, Williams (discussed further in section V below):

> *King* [in disguise]. Methinks I could not die anywhere so contented as in the king's company, his cause being just and his quarrel honorable.
> *Williams*. That's more than we know.
> . . . .
> *Williams*. But if the cause be not good, the king himself hath a heavy reckoning to make when all those legs and arms and heads chopp'd off in a battle shall join together at the latter day . . . . Now if these men do not die well, it will be a black matter for the king that led them to it . . . .   [4, 1, 126–45]

---

[27] On St. Thomas Aquinas's views on just war, see G. WEIGEL, TRANQUILLITAS ORDINIS 36–38 (1987); on St. Augustine's theory of just war, see *id.* at 29–30. *See also* T. FRANCK, THE POWER OF LEGITIMACY AMONG NATIONS 80–81 (1990).

[28]

> [H]e protested unto them, that neither the ambitious desire to inlarge his dominions, neither to purchase vaine renowme and worldlie fame, nor anie other consideration had mooved him to take the warres in hand; but onelie that in prosecuting his just title, he might in the end atteine to a perfect peace, and come to enjoie those peeces of his inheritance, which to him of right belonged: and that before the beginning of the same warres, he was fullie persuaded by men both wise and of great holinesse of life, that upon such intent he might and ought both begin the same warres, and follow them . . . and that without all danger of Gods displeasure or perill of soule.

R. HOLINSHED, *supra* note 3, at 129–30.

Writers on *jus gentium* in Shakespeare's era often linked spiritual and secular elements as components of the just war doctrine. Thus, Suárez advanced a combination of moral, humanistic and legal considerations as reasons for limiting lawful resort to war to unquestionably just wars. He observed that since, "in war, men are despoiled of their property, their liberty, and their lives[,] ... to do such things without just cause is absolutely iniquitous, for if this were permissible, men could kill one another without cause."[29] He also pointed out that aggressive war is frequently waged against foreign nationals ("non-subjects"), who would deserve neither punishment nor subjection to foreign jurisdiction unless they "have committed some wrong on account of which they render themselves subjects."[30]

Of the possible secular causes for a just war, the cause most directly relevant to King Henry was the recapture of the French territory that he considered to belong to England, or to the Lancastrians as descendants of the Plantagenets. According to writers on international law contemporaneous with Shakespeare, a war aimed at repossessing property captured by an enemy would be a defensive, not an aggressive, war.[31] "[T]he seizure by a prince of another's property, and his refusal to restore it," was the very first example of a just cause of war given by Suárez.[32] Vitoria, too, regarded a war designed to repossess property as a defensive, and necessarily just, war.[33] In those circumstances, it was "permissible to recapt everything that has been lost."[34]

In reality, of course, the situation was more complex, because each party to the conflict was likely to maintain that its cause was just (*bellum nostrum justum*).[35] Yet, under medieval legal theory, war could be just for one side only. More realistically, and perhaps ahead of his time, Gentili believed that a war might objectively be just on both sides.[36] "It is the nature of wars for both sides to maintain that they are supporting a just cause."[37] In most cases, it is difficult to determine on which side justice rests, "and if each side aims at justice, neither can be called unjust."[38]

[29] 2 F. SUÁREZ, SELECTIONS FROM THREE WORKS 816 (Carnegie ed., G. Williams, A. Brown & J. Waldron trans. 1944) (1612, 1613, 1621).

[30] *Id. See also* P. HAGGENMACHER, *supra* note 6, at 409–26.

[31] F. SUÁREZ, *supra* note 29, at 804.   [32] *Id.* at 817.

[33] F. VICTORIA, *The Second Relectio on the Indians, or on the Law of War made by the Spaniards on the Barbarians*, in DE INDIS ET DE IURE BELLI RELECTIONES 166–67(1) (Carnegie ed., J. P. Bate trans. 1917). These lectures were published posthumously in 1557.

[34] *Id.* at 171(16).   [35] M. KEEN, *supra* note 7, at 71.

[36] A. NUSSBAUM, *supra* note 17, at 97. *See also* P. HAGGENMACHER, *supra* note 6, at 203–23, 279–311; text at and note 54 *infra*.

[37] 2 A. GENTILI, DE JURE BELLI LIBRI TRES 31 (Carnegie ed., trans. J. Rolfe 1933) (This is the 1931 translation of the 1612 edition. *Prima commentatio de jure belli* was published in 1588, the second and third parts in 1589. The three books appeared, as a new work, in 1598 under the title *De jure belli libri tres. See* Phillipson, *Introduction* to *id.* at 14a).

[38] *Id.* at 32.

This view was also taken by another contemporary of Shakespeare, Balthazar Ayala (1548–1584), who related the just war doctrine to the duties of the religious man. He believed that a war between legitimate sovereigns, lawfully conducted, might be just for both sides.[39] But Suárez argued that if purposes such as ambition or avarice were sufficient to justify resort to war, "any state whatsoever could aspire to these ends; and hence, a war would be just on both sides, essentially and apart from any element of ignorance. This supposition is entirely absurd; for two mutually conflicting rights cannot both be just."[40] "Excluding cases of ignorance," the war cannot "incidentally be just for both sides." Suárez conceded, however, that a war could be *unjust* for both sides,[41] for example, when waged by mutual agreement.[42]

That mere expansionism ("extension of empire") could not be a just cause of war was already suggested by Vitoria. Otherwise, he claimed, "each of the two belligerents might have an equally just cause and so both would be innocent .... [T]he consequence [would be] that it would not be lawful to kill them and so imply a contradiction, because it would be a just war."[43] Presumably, Henry's counsel would distinguish between recapturing property lost to another prince, which would constitute a just cause of the war, and extension of the empire, which would not. The King of France, however, would surely believe that Henry was expanding his empire, not reclaiming property lost to France.

In such circumstances, the right of every prince to judge whether or not his cause was just appears inherently arbitrary, self-serving and even hypocritical. Shakespeare's contemporaries were not unaware of these difficulties. They are hardly dispelled by the fact that Shakespeare's King of England, like Holinshed's Henry, defers to the moral and religious authority of the senior English ecclesiastic (the Archbishop of Canterbury) for assurance of the justness of the English cause.

Actually, advancing an idea that has yet to gain acceptance, Vitoria stated that:

---

[39] A. NUSSBAUM, *supra* note 17, at 92.

[40] F. SUÁREZ, *supra* note 29, at 816. Vitoria implied, *supra* note 33, at 177(32), that ignorance may make the war just for both sides. He wrote that "[a]part from ignorance [a war cannot be just on both sides] ... for if the right and justice of each side be certain, it is unlawful to fight against it ...." However, "[a]ssuming a demonstrable ignorance either of fact or of law," he continued, "it may be that on the side where true justice is the war is just of itself, while on the other side the war is just in the sense of being excused from sin by reason of good faith, because invincible ignorance is a complete excuse." *Id.*

[41] F. SUÁREZ, *supra* note 29, at 850–51. *Compare* Abraham Lincoln's statement: "In great contests each party claims to act in accordance with the will of God. Both *may* be, and one *must* be wrong." *Quoted by* W. SAFIRE, FREEDOM 787 (1987).

[42] *See* P. HAGGENMACHER, *supra* note 6, at 436–37.

[43] F. VICTORIA, *supra* note 33, at 170(11).

if there were any competent judge over the two belligerents, he would have to condemn the unjust aggressors and authors of wrong, not only to make restitution of what they have carried off, but also to make good the expenses of the war to the other side, and also all damages.[44]

Absent such a third-party determination, "a prince who is carrying on a just war is as it were his own judge."[45] "[A] superior judge has competence to mulct the author of a wrong by taking away from him a city ... or a fortress .... [In the same way] a prince who has suffered wrong can do this too, because by the law of war he is put in the position of a judge."[46]

Suárez appears to have been less troubled by the privilege of every prince to determine the justness of his own cause. In discussing the possibility of a king's claiming a certain city "as falling newly to him by hereditary right" (such as Henry's claim to France), he wrote that, "when the case of each side contains [an element of] probability, then the king ought to act as a just judge .... [I]f he finds that the opinion favouring his own side is the more probably true, he may, even justly, prosecute his own right ...."[47]

Just cause concerned not only *jus ad bellum* (the right to resort to war), but also *jus in bello* (the law governing the conduct of war), since it had bearing on the effects of war. Because medieval legal doctrine taught that the lawfulness of the title to the spoils of war turned on the justness of its cause, Henry required a good cause to realize his objectives. Thus, Vitoria emphasized that in a just war it was lawful "to recover things taken from us."[48] Subject to certain limits, which he suggested, "everything captured in a just war vests in the seizor .... This needs no proof, for that is the end and aim of war."[49]

There therefore continued into Shakespeare's era a much closer link than remains today between *jus ad bellum* and *jus in bello*. As Keen has pointed out, the first concern of the medieval soldier was to show that "his booty was *prise de bonne guerre*, that is, taken in just war. If it was not taken in these circumstances, restitution could be demanded."[50] A just war could legitimize criminal acts and create a legal title to goods whose taking in other circumstances would be considered robbery.[51] Only in a just war could spoils and prisoners be taken lawfully.[52] Whether or not a captor would acquire a property right in the person of prisoners and the consequent right to the payment of ransom hinged on whether or not the war was just.[53]

---

[44] F. VICTORIA, *supra* note 33, at 171(17).   [45] *Id.*

[46] *Id.* at 186(56). *See also* P. HAGGENMACHER, *supra* note 6, at 409–26.

[47] F. SUÁREZ, *supra* note 29, at 828.   [48] F. VICTORIA, *supra* note 33, at 182(44).

[49] *Id.* at 184(50).

[50] M. KEEN, *supra* note 7, at 139. *See also* P. HAGGENMACHER, *supra* note 6, at 300–05.

[51] M. KEEN, *supra* note 7, at 65.   [52] *Id.* at 70.   [53] *Id.* at 137.

Cracks already began to appear in this rigid doctrine during the fourteenth and fifteenth centuries. In discussing *jus in bello*, Keen explains that, according to the canonists, rights to the spoils of a public war – that is, a war declared by a prince, waged on his authority and governed by *jus gentium* – were in theory dependent on the satisfaction of several standards of justice, in addition to that of authority to wage war. However, because there was no superior or third party to judge the justice of the cause, "[i]n practice . . . a just war . . . and a public war meant the same thing."[54]

The jurists of Shakespeare's time departed even more sharply from the medieval doctrine. Suárez stated that only in a just war may the prince seize cities and provinces,[55] but he conceded that in a war that is unjust for both sides, the victor would acquire the property of the vanquished as a result of the agreement to wage war, i.e., by a sort of implied contract theory.[56]

Gentili suggested that the belligerents' rights to prisoners and booty do not depend on the war's justness.[57] By insisting, with considerable sophistication, that war may be just on both sides, he reached the conclusion that the law must be impartial to both sides. He thus paved the way for the uniform applicability of *jus in bello*,[58] an approach inherently less subject to abuse that is characteristic of modern international law. The rights of war, Gentili wrote, belong to both contestants, "mak[ing] what is taken on each side the property of the captors."[59]

Gentili thus felt that the distinction between just and unjust war was sophistry, at least to a large extent. While not unique, however, he was not typical of his times. Moreover, like Ayala, he wrote about 175 years after the discussion Shakespeare ascribes to Henry and the Archbishop of Canterbury, in which the justness of Henry's cause is so central.

In the same vein, Ayala held that "[n]othing more is needed . . . so far as concerns the legal effects which are produced and the bringing into operation of the laws of war, than that the war should be waged by parties who are within the definition of 'enemies' and who have the right to wage war."[60] Nevertheless, a soldier who is summoned to fight in an

---

[54] *Id.* at 71. Keen cites the fourteenth-century BARTHOLOMEW OF SALICETO, SUPER VIII COD., tit. 51, *l.* 12: "It is tacitly assumed that it is in the nature of war waged by kings and lords, that it is public and general on both sides," and the ca. 1396 disputations of ANGELUS OF PERUSIA, DISPUTATIO, INC. "RENOVATA GUERRA" (printed ca. 1490, unpag.): "propter dubium ex utroque latere dicere possumus guerram justam." M. KEEN, *supra* note 7, at 71 n. 1.

[55] F. SUÁREZ, *supra* note 29, at 850.

[56] *Id.* at 851–52. *See* P. HAGGENMACHER, *supra* note 6, at 426–37.

[57] A. NUSSBAUM, *supra* note 17, at 97.

[58] *See generally* P. HAGGENMACHER, *supra* note 6, at 597–612.

[59] A. GENTILI, *supra* note 37, at 33. *See generally* P. HAGGENMACHER, *supra* note 6, at 74–139.

[60] B. AYALA, THREE BOOKS ON THE LAW OF WAR AND ON THE DUTIES CONNECTED WITH WAR AND ON MILITARY DISCIPLINE 23 (Carnegie ed. 1912, J. Bate trans.) (1582). It follows that things captured in war become the property of the captors. *Id.* at 35.

unjust war "has no action at law either for the recovery of pay or for reimbursement of loss, for no right of action is allowed to arise out of circumstances of disgrace [*ex turpi causa nulla datur actio*]."[61] Since the right of combatants to engage in war and hence to be protected by the laws of war also depended on the justness of the war, demonstrating just cause was important for many practical reasons, including raising troops and maintaining morale.

To give rise to combatant privileges, the war had to be declared by a prince, acting on behalf of the state. A state could wage war if it constituted "[a] perfect State or community ... [i.e.,] one which is complete in itself, that is, which is not a part of another community."[62] According to Suárez, war could be waged only by a power entitled to declare war, i.e., a sovereign prince who has no superior in temporal affairs.[63] Indeed, whether war had been declared by a sovereign prince was an important practical test of the justness of the conflict and its public nature.[64]

Suárez argued that the captured soldiers of a prince who waged an unjust war would not enjoy the protection of the *jus gentium* and could be killed, but he favored such protection of mercenary soldiers, who were innocent in the sense that they did not know any reasons indicating the justness of the other side's cause.[65] Neither unjust war nor those participating in it had standing in law.[66]

In contrast to medieval law, most modern rules of warfare (e.g., on requisitioning property and the treatment of prisoners of war and civilians, that is, *jus in bello*) apply equally to a state fighting a war of aggression and to one involved in lawful self-defense. Prisoner-of-war status and combatant privileges in modern international law depend, in principle, on the combatants' conformity with conditions of openness and respect for the laws and customs of war enumerated in Article 4 of the third Geneva Convention of 1949[67] and in Articles 43 and 44 of Additional

---

[61] *Id.* at 23, 25.

[62] F. VICTORIA, *supra* note 33, at 169(7).

[63] F. SUÁREZ, *supra* note 29, at 805. Gentili criticized Spain for not treating as "lawful enemies' some Frenchmen captured in a war with Portugal who held letters from a king unrecognized by Spain. A. GENTILI, *supra* note 37, at 26.

[64] M. KEEN, *supra* note 7, at 72.

[65] A. NUSSBAUM, *supra* note 17, at 90.

[66] M. KEEN, *supra* note 7, at 65 (citing Nicholas of Tudeschi, who wrote in 1524).

[67] Convention Relative to the Treatment of Prisoners of War (Geneva Convention No. III), Aug. 12, 1949, 6 UST 3316, TIAS No. 3364, 75 UNTS 135.

Professor Haggenmacher aptly suggests that in contrast to the medieval doctrine of just war, which focused on the justness of the cause of war, the modern law of war, which underlies the Hague Regulations and the Geneva Conventions for the Protection of Victims of War, focuses on whether the war constitutes a "regular war," i.e., on its "formal aspects." Haggenmacher, *La doctrine de la guerre juste chez les théologiens et les juristes du siècle d'or*, in L'ESPAGNE ET LA FORMATION DU DROIT DES GENS MODERNE 27, 28–29 (G. Van Hecke ed. 1988).

Protocol I,[68] regardless of the cause of the conflict. *Jus ad bellum* has survived in such matters as the right of self-defense (Article 51 of the United Nations Charter) and action necessary to maintain international peace and security (Articles 42–43 of the UN Charter). An echo of the medieval doctrine of just war can be found in the modern principle outlawing the annexation of territory acquired in a war of aggression.[69]

IV   DECLARATION OF WAR

On the basis of the Archbishop of Canterbury's reassurances about the justness of Henry's cause, the King's ambassador and special envoy to the court of France, the Duke of Exeter, addresses the following ultimatum to the King of France:

That you divest yourself and lay apart
The borrow'd glories that by gift of heaven,
By law of nature and of nations, 'longs
To him and to his heirs – namely, the crown
And all wide-stretched honors that pertain
By custom and the ordinance of times
Unto the crown of France. ...
    King. Or else what follows?
    Exeter. Bloody constraint ....

---

[68] Protocol Additional to the Geneva Conventions of 12 August 1949, and Relating to the Protection of Victims of International Armed Conflicts (Protocol I), *opened for signature* Dec. 12, 1977, 1125 UNTS 3.

[69] This doctrine has been applied by the United Nations rather selectively. The General Assembly's Resolution on the Definition of Aggression of December 14, 1974, reaffirms that "the territory of a State shall not be violated by being the object, even temporarily, of military occupation or of other measures of force ... and ... shall not be the object of acquisition by another State resulting from such measures or the threat thereof." GA Res. 3314, 29 UN GAOR Supp. (No. 31) at 142, UN Doc. A/9631 (1975).

By Resolution 662 of August 9, 1990 (*reprinted in* 29 ILM 1327 (1990)), the Security Council asserted its determination "to restore the sovereignty, independence and territorial integrity of Kuwait" and decided "that annexation of Kuwait by Iraq under any form and whatever pretext has no legal validity, and is considered null and void." *See also* SC Res. 687A of April 3, 1991 (*reprinted in* 30 ILM 847 (1991)); Schachter, *United Nations Law in the Gulf Conflict*, 85 AJIL 452, 454 (1991).

In the more general context of the blueprint for settling the Six-Day War between Israel and the neighboring Arab states, for whose outbreak responsibility has not been authoritatively established, the Security Council emphasized in Resolution 242 of November 22, 1967, "the inadmissibility of the acquisition of territory by war."

On some contemporary aspects of just war, see Y. Dinstein, War, Aggression and Self-Defence 66–74 (1988); Schachter, *In Defense of International Rules on the Use of Force*, 53 U. Chi. L. Rev. 113, 142–44 (1986).

Deliver up the crown, and ... take mercy
On the poor souls for whom this hungry war
Opens his vasty jaws ....[70]

[2, 4, 78–105]

Here Shakespeare renders in dramatic form a declaration of war, or an ultimatum that in effect amounted to a declaration of war, required by the *jus gentium* of both the medieval and the Renaissance periods. The message states the claim to the crown of France, the legal basis for that claim *in the law of nature and the law of nations*, and the consequences of noncompliance with its demands, i.e., war.

In the Middle Ages, the requirement that a war be publicly declared was commonly met by issuing letters of defiance; later Elizabethan doctrine required not only that the cause of war be just, but also that the procedures of war be followed,[71] and, in particular, that resort be made to a formal declaration of war.[72] Accordingly, Queen Elizabeth published, in 1585, A Declaration of the Causes Mooving the Queene of England to Give Aide to the Defence of the People Afflicted and Oppressed in the Lowe Countries and, in 1596, A Declaration of the Causes Moving the Queenes Majestie of England, to Prepare and Send a Navy to the Seas, for the Defence of Her Realmes against the King of Spaines Forces.[73] Shakespeare's Henry faithfully reflects this doctrine in the message carried by the Duke of Exeter to the court of France. The dramatist's version finds support in Hall's *Chronicle*:

> The Kyng like a wise prince and pollitique governor, entendyng to observe the auncient orders of famous kynges and renoumed potentates used aswel emong Paynimes as Christians, which is, not to invade another mannes territory without open war and the cause of the same to hym published and declared, dispatched into Fraunce his uncle the duke of Excester ....[74]

A similar declaration of war can be found in Shakespeare's *King John*:

> K[ing] John. Now, say, Chatillon, what would France with us?
> Chatillon. Thus, after greeting, speaks the King of France ....

---

[70] *Compare The final demands of Henry V's ambassadors, March 1415, reprinted in* 4 ENGLISH HISTORICAL DOCUMENTS 1327–1485, at 209 (D. Douglas ed. 1969); R. HOLINSHED, *supra* note 3, at 12–13. For an English translation of some of the correspondence between Henry V and Charles VI, see H. NICOLAS, A HISTORY OF THE BATTLE OF AGINCOURT, App. 1 (2d ed. 1832). For the French text of part of the correspondence, see 5 CHRONIQUE DU RELIGIEUX DE SAINT-DENYS 507–11, 527–31 (Collection de Documents Inédits sur l'Histoire de France, 1ère série, 1844). For the Latin version, see 4 T. RYMER, FOEDERA, pt. 2 at 106 (Hague ed. 1740). See also the self-justifying account of the negotiations in GESTA HENRICI QUINTI 14–15 (F. Taylor & J. Roskell eds. 1975).

[71] L. CAMPBELL, *supra* note 1, at 287, regards Henry's demand for the surrender of Harfleur, to be discussed further in this essay, as an example of observance of such procedures.

[72] *Id.* at 285–86.   [73] *Id.*   [74] E. HALL, *supra* note 4, at 57.

....

> *Châtillon.* Philip of France, in right and true behalf
> Of thy deceased brother Geffrey's son,
> Arthur Plantagenet, lays most lawful claim
> To this fair island and the territories,
> To Ireland, Poitiers, Anjou, Touraine, Maine, ...
> And put the same into young Arthur's hand,
> Thy nephew and right royal sovereign.
>   *K. John.* What follows if we disallow of this?
>   *Châtillon.* The proud control of fierce and bloody war,
> To enforce these rights so forcibly withheld.[75]

[1, 1, 1–18]

Actually, Henry's invasion of France in August 1415 did not start a new war but continued the war that legally was still extant. The Hundred Years' War was renewed with the collapse in 1369 of the Treaty of Brétigny (1360) after the rejection, or "defiance," by France of Edward III's ultimatum. Since then, the conflict had been interrupted only by truces, which, according to medieval doctrine, suspended, but did not end, the war. Because truces suspended the fighting for an agreed period of time only, it was not even necessary, as a matter of law, to declare war when they came to an end.[76]

Henry's negotiations with France made it clear that additional extensions of the truces depended on the satisfaction of his demands. Indeed, to press for faster negotiations and concessions, Henry refused to extend the passports or safe conducts of the French ambassadors beyond June 8, 1415. The invasion started on August 13 after the expiration of the truce as last prolonged, there being no record of a definitive rejection of the English demands. Such a rejection was contained only in Charles's letter to Henry of August 24, which followed the English invasion. Although Henry took an uncompromising stand in the negotiations, insisting on "justice" and the restoration of his right to the French crown rather than on this or that French duchy, he certainly could not be accused of having failed to give ample and public notice of his intention to resume hostilities. Henry's ultimatums, although possibly not drafted in the form of

---

[75] Kittredge, *supra* note 2.

[76] Regarding termination of the Treaty of Brétigny, see 4 R. DELACHENAL, HISTOIRE DE CHARLES V, at 134–45 (1928). On the status of truces in medieval war, see M. KEEN, *supra* note 7, at 206–17; A. GENTILI, *supra* note 37, at 187 ("it is not necessary to declare war when such truces come to an end"). On the extension of truces in 1415 and their expiration, see 1 J. WYLIE, *supra* note 26, at 444. Henry's dispatch on July 28 of a herald bearing a letter to the King of France "was no doubt intended as a formal defiance to war, and as such the French accepted it." C. KINGSFORD, *supra* note 26, at 122; *accord*, J. WYLIE, *supra*, at 493–94. For the text of the letter of July 28, see H. NICOLAS, *supra* note 70, at 5. On the "ultimatum" of Bishop Beaufort, see J. WYLIE, *supra*, at 491.

declarations of war, undoubtedly satisfied the requirements of an open
and public war.

George Keeton, a modern commentator, believes that in Shakespeare's
times declarations of war were becoming obsolete and "nations not
infrequently found themselves at war without any further notification
than the appearance of the army of one belligerent in the territory of
another .... In the Historical plays, however, where Shakespeare was
following the Chronicles, a formal declaration of war by a herald or
ambassador precedes hostilities ...."[77] Regardless of the practice in
Renaissance Europe, contemporaneous legal theory clearly articulated
the duty to declare war. Gentili asserted that the "enemy are those who
have officially declared war upon us, or upon whom we have officially
declared war."[78] Those who did not declare war would be considered
pirates or brigands, i.e., nonprivileged combatants in contemporary
usage. The "war on both sides must be public and official and there
must be sovereigns on both sides to direct the war."[79] In his 1929 introduction to the Carnegie edition of Gentili's *De jure belli libri tres*, Coleman
Phillipson explains Gentili's insistence on the obligation to declare war
prior to resorting to hostilities:

> [I]n the time of Gentili, though we find a few instances in which heralds were
> dispatched to announce the commencement of hostilities, the practice of declar-
> ing war was generally falling into disuse; so that Gentili was performing a great
> service by protesting so vigorously against its discontinuance and by demand-
> ing a long interval in accordance (in his view) with the old-established law of
> nations as well as with Divine injunctions.[80]

Grotius stated that "[d]eclarations of war in fact ... were wont to be
made publicly, with a statement of the cause, in order that the whole
human race as it were might judge of the justness of it."[81] Referring to past
events that suggested that "most wars begin without declaration,"[82]
Grotius observed:

> [B]efore the possessor of sovereign power is attacked for the debt or crime of a
> subject, a demand for settlement should be made, which may place him in the

---

[77] G. Keeton, *supra* note 11, at 89; *see also* G. Keeton, *supra* note 18, at 72–73.

[78] A. Gentili, *supra* note 37, at 15 (citing Pomponius).

[79] *Id.* "[I]f war is not declared when it ought to be declared, then war is said to be carried
on treacherously; and such a war is unjust, detestable, and savage. [That is] because it is
waged according to none of the laws of war...." *Id.* at 140. *See also* F. Suárez, *supra* note 29, at
837–38.

[80] A. Gentili, *supra* note 37, at 39a.

[81] H. Grotius, De jure belli ac pacis libri tres, bk. II, ch. XXVI, pt. IV(7) (Carnegie ed.,
F. Kelsey trans. 1925) (1646). Kelsey translated the 1646 edition rather than the first, 1625,
edition.

[82] *Id.*, bk. III, ch. III, pt. VI(1).

wrong, and in consequence of which he may be held either to be causing us loss or to be himself committing a crime, according to the principles which have previously been discussed.

But even in case the law of nature does not require that such a demand be made, still it is honourable and praiseworthy to make it, in order that, for instance, we may avoid giving offence, or that the wrong may be atoned for by repentance and compensation, according to what we have said regarding the means to be tried to avoid war ....

... But by the law of nations a proclamation is required in all cases in order to secure [the] ... particular effects [of war]. ...[83]

Whatever their normative status, since Henry's era declarations of war have proved remarkably resilient. The question of the duty to declare war may have been rendered moot by the law of the United Nations Charter, with its categorical prohibition of resort to war (subject to the inherent right of individual or collective self-defense). In determining whether the duty to declare war is firmly rooted in customary law, examples of the failure of states to issue declarations of war must be taken into account. As for conventional law, Article 1 of the 1907 Hague Convention Relative to the Opening of Hostilities, which is still in force between forty-two states, including all the permanent members of the UN Security Council except China, provides that the "Contracting Powers recognize that hostilities between themselves must not commence without previous and explicit warning, in the form either of a reasoned declaration of war or of an ultimatum with conditional declaration of war."[84] At least as between the parties to this Convention, the law remains formally[85] as it was during the reign of Henry V.

V RESPONSIBILITY OF PRINCES

On the eve of the battle of Agincourt, Shakespeare has Henry circulate among his troops in disguise. The King's exchange with the soldier

---

[83] *Id.*, (2)–(3).

[84] Oct. 18, 1907, 36 Stat. 2259, 2271 (pt. 2), TS No. 538, 1 Bevans 619. In a note to the entry on China, *Treaties in Force*, published by the U.S. Department of State, indicates that this Convention is "applicable only to Taiwan."

[85] *See* 2 L. Oppenheim, International Law 293 (H. Lauterpacht 7th ed. 1952); [United Kingdom] War Office, The Law of War on Land, Being Part III of the Manual of Military Law 7–8 (1958).

Williams[86] concerns the spiritual responsibility of princes[87] for the death
of soldiers in war, whether just or not. They discuss the King's responsibility both from a Christian perspective, reflecting the doctrine that persons dying without having had a chance to repent are doomed to eternal
damnation, and from a legal viewpoint. In explaining whether the King
should be held responsible for the damnation of soldiers killed in battle
with "many irreconcil'd iniquities" on their conscience, Henry makes a
clear distinction between authorized acts, committed by soldiers in their
official capacity, for which the King is indeed responsible ("every subject's duty is the king's"), and private acts, for which he is not ("but every
subject's soul is his own").

Modern commentators such as Edward White have already observed
that Henry's statement is faithful to the basic common law principle
respondere non sovereign, an exception to *respondeat superior*.[88] The rule
that the principal is liable for the acts of his agents, even negligent acts,
performed pursuant to authority or powers delegated to them was thus
inapplicable to the King. These rules, of course, govern civil responsibility; penal responsibility in common law is usually personal. Henry's
discourse merits consideration in this essay not because it is faithful to
the common law but because of what it implies about the important
question of the King's responsibility for the unauthorized or criminal
acts of soldiers in war. The emphasis in act 4, scene 1, on the King's
exemption from responsibility for his soldiers' misdeeds such as pillage
and murder is unremarkable for an era in which the concept of central
authority over the army was still rudimentary.

---

[86] For the beginning of the exchange, see text following note 28 *supra*. The King continues:

> *King*. So, if a son that is by his father sent about merchandise do sinfully miscarry
> upon the sea, the imputation of his wickedness, by your rule, should be imposed upon
> his father that sent him. Or if a servant under his master's command transporting a sum
> of money be assailed by robbers and die in many irreconcil'd iniquities, you may call
> the business of the master the author of the servant's damnation. But this is not so. The
> king is not bound to answer the particular endings of his soldiers, the father of his son,
> nor the master of his servant. For they purpose not their death when they purpose their
> services. Besides, there is no king, be his cause never so spotless, if it come to the
> arbitrament of swords, can try it out with all unspotted soldiers. Some peradventure
> have on them the guilt of premeditated and contrived murther; some, of beguiling
> virgins with the broken seals of perjury; some, making the wars their bulwark, that have
> before gored the gentle bosom of peace with pillage and robbery. Now if these men
> have defeated the law and outrun native punishment, though they can outstrip men,
> they have no wings to fly from God. . . . Then if they die unprovided, no more is the king
> guilty of their damnation than he was before guilty of those impieties for the which they
> are now visited. Every subject's duty is the king's, but every subject's soul is his own . . .
>
> *Williams*. "Tis certain every man that dies ill, the ill upon his own head – the king is
> not to answer it.   [4, 1, 148–89]

[87] *See generally* F. SHELLING, SHAKESPEARE AND "DEMI-SCIENCE" 97 (1927); J. O'MALLEY,
supra note 20, at 46–47.

[88] E. WHITE, *supra* note 20, at 291–92.

Responsibility for the treatment of prisoners depended to a large extent on who possessed them. In modern law, Article 12 of the third Geneva Convention provides that "[p]risoners of war are in the hands of the enemy Power, but not of the individuals or military units who have captured them"; and that "[i]rrespective of the individual responsibilities that may exist, the Detaining Power is responsible for the treatment given them." In medieval law, however, it was not always clear whether a prisoner of war "belonged" to the captor or the prince.[89]

---

[89] *See* Geneva Convention No. III, *supra* note 67. Compare the conflict between Henry IV and Hotspur over the prisoners that Hotspur took. Shakespeare, *The First Part of King Henry the Fourth*, act 1, scenes 1 & 3.

English indentures commonly show the king reserving certain classes of prisoners to himself (e.g., high-ranking officials, members of the opposing royal family). A captor normally owed a share of his ransom money to his captain, and a captain a share to the king. After all, the right to make such captures only arose because the war was "licensed" by the king and waged on his authority. What Honoré Bonet [Bouvet] said about spoil in his late fourteenth-century work is indicative of how difficult the problem was seen to be:

> [T]he law on the matter is ... by no means clear, and expressed opinion is doubtful. According to one law it is thought that the chattels a man wins should be his, but another law says that if a man comes into possession of chattels in war, he must deliver them to the duke of the battle [i.e., the commander, the prince or the lieutenant]. For my part I say that what a man gains from his enemies belongs to him, if we bear in mind that previously it belonged to his enemies, who have lost their lordship over it; but it does not belong to the captor to the extent that he is not obliged to hand it over to the duke of the battle; and the duke should share the spoils out among his men ....

H. BONET, THE TREE OF BATTLES 150 (G. Coopland ed. 1949) (trans. of Nys ed. 1883). More directly, Bouvet's discussion of prisoners points to similar difficulties:

> I ask now, if a soldier has captured [a duke or marshal] ..., to whom should he belong as prisoner, to the soldier, or to that soldier's lord; for according to these laws it would appear that he is the soldier's prisoner because the laws say that the captive is at the disposal of the captor. I assert, however, the contrary; for, if it is the case that the soldier is in the king's pay, or in that of another lord, the prisoners or other possessions acquired should be the lord's in whose pay the soldier is. And with regard to this the decretal says that all the booty should be at the king's disposal, and he should dispose of it at his pleasure to those who, according to his estimation, have helped him to win. And, if anyone said the contrary, he could not maintain it according to written law, for if a prisoner must belong to him who has taken and conquered him, by similar reasoning every strong castle and fortified town should be his if he took them. And it would not be reasonable that at the king's cost and expense he should gain land, for he does all that he does as a deputy of the king or of the lord in whose pay he is. Therefore what he conquers should be his lord's; for what he does he does not by his own industry or his own initiative.

Id. at 134–35. *See also* M. KEEN, *supra* note 7, at 144–45. While acknowledging that views on this question differed, C. DE PISAN, *supra* note 5, at 223, believed that both prisoners and other spoils of war were "atte wille of the prynce whom apparteyneth to dystrybute them after dyscrecyon."

The Ordinances of War attributed to King Henry V provided that soldiers pay their captains one-third of war booty ("wynnyng by werr") (para. 16). As regards prisoners, the ordinances required that the captor bring his prisoners to his captain or master. The penalty for noncompliance was forfeiture of the captor's part of the ransom to his captain or master. Within eight days, the captain or the master was to bring the prisoner to the king, constable or marshal (para. 20). If he failed to do so, he forfeited his share to whoever first gave notice

Contemporary legal doctrine was probably consistent with the denial of responsibility by Shakespeare's King for the improper acts of his troops when acting in their private capacity. Nevertheless, in view of the feudal structure of fifteenth-century armies, it would be misleading to regard the fighting men of France and England exclusively as soldiers of the realm whose sole duty of fealty was to their prince. The medieval system was quite different from the absolutist monarchical state later advocated by Jean Bodin.[90] The connection between a soldier and his immediate captain or lord was extremely important; soldiers were thus enmeshed in a web of relationships involving both king and captain. Keen observes that "[a] company was a *societas*, a corporate body of itself; ... [the captain] was its head .... As such he could be held liable for unauthorised pillaging by his men .... He might even, by the terms of his contracts with his soldiers, be bound to ransom them ...."[91] Although the king could deny responsibility for the improper acts of his soldiers, this was not necessarily true of their captain. That the captain could and should be held criminally responsible for such acts by his men, including illegal pillaging, is manifested by the ordinance issued by Charles VII of France in 1439.[92]

Gentili addressed the broader question whether the faults of individuals could be "charged against a community."[93] In principle, the act of a private citizen, not necessarily including soldiers, does not involve the entire community, the wrong not being caused "by act of the state."[94] But the state may become responsible if it fails to right the wrong. Since

to the constable or marshal. *Id. Ordinances of War made by King Henry V at Mawnt* [Mantes], *reprinted in* MONUMENTA JURIDICA, THE BLACK BOOK OF ADMIRALTY, App. at 459 (Travers Twiss ed. 1871). Sir Travers believes that these ordinances were probably issued by King Henry V in July 1419, when he was negotiating a treaty with the Duke of Burgundy and the Queen of France. Another text, The Statutes and Ordinaunces to be Keped in Time of Werre, although attributed to King Richard II, is probably a translation into English of a Latin version of Henry's ordinances; this version omits nine of the ordinances found in the Mantes version. *See* THE BLACK BOOK OF ADMIRALTY, *supra*, at 282 ed. nn. 1 & 2.

[90] J. BODIN, SIX LIVRES DE LA RÉPUBLIQUE (1577), *translated as* THE SIX BOOKES OF A COMMONWEALE (K. McRae ed. 1962) (facsimile reprint of Eng. trans., 1606).

[91] M. KEEN, *supra* note 7, at 150–51 (footnotes omitted).

[92] *See* Lettres de Charles VII, Pour obvier aux pilleries et vexations des gens de guerre (Orléans, le 2 Novembre, 1439), 13 ORDONNANCES DES ROIS DE FRANCE 306, 308 (Paris 1782):

cl. 18) Item, Ordonne le Roi, que chacun Capitaine ou Lieutenant sera tenu des excès, maux & outrages commis par ceux de sa compagnie, ou aucun d'eux, en tant que sitost que plainte ou clameur sera faite au Capitaine, de ses gens, ou d'aucun d'eux, d'aucun malfait ou excès, que incontinent il prenne le délinquant, et le baille à Justice pour en estre faite punition, selon son délit, raisonnable, selon ces présentes Ordonnances: & en cas qu'il ne le fera ou dissimulera ou delayera en quelque maniere que ce soit, ou que par négligence ou autrement le délinquant évadera & s'en ira, en telle maniere que punition & justice n'en soit faite, le Capitaine sera tenu du délit, comme celui qui l'aura fait, & en souffrira pareille peine qu'eust fait le délinquant.

See also M. KEEN, *supra* note 7, at 150.

[93] A. GENTILI, *supra* note 37, at 99.   [94] *Id.* at 100.

the community "can hold its citizens to their duty, and indeed is bound to hold them, it does wrong if it fails to do so."[95] The state has a clear duty to prevent wrongs of which it has notice and which it has the power to prevent: "the state, which knows because it has been warned, and which ought to prevent the misdeeds of its citizens, and through its jurisdiction can prevent them, will be at fault and guilty of a crime if it does not do so."[96] In language anticipating Article 18 of the UN International Law Commission's draft articles on state responsibility,[97] Gentili observed that "a state is liable for such offences of its citizens as are not for the moment but are *successive and continuous*; but even then, only if it knew of them and could have prevented them."[98] Had Gentili applied the same, if not a higher, duty of care to the acts of soldiers and sailors, the king would have been responsible for those wrongs he had known about and could have prevented.

Grotius took a similar approach: "Kings and public officials are liable for neglect if they do not employ the remedies which they can and ought to employ for the prevention of robbery and piracy,"[99] but their responsibility is limited to the punishment and "surrender" (extradition) of the guilty persons and the confiscation of the plundered goods. He added that if persons authorized to make captures from enemies at sea unlawfully captured the property of friends, a claim for restitution would not be acceptable even if the assertion were made that the rulers "utilized the services of wicked men, or ... had not required a bond."[100] Grotius appears to have distinguished between liability for neglect and nonliability for acts disobeying specific orders. As regards the latter, he categorically denied a prince's responsibility under the law of nations for those acts committed by his troops "contrary to orders": "this rule has been approved by witness of France and England. The liability of one for the acts of his servants without fault of his own does not belong to the law of nations, according to which this question has to be settled, but to municipal law ...."[101]

The principle of civil responsibility of the state for the unauthorized acts of its soldiers is relatively recent. Recognized in international

---

[95] *Id.*   [96] *Id.*

[97] *See* Article 18 and Commentary:

   [T]hree different cases are treated separately in the three paragraphs mentioned: that of a single State act of a continuing character extending over a period of time (continuing act); that of an act consisting of a systematic repetition of actions or omissions relating to separate cases (composite act); and that of an act consisting of a plurality of different actions or omissions by State organs relating to a single case (complex act).

[1976] 2 Y.B. INT'L L. COMM'N, pt. 2 at 88, UN Doc. A/CN.4/SER.A/1976/Add. 1 (Pt. 2).

[98] A. GENTILI, *supra* note 37, at 101 (emphasis added).

[99] H. GROTIUS, *supra* note 81, bk. II, ch. XVII, pt. XX(1).

[100] *Id.*   [101] *Id.*, pt. XX(2).

arbitrations,[102] its most authoritative statement is found in Article 3 of the
Hague Convention (No. IV) Respecting the Laws and Customs of War on
Land.[103] This provision, now accepted as customary law,[104] goes beyond
the generally applicable rules governing the international responsibility
of states, which are based on the distinction between official capacity and
private capacity, to establish a more stringent standard for members of
the armed forces. Article 3 constitutes "a veritable guarantee covering all
damage that might be caused by armed forces, whether they had acted as
organs [of the state] or as private persons."[105] This special rule, however,
addresses the *consequences* of acts by a particular category of state agents
rather than the attribution of their acts to the state.[106] In contrast to the
statement by Shakespeare's Henry, Article 3 holds the state responsible

---

[102] *See, e.g.*, Jeannaud v. United States, 3 J. MOORE, HISTORY AND DIGEST OF THE INTERNA-
TIONAL ARBITRATIONS TO WHICH THE UNITED STATES HAS BEEN A PARTY 3000 (1898); Zafiro
case (Gr. Brit. v. U.S.), 6 R. Int'l Arb. Awards 160 (1925). *See also* I. BROWNLIE, PRINCIPLES OF
PUBLIC INTERNATIONAL LAW 452 (4th ed. 1990).

[103] Oct. 18, 1907, 36 Stat. 2277, TS No. 539, 1 Bevans 631. Article 3 provides that a
belligerent party "shall be responsible for all acts committed by persons forming part of its
armed forces." On responsibility of states under Article 3, see Affaire des Biens Britanniques
au Maroc Espagnol (Spain v. U.K.), Report III (Oct. 23, 1924), 2 R. Int'l Arb. Awards 615, 645
(1925).

Article 3, of course, constitutes *lex specialis*. Regarding the general customary law rules on
attribution, see F. GARCÍA-AMADOR, L. SOHN & R. BAXTER, RECENT CODIFICATION OF THE
LAW OF STATE RESPONSIBILITY FOR INJURIES TO ALIENS 247–49 (1974); Meron, *International
Responsibility of States for Unauthorized Acts of Their Officials*, 33 BRIT. Y.B. INT'L L. 85 (1957).
See also Condorelli, *L'Imputation à l'Etat d'un fait internationalement illicite: solutions classiques et
nouvelles tendances*, 189 RECUEIL DES COURS 9, 147–48 (1984 VI); Christenson, *The Doctrine of
Attribution in State Responsibility*, in INTERNATIONAL LAW OF STATE RESPONSIBILITY FOR
INJURIES TO ALIENS 321 (R. Lillich ed. 1983); T. MERON, HUMAN RIGHTS AND HUMANITARIAN
NORMS AS CUSTOMARY LAW 155–71 (1989). For other scholarly writings on attribution to
states of *ultra vires* acts of state organs, see [1975] 2 Y.B. INT'L L. COMM'N 66 nn. 71–72, UN
Doc. A/CN.4/SER.A/1975/Add.1 (1976).

[104] [1975] 1 Y.B. INT'L L. COMM'N 7, UN Doc. A/CN.4/SER.A/1975 (comments of Prof.
Reuter); *see also* T. MERON, *supra* note 103, at 225–26.

[105] [1975] 1 Y.B. INT'L L. COMM'N, *supra* note 104, at 16 (comments by Special Rapporteur
Roberto Ago). The ILC observed that "article 3 ... attributes to the State responsibility ...
whether [the actors] acted as organs or as individuals." 2 *id., supra* note 103, at 69 (footnote
omitted). *See also* 1 L. OPPENHEIM, INTERNATIONAL LAW 363 n. 1 (H. Lauterpacht 8th ed.
1955). Article 3 was also intended to apply to cases "in which negligence cannot be attributed
to the government itself," i.e., violations committed "without the knowledge of governments, or against their will." Sandoz, *Unlawful Damage in Armed Conflicts and Redress under
International Humanitarian Law*, INT'L REV. RED CROSS, No. 228, May–June 1982, at 131, 136–
37. *See also* Kalshoven, *State Responsibility for Warlike Acts of the Armed Forces*, 40 INT'L &
COMP. L.Q. 827, 837–38 (1991).

[106] Note the opinion of Professor Brownlie that "[i]mputability would seem to be a
superfluous notion, since the major issue in a given situation is whether there has been a
breach of duty: the content of 'imputability' will vary according to the particular duty, the
nature of the breach, and so on." I. BROWNLIE, SYSTEM OF THE LAW OF NATIONS: STATE
RESPONSIBILITY, PART I, at 36 (1983) (footnote omitted). *See also* Arangio-Ruiz, Second Report
on State Responsibility, UN Doc. A/CN.4/425/Add.1, para. 173 (1989) ("in the case of States
as international persons a *legal* attribution seems actually to be an error and a redundancy").

for the misdeeds of the members of its armed forces even when their acts cannot be imputed to the state.

The recognition of the leader's penal responsibility for acts committed by members of the armed forces in violation of the law of war came still later with the "*Yamashita* doctrine."[107] Nevertheless, the *Yamashita* doctrine, which can be regarded as a statement of customary law, was not expressed in the Geneva Conventions of 12 August 1949 for the Protection of Victims of War[108] and it found explicit recognition in a treaty only in 1977.[109]

---

[107] In 1946 General Tomuyuki Yamashita, the commander of the Japanese armed forces in the Philippines in 1944–1945, voiced a defense that echoed Henry's plea of *respondere non sovereign*. Charged with failing to discharge his duty to control the operations of the persons subject to his command who had violated the laws of war by committing massacres, acts of violence, cruelty, homicide, pillage and destruction against the civilian population and prisoners of war, Yamashita maintained that the charge did not allege that he personally had either committed or directed the commission of these acts and that he could therefore not be held responsible for any violation of the law of war. On a petition of certiorari from a U.S. military commission, the U.S. Supreme Court considered a military commander's criminal liability for such violations and stated that the aim of protecting civilian populations and POWs from brutality would largely be defeated if the commander of an invading army "could with impunity neglect to take reasonable measures for their protection. Hence the law of war presupposes that its violation is to be avoided through the control of the operations of war by commanders who are to some extent responsible for their subordinates." *In re* Yamashita, 327 U.S. 1, 15 (1945). Extrapolating from provisions of the Hague Convention No. IV and other treaties, Chief Justice Stone concluded that they "plainly imposed on petitioner ... an affirmative duty to take such measures as were within his power and appropriate in the circumstances to protect prisoners of war and the civilian population. This duty of a commanding officer has heretofore been recognized, and its breach penalized by our own military tribunals." *Id.* at 16. See the criticism of this decision by M. WALZER, JUST AND UNJUST WARS 319–22 (1977).

In *United States v. Sadao Araki*, the International Tribunal for the Far East followed the *Yamashita* doctrine with regard to the responsibility of members of the Japanese cabinet for mistreatment of POWs. "even though they delegate the duties of maintenance and protection to others." U.S. NAVAL WAR COLLEGE, INTERNATIONAL LAW STUDIES, VOL. 60, DOCUMENTS ON PRISONERS OF WAR 437, 438 (H. Levie ed. 1979). The Tribunal held that members of the government and military and civilian officials with control over POWs fail in their duty and become responsible for ill-treatment of prisoners if they do not establish and secure the efficient functioning of a system aimed at preventing such treatment. *Id.* at 438. Only for the last two centuries, however, had prisoners of war and civilian internees been considered to be in the power of the captor sovereign. *Id.* at 437. The principle of the responsibility of the state for the POWs captured by its troops is stated in the nineteenth- and twentieth-century law of war instruments.

[108] The authoritative Commentary on Article 146 of the Geneva Convention (No. IV) Relative to the Protection of Civilian Persons in Time of War, Aug. 12, 1949, 6 UST 3516, TIAS No. 3365, 75 UNTS 287, prepared by the International Committee of the Red Cross, mentions the guilty verdicts in several cases in Allied courts and observes: "In view of the Convention's silence on this point, it will have to be determined under municipal law either by the enactment of special provisions or by the application of the general clauses which may occur in the penal codes." COMMENTARY ON THE GENEVA CONVENTIONS OF 12 AUGUST 1949: GENEVA CONVENTION RELATIVE TO THE PROTECTION OF CIVILIAN PERSONS IN TIME OF WAR 591–92 (O. Uhler & H. Coursier eds. 1958).

[109] Article 86(2) of Protocol I Additional to the Geneva Conventions, *supra* note 68.

This principle of responsibility, *respondere sovereign*, was incorporated into modern international customary and conventional law as necessary to ensure the effectiveness of the law of war. It is a far cry from Henry's statement on his own responsibility in act 4, scene 1.

VI   THE SIEGE OF HARFLEUR AND TREATMENT OF OCCUPIED TERRITORY

A commentator on the modern law of war would be hard pressed to offer a more terrifying catalog of violations of the law of war than that contained in the speech by Shakespeare's Henry before the walls of Harfleur, threatening cruel retribution should Harfleur refuse to surrender:[110]

110

       King. How yet resolves the governor of the town?
This is the latest parle we will admit.
Therefore to our best mercy give yourselves,
Or like to men proud of destruction
Defy us to our worst. For, as I am a soldier,
A name that in my thoughts becomes me best,
If I begin the batt'ry once again,
I will not leave the half-achiev'd Harflew
Till in her ashes she lie buried.
The gates of mercy shall be all shut up,
And the flesh'd soldier, rough and hard of heart,
In liberty of bloody hand shall range
With conscience wide as hell, mowing like grass
Your fresh fair virgins and your flow'ring infants.
What is it then to me if impious War,
Array'd in flames like to the prince of fiends,
Do with his smirch'd complexion all fell feats
Enlink'd to waste and desolation?
What is't to me, when you yourselves are cause,
If your pure maidens fall into the hand
Of hot and forcing violation?
What rein can hold licentious wickedness
When down the hill he holds his fierce career?
We may as bootless spend our vain command
Upon th' enraged soldiers in their spoil
As send precepts to the leviathan
To come ashore. Therefore, you men of Harflew,
Take pity of your town and of your people
Whiles yet my soldiers are in my command,
Whiles yet the cool and temperate wind of grace
O'erblows the filthy and contagious clouds
Of heady murther, spoil, and villainy.
If not – why, in a moment look to see
The blind and bloody soldier with foul hand
Defile the locks of your shrill-shrieking daughters,
Your fathers taken by the silver beards

denying quarter; killing or wounding an enemy who, having laid down his arms or no longer having a means of defense, has been captured;[111] ignoring the principle of distinction between combatants and civilians; attacking civilians;[112] enforcing collective penalties; resorting to measures of intimidation and terrorism; and engaging in pillaging and rape.[113] Of course, Henry cannot be judged by modern international norms, which in any case are too often honored only in the breach.[114] Rather, the relevant questions are, first, how did the real Henry treat the conquered inhabitants of Harfleur? Did he actually "use mercy to them all"? Second, to what extent did the speech of Shakespeare's Henry and the conduct of the real Henry's troops comport with the then-prevailing standards?

Of considerable legal importance is the fact that, in the negotiations preceding its surrender, the leaders of Harfleur had offered "to deliver the towne into the kings hands, their lives and goods saved." This offer, however, was refused, the King having successfully insisted on "their bodies and goods to stand at the kings pleasure."[115] After the surrender, which was achieved by agreement ("composition"),[116] "[t]he souldiors

> And their most reverend heads dash'd to the walls,
> Your naked infants spitted upon pikes
> Whiles the mad mothers with their howls confus'd
> Do break the clouds, as did the wives of Jewry
> At Herod's bloody-hunting slaughtermen.
> What say you? Will you yield, and this avoid,
> Or, guilty in defense, be thus destroy'd?
>   *Governor.* . . . We yield our town and lives to thy soft mercy.
> Enter our gates, dispose of us and ours,
> For we no longer are defensible.
>   *King.* Open your gates. Come, Uncle Exeter,
> Go you and enter Harflew. There remain,
> And fortify it strongly 'gainst the French.
> Use mercy to them all.
>
>   [3, 3, 1–54]

Compare White, *Shakespeare and Psychological Warfare*, 12 PUB. OPINION Q. 68, 70–72 (1948).

[111] *Compare* Hague Regulations annexed to Convention No. IV, *supra* note 103, Art. 23(c)–(d). In negotiating the terms of surrender of Rone, Henry insisted that "the gunners that had discharged anie peece against the Englishmen should suffer death." R. HOLINSHED, *supra* note 3, at 69.

[112] Additional Protocol I, *supra* note 68, Art. 51.

[113] Geneva Convention No. IV, *supra* note 108, Arts. 33 and 27, respectively.

[114] E.g., the treatment of Kuwaiti civilians by Iraq in 1990. *See, e.g.,* SC Res. 674 (Oct. 29, 1990), *reprinted in* 29 ILM 1561 (1990); and UN Doc. A/C.3/45/L.90 (Nov. 27, 1990).

[115] R. HOLINSHED, *supra* note 3, at 23–24. Sir Harris Nicolas writes that King Henry intimated to the French that, unless they would yield at discretion, they must not expect any terms. H. NICOLAS, *supra* note 70, at 62. After the surrender, the King is reported to have stated that, although Harfleur had defied him, "in consideration of their having submitted to his clemency, he would not entirely withhold his mercy from them." *Id.* at 66. This version is not mentioned in Holinshed or Hall and is therefore unlikely to have been known to Shakespeare. *See also infra* text at and notes 165–66.

[116] 2 J. WYLIE, *supra* note 26, at 50 (1919).

were ransomed, and the towne sacked, to the great gaine of the Englishmen."[117] The wealthy were allowed to pay ransom in return for permission
to stay,[118] but "a greate part of the women and children"[119] were "expelled
out of their habitations ... parents with their children, yoong maids and old
folke went out of the towne gates with heavie harts."[120] "The priestes had
licence to depart leuyng behinde them their substaunce."[121] The King then
issued a proclamation in England "that whosoever ... would inhabit in
Harflue, should have his dwelling given him gratis."[122] Although from the
modern viewpoint the treatment of the captured Harfleur cannot easily be
seen as merciful, more massive violations, particularly widespread killing
of the population such as that resorted to by Henry's troops in taking
Caen,[123] were avoided. Not surprisingly, Henry's contemporaries, including the French chronicler the Religieux de Saint-Denys, thus considered
the treatment of Harfleur lenient.[124]

Turning from the facts to the prevailing law, it must be made clear that
some norms regulating warfare were agreed upon, at least in theory.

The canonistic doctrine of privilege "was rooted in the notion that the
public welfare could be promoted in certain circumstances by granting
special rights to groups who served the general interests of the community"[125] (e.g., scholars and clerics). The concept of Peace of God,[126]

---

[117] R. HOLINSHED, *supra* note 3, at 24. But see H. HUTCHISON, KING HENRY V, at 114 (1967),
who argues that Harfleur was not sacked. He explains the deportation order as based on
Henry's belief that Harfleur belonged to him, and on his wish to settle Englishmen in place of
the departed natives. *See also* D. SEWARD, HENRY V, at 67–68 (1988); and E. JACOB, HENRY V,
supra note 26, at 90. Jacob mentions Henry's order prohibiting the sacking of Harfleur. *Id.* G.
TOWLE, THE HISTORY OF HENRY THE FIFTH 304 (1866), wrote that Henry tried to prevent
pillage, but in vain. Despite Holinshed's statement that Harfleur was sacked, historians thus
obviously differ on whether it was. Because of his familiarity with Holinshed, Shakespeare
must have assumed that Harfleur was sacked.

[118] E. HALL, *supra* note 4, at 63; 2 J. WYLIE, *supra* note 116, at 58–59.

[119] E. HALL, *supra* note 4, at 63.

[120] R. HOLINSHED, *supra* note 3, at 24. THE FIRST ENGLISH LIFE OF KING HENRY THE FIFTH,
supra note 26, at 41, does not mention the deportation. *See also* H. NICOLAS, *supra* note 70, at
68–69.

[121] E. HALL, *supra* note 4, at 63.

[122] R. HOLINSHED, *supra* note 3, at 24. *Compare* Geneva Convention No. IV, *supra* note 108,
Art. 49 (which categorically prohibits deportation of the population of occupied territories
and transfer of the occupying power's population to occupied territory). Henry also expelled
French population elsewhere, e.g., in Caen. R. HOLINSHED, *supra*, at 58. In Rone, however, the
terms of surrender included the right of the townspeople to remain in their dwellings.

[123] M. KEEN, *supra* note 7, at 121.

[124] 2 J. WYLIE, *supra* note 116, at 59. "Il [Henry V] traita les chevaliers et les écuyers qui
avaient été faits prisonniers avec plus de douceur et de générosité qu'on s'y attendait." 5
CHRONIQUE DU RELIGIEUX DE SAINT-DENYS, *supra* note 70, at 545.

[125] J. BRUNDAGE, MEDIEVAL CANON LAW AND THE CRUSADER 140 (1969). The foundations
of this doctrine can be found in Gratian's *Decretum. Id.* at 141. On the latter, see notes 127, 130
infra.

[126] Brundage does not appear to distinguish between the Truce of God and the Peace of
God. *See* J. BRUNDAGE, *supra* note 125, at 13 n. 40, 161.

a canonical attempt to humanize warfare, was instrumental in establishing the principle of the immunity of noncombatants, though it was frequently disrespected in practice. That concept, which was developed considerably earlier,[127] was incorporated into canon law during the papacy of Gregory IX in the thirteenth century. *De treuga et pace* (Of Truces and Peace) listed eight categories of persons "who should have full security against the ravages of war: clerics, monks, friars, other religious, pilgrims, travelers, merchants and peasants cultivating the soil";[128] they were also to be accorded protection for at least some of their property. These classes were composed of persons whose social functions precluded their engaging in war; reciprocity required that war not be waged against them.[129] In elaborating this list, the church took good care of its own. Strikingly, the classification did not include women, children and the aged, i.e., those physically unable to bear arms.[130] In theory, however, these groups benefited from the parallel, secular code of chivalry, which required the protection of broader categories of persons, defined by weakness and innocence, i.e., women, children, the aged, the sick and other peaceable persons.[131]

Account must also be taken of various ordinances of war and admiralty promulgated by the Kings of England in the Middle Ages.[132] Of these, the most comprehensive and important regarding war on land are the Ordinances of War made by King Richard II at Durham (1385)[133] and the Ordinances of War made by King Henry V at Mantes (1419).[134] The latter obviously drew on the former, particularly in the provision that prohibited stealing from the church and the killing or raping of women.[135] The penalty for violating these prohibitions was death. Apart from military discipline, the ordinances of Henry V imposed such humanitarian

---

[127] For a discussion of Gratian's *Decretum* (ca. 1140), see F. RUSSELL, THE JUST WAR IN THE MIDDLE AGES 55, 70 (1975). Gratian proclaimed immunity from violence for pilgrims, clerics, monks, women and the unarmed poor. *Id.* at 70.

[128] J. JOHNSON, JUST WAR TRADITION AND THE RESTRAINT OF WAR 127 (1981); P. HAGGENMACHER, *supra* note 6, at 268–72. The Magna Carta (June 12, 1215), *reprinted in* SOURCES OF OUR LIBERTIES 11, 17 (R. Perry & J. Cooper eds. 1959), Art. 41, already recognized, on the basis of reciprocity, the immunity of merchants in time of war.

[129] J. JOHNSON, *supra* note 128, at 132.

[130] Women and the unarmed poor, however, were included in the protected categories in Gratian's *Decretum*. F. RUSSELL, *supra* note 128, at 70.

[131] J. JOHNSON, *supra* note 128, at 135–36. Both women and unarmed priests were protected by King Henry V's Ordinances of War, *supra* note 89; *see also infra* note 196.

[132] *See generally* Twiss, *Introduction* to THE BLACK BOOK OF ADMIRALTY, *supra* note 89, at lviii–lxxvii.

[133] These ordinances are in French. *See id.* at lxxvi. On the official use of French in England in the thirteenth and fourteenth centuries, see *id.* at xlv–lvi.

[134] *Supra* note 89. These ordinances were probably written in Latin, but there is no complete Latin text extant. Editor's Notes, THE BLACK BOOK OF ADMIRALTY, *supra* note 89, at 282–83. For the earliest English form of these ordinances, see *supra* note 89.

[135] *See infra* note 196.

measures as prohibiting the taking of children under the age of fourteen as prisoners and protecting women confined by childbirth[136] and peasants, whose agricultural tools and work animals were safeguarded from seizure. This was not the first time that Henry had promulgated laws protecting the civilian population of France from the excesses of his soldiery. Soon after reaching Harfleur in 1415, Henry issued a proclamation, mentioned by Holinshed, prohibiting, under penalty of death, such crimes as setting houses on fire and violating churches or the person of women and priests, unless any of the latter were armed[137] (in reality, ecclesiastics often engaged in warfare). Henry found it necessary to reaffirm these strictures by issuing a similar proclamation after the conquest of Harfleur, forbidding his troops to devastate the area or to plunder the inhabitants, except for food and other necessities of life.[138]

Writers on *jus gentium* contemporaneous with Shakespeare recognized several protected categories of noncombatants. Vitoria asserted that even when fighting against Turks it was unlawful to kill children, because they are innocent, and women, because they are presumed innocent.[139] In war between Christians, "harmless agricultural folk," other "peaceable civilian population," "foreigners or guests," "clerics and members of a religious order" are all presumed innocent and therefore could not be killed.[140] The presumption of innocence could be rebutted by showing that the person concerned took part in the hostilities. Although Vitoria subjected the prohibition on killing innocents to the necessities of war ("when there is no other means of carrying on the operations of a just war"),[141] he articulated a precursor of the modern principle of proportionality:[142]

> [If] little effect upon the ultimate issue of the war is to be expected from the storming of a fortress ... wherein are many innocent folk, it would not be right,

---

[136] *See also infra* note 202.

[137] H. NICOLAS, *supra* note 70, at 52–53. According to Holinshed:

> At his first comming on land, he caused proclamation to be made, that no person should be so hardie on paine of death, either to take anie thing out of anie church that belonged to the same, or to hurt or doo anie violence either to priests, women, or anie such as should be found without weapon or armor, and not readie to make resistance ....

R. HOLINSHED, *supra* note 3, at 21–22.

[138] H. NICOLAS, *supra* note 70, at 81–82. *See also infra* text at notes 196–204; H. HUTCHISON, *supra* note 117, at 111. Hutchison believes that "such regulations were common to most medieval armies, and the fact that they were issued at all argues as much for their regrettable necessity as for the mercy ... of those who made them." *Id.*

[139] F. VICTORIA, *supra* note 33, at 179(36).

[140] *Id.*

[141] *Id.* at 179(37).

[142] *See* Additional Protocol I, *supra* note 68, Art. 51(5)(*b*), which prohibits as indiscriminate an attack "which may be expected to cause incidental loss of civilian life, injury to civilians, damage to civilian objects, or a combination thereof, which would be excessive in relation to the concrete and direct military advantage anticipated."

for the purpose of assailing a few guilty, to slay the many innocent by use of fire or engines of war or other means likely to overwhelm indifferently both innocent and guilty.[143]

Gentili, for his part, insisted that "[c]hildren should always be spared, and so should women."[144] "[W]omen, because they cannot handle arms, are treated like the clergy .... [T]hey are spared."[145] He also advocated the protection of farmers, traders and foreigners.[146] Suárez argued that the innocent include children, women and all those unable to bear arms, by virtue of natural law; ambassadors, by virtue of *jus gentium;* and members of religious orders and priests, by virtue of canon law. All other persons forming part of a hostile state (which excludes strangers and foreigners) are considered enemies.[147] In practice, these rules may have been breached more than respected, as was claimed by the military law expert Ayala, who wrote that the canons requiring that "clergy, monks, converts, foreigners, merchants, and country folk" be spared had been abrogated by contrary usage.[148]

The 1785 Treaty of Amity and Commerce between the United States and Prussia exemplifies the convergence of the canonical and chivalric lists of protected persons. This Treaty, cited by the U.S. Supreme Court in *The Paquete Habana,*[149] reflects the medieval concepts of both innocence and social function. Modern international law differs in that it is informed primarily by the notions of civilian status and the immunity of civilians from attack, into which the concept of innocence metamorphosed. It focuses on the protection of individual civilians and the civilian

---

[143] F. VICTORIA, *supra* note 33, at 179(37). *See* P. HAGGENMACHER, *supra* note 6, at 275–76.

[144] A. GENTILI, *supra* note 37, at 251.

[145] *Id.* Gentili believed that women (*id.* at 251–54) and clergy (*id.* at 427–28) who take up arms lose their immunity. Regarding armed clergy's loss of protection from acts of war, see also C. DE PISAN, *supra* note 5, at 235–36, 257, 283.

[146] A. GENTILI, *supra* note 37, at 261–69.

[147] F. SUÁREZ, *supra* note 29, at 843.

[148] B. AYALA, *supra* note 60, at 45.

[149] 175 U.S. 677, 690–91 (1900). Article XXIII of the Treaty of Amity and Commerce between the United States and Prussia, July 9 and Sept. 10, 1785, provided that in case of war:

the merchants of either country then residing in the other shall be allowed to remain nine months to collect their debts and settle their affairs, and may depart freely, carrying off all their effects without molestation or hindrance. And all women and children, scholars of every faculty, cultivators of the earth, artizans, manufacturers, and fishermen, unarmed and inhabiting unfortified towns, villages, or places, and in general all others whose occupations are for the common subsistence and benefit of mankind, shall be allowed to continue their respective employments, and shall not be molested in their persons, nor shall their houses or goods be burnt or otherwise destroyed, nor their fields wasted by the armed force of the enemy, into whose power by the events of war they may happen to fall; but if anything is necessary to be taken from them for the use of such armed force, the same shall be paid for at a reasonable price.

8 Stat. 84, TS No. 292, 8 Bevans 78, 85–86.

population,[150] with the exception of the special protection granted to the
Red Cross and other humanitarian organizations.[151] Additional measures
regarding children and women are subsumed under the protection of the
civilian population. With the exception of the Red Cross and medical and
religious personnel, beneficial social function as a criterion for protection
has become obsolete.

How, then, can the dire threats of Shakespeare's Henry be reconciled
with the existing and emerging norms protecting women and others
from the ravages of war? The distinction in medieval law between
the treatment of both combatants and civilians in captured territory
or on the battlefield, on the one hand, and their treatment in a besieged
city or fortress[152] that was taken by "assault,"[153] on the other hand,
suggests an explanation. Unmitigated brutality was reserved for the
latter:

> In a city taken by storm almost any licence was condoned by the law. Only
> churches and churchmen were technically secure, but even they were not often
> spared. Women could be raped, and men killed out of hand. All the goods of the
> inhabitants were regarded as forfeit.... The prospect of this free run of his lusts
> for blood, spoil and women was a major incentive to a soldier to persevere in
> the rigours which were likely to attend a protracted siege.[154]

Notwithstanding the importance of such famous battles as Crécy and
Agincourt, medieval warfare turned far more on sieges of strongholds
than on pitched battles.[155] Only through the conquest of fortresses could a
territory be effectively occupied. Resistance therefore was grimly viewed
and severely punished. Both the goods and the lives of the inhabitants of a
conquered town "were forefeit [*sic*] for the contumacious disregard of a
prince's summons to surrender.... [S]poliation was not an act of war, but

---

[150] *See, e.g.*, Additional Protocol I, *supra* note 68, Arts. 50–52.

[151] *Id.*, Art. 81.

[152] On sieges, see generally M. WALZER, *supra* note 107, ch. 10.

[153] i.e., following an unconditional surrender, whether or not the city was stormed. M.
KEEN, *supra* note 7, at 122. A city that did not surrender by a treaty (*appointment*) could be
taken by assault. *Id.* at 119. Medieval strategists taught that a fortress could be reduced "by
methods of drought [poisoning or cutting the supply of water], famine [blockade] or fight
[assault]." 2J. WYLIE, *supra* note 116, at 32.

The prohibition of starvation of civilians as a method of warfare is of quite recent origin.
See Additional Protocol I, *supra* note 68, Art. 54. Interpreting its Resolution 661 of August 6,
1990 (*reprinted in* 29 ILM 1325 (1990)), which imposed sanctions on Iraq and prohibited
importation of foodstuffs, except in humanitarian circumstances, the Security Council recognized, in Resolution 666 of September 13, 1990 (*reprinted in* 29 ILM at 1330), that foodstuffs
might have to be supplied to the civilian population of Iraq or Kuwait to relieve human
suffering.

[154] M. KEEN, *supra* note 7, at 121–22.

[155] J. JOHNSON, *supra* note 128, at 133. Keen writes that the "stories of great sieges ... loom
large in the history of the Hundred Years War; in fact they are its turning points." M. KEEN,
supra note 7, at 119. *See also* G. PARKER, THE MILITARY REVOLUTION 7–9 (1988).

the sentence of justice."[156] A city such as Harfleur, which "held out till it had to yield unconditionally was at the mercy of its captor, to be given up to plunder or ransomed according to his will. Its population [could be] ... subjected to pillage, slaughter and rape ...."[157]

Vitoria's later, reluctant recognition that the sacking of a city was legal if it was "necessary for the conduct of the war or as a deterrent to the enemy or as a spur to the courage of the troops"[158] indicates that the threats made by Shakespeare's Henry measured up to the norms prevailing during the Hundred Years' War. However, because such sacking resulted "in many horrors and cruelties, enacted beyond all humane limits by a barbarous soldiery, such as slaughter and torture of the innocent, rape of virgins, dishonor of matrons, and looting of temples,"[159] delivering up a city to be sacked "without the greatest necessity and weightiest reason" was unjust.[160]

These harsh norms, seldom questioned in medieval times, were challenged by Renaissance writers on international law. As was often the case, Gentili led the way in promoting the humanization of the law.[161] With eloquence and clarity, he proclaimed that "[t]hese are called the rights of humanity and the laws of war, which order the sparing of those who surrender."[162] If conditions of surrender are stipulated, the law of nature requires that they be observed.[163] Even unconditional surrenders, "surrender ... at discretion," may not lead to license with regard to "property, life, and honour" because discretion ought to be understood as "the discretion of a good man."[164] If Henry's speech reflected the medieval norms contemporaneous with the siege of Harfleur, Henry's command to Exeter to "use mercy" may well have reflected the wide medieval recognition of the injunction to use mercy (the word "mercy" appears four times in the speech), a secular counterpart and reflection of the Christian concept of charity or *caritas*.[165] Be that as it may, Shakespeare probably wanted to emphasize Henry's humanity, for the order to use mercy is

---

[156] M. KEEN, *supra* note 7, at 123. While the penalties for holding out against a siege were brutal, a captain who surrendered a town without siege while there was a chance of defending it would be guilty of treason toward another prince. *Id*. at 124–25. *See also* B. AYALA, *supra* note 60, at 233.

[157] E. CHEYNEY, THE DAWN OF A NEW ERA: 1250–1453, at 165 (1936).

[158] F. VICTORIA, *supra* note 33, at 184(52).   [159] *Id*. at 184–85(52).

[160] *Id*. at 185(52).   [161] *See also* P. HAGGENMACHER, *supra* note 6, at 277.

[162] A. GENTILI, *supra* note 37, at 216. Invoking the law of Lycurgus and the Greeks, Gentili wrote that "when the victory was assured the slaying of the enemy should cease." *Id*. at 211.

[163] *Id*. at 219.   [164] *Id*. at 227.

[165] On the concept of mercy, see J. JOHNSON, *supra* note 128, at 6–10; P. RAMSEY, THE JUST WAR: FORCE AND POLITICAL RESPONSIBILITY 150–51 (1968). In discussing war, St. Thomas Aquinas cited Augustine:

Among true worshippers of God those wars are looked on as peace-making which are waged neither from aggrandisement nor cruelty, but with the object of securing peace, of repressing the

mentioned neither by Holinshed nor by Hall,[166] and both the sack of Harfleur and the deportations that followed are passed over in silence in the play, though related by Holinshed (Hall mentioned the sack of Harfleur but not the deportations).

Three of the elements in Henry's ultimatum merit more detailed comment: the denial of quarter, and the threats of rape and of pillage. The chivalric code of conduct "required that a knight vanquished in battle be given quarter rather than being killed, that when taken prisoner he must be treated as a gentleman, and that he be ransomed for a reasonable sum not beyond his means to pay."[167] Of course, a knight who surrendered might refuse to enter into a contract to pay ransom and would be killed or condemned to captivity, or would have to fight on and risk being killed on the battlefield. The latter possibility is heroically depicted by Shakespeare's Henry:

> *King*. . . . Herald, save thou thy labor.
> Come thou no more for ransom, gentle herald.
> They shall have none, I swear, but these my joints,
> Which if they have as I will leave 'em them,
> Shall yield them little, tell the Constable.
>
> [4, 3, 121–25]

It was unclear, however, to what extent these protective rules applied to "non-knightly infantry" (commoners and peasants who, not infrequently, were massacred[168]) and to non-Christians.[169] It should not be assumed that only gentlemen were given the chance to ransom themselves. Honoré Bouvet, writing before Agincourt, thus complained that "excessive payments and ransoms [were demanded] without pity or mercy . . . from the poor labourers who cultivate lands and vineyards."[170]

evil and supporting the good. . . . The craving to hurt people, the cruel thirst for revenge, the unappeased and unrelenting spirit, the savageness of fighting on, . . . all these are rightly condemned in wars.

35 SUMMA THEOLOGIAE: CONSEQUENCES OF CHARITY, Question 40, at 83 (Blackfriars ed. 1972). See also Question 44, on the commands to love, *Id.* at 143, 155, 157.

Grotius recognized that history abounded with accounts of "the destruction of whole cities, or the levelling of walls to the ground, the devastation of fields, and conflagrations. . . . [They were] permissible also against those who have surrendered." H. GROTIUS, *supra* note 81, bk. III. ch. V, pt. I. However, both in battle and in a siege, a "surrender of those who yield upon condition that their lives be spared ought not to be rejected," *id.*, ch. XI, pt. XIV(1), and "[t]he same sense of justice bids that those be spared who yield themselves unconditionally to the victor, or who become suppliants." *Id.*, pt. XV.

See also supra note 115.

[166] *See* R. HOLINSHED, *supra* note 3, at 23–25; E. HALL, *supra* note 4, at 62–63.

[167] J. JOHNSON, *supra* note 128, at 126.   [168] *Id.* at 137.

[169] F. VICTORIA, *supra* note 33, at 183(48). However, even in war with the Turks, it was not lawful to kill women, who were presumed innocent, or children. *Id.* at 179(36).

[170] H. BONET, *supra* note 89, at 153.

Nevertheless, a lowly prisoner could call upon his lord's duty to him when it came to ransom, which might encourage the captor to treat him kindly.[171]

Even knights could not always rely on an offer of quarter on the battle-field.[172] In his important fourteenth-century work on the law of war, John of Legnano (Giovanni da Legnano)[173] favored sparing captured generals but made the grant of quarter subject to the necessities of war:

> [Q]uarter should be granted to one who humbles himself and does not try to resist, unless the grant of quarter gives reason for fearing a disturbance of the peace, in which case he must suffer. ... [Q]uarter is to be granted only when disturbance of the peace is not feared, and otherwise not.[174]

According to the modern historian James Hamilton Wylie, word had circulated among Henry's troops in Agincourt "that the Frenchmen meant to give no quarter save to the king and his nobles, for whose captivity ... they had already begun to make arrangements, while the rumour ran that they would cut off every archer's right hand."[175] The practice of denying quarter even on the battlefield found support among some writers on *jus gentium* in Shakespeare's era. Thus, Vitoria stated that "[a]ll the doubt and difficulty [was] ... to know whether, when we have won our victory and the enemy is no longer any danger to us, we may kill all who have borne arms against us. Manifestly, yes."[176] He justified this license to kill on the basis of its promise of future security through the

---

[171] M. KEEN, *supra* note 7, at 150–51, points out that by the terms of his contracts with his soldiers, the captain might be bound to ransom them. *See also* P. LEWIS, *supra* note 22, at 212 ("It was possible to get help with one's ransom from one's lord: from the king or from one's commander").

[172] H. BONET, *supra* note 89, at 152, wrote that "if a knight, captain, or champion, take another in battle he may freely kill him. ... [B]ut out of battle no man may kill another save in self-defence ...."

[173] M. KEEN, *supra* note 7, at 7, regards John of Legnano and Honoré Bonet (*supra* note 89) as the most famous academic lawyers (actually, Bonet was a monk, rather than an academic lawyer) who wrote about the law of war. Holland describes Legnano's work as "the earliest attempt to deal, as a whole, with the group of rights and duties which arise out of a state of War." Holland, *Introduction* to GIOVANNI DA LEGNANO, TRACTATUS DE BELLO, DE REPRESALIIS ET DE DUELLO, at b (T. Holland ed. 1917) (Bologna ms. ca. 1390). Legnano completed his work in 1360, but it was published in 1477 and in better-known editions in 1487 and 1584. *Id.* at xxvii–xxix.

[174] G. DA LEGNANO, *supra* note 173, ch. XXX, at 253–54. *See also id.*, ch. LXIX, at 274 ("Should mercy be shown to persons captured in a lawful war? We must say that it should, unless by sparing them there is fear of a disturbance of the peace").

[175] 2 J. WYLIE, *supra* note 116, at 154.

[176] F. VICTORIA, *supra* note 33, at 182(45). F. SUÁREZ, *supra* note 29, at 845, argued for the protection from killing of innocent persons, even if the punishment inflicted upon their state was insufficient; but he favored allowing, in these circumstances, the killing of some additional guilty individuals after the war. *Id.* at 841. "[T]he slaying of a great multitude would be thus permissible only when there was most urgent cause, nevertheless, even such slaughter may sometimes be allowed, in order to terrify the rest ...." *Id.*

deterrent effect of punishment.[177] He attempted to temper the severity of
the law by invoking the need "to take into account the nature of the wrong
done by the enemy and of the damage they have caused ... and from that
standpoint to move to our revenge and punishment, without any cruelty
and inhumanity."[178] Gentili, however, advocated greater humanity.[179]

In contrast to combat on the battlefield, siege warfare was waged in
accordance with the rule of "war to the death without quarter (though
the rule could be waived for anyone, and a prisoner who could pay a good
ransom was likely enough to be spared)."[180] The rule applied "not against
soldiers only, but against all the able-bodied inhabitants of the town."[181]
Disregarding those cases where the attacking prince insisted on unconditional surrender, Vitoria argued that, if a city surrendered unconditionally
without providing in the conditions of capitulation for the safety of its
inhabitants, it would be permissible, subject to some qualifications, to put
"the more notorious offenders" to death.[182] Nevertheless, guided by his
theory of innocence, Vitoria believed that troops engaged in defending or
attacking cities, whether in a just or an unjust war, should not be killed if the
presumption was "that they entered on the strife in good faith."[183] Gentili
criticized the denial of quarter more directly. Specifically in the context of
siege warfare, he admitted that there might be reasons for refusing to
accept a surrender, "but if there is no such cause, it surely seems right to
accept it; otherwise we have a war of extermination."[184] He regarded an
order to kill a large number of warriors "who surrendered themselves and
threw down their arms on the ground ... [as a grave] crime."[185]

I turn now to the second element specified in Shakespeare's ultimatum:
the rape of women. Henry's speech, which implies that violation of
women would be inevitable because soldiery could not be controlled in
the heat of battle, falls short of the real Henry's severe prohibition of
rape,[186] though rape in a town taken by assault following a siege would
have been more leniently treated. Here, Shakespeare's Henry may have
reflected the difficulties of the real Henry. The latter's Ordinances of War
attempted to protect the noncombatant, but enforcing compliance with
the norms was – and remains – a real problem. Keen observes that "[w]hat
is important is not that the law of arms tolerated outrages (which it did
not do); but that it was not effectively enforced throughout most of the
Hundred Years War."[187]

---

[177] F. VICTORIA, *supra* note 33, at 182(46).   [178] *Id.* at 182–83(47).
[179] *See supra* text at notes 144–46, 162–64.   [180] M. KEEN, *supra* note 7, at 121.
[181] *Id.*   [182] F. VICTORIA, *supra* note 33, at 183–84(49).
[183] *Id.* at 183(48).   [184] A. GENTILI, *supra* note 37, at 218.
[185] *Id.* at 223.   [186] *See infra* note 196.
[187] M. KEEN, *supra* note 7, at 192; *see also id.* at 190. Compare common Article 1 of the
Geneva Conventions, which requires the parties "to respect and to ensure respect for
the present Convention in all circumstances." The authoritative Commentary prepared by

The reality was even grimmer. I have already cited Keen's observation that the license to rape was considered a major incentive for the soldier involved in siege warfare. While urging generals to forbid and prevent rape during the sacking of a city, Vitoria reluctantly admitted the lawfulness of allowing soldiers to sack a city if "the necessities of war" required it, "or as a spur to the courage of the troops,"[188] even when rape would result. These cruel rules, however, were rejected by Gentili:

> Further, to violate the honour of women will always be held to be unjust. For although it is not contrary to nature to despoil one whom it is honourable to kill, and although where the law of slavery obtains it is permitted according to the laws of war to sell the enemy together with his wives and children, yet it is not lawful for any captive to be visited with insult. ... I make no allowance for retaliation. ...
>
> At some time the enemy [who allows raping women] ... will surely render an account to ... the rest of the world, if there is no magistrate here to check and punish the injustice of the victor. He will render an account to those sovereigns who wish to observe honourable causes for war and to maintain the common law of nations and of nature.[189]

Under modern international law, despite the prohibition of "all rape" in Lieber's Code of 1863,[190] the protection of women's rights does not appear to have been a priority item. The Hague Regulations provide only indirect and partial protection against rape.[191] The 1929 Geneva Convention on Prisoners of War contained a general provision too vague to afford effective protection to women prisoners.[192] During the Second World War, rape was tolerated and, horrifyingly, was even utilized in some instances as an instrument of policy. Walzer recounts that Moroccan

the International Committee of the Red Cross adds: "[T]he Party to the conflict is responsible for the treatment accorded to protected persons. It would not, for example, be enough for a State to give orders or directions. ... It is for the State to supervise the execution of the orders it gives." COMMENTARY ON THE GENEVA CONVENTIONS OF 12 AUGUST 1949, *supra* note 108, at 16.

[188] F. VICTORIA, *supra* note 33, at 184–85(52).

[189] A. GENTILI, *supra* note 37, at 257. *See also* Meron, *supra* note 5, at 115–16. Although Grotius mentioned the argument that rape should be legal on the ground that "it is not inconsistent with the law of war that everything which belongs to the enemy should be at the disposition of the victor," he reasoned that, being unrelated to either security or punishment, rape "should consequently not go unpunished in war any more than in peace. The latter view is the law not of all nations, but of the better ones." H. GROTIUS, *supra* note 81, bk. III, ch. IV, pt. XIX(1).

[190] F. Lieber, *Instructions for the Government of Armies of the United States in the Field*, Art. 44, originally published as U.S. WAR DEPARTMENT, ADJUTANT GENERAL'S OFFICE, GENERAL ORDERS No. 100 (Apr. 24, 1863), *reprinted in* R. HARTIGAN, LIEBER'S CODE AND THE LAW OF WAR 54 (1983).

[191] *Supra* note 111, Art. 46.

[192] (Geneva) Convention Relative to the Treatment of Prisoners of War, July 27, 1929, Art. 3, 47 Stat. 2021, 2031 (pt. 2), TS No. 846, 2 Bevans 932 ("Women shall be treated with all the regard due to their sex").

mercenary troops fought with Free French forces in Italy in 1943 on "terms [which] included [as a spur to masculine courage] license to rape."[193] In occupied Europe, thousands of women were subjected to rape and thousands more were forced to enter brothels for Nazi troops. Rape of German women by Soviet soldiers appears to have been tolerated. Only in the fourth Geneva Convention of 1949 was an unequivocal prohibition of rape established.[194] Even so, infringement of this provision was not listed among the "grave breaches" of the Convention, which require the imposition of penal sanctions or extradition.[195]

We return to consideration of a third element in the King's ultimatum, pillage. With the exception of siege warfare, Henry's prohibition of pillage in occupied territories is best reflected by the previously mentioned incident of the stolen pyx, reported to Captain Fluellen by Lieutenant Pistol:

> *Pistol.* Fortune is Bardolph's foe, and frowns on him,
> For he hath stol'n a pax, and hanged must a' be –
> A damned death!
> Let gallows gape for dog, let man go free,
> And let not hemp his windpipe suffocate.
> But Exeter hath given the doom of death
> For pax of little price.
> Therefore go speak – the duke will hear thy voice,
> And let not Bardolph's vital thread be cut
> With edge of penny cord and vile reproach.
> Speak, captain, for his life, and I will thee requite.
> . . . .

---

[193] M. WALZER, *supra* note 107, at 133.

[194] "Women shall be especially protected against any attack on their honour, in particular against rape, enforced prostitution, or any form of indecent assault." Geneva Convention No. IV, *supra* note 108, Art. 27. For a similar prohibition, see Additional Protocol I, *supra* note 68, Art. 76(1).

[195] Geneva Convention No. IV, *supra* note 108, Arts. 146–47. Rape and enforced prostitution were not included in the list of grave breaches in Article 85 of Additional Protocol I, *supra* note 68. *See generally* Krill, *The Protection of Women in International Humanitarian Law*, INT'L REV. RED CROSS, No. 249, November-December 1985, at 337, 341. A useful precedent for the international criminalization of rape as inhuman treatment, or even as torture, was established by the European Commission of Human Rights in Cyprus v. Turkey, Applications Nos. 6780/74 and 6950/75 (July 10, 1976). As regards rape committed by Turkish soldiers and officers, members of the armed forces of an occupying power, the Commission ruled that those acts which could be imputed to the occupying power constituted "inhuman ... treatment" in the sense of Article 3 of the European Convention on the Protection of Human Rights and Fundamental Freedoms, *opened for signature* Nov. 4, 1950, 213 UNTS 221. Nos. 6780/74, 6950/75, paras. 373–74. The Commission emphasized that "[i]t has not been shown that the Turkish authorities took adequate measures to prevent this happening or that they generally took any disciplinary measures following such incidents." *Id.*, para. 373. *See generally* Byrnes, *The Committee against Torture*, in THE HUMAN RIGHTS ORGANS OF THE UNITED NATIONS (P. Alston ed. forthcoming); Bunch, *Women's Rights as Human Rights: Toward a Re-Vision of Human Rights*, 12 HUM. RTS. Q. 486 (1990).

Fluellen. .... [I]f, look you, he were my brother, I would desire the duke to use his good pleasure and put him to execution, for discipline ought to be used.

[3, 6, 39–57]

As we have seen, when Fluellen later tells the King about Bardolph's offense and likely execution, Henry endorses the harsh punishment and orders that "in our marches through the country there be nothing compell'd from the villages, nothing taken but paid for, none of the French upbraided or abused in disdainful language" (*id.*, 112–15).

Shakespeare based the story of the stolen pyx on Holinshed, who reported that, despite the needs of the English troops, nothing was taken from the local population without payment and no offenses were committed

> except one, which was, that a souldiour tooke a pix out of a church, for which he was apprehended, and the king not once remooved [did not move at all, halted] till the box was restored, and the offendor strangled. The people of the countries thereabout, hearing of such zeale in him, to the maintenance of justice, ministered to his armie victuals, and other necessaries, although by open proclamation so to doo they were prohibited.[196]

The real Henry indeed ordered that churches and their contents be left unharmed and that no man lay hands on priests or women unless they were actually armed or planning a violent attack. "[A]ll victuals which might be useful for the support of the army were to be spared from waste and pillage."[197] These rules did not originate with Henry but preceded him. Christine de Pisan, who compiled the medieval laws of war and customs of chivalry in 1408–1409, supported the death penalty for soldiers

---

[196] R. HOLINSHED, *supra* note 3, at 30; *see also* E. HALL, *supra* note 4, at 64. According to 2 J. WYLIE, *supra* note 116, at 117, "A cry was at once raised, the battalion was halted and the king refused to advance till the thief was caught. He was dragged out before the gazing files and hanged on a tree beside the church where the theft had been committed; the pyx was restored..." *See also* H. NICOLAS, *supra* note 70, at 91–92. The incident of the pyx is also reported in the contemporary account GESTA HENRICI QUINTI, *supra* note 70, at 69. The hanging of the offender appears to have been consistent with paragraph 3 of King Henry V's Ordinances of War, *supra* note 89:

> [A]lso, that no manner of man be so hardy to robbe ne to pille holy Church of no goode, ne ornament, that longeth to the Church, ne to sle no man of holy Church, religious, ne none other, but if he be armed, upon peyne of deth, noper that noman be so hardy to sle ne enforce no woman uppon the same peyn. And that noman take no woman prisoner, man of holy Churche, ne none oper religious, but if he be armed, uppon peyn of enprisonement and his body at the Kynges will.

Although these ordinances were promulgated in 1419, the earlier proclamations of King Henry appear to have contained similar prohibitions. *See supra* text at notes 137–38. According to R. HOLINSHED, *supra* note 3, at 58, Henry found a large amount of money at Caen castle, which he fully restored to the inhabitants.

[197] 2 J. WYLIE, *supra* note 116, at 20–22. The story of the pyx is confirmed by THE FIRST ENGLISH LIFE OF KING HENRY THE FIFTH, *supra* note 26, at 44–45.

committing pillage,[198] strongly advocated the protection of noncombatants,[199] and proclaimed prohibitions on the killing of prisoners[200] and, anticipating Article 23(a) of the Hague Regulations, the use of poisoned weapons, which she considered so inhumane as to be against the law of war for Christians.[201]

Henry V promulgated ordinances on warfare not only to maintain the necessary discipline among his troops, but also to promote various humane practices.[202] The army, however, disrespected these protective rules to such an extent, particularly through plunder, that six years later they had to be solemnly reissued.[203] Nevertheless, Henry's "humane intentions ... had made so deep an impression in France that one of the most high-minded of the French ecclesiastics appealed to him to protect French churches from the plundering violence of their own people."[204]

Henry's conduct may seem surprising, as medieval rules of war liberally allowed the taking of spoils. In certain circumstances, real estate could be appropriated by the victorious prince;[205] but movables, including those not taken on the battlefield, could become the property of the captor himself (depending on certain qualifications and the hazy entitlements of the prince and the captor, respectively).[206] Normally, movables would be distributed among the various parties, including the captor, his captain and the prince.[207]

Vitoria maintained that "[a]ll movables vest in the seizor by the law of nations, even if in amount they exceed what will compensate for damages sustained."[208] Although Vitoria advocated the protection of innocent civilians ("agricultural population and other innocent folk ... ought not to be despoiled" if the war can be carried out effectively without their spoliation), he gave priority to the requirements of war by emphasizing that in a just war it is lawful to despoil even innocent enemy subjects so as

---

[198] C. De Pisan, *supra* note 5, at 44; *see also id.* at 217.

[199] *Id.* at 224–35.

[200] *Id.* at 222, 64–65, and *infra* note 245. Like writers on modern law of war, Christine de Pisan considered the use of ruses permissible, but not perfidy. C. de Pisan, *supra* note 5, at 213–14.

[201] C. de Pisan, *supra* note 5, at 184.

[202] E.g., the prohibition against making captives of children under 14 years of age, or requiring that an occupied lying-in room be spared. 2 J. Wylie, *supra* note 116, at 22.

[203] *Id.* at 23–24. *See also supra* text at note 138.

[204] 2 J. Wylie, *supra* note 116, at 24.

[205] *See* F. Victoria, *supra* note 33, at 185–86(56); H. Grotius, *supra* note 81, bk. III, ch. VI, pt. XI.

[206] M. Keen, *supra* note 7, at 137, 139–40; H. Bonet, *supra* note 89, at 150.

[207] John of Legnano wrote that movables "become the property of the captor; but he is bound to assign them to the general of the war, who will distribute them according to deserts." G. da Legnano, *supra* note 173, ch. LXI, at 270. *See also* King Henry V's Ordinances of War, *supra* note 89.

[208] F. Victoria, *supra* note 33, at 184(51).

to sap the enemy's strength.[209] Vitoria was less concerned about protecting enemy subjects' property than about ensuring that soldiers not loot without the authority of the prince or general.[210] Suárez similarly wrote that soldiers may take from their "hosts" only what the king has authorized.[211]

The harshness of the punishment meted out to the soldier who stole the pyx can be explained in part by the unauthorized nature of the taking, the King's desire to maintain law and order and, perhaps, the violation of protected religious objects (i.e., the church and pyx). Moreover, Henry felt that he was reclaiming his own duchy: he had no interest in pillaging or destroying what he regarded as rightfully his own. His political and propagandistic purpose was to befriend, not antagonize, the population. Nevertheless, Henry's proscriptions, as described by Shakespeare, against molesting the inhabitants and taking any goods from them without proper payment were quite advanced for their era and are comparable to nineteenth- and twentieth-century texts such as the Lieber Rules,[212] the Oxford *Manual*[213] and the Hague Regulations.[214] These texts are based on the distinction between private and public property, which was not central for writers on *jus gentium* in Shakespeare's era, and they grant far greater protection to the former. In contrast to the period of the Hundred Years' War, today the right to appropriate property in occupied territory has become a monopoly of the state and individual pillage is outlawed by both customary rules (of which Henry's ordinances are an important antecedent) and conventional rules. The taking of private property is strictly regulated and, in principle, is allowed only when required by the army. Requisitioned goods must be paid for, as ordered by Henry. The distinction between movable and immovable property has survived, but it has acquired a new meaning. Movables belonging to the state (public property) may still be appropriated by the occupying state, but not those belonging to individuals (private property) unless particularly suited to a military purpose. The latter may be requisitioned, but they must be restored and compensation paid when peace is concluded. Immovable property, even that belonging to the state, is protected from expropriation by the occupying power, whose rights may not exceed those of an administrator and usufructuary.

---

[209] *Id.* at 180 (39)–(40). A. GENTILI, *supra* note 37, at 270, wrote that "booty is commonly reckoned as a part of the fruits of victory."

[210] Soldiers who loot without a prince's permission are bound to make restitution. F. VICTORIA, *supra* note 33, at 185(53).

[211] F. SUÁREZ, *supra* note 29, at 837.

[212] *Supra* note 190, sec. II.

[213] THE LAWS OF WAR ON LAND (OXFORD MANUAL), pt. II and Art. 32 (adopted by the Institute of International Law at Oxford, 1880), *reprinted in* THE LAWS OF ARMED CONFLICTS 35 (D. Schindler & J. Toman eds. 1988).

[214] *Supra* note 115, Arts. 23(g), 28, 46, 47, 52, 53, 55, 56.

VII AGINCOURT: PRISONERS OF WAR AND
SERVANTS

As the battle of Agincourt wore on, the outnumbered English appeared to have the upper hand. The fear that another French charge was about to begin, the presence on the battlefield of a large number of French prisoners, who, though disarmed, could have risen against their English captors, and a French attack on the English baggage train possibly involving loss of life among the attendants – all combined to trigger an unexpected order by the King. Shakespeare's Henry, hearing a sudden call to arms, cries out:

> *King*. But hark! What new alarum is this same?
> The French have reinforc'd their scatter'd men.
> Then every soldier kill his prisoners.
> Give the word through.
>
> [4, 6, 35–38]

The play reveals another reason for this order in the next scene:

> *Fluellen*. Kill the poys and the luggage! 'Tis expressly against the law of arms. 'Tis as arrant a piece of knavery, mark you now, as can be offert. In your conscience, now, is it not?
> *Gower*. 'Tis certain there's not a boy left alive, and the cowardly rascals that ran from the battle ha' done this slaughter. Besides, they have burned and carried away all that was in the king's tent, wherefore the king most worthily hath caus'd every soldier to cut his prisoner's throat. O, 'tis a gallant king!   [4, 7, 1–11]

After this disclosure, the King elaborates on his order regarding the prisoners:

> *King*. I was not angry since I came to France
> Until this instant. Take a trumpet, herald.
> Ride thou unto the horsemen on yon hill.
> If they will fight with us, bid them come down,
> Or void the field. They do offend our sight.
> If they'll do neither, we will come to them
> And make them skirr away as swift as stones
> Enforced from the old Assyrian slings.
> Besides, we'll cut the throats of those we have,
> And not a man of them that we shall take
> Shall taste our mercy. Go and tell them so.
>
> [*id.*, 56–66]

Shakespeare thus explains Henry's cruel order to kill the French prisoners on two grounds: necessity, as the French appeared to be regrouping to attack; and reprisal for the unlawful attack on the servants[215] guarding the rear camp and its plunder. Attempting to highlight Henry's humanity, Shakespeare focuses on the King's impetuous anger ("I was not angry since I came to France until this instant"). However, Holinshed offers a different version of the facts:

[C]erteine Frenchmen on horssebacke ... to the number of six hundred horssemen, which were the first that fled, hearing that the English tents and pavillions were a good waie distant from the armie, without anie sufficient gard to defend the same ... enterd upon the kings campe, and there spoiled the hails, robbed the tents, brake up chests, and carried awaie caskets, and slue such servants as they found to make anie resistance. ...

But when the outcrie of the lackies and boies, which ran awaie for feare of the Frenchmen thus spoiling the campe, came to the kings eares, he doubting least his enimies should gather togither againe, and begin a new field; and mistrusting further that the prisoners would be an aid to his enimies ... contrarie to his accustomed gentlenes, commanded by sound of trumpet, that everie man (upon paine of death) should incontinentlie slaie his prisoner.[216]

Accordingly, the chronicler whom Shakespeare most closely followed recorded that the French killed only those servants who offered resistance.[217] Holinshed's version of the story formed a part of the mythology of Agincourt by his time. Shakespeare modified the story, apparently to cast Henry's order in the best possible light.

Modern accounts by both Wylie[218] and Winston Churchill[219] speak of plunder but not killing. John Keegan refers to plunder by a body of armed peasants who were led by three mounted knights; they stole some objects and "inflicted some loss of life."[220] The anonymous early sixteenth-century biographer of Henry V explained that the King's order to kill the prisoners was triggered by his fear that he would have to fight them as

[215] Lackeys, boys, pages, sutlers, waggoners and servants of the camp. 2 J. WYLIE, *supra* note 116, at 148 n.6.

[216] R. HOLINSHED, *supra* note 3, at 38.

[217] But E. HALL, *supra* note 4, at 69, stated that the French killed servants they could find. *Compare* Hague Convention No. IV, *supra* note 103, Art. 13; the 1929 Geneva POW Convention, *supra* note 192, Art. 81; Geneva Convention No. III, *supra* note 67, Art. 4(A)(4). Under such provisions, service personnel accompanying the armed forces, without actually being members thereof, would be entitled to POW status but, as noncombatants, would not be a lawful object of attack unless they took a direct part in the hostilities. Additional Protocol I, *supra* note 68, Art. 51(3).

[218] 2 J. WYLIE, *supra* note 116, at 171. In his discussion of the attack on the King's baggage, Hibbert does not mention any loss of life. C. HIBBERT, AGINCOURT 127 (1964).

[219] 1 W. CHURCHILL, A HISTORY OF THE ENGLISH-SPEAKING PEOPLE 319 (1956). *See also* J. DAVIES, HENRY V, at 190 (1935).

[220] J. KEEGAN, THE FACE OF BATTLE 84 (1978).

well as the attacking French forces. This author did not even mention the assault on the baggage train.[221]

If Holinshed's version is correct, the French raid is unlikely to have violated any laws of war. The English rear camp constituted a lawful object of attack. In the absence of resistance, the immunity of persons serving the troops would have depended on whether they met the prevailing standards of innocence.[222] Assuming that the pages were not entitled to the immunity of children[223] and were to be treated as "youths," their right to be spared would have turned on their surrender, either on "fair terms" or unconditionally.[224] At least some medieval jurists regarded noncombatant servants of an army as a legitimate military objective even when they were not involved in any fighting, either defensive or otherwise.[225] Perhaps Shakespeare himself was not quite persuaded that Fluellen's version of the law sufficiently justified the order to kill the prisoners. The sarcasm in Gower's response appears to be aimed both at the Welshman Fluellen and at the King. Indeed, the real Henry may later have been embarrassed by the order. In his eyewitness account of the Agincourt campaign, the anonymous English cleric attached to Henry's court clearly intended to justify Henry's foreign policy and to present him as a devout and humane Christian prince who was seeking peace with justice. Yet, in describing the killing of the prisoners ("by the swords either of their captors or of others following after, lest they should involve us in utter disaster in the fighting that would ensue"), he never mentioned the provocation of the French attack on the luggage train or even the existence of Henry's command.[226]

Although some of the French participants in the attack were subsequently punished by France for committing "treason" and leaving their camp for private plunder,[227] those punitive measures were motivated not by the violation of the laws of war, but by the "causing [of] the rumour [of a French counterattack] which led to the hideous massacre of the

---

[221] THE FIRST ENGLISH LIFE OF KING HENRY THE FIFTH, *supra* note 26, at 60–61. H. NICOLAS, *supra* note 70, at 124, writes that King Henry was advised that the French had attacked his rear and plundered his baggage, but he does not mention any loss of life among the baggage attendants. Many other historians also mention the attack on the baggage train, but not loss of life among the attendants. *See* E. JACOB, HENRY V, *supra* note 26, at 105; G. TOWLE, *supra* note 117, at 340; D. SEWARD, *supra* note 117, at 80; R. MOWAT, HENRY V, at 159 (1920).

[222] F. VICTORIA, *supra* note 33, at 180(38)–(39).

[223] *See* H. GROTIUS, *supra* note 81, bk. III, ch. XI, pt. IX.

[224] *Id.*, pts. XIII(2), XIV, XV; *see also* A. GENTILI, *supra* note 37, at 216.

[225] "Should those who attend in a war, but who cannot fight, enjoy the immunities [status] of combatants? Say that they should, provided that they are useful in counsel in other ways ...." G. DA LEGNANO, *supra* note 173, ch. LXXI, at 274.

[226] GESTA HENRICI QUINTI, *supra* note 70, at 93. *See also Introduction by the Editors, id.* at xviii, xxiii, xxviii.

[227] R. HOLINSHED, *supra* note 3, at 38.

prisoners on the battlefield."[228] Under the circumstances, Fluellen's invocation of the law of arms may have reflected Shakespeare's desire to place the most favorable interpretation on the King's order; but, legally, it was flawed.

Without a manifest breach of the law by the French, Henry could not claim the defense of reprisal, which was then generally permissible[229] and, according to some views, was even allowed against innocent private persons.[230] Indeed, it did not occur to Gentili, in his discussion of Agincourt (see below), that reprisals might be relevant. The usually humane Gentili, while pleading for compassion "towards those who really suffer [retaliation] for the faults of others,"[231] nonetheless, as a matter of law, accepted the principle of collective responsibility as manifested by reprisals:

> [I]t avails not in this case to say that those who were punished were not the ones who acted cruelly, and that hence they ought not to have been treated cruelly; for the enemy make up one body, just as an army is a single body . . . [T]he individuals are responsible, even if a fault was committed by all in common.[232]

Writing soon after Gentili, Grotius challenged the legality of reprisals against prisoners, except in those cases of individual responsibility for a previously committed crime that "a just judge would hold punishable by death."[233] Grotius argued that collective responsibility was a fiction and should not be invoked to justify reprisals against innocent persons: "nature does not sanction retaliation except against those who have done

---

[228] 2 J. WYLIE, *supra* note 116, at 171 (footnotes omitted); *see also* R. HOLINSHED, *supra* note 3, at 38.

[229] See the discussion of the breadth of permissible reprisals by G. DA LEGNANO, *supra* note 173, chs. CXXIV–CLXVI, at 308–30. Reprisals against prisoners of war are now outlawed. *See, e.g.,* Geneva Convention No. III, *supra* note 67, Art. 13.

[230] A rule protecting innocent private persons against reprisals was justified by Jacobus de Belvisio on the basis of the principle of individual responsibility: "a man ought not to be punished for another's offence." *Cited by* G. DA LEGNANO, *supra* note 173, ch. CXLIV, at 321. John of Legnano disagrees. *Id.*

[231] A. GENTILI, *supra* note 37, at 232.

[232] *Id. Compare Genesis* 18:23–26:

> 23. And Abraham drew near, and said, Wilt thou also destroy the righteous with the wicked?
>
> 24. Peradventure there be fifty righteous within the city: wilt thou also destroy and not spare the place for the fifty righteous that are therein?
>
> 25. That be far from thee to do after this manner, to slay the righteous with the wicked: and that the righteous should be as the wicked, that be far from thee: Shall not the Judge of all the earth do right?
>
> 26. And the Lord said, If I find in Sodom fifty righteous within the city, then I will spare all the place for their sakes.

[233] H. GROTIUS, *supra* note 81, bk. III, ch. XI, pt. XVI(1).

wrong. It is not sufficient that by a sort of fiction the enemy may be conceived as forming a single body ....'[234]

If the massacre of the French prisoners, whose horror was vividly described by Holinshed,[235] was not excusable as a reprisal, could it have been justified on grounds of necessity? Alluding to the necessities of war, the eminent medieval jurist John of Legnano recognized the captor's right to kill prisoners where there was "fear of a disturbance of the peace."[236] Holinshed's account suggests that the King's fear of an impending attack, in which the French prisoners would join, was real.[237] The heavily outnumbered English would have had difficulty repelling another attack while guarding their numerous prisoners. In the same vein, Wylie, basing himself on the chroniclers, writes that the danger of a new assault triggered the King's order. But this explanation is undercut by the fact that the King made an exception for dukes, earls and other high-placed leaders "as fell [insofar as ransom was concerned] to the king's own share."[238] Mindful of their expected ransoms, the captors were reluctant to carry out the order, "but the king threatened to hang any man that disobeyed and told off 200 of his ever-handy archers to begin the bloody work."[239] Churchill, defending Henry, claims that the King ordered the killing of the prisoners in the belief that he was being attacked from the rear; although "[t]he alarm in the rear was soon relieved," by then the massacre was almost over.[240] Less categorically, Keegan writes that the order to kill the prisoners was prompted by either the attack on the rear camp or the continued menace of the French.[241]

---

[234] *Id.*, pt. XVI(2). "[R]etaliation that is lawful ... must be inflicted upon the very person who has done wrong ...." *Id.*, ch. IV, pt. XIII(1).

[235] R. HOLINSHED, *supra* note 3, at 38–39.

[236] G. DA LEGNANO, *supra* note 173, at 274. Many historians believe that necessity justified Henry's order to kill the prisoners. Thus, H. HUTCHISON, *supra* note 117, at 124, observes that "[b]y medieval standards Henry was obeying his soldier creed – military necessity justified any butchery ...." *See also* G. TOWLE, *supra* note 117, at 339–40. D. SEWARD, *supra* note 117, at 81, strongly dissents: "In reality, by fifteenth-century standards, to massacre captive, unarmed noblemen who, according to the universally recognized international laws of chivalry, had every reason to expect to be ransomed if they surrendered formally, was a peculiarly nasty crime ...."

[237] *Supra* text at note 216. H. NICOLAS, *supra* note 70, at 124, believes that "[i]mperative necessity" dictated the King's order.

[238] 2 J. WYLIE, *supra* note 116, at 171. Hutchison, who supports the traditional justification of necessity, argues that the fact that Henry's own rich prisoners were exempted from being killed tallied with Henry's reputation for "shrewd common sense – he simply could not afford to miss the chance of spectacular ransoms." H. HUTCHISON, *supra* note 117, at 124.

[239] 2 J. WYLIE, *supra* note 116, at 171–72. The archers, not being knights, may have had fewer scruples about killing members of the French nobility. Moreover, under the law of chivalry, only knights could enforce agreements to pay ransom. M. KEEN, *supra* note 7, at 19–20. 1 F. GROSE, MILITARY ANTIQUITIES 345 (1786), cynically observed that "[t]he hopes of ransom frequently acted in the place of humanity, avarice assuming the place of mercy ...."

[240] 1 W. CHURCHILL, *supra* note 219, at 319–20.

[241] J. KEEGAN, *supra* note 220, at 84.

However genuine the King's fear of an attack on his outnumbered troops may have been, the order to kill the French prisoners, already *hors de combat*, could hardly be justified on the ground that they might have joined the ranks of the attackers. The captured French were still encumbered by their heavy armor, as their basinets (helmets) alone had been removed.[242] Dismounted, defenseless, and barely able to move, they were not a menace to the English troops. In the face of real necessity, a threat of execution would not have been required to enforce Henry's order.

Did the order violate the applicable laws of war? While maintaining that, "speaking absolutely, there is nothing to prevent the killing of those who have surrendered or been captured in a just war so long as abstract equity is observed,"[243] Vitoria suggested that this harsh rule had been tempered by the law of nations and the customs of war; consequently, "after victory has been won ... and all danger is over, [they] are not to be killed."[244] Because Henry believed that the victory had not been won and that the danger persisted, he would not have violated Vitoria's standards, and certainly not the earlier medieval norms described by John of Legnano. But such medieval writers as Bouvet and Christine de Pisan advocated the prohibition of the killing of prisoners, though subject to some reservations.[245]

Gentili's humane position on the duty to give quarter has already been discussed. Faithful to the chivalric code of conduct,[246] Gentili suggested that an implied contract is formed between the captor and the captive, "a bargain with the enemy for his life." The "rights of humanity and the laws of war ... order the sparing of those who surrender."[247] Gentili did not agree that danger justified the killing of captives and he praised those that

---

[242] 2 J. Wylie, *supra* note 116, at 171.

[243] F. Victoria, *supra* note 33, at 183(49).   [244] *Id.*

[245] H. Bonet, *supra* note 89, pt IV, ch. XIII, argued that "he who in battle has captured his enemy, especially if it be the duke or marshal of the battle ... should have mercy on him, unless by his deliverance there is danger of having greater wars." Elsewhere, he explains that "to kill an enemy in battle is allowed by law and by the lord, but out of battle no man may kill another save in self-defence, except the lord, after trial." *Id.*, ch. XLVI. C. de Pisan, *supra* note 5, at 222, would prohibit the killing of prisoners even in battle: "Soo saye I to the well that it is ayenst all ryght and gentylnesse to slee hym that yeldeth hym." Arguing against "a thynge Inhumayne and to grete a cruelness" and answering critics who invoked the ancient right of the captor to kill his prisoners, sell them, or otherwise dispose of them, she asserted that "amonge crysten folke where the lawe is altogyder grounded vpon myldefulnes and pyte [it] is not lycyte nor accordynge to vse of suche terannye whyche be acursed and reproued." *Id.* Nevertheless, after the battle, she would allow the prince to kill a prisoner who would be dangerous to the prince if allowed to go free. *Id.*

[246] *See supra* text at notes 167, 162, 182–83.

[247] A. Gentili, *supra* note 37, at 216. *Compare* H. Grotius, *supra* note 81, bk. III, ch. IV, pt. X(2) ("So far as the law of nations is concerned, the right of killing such slaves, that is, captives taken in war, is not precluded at any time, although it is restricted, now more, now less, by the laws of states"). Elsewhere, however, Grotius advocated sparing captives who have surrendered unconditionally. *Id.*, ch. XI, pt. XV.

"did not slay their captives, no matter how great danger threatened them."[248] He had harsh words for Henry:

> I cannot praise the English who, in that famous battle in which they overthrew the power of France, having taken more prisoners than the number of their victorious army and fearing danger from them by night, set aside those of high rank and slew the rest. "A hateful and inhuman deed," says the historian, "and the battle was not so bloody as the victory."[249]

Perhaps Gentili's stricture on Henry's action, had it been known to Shakespeare, would explain his sensitivity and his desire to depart from Holinshed's account. But Shakespeare's apparently deliberate departure from Holinshed can plausibly be explained, without reference to Gentili, as an attempt to put Henry's order in the best possible light.

Notwithstanding Gentili's condemnation, it cannot be concluded that Henry clearly violated contemporary standards. Wylie reports that, even though the writers of the time regarded the massacre as an inhuman deed, his French critics refrained from blaming Henry because "in those days the French would have done the same themselves had they been in so perilous a case."[250] Killing prisoners in an emergency was not unprecedented[251] and, while quarter was normally granted in Anglo-French wars, the virtual absence of "contemporary criticism" of Henry's action[252] suggests that, cruel though it was, his order did not violate the accepted norms of behavior.

VIII   HERALDS, AMBASSADORS AND THE TREATY OF TROYES

The scene on the battlefield at Agincourt, when the English appeared to have won and the French herald Montjoy arrived on yet another mission to Shakespeare's Henry, is vividly described by the playwright:

> *Exeter*. Here comes the herald of the French, my liege.
> *Gloucester*. His eyes are humbler than they us'd to be.
> *King*. How now! What means this, herald? Know'st thou not
> That I have fin'd these bones of mine for ransom? . . . [253]
> *Montjoy*.   No, great king.

---

[248] A. GENTILI, *supra* note 37, at 211–12.   [249] *Id.*

[250] 2 J. WYLIE, *supra* note 116, at 175. C. HIBBERT, *supra* note 218, at 129, observes: "Even the French chroniclers write of [Henry's] action as though it were dictated by painful necessity."

[251] M. KEEN, CHIVALRY 276 n. 7 (1984).

[252] *Id.* at 221. Note the matter-of-fact, nonjudgmental reference to the massacre by the French chronicler the Religieux de Saint-Denys: "Le roi d'Angleterre, croyant qu'ils [the French] voulaient revenir à la charge, ordonna qu'on tuat tous les prisonniers." 5 CHRONIQUE DU RELIGIEUX DE SAINT-DENYS, *supra* note 70, at 565.

I come to thee for charitable license,
That we may wander o'er this bloody field
To book our dead, and then to bury them,
To sort our nobles from our common men.
For many of our princes – woe the while! –
Lie drown'd and soak'd in mercenary blood.
So do our vulgar drench their peasant limbs
In blood of princes, and their wounded steeds
Fret fetlock-deep in gore and with wild rage
Yerk out their armed heels at their dead masters,
Killing them twice. O, give us leave, great king,
To view the field in safety and dispose
Of their dead bodies!
King. I tell thee truly, herald,
I know not if the day be ours or no,
For yet a many of your horsemen peer
And gallop o'er the field.
Montjoy.   The day is yours.[254]

[4, 7, 67–87]

Heralds performed an important role in medieval warfare, as is seen in the play.[255] The herald's function derives from an ancient tradition. The institution of the herald's office was mythically attributed to as ancient a source as Julius Caesar.[256] Attired in distinctive habits designed to protect them from acts of violence ("*Montjoy.* You know me by my habit" (3, 6, 118)), heralds carried messages between the warring parties; mediated and arranged the time and place of important battles (including Agincourt) in such a manner that, according to "the etiquette of chivalry ... [neither side would] take ... unfair advantage of the other";[257] and arranged truces.[258] They were the recognized experts on the code of chivalry,[259] whose verdicts were decisive for members of the

---

[253] See also the heroic answer by Shakespeare's Henry to the French herald Montjoy before the battle of Agincourt, in which Henry ruled out the possibility of being ransomed in case of defeat:

Herald, save thou thy labor.
Come thou no more for ransom, gentle herald.
They shall have none, I swear, but these my joints,
Which if they have as I will leave 'em them,
Shall yield them little, tell the Constable.

[4, 3, 121–25]

[254] *See also* act 3, scene 6, and act 4, scene 3.
[255] G. KEETON, *supra* note 18, at 70–71; G. KEETON, *supra* note 11, at 87–88. See also the oath of heralds in THE BLACK BOOK OF ADMIRALTY, *supra* note 89, at 297, and the oath of "kynges of armes," *id.* at 295.
[256] M. KEEN, *supra* note 7, at 57.   [257] 2J. WYLIE, *supra* note 116, at 140.
[258] On the role of Montjoy at Agincourt, see R. HOLINSHED, *supra* note 3, at 39–40.
[259] M. KEEN, *supra* note 7, at 16, 50; *see also* M. KEEN, *supra* note 251, at 137–40.

"international order of knighthood,"[260] including even princes. They "refereed" tournaments and at battles recorded those who were present, those who had distinguished themselves, and those who had died. At Agincourt, Montjoy advised the winner of his victory.[261] However, the latter episode has few parallels in other engagements. Heralds carefully refrained from participating in hostilities.[262]

In some European countries, especially in France, heralds were soon to disappear, together with the medieval social order and the rules of chivalry. There are still heralds in England, however, serving as the sovereign's official and salaried officers of arms.

Heralds should be distinguished from envoys. Heralds regularly acted as privileged messengers (Henry V himself sent a herald to deliver a letter to Charles VI during the negotiations that preceded the campaign described in Shakespeare's play); hence, they had a function in diplomatic exchanges (such as by delivering ultimatums and defiances, collecting safe conducts for embassies and carrying messages between belligerents) but did not perform in a real plenipotentiary capacity. That seems always to have involved envoys or ambassadors. Heralds did not have the status and were not expected to have the expertise to fit them to act as ambassadors.

Ambassadors, who play significant roles in *Henry V* as special envoys, or, in modern parlance, heads of special missions[263] (rather than permanent diplomatic missions[264]), were to become a permanent institution.[265] Shakespeare's ambassadors deliver messages between the courts of France and England[266] that include territorial claims, an ultimatum, a declaration of war and the corresponding replies. Like heralds, ambassadors enjoyed immunity,[267] but the rules of immunity must still have been relatively "soft" and unreliable for Henry's ambassador, Exeter, to feel impelled to threaten the King of France with Henry's might:

---

[260] M. KEEN, *supra* note 7, at 50.

[261] R. HOLINSHED, *supra* note 3, at 39–40; *see also* C. HIBBERT, *supra* note 218, at 134.

[262] "Throughout the battle of Agincourt the heralds of both sides stood together on a hill, away from the fighting in which their order had no part ...." M. KEEN, *supra* note 7, at 195.

[263] Within the meaning of Article 1 of the Convention on Special Missions, *opened for signature* Dec. 16, 1969, Annex to GA Res. 2530 (XXIV), 24 UN GAOR Supp. (No. 30) at 99, UN Doc. A/7630 (1970).

[264] *See* Vienna Convention on Diplomatic Relations, *done* Apr. 18, 1961, 23 UST 3227, TIAS No. 7502, 500 UNTS 95.

[265] *See* H. NICOLSON, DIPLOMACY 30–31 (1963).

[266] *See* act 1, scene 2; act 2, scene 4.

[267] H. GROTIUS, *supra* note 81, bk. II, ch. XVIII. For a fourteenth-century statement of the immunity of ambassadors from reprisals, see G. DA LEGNANO, *supra* note 173, ch. CXXXIX, at 319. For an example of early fifteenth-century inviolability of ambassadors and their property, see C. DE PISAN, *supra* note 5, at 234–35.

    Exeter. Dispatch us with all speed, lest that our king
Come here himself to question our delay,
For he is footed in this land already.
    King. You shall be soon dispatch'd with fair conditions.
A night is but small breath and little pause
To answer matters of this consequence.

[2, 4, 141–46]

Equally interesting was the role entrusted to ambassadors by Henry V in negotiating the treaty of peace:

    King Henry. If, Duke of Burgundy, you would the peace
Whose want gives growth to th' imperfections
Which you have cited, you must buy that peace
With full accord to all our just demands,
Whose tenors and particular effects
You have, enschedul'd briefly, in your hands.
    Burgundy. The king hath heard them, to the which as yet
There is no answer made.
    King Henry.   Well then, the peace
Which you before so urg'd lies in his answer.
    France. I have but with a cursitory eye
O'erglanc'd the articles. Pleaseth your grace
To appoint some of your council presently
To sit with us once more, with better heed
To resurvey them, we will suddenly
Pass our accept and peremptory answer.
    King Henry. Brother, we shall. Go, uncle Exeter,
And brother Clarence, and you, brother Gloucester,
Warwick, and Huntingdon, go with the king.
And take with you free power to ratify,
Augment, or alter, as your wisdoms best
Shall see advantageable for our dignity,
Anything in or out of our demands,
And we'll consign thereto.

[5, 2, 68–90]

The negotiation of the Treaty of Troyes (1420) lasted several months.[268] Although Henry himself took a leading role,[269] Shakespeare's Henry, echoing Holinshed,[270] provides here a prime example of ambassadors'

---

[268] *Henry V*, 13 ENCYCLOPAEDIA BRITANNICA 285 (11th ed. 1910). For the English text of the Treaty, see 4 T. RYMER, *supra* note 70, pt. 3, at 179. For a detailed discussion of the negotiations, see P. BONENFANT, DU MEURTRE DE MONTEREAU AU TRAITÉ DE TROYES (1956).

[269] R. HOLINSHED, *supra* note 3, at 84–86; *see also* J. DAVIES, *supra* note 219, at 250.

[270] "[T]he king of England should send in the companie of the duke of Burgognie his ambassadours unto Trois in Champaigne sufficientlie authorised to treat and conclude of so great matter." R. HOLINSHED, *supra* note 3, at 94. Henry V complained of the futility of the pre-invasion negotiations with Charles VI on the ground that the French ambassadors "did

full powers to negotiate and conclude a treaty of peace.[271] With the advent of modern communications technology, which permits rapid communication between capitals and negotiators, the practice of granting ambassadors such full powers has almost fallen into desuetude, particularly in negotiations of vital importance.

The Anglo-French bargaining, in which both parties were assisted by competent lawyers, involved delicate points of law. As a part of the terms of peace, Henry was to marry King Charles's daughter Catherine. He therefore sought to secure his right to the crown of France, for which he had gone to war, without the embarrassment of deposing his future father-in-law. In fact, Henry wanted the immediate right to govern France, as well as a guarantee that the title to France would be transferred to him upon the death of Charles. The solution was to recognize Henry as the heir of the King of France, instead of Charles's legitimate son, the Dauphin, and France's regent.[272] In the concluding scene, Shakespeare portrays the negotiations that led to this resolution and the promise of peace that it held:

> *Westmoreland.* The King hath granted every article:
> His daughter first, and then in sequel all,
> According to their firm proposed natures.
> *Exeter.* Only he hath not yet subscribed this: Where your majesty demands that the King of France, having any occasion to write for matter of grant, shall name your highness in this form and with this addition, . . . ''Notre très-cher fils Henri, Roi d'Angleterre, Héritier de France'' . . .
> *French King.* Nor this I have not, brother, so denied,
> But your request shall make me let it pass.

not have full power to treat'' (letter of April 7, 1415), and he demanded that the powers of the French ambassadors about to be sent should be ''sufficiently ample'' (letter of April 15, 1415). H. NICOLAS, *supra* note 70, App. 1 at 3. *See also* C. KINGSFORD, *supra* note 26, at 113. Regarding the English ambassadors' argument that they lacked power to conclude an agreement, see 1 J. WYLIE, *supra* note 26, at 442.

[271] *See* E. SATOW, GUIDE TO DIPLOMATIC PRACTICE 58–59 (Gore-Booth ed. 1979). An ancient chronicle notes:

> He [Henry] there found the King and Queen of France, their daughter . . . and the Duke of Burgundy, who then ratified and confirmed every article of the treaty which had been agreed upon by their ambassadors, according to the stipulations made between the two kings and the Duke of Burgundy, with the consent of the citizens of Paris . . . .

A Fragment of the Chronicle of Normandy from the Year 1414 to the Year 1422 (ca. 1581), *reprinted in* HENRICI QUINTI ANGLIAE REGIS GESTA 252 (B. Williams ed. 1850). On the background of the *Chronicle*, see the editor's *Preface* at viii.

[272] R. HOLINSHED, *supra* note 3, at 95, 102–03. Holinshed reports: ''It was also agreed, that king Henrie, during his father in lawes life, should in his steed have the whole government of the realme of France, as regent thereof . . . .'' *Id.* at 95. The grant to Henry of the right to govern France was justified on the ground that Charles ''is withholden with diverse sickenesse, in such manner as he maie not intend in his owne person for to dispose for the needs of the foresaid realme of France.'' *Id.* at 99. It was provided that during his lifetime, Charles would possess the crown of France, ''and dignitie roiall of France, with rents and profits for the same.'' *Id.* at 98. *See also* J. DAVIES, *supra* note 219, at 250–51.

 King Henry. I pray you, then, in love and dear alliance,
Let that one article rank with the rest,
And thereupon give me your daughter.
 French King. Take her, fair son, and from her blood raise up
Issue to me, that the contending kingdoms
Of France and England, whose very shores look pale
With envy of each other's happiness,
May cease their hatred ...

[5, 2, 341–61]

Rather than follow the model of the Treaty of Brétigny, which transferred various French territories to English sovereignty, Henry intended to use the Treaty of Troyes, upon his marriage to Catherine, to change the French line of succession. By having himself described in the Treaty as Charles's son and heir of France, Henry hoped to avoid a direct conflict with the Salic law prohibiting the passing of the French crown through females or the female line. Accordingly, the carefully drafted Treaty of Troyes made no reference to the Plantagenet claim to the crown of France. To avoid future challenges to its validity, on the ground either of Charles's madness or of his lack of authority to alienate the crown or change the Valois succession, the Treaty required that it be ratified by the estates of both kingdoms.[273] Nevertheless, the Treaty would not long survive the nationalistic opposition that it provoked in France, which led to its eventual abrogation by the Burgundian French in 1435. The Salic law returned to haunt the English monarchs: the French jurists opposed to the Treaty invoked the law in a new and expanded interpretation as a fundamental constitutional principle prohibiting the alienation of the French crown to a foreigner.[274]

For international lawyers, the Treaty of Troyes is an instrument of extraordinary interest. Although the Treaty deals with the personal union of two kingdoms,[275] while the Hague Regulations of 1907[276] and

---

[273] The above discussion draws on Keen's excellent analysis of the Treaty of Troyes, *Diplomacy*, in HENRY V, at 181–99 (G. Harriss ed. 1985).

[274] *See* Potter, *supra* note 22, at 249–53.

[275] *See* E. JACOB, HENRY V, *supra* note 26, at 149. Both realms would be "under the same person[,] ... keeping neverthelesse in all maner of other things to either of the same realmes, their rights, liberties, customes, usages, and lawes, not making subject in any maner of wise one of the same realmes, to the rights, lawes, or usages of that other." R. HOLINSHED, *supra* note 3, at 103.

[276] *Supra* note 111 (particularly Arts. 43, 46, 48). *See also* E. JACOB, HENRY V, *supra* note 26, at 155. Compare Article 48 of the Hague Regulations to this provision of the Treaty of Troyes:

 Also that we shall put none impositions or exactions, or doo charge the subjects of our said father without cause reasonable and necessarie, ne otherwise than for common good of the realme of France, and after the saieng and asking of the lawes and customes reasonable approved of the same realme.

R. HOLINSHED, *supra* note 3, at 103.

the fourth Geneva Convention of 1949[277] concern occupied territories, the former anticipates the latter in providing for the maintenance of French laws, courts and other institutions.[278]

IX CONCLUDING REMARKS

Holinshed wrote about public affairs of state, and *jus gentium*, including the ordinances and proclamations of war of King Henry V, was an important element in those affairs. It was therefore only natural that Shakespeare, who was an ardent student of Holinshed and who explored the law of the land in such nonhistorical plays as *The Merchant of Venice*, should take a keen interest in *jus gentium* in *Henry V*, a history.[279]

A lawyer studying the play is impressed by Shakespeare's attention to historical detail and rules of law in international relations and diplomacy. One need only recall his careful formulation of the ultimatum to France, which contains a statement of the claim, its legal basis and the consequences of noncompliance.

We have examined clusters of norms that underlie Shakespeare's account of a phase of the Hundred Years' War. These clusters concern the just war doctrine, declarations of war, the responsibility of princes, the treatment of the population of occupied territory – including in the case of siege – and prisoners of war, and the conduct of diplomacy. We have used the play as a vehicle to analyze the law of war issues that governed, or

---

[277] *Supra* note 108 (particularly Arts. 54, 64).

[278] Consider these excerpts from Holinshed's version:

> Also that we of our owne power shall doo the court of parlement in France to be kept and observed in his authoritie and sovereignetie . . . .
>
> Also we to our power shall defend and helpe all and everie of the peeres, nobles, cities, townes, communalties, and singular persons, now or in time comming, subjects to our father in their rights, customes, privileges, freedomes, and franchises, longing or due to them in all manner of places now or in time comming subject to our father.
>
> Also we diligentlie and truelie shall travell to our power, and doo that justice be administred and doone in the same realme of France after the lawes, customes, and rights of the same realme . . . .
>
> Also we to our power shall provide, and doo to our power, that able persons and profitable beene taken to the offices as well of justices and other offices belonging to the governance of the demaines, and of other offices of the said realme of France, for the good right and peaceable justice of the same, and for the administration that shall be committed unto them . . . .

R. HOLINSHED, *supra* note 3, at 99–100. On the Treaty of Troyes, see also H. HUTCHISON, *supra* note 117, at 186–89; E. JACOB, HENRY V, *supra* note 26, at 148–55; G. TOWLE, *supra* note 117, at 410–13; R. MOWAT, *supra* note 221, at 229–37; D. SEWARD, *supra* note 117, at 145–46; 3 J. WYLIE & W. WAUGH, THE REIGN OF HENRY THE FIFTH 198–204 (1968).

[279] In his other histories, Shakespeare, however, focused far less on *jus gentium*.

should have governed, that conflict, and to develop an intertemporal, historical perspective on the law of war and its evolution.

Because Shakespeare wrote about a medieval war during the Elizabethan Renaissance, it would be comforting to suggest that during the 179 years that elapsed between the Treaty of Troyes and the writing of the play, the law had significantly progressed toward greater humanity. Yet major progress cannot be discerned when one considers, for example, the cruelty of the Thirty Years' War (1618–1648), which was soon to break out and was conducted without the constraints of chivalric rules.

Our analysis of such detailed rules as those pertaining to necessity, reprisals and the protection of prisoners of war and civilians, especially women, reveals that resort to humane principles, which was advocated by Renaissance scholars, particularly Gentili, was frequently rejected by other Renaissance writers on *jus gentium*, who gave preference to harsher, *Kriegsraison* rules. A more humane approach, however, was not alien to some medieval writers, especially Christine de Pisan, who insisted that religious and chivalric principles demanded a high degree of respect and mercy for the human person.

Indeed, in medieval times interest in *jus gentium* was not limited to scholars. Medieval English Kings, such as Richard II and Henry V, promulgated detailed proclamations and ordinances on war. The latter's proclamations, which attracted the attention of Holinshed and Shakespeare, were informed both by pragmatic concerns of good order and military discipline and by considerations of humanity. They were addressed to such matters as the right to ransom and other spoils of war, the prohibition of pillage, and the protection of women, ecclesiastics, and churches. Here considerations of humanity, frequently compelled by religious principles,[280] blended with the imperatives of military order to result in a higher standard of protection for the civilian population.

Like their twentieth-century counterparts, both medieval and Renaissance works on the law of war mirror the tension between principles of humanity and military necessity, broadly construed. Their authors defined some of the issues still central to the law of war and often enunciated policies and principles that shaped norms of modern international law on matters such as combatant privileges and the protection of civilians. The ancestry of these protective rules was recently acknowledged by the U.S. Department of Defense in a report to Congress on the conduct of the gulf war[281] and will weigh heavily in determining their

---

[280] *See, e.g., supra* text at notes 201, 245.

[281] The report notes:

> The law of armed conflict ... with respect to collateral damage and collateral civilian casualties is derived from the Just War tradition of discrimination; that is, the necessity for distinguishing combatants from noncombatants and legitimate military targets

character as customary law. That ordinances of war dating from the Middle Ages prohibited pillage and protected women goes far beyond the Hague Regulations or the Lieber Code in helping to establish the customary law pedigree of these rules.

The medieval umbilical cord connecting *jus ad bellum* and *jus in bello*, still conventional to the contemporaries of Shakespeare, was eventually cut, giving rise to the uniform and more equitable application of the law of war. But echoes of the medieval doctrine of just war can still be heard, as we have attempted to show, in some theories of modern international law.

The principle of *respondere non sovereign* had to give way to the much stricter modern concepts of attribution and responsibility, so essential to the effectiveness of international law. Although necessity has not been eliminated from the lexicon of the law of war, persons *hors de combat*, including prisoners of war, are now protected from both reprisal and slaughter on the altar of state necessity, in contrast to the unfortunates at Agincourt. In Henry's times, as still today, disrespect for the existing rules, rather than the absence of rules, was the principal problem.

Henry V illustrates the underlying issues implicated in the law of war. While, for the most part, Shakespeare is faithful to Holinshed's version of the facts, he departs from that version in two major instances: the addition of Henry's admonition to Exeter at Harfleur to "use mercy," and the favorable gloss put on the order to kill the French prisoners at Agincourt. There is no mention of "mercy" in Holinshed. Yet Shakespeare not only highlights it as the principal order issued by the King in Harfleur, but also passes over in silence the harsh measures taken by the English in Harfleur, including the deportation of its indigent population. The medieval concept of mercy on which the dramatist drew evolved into the concept of obligations of humanity in the modern law of war. What, after all, are the latter if not legally binding progeny of the former?

In these two deviations from Holinshed's *Chronicles*, the dramatist probably was simply trying to portray the heroic King to his best advantage. But, in so doing, Shakespeare aligned himself with the advocates of greater adherence to humane laws of war, whether medieval or Renaissance.

from civilian objects ... [T]his tradition is a major part of the foundation on which the law of war is built ....

U.S. DEPARTMENT OF DEFENSE, CONDUCT OF THE PERSIAN GULF CONFLICT: AN INTERIM REPORT TO CONGRESS PURSUANT TO TITLE V PERSIAN GULF CONFLICT SUPPLEMENTAL AUTHORIZATION AND PERSONNEL BENEFITS ACT OF 1991 (Public Law 102–25), at 12–2 (1991).

III

Crimes and Accountability in Shakespeare*

Accountability for crimes, a theme central to Shakespeare's plays, is also extraordinarily pertinent to our times. Newspapers have reported on the care taken by the leaders of the former Yugoslavia to order atrocities against "enemy" populations only in the most indirect and euphemistic way. Even the Nazi leaders constantly resorted to euphemisms in referring to the Holocaust. No explicit written order from Hitler to carry out the final solution has ever been found. At the height of their power, the Nazis treated the data on the killing of Jews as top secret.[1] Similarly, a high-ranking member of the former security police told the South African Truth and Reconciliation Commission that written instructions to kill antiapartheid activists were never given; squad members who carried out the killings simply got "a nod of the head or a wink-wink kind of attitude."[2]

For a generation that grew up with the memory of the Holocaust, and witnessed the genocide in Cambodia, as well as the atrocities in Kurdistan, Yugoslavia and Rwanda, no question can be more cogent than personal responsibility. Shakespeare's treatment of the accountability of leaders sheds light on the antecedents of our notions of personal responsibility. Throughout recorded history, most egregious crimes – the mass atrocities, the genocides and the crimes against humanity – have been ordered by leaders; it is they who must be held primarily accountable. But Shakespeare also pondered the roles of executioners and courtiers – in modern terms, aides, staffers and bureaucrats.

In this essay, I intend to show how, in his works, Shakespeare dealt with crimes committed or ordered by leaders, as well as such related, but different, concepts as the arrogance of power; constraints on the prince's power; commitment versus interest; the leader's special responsibility;

* This essay draws on my book, *Bloody Constraint: War and Chivalry in Shakespeare* (O.U.P. 1998). I am grateful to the Filomen D'Agostino and Max E. Greenberg Research Fund of New York University Law School for its generous support of this study, to Professors John Baker, Liam Murphy, Thomas Nagel, Benedict Kingsbury, Detlev Vagts and Julie Peters, and Monroe Leigh for their comments and advice, and Aryeh Neier for suggesting some important sources. Thanks also to Ronald Brown of the NYU Law Library, my research assistant Laurie Rosensweig, and my secretary Sharon Town.

[1] Philippe Burrin, Hitler et les Juifs 142, 148, 163, 166–67, 172 (1989).
[2] N.Y. Times, Nov. 6, 1996, at A5.

command responsibility; superior orders and the responsibility of the ruler's advisers and intermediaries; responsibility for thought alone; the observance of forms of law; capitulation to pressure to commit crimes; Richard III as a Machiavellian prince; and responsibility for war crimes such as the massacre of French prisoners of war at Agincourt.

Not a literary critic, I do not purport to write as one. Rather, I write as a scholar of international law who is interested in history and literature. I focus not only on Shakespeare the poet and dramatist, but also on the Shakespeare who read the chronicles, Plutarch, and the literature and poetry of chivalry; who had an acute understanding of affairs of state and war; and who often recreated historical events and the mores of times past in his plays. In analyzing Shakespeare's portrayal of crimes and responsibility, I touch on the intellectual genealogy of our modern humanitarian law. His writings thus constitute an early literary reflection of this law and a vast source of questions still important today. Shakespeare raises critical questions whose complexity he recognizes and cannot, or prefers not, to resolve. Although I relate some of these questions to modern international law, I do not attempt to align them perfectly with that law. Any such attempt would be based on the false assumption that the issues – and the solutions – were the same for Shakespeare as they are for us.

Although some of the crimes I discuss were committed in international wars or their medieval or earlier counterparts, most of these offenses occurred during periods of civil war, internal strife or tyrannical repression. However, "internal" crimes should bear just as much significance for international lawyers as "international" crimes, for several reasons. First, the concepts of guilt and responsibility are easily carried over from one type of crime to another. Second, modern international law increasingly

TABLE 1.   ENGLISH KINGS IN SHAKESPEARE'S HISTORIES*

KINGS	ACCESSION DATE	LENGTH OF REIGN	PLAYS
John	May 27, 1199	18	*The Life and Death of King John*
Richard II	June 22, 1377	23	*Richard II*
Henry IV	September 30, 1399	14	*1 Henry IV*
			2 Henry IV
Henry V	March 21, 1413	10	*Henry V*
Henry VI	September 1, 1422	39	*1 Henry VI*
			2 Henry VI
			3 Henry VI
Edward IV	March 4, 1461	23	*Richard III*
Richard III	June 26, 1483	3	*Richard III*
Henry VIII	April 22, 1509	38	*All is True* (*Henry VIII*)

* Some of the information in this table is taken from Black's Law Dictionary 1657 (6th ed. 1990).

recognizes that crimes against humanity can be committed within a single country and without any nexus to war, and that certain war crimes can be committed in civil as well as international wars. Third, international human rights treaties penalize the perpetrators of egregious violations such as torture and inhuman or degrading treatment and punishment.

I ARROGANCE, RESPONSIBILITY AND CONSTRAINTS ON THE PRINCE'S POWER

Tyrannical rulers demonstrate arrogance of power by refusing to account for their acts. This arrogance stems both from the physical force of soldiers and from claims of legislative and judicial authority. For example, Lady Macbeth encourages her husband by reminding him that his superior forces offer ample protection. "Fie, my lord, fie, a soldier and afeard? What need we fear who knows it when none can call our power to account?" (*Macbeth*, V.i.34–36).[3] Further, such leaders make the laws and refuse to have them interpreted and applied against themselves. Goneril makes the ultimate claim of the absolute ruler: "Say if I do, the laws are mine, not thine. / Who can arraign me for't?" (*King Lear*, folio text, V.iii.149). In "To be, or not to be," Hamlet complains of "[t]he insolence of office" (*Hamlet*, III.i.75).

The plays show the resilience of the concept of accountability, which Shakespeare refers to in both secular (e.g., *Coriolanus*, IV.vii.18–19; *Macbeth*, V.i.34–36) and spiritual senses (e.g., *Hamlet*, I.v.79; *King John*, IV.ii.217). The tyrants' secular political nemeses are the barons who, as in *Macbeth* and *King John*, unite against murder and tyranny and fight for the restoration of the social compact that governs relations between the sovereign and his subjects. Shakespeare understood that, in the case of egregious excesses, the rudimentary system of checks and balances of medieval society could direct the enforcement of these basic rules against the sovereign himself, just as in our contemporary law, violations of international humanitarian law, or war crimes, can be avenged against the rulers.

There was thus a normative system to which even the mighty were bound to pay lip service, if not obey. On his ascension to the throne, Henry V renounces his earlier juvenile, even criminal, behavior, and accepts the supreme authority of the law and regal obligations. The Chief Justice, concerned lest the new King make him pay for his attempts to enforce the law against Henry when he was the crown prince, pleads:

---

[3] All citations of the canon are to WILLIAM SHAKESPEARE, THE COMPLETE WORKS (Stanley Wells & Gary Taylor eds., 1988). References are to act, scene and line. Some of the information in table 1, above, is taken from BLACK'S LAW DICTIONARY 1657 (6th ed. 1990).

I then did use the person of your father.
The image of his power lay then in me;
And in th'administration of his law,
Whiles I was busy for the commonwealth,
Your highness pleasèd to forget my place,
The majesty and power of law and justice,
The image of the King whom I presented,
And struck me in my very seat of judgement;
Whereon, as an offender to your father,
I gave bold way to my authority
And did commit you.

(2 Henry IV, V.ii.72–82)

And Prince Harry, now King, responds:

You are right Justice, and you weigh this well.
Therefore still bear the balance and the sword.

(Id., 101–02)

This scene was inspired by the anonymous play *Famous Victories of Henry the Fifth*[4] and by Holinshed,[5] but Shakespeare goes further in elevating the concept of supremacy of the law over princes. Shakespeare's contemporary, the great common lawyer and Chief Justice Sir Edward Coke, inevitably comes to mind. In his disputes with King James I, Coke argued that the king was subject to a dual set of restraints, the orders of the Almighty and the common law. Using the thirteenth-century maxim of Henry de Bracton, Coke developed a theory of government under God and law, *non sub homine sed sub deo et lege.*[6] Although such principles were in the air, Shakespeare's play was printed in 1600, well before Coke became Chief Justice of the Court of Common Pleas in 1606.

---

[4] 4 NARRATIVE AND DRAMATIC SOURCES OF SHAKESPEARE 260, 324–25 (Geoffrey Bullough ed., 1966) [hereinafter SOURCES OF SHAKESPEARE].

[5] W. G. BOSWELL-STONE, SHAKESPEARE'S HOLINSHED: THE CHRONICLE AND THE PLAYS COMPARED 161–63 (1968).

[6] THEODORE F. T. PLUCKNETT, A CONCISE HISTORY OF THE COMMON LAW 49 (5th ed. 1956). The issues pertaining to the authority of the king, judges, and Parliament were clearly joined in 1607, when the king argued that Coke's views on the supremacy of the common law and the judges' authority to be the uncontrolled interpreters of this law meant that "I shall be under the law, which it is treason to affirm; to which, says Coke, I replied that Bracton saith, *quod Rex non debet esse sub homine, sed sub Deo et lege.*" 5 W. S. HOLDSWORTH, A HISTORY OF ENGLISH LAW 430 & nn.2–3 (4th rev. ed. 1927). Although this is not the place to discuss the dynamics of executive acceptance of decisions of the judiciary, one might consider Truman's prompt acceptance of the decision of the U.S. Supreme Court in Youngstown Sheet & Tube Co. v. Sawyer, 343 U.S. 579 (1952), that the confiscated steel mills should be returned to the owners; and Nixon's eventual surrender of the tapes in response to the Court's ruling in United States v. Nixon, 418 U.S. 683 (1974), *see* STANLEY I. KUTLER, THE WARS OF WATERGATE 409, 513–16 (1990). On "culture of compliance," see Louis Henkin, *International Law: Politics, Values and Functions*, 216 RECUEIL DES COURS 71 (1989 IV).

Also in the air was the influence of the great Dutch humanist Erasmus, whose ideas, Kaiser suggested, "had filtered down through the century and become a part of the ideological climate of Shakespeare's world."[7] Moreover, one of Erasmus's plays may have been among the inspirations for *The Taming of the Shrew*[8] and Shakespeare's Falstaff may have been influenced by Erasmus's *Stultitia*.[9] For me, Henry's acceptance of the supremacy of the law echoes Erasmus's *The Education of a Christian Prince*, written in 1516.[10] Although this work was first translated into English only after Shakespeare's death, Shakespeare probably knew enough Latin to read the original. According to divine law, Erasmus wrote, the prince is subject to earthly law and must obey it, even though his will has the force of law.[11] Justice "restrains bloodshed, punishes guilt, defends possessions, and keeps the people safe from oppression."[12] In contrast to Niccolò Machiavelli, whose prince I shall discuss as a model for Richard III, Erasmus believed that "there can be no good prince who is not also a good man."[13] Our own private standards of integrity, morality and goodness should therefore govern our comportment as public officials and in the public domain generally. Machiavelli, "a hated name" in Shakespeare's England[14] – it was fashionable to highlight as cynical and amoral his espousal of the interests of the Prince – had an important impact on the England of the 1590s, and, as I shall show, on Shakespeare. Invoking *The Discourses*, Gentili defended Machiavelli against calumnies triggered by *The Prince*. He described Machiavelli as a misunderstood "eulogist of democracy" and "a supreme foe of tyranny." In *The Discourses*, in contrast to *The Prince*, Machiavelli supported the democratic republic and the concept of mass consent.[15]

For his part, Erasmus argued that the prince must be religious, refrain from plunder and violence, and not let his personal ambitions override concern for the state. He should govern with "wisdom, integrity and beneficence."[16] Shakespeare's Henry V amply reflects Erasmus's ideal of a Christian prince: he is pious, worried about the right decisions and causing loss of life through war, uninterested in material pursuits, chivalrous and patriotic. Replete with warnings against tyranny, Erasmus's

---

[7] WALTER KAISER, PRAISERS OF FOLLY: ERASMUS, RABELAIS, SHAKESPEARE 210 (1963).

[8] DAVID BEVINGTON, THE COMPLETE WORKS OF SHAKESPEARE at A-25 (1997).

[9] KAISER, *supra* note 7, at 209–10.

[10] DESIDERIUS ERASMUS, THE EDUCATION OF A CHRISTIAN PRINCE (Lester K. Born trans., 1936) (1540).

[11] *Id.* at 113.   [12] *Id.* at 122–23.   [13] *Id.* at 189.

[14] BEVINGTON, *supra* note 8, at xxiv.

[15] ALBERICO GENTILI, DE LEGATIONIBUS LIBRI TRES 156 (Carnegie ed., Gordon J. Laing trans. 1924) (1594); Max Lerner, *Introduction* to NICCOLÒ MACHIAVELLI, THE PRINCE AND THE DISCOURSES at xxxvi–xxxvii (Max Lerner ed., 1950).

[16] ERASMUS, *supra* note 10, at 163.

book expounds his justification for tyrannicide. Since tyrants void the mutual compact with the people through their oppressive behavior, violence against them is not unlawful and can even be justified.[17]

Despite the extremely broad powers and command over the law enforcement and military apparatus of English kings, the criminalization of acts or speech against them as treason, and their claim to a divine right to govern (e.g., *Richard II*, III.ii.50–53), they did not have unlimited power. In 1215 King John was compelled by the barons to issue the Magna Carta, a foundation of English constitutional freedoms. The barons, the commons, the judges and the common law, the church, and the need to obtain funds – all effectively limited the power of the medieval kings. The feudal system of relationships between vassals and sovereign also gave rights to the vassals.

Although Shakespeare may overstate the powers of the kings for dramatic purposes, he effectively shows that egregious violations of governing principles may have caused rebellions or strife by the barons, an important restraint on abuses by the monarch. Sometimes Shakespeare's kings thus choose to reject and disclaim illegal orders that violate the norms of chivalry and contravene the social compact between the kings and the nobility.

Shakespeare advocates the right to rebel against absolutely tyrannical, evil, murderous kings in *Richard III* and *Macbeth*. However, when faced with abusive kings who do not rise to the supreme evil of Richard III, Shakespeare expresses qualms about rebellion, a caution that may reflect sensitivity imposed by the censorship of Elizabeth, the granddaughter of the victorious rebel Henry VII. In any event, maligning Richard III may have been the "party line" for the descendants of Henry VII.

The necessity of justifying Elizabeth's and James's reigns (and the history that led up to them) required Shakespeare to do a delicate balancing act in some places. How could one justify the history of regicide and usurpation that led to the Tudor/Stuart reigns without endorsing regicide and usurpation generally, hence destabilizing those very monarchies? Although Richard III's evil tyranny served as justification for Henry of Richmond's rebellion and regicide, to sustain this justification fully required claiming that Richard was a usurper (*Richard III*, V.v.193–216).

Elsewhere, Shakespeare's general message is that rebellion is a serious matter; it causes great disorder and suffering, and can be justified only in extreme circumstances. The nobles voice their complaints against Richard II's abuses: unjust taxation, the seizure of Bolingbroke's inheritance, the

---

[17] ERASMUS, *supra* note 10, at 113, 117.

King's incompetence, which is central to the loss of his crown, and the unfortunate state of the nation. Although they hold Richard responsible for these wrongs (*Richard II*, II.i), Shakespeare does not grant them a moral imprimatur for rebellion and leaves the question of the right of rebellion unanswered.

As James Boyd White argues, *Richard II* does not speak with the voice of a general theorist of constitutional law; the voices are of particular characters, addressing particular situations and positions. The play thus "works on the principle that the truth cannot be said in a single speech or language, but lies in the recognition that against one speech or claim or language is always another one."[18] White's interpretation therefore seems to be that, for Shakespeare, there cannot be a simple statement of unique truths but, rather, a continuous, unresolved dialogue about fundamental questions in which it is difficult to discern a single, unified position that is Shakespeare's own. My view is different. I suggest that with regard to crimes and accountability – in contrast, perhaps, to constitutional theory – Shakespeare presents something close to his own moral voice in the language of his protagonists. Of course, Shakespeare's view is not condensed into the lines of any one character, but it nevertheless emerges by analyzing the dialogue with reference to the situations of the characters. While one finds many emphatic statements underlying accountability, there are hardly any categorical denials of this concept. Shakespeare thus has a resolved moral view of accountability for crimes that is valid across time and in different places.

Shakespeare's Bishop of Carlisle pleads eloquently against overthrowing Richard II, God's anointed King, censures trying him *in absentia*, and warns against the social upheavals his removal would generate:

> What subject can give sentence on his king?
> And who sits here that is not Richard's subject?
> Thieves are not judged but they are by to hear,
> Although apparent guilt be seen in them;
> And shall the figure of God's majesty,
> His captain, steward, deputy elect,
> Anointed, crownèd, planted many years,
> Be judged by subject and inferior breath,
> And he himself not present? O, forfend it, God.

> (*Richard II*, IV.i.112–20)

John of Gaunt also refuses to rebel against Richard II, despite the Duchess of Gloucester's entreaties that he avenge her husband and Gaunt's brother's death. He states:

---

[18] JAMES BOYD WHITE, ACTS OF HOPE 50 (1994).

God's is the quarrel; for God's substitute,
His deputy anointed in his sight,
Hath caused his death; the which if wrongfully,
Let heaven revenge, for I may never lift
An angry arm against his minister.

(Id., I.ii.37–41)

Pressured by Bolingbroke to join the rebels against Richard II, York, by nature a loyalist and a legalist, agonizes over his decision: "It may be I will go with you – but yet I'll pause, / For I am loath to break our country's laws" (*id.*, II.iii.167–68).

Throughout the Histories, the protagonists engage in calculation and rationalization in deciding whether kings' wrongs justify resort to the ultimate and dangerous recourse of rebellion. In *2 Henry IV*, the Archbishop of York weighs the rights and wrongs of rebellion against an abusive monarch. York invokes the mismanagement of the kingdom, the giving away of Anjou and Maine for Margaret's hand, and the loss of France, but the principal cause of the rebellion, and the one for which Shakespeare appears to have the greatest sympathy, is York's seemingly better claim to the Crown. Henry V fears that, despite his efforts to atone, he will be held to account for his father's crime in usurping the Crown and will also bear responsibility for the death of Richard II (*Henry V*, IV.i.289–302).

Although some chivalric writers supported the right of rebellion against a prince who was acting unlawfully and outside his authority, Shakespeare made his heroes distinctly unsympathetic to rebels and rebellions, which he denigrates in particularly sharp language.[19] This approach extends beyond the Histories. Thus, in *Julius Caesar*, Shakespeare affirms stability, legitimacy and empire and voices strong reservations about the overthrow of Caesar and republicanism.

Because of the ever-present danger of an uprising by the barons, Shakespeare's kings – like other leaders throughout history – resort to euphemisms to mask their murderous orders, and disown the deeds after their execution. These practices lead to complicated issues of accountability.

II   COMMITMENT VERSUS INTEREST

Even oaths and solemn promises, the foundation (*Grundnorm*) of the medieval honor system, may yield to the interests of power. A knight

---

[19] Theodor Meron, Henry's Wars and Shakespeare's Laws 199–202 (1993). *See also* Jack Benoit Gohn, Richard II: *Shakespeare's Legal Brief on the Royal Prerogative and the Succession to the Throne*, 70 Geo. L. J. 943 (1982).

who broke an oath of loyalty to his king, his lord, his captor or others was a perjurer and a traitor to his faith,[20] the king and chivalry. He was thus subject to the severe sanction of dishonor. For example, Fluellen declares that a soldier who does not keep his vow to resort to a duel is "a craven and a villain" (*Henry V*, IV.vii.130). Promises to pay ransom enjoyed high status and were seldom breached; violations were subject to severe punishment. A knight's oath was his word of honor, a pledge of his faith. Some oaths involved important matters of peace and war and governance. But even these promises proved ineffective in binding kings and rulers. Shakespeare's plays incorporate the entire spectrum of chivalric oaths and vows and illuminate in particular the tension between principle and necessity.[21] I shall mention only a few examples of special interest to international lawyers.

One formal use of oaths of allegiance was to complete and guarantee peace agreements with "foreign" princes, and the renunciation of such an oath could amount to *lèse majesté* and treason. The victorious Henry V requires the oaths of the Duke of Burgundy and the French peers "for surety of our leagues" (*id.*, V.ii.367). Gloucester forces the Governor of Paris to swear allegiance to Henry VI: "Now, Governor of Paris, take your oath / That you elect no other king but him; / Esteem none friends but such as are his friends" (*1 Henry VI*, IV.i.3–4). To avoid further killing, Charles, the Dauphin, accepts the request of Richard, Duke of York, that he

> swear allegiance to his majesty,
> As thou art knight, never to disobey
> Nor be rebellious to the crown of England,
> Thou nor thy nobles, to the crown of England.
> [*They swear*]
> So, now dismiss your army when ye please.
>
> (*Id.*, V.vi.169–73)

Nonetheless, Alençon already hints at the fragility of this agreement in his whispered aside to Charles to "break [the truce] when your pleasure serves" (*id.*, 164).

The keeping of oaths must contend with papal pressure and the threat of excommunication in *King John*. King Philip of France and England's King John have just concluded a solemn pact involving the marriage of Blanche, John's niece, to Louis, the Dauphin. In the treaty, the French renounced support for Prince Arthur's claim to the throne of England. Pandolph, the papal envoy, wants King Philip to abrogate the pact and resume the war against John, because John objects to the pope's appointment of Stephen

---

[20] Maurice H. Keen, The Laws of War in the Late Middle Ages 162 (1965).

[21] For a fuller discussion, see Theodor Meron, Bloody Constraint: War and Chivalry in Shakespeare, ch. VIII (1998).

Langton to the Archbishopric of Canterbury. Pandolph threatens to place
a curse on Philip's head if he refuses. In response to this pressure, John
appeals to nationalistic and antipapal arguments and is promptly excom-
municated. Philip then invokes his obligation to honor the sacred vows
underlying his pact with King John (*King John*, III.i.154–58, 188). Pandolph
responds by invoking a theory of the supremacy of Philip's earlier religious vows of obedience to the church over later secular vows (*id.*, 189–92,
205–06, 214–15). Ultimately, threatened with excommunication, Philip
yields and breaks his pact with King John.

All normative systems, including chivalry, have escape valves based on
public policy that allow or even require the disavowal of existing obligations. Knights were therefore excused from participating in obviously
unjust wars. Similarly, they did not owe their princes the duty to engage
in wars against the church, despite vows of allegiance.[22] Sinful orders did
not require compliance[23] and a person could even fight against a superior
who acted unlawfully.[24] In addition, any promise obtained through
threats or fraud and any oath subjecting imprisoned knights to ill treatment could be disowned.[25] For the same reasons, oaths extorted through
fraud, made under misapprehension, compulsion, or in the service of
injustice or tyrants did not have to be honored.[26]

Shakespeare's treatment of oaths demonstrates mastery of the subject
and the legalisms and sophistry advanced to justify withdrawal from
existing obligations. The higher one's rank, the greater the latitude one
had for such renunciation.

Although Shakespeare's plays abound in references to honor and dishonor, accentuating the critical importance of shame in ensuring respect
for the norms, they also reveal the limitations on the effectiveness of the
appeal to dishonor. Despite the impact and ignominy of the sanction, the
normative system could not be enforced against sovereigns and was not
applicable to commoners. For when it comes to high politics, kings and
princes could resort to various safety valves, crude or sophisticated, to
renege on their promises, and they did so more often than ordinary
knights, against whom the sanction of dishonor could more effectively
be applied. As Frances Shirley observed, Shakespeare's plays demonstrate how allegiances evaporate, sometimes with legalistic justifications,

---

[22] Giovanni da Legnano, Tractatus de bello, de represaliis et de duello 234 (Carnegie ed., J.L. Brierly trans. 1917) (completed 1360).

[23] Honoré Bonet (Bouvet), The Tree of Battles, ch. lxxii, at 169 (G. W. Coopland ed.,
1949) (*c.*1387).

[24] Legnano, *supra* note 22, at 289.   [25] Meron, *supra* note 19, at 14–15.

[26] 2 Alberico Gentili, De jure belli libri tres 152–53 (Carnegie ed., John C. Rolfe trans.
1933) (1612). This is the 1931 translation of the 1612 edition. The first part of the book was first
published in 1588, the second and third parts in 1589. Gentili argued that kings were not
allowed to alienate their subjects. *Id.* at 373. *See also* Meron, *supra* note 19, at 189.

sometimes with mere verbiage: "every regicide, every friend-turned-rival" finds excuses for breaking oaths; men of power turn oaths into air.[27] Facing the pressure of self-interest, Shakespeare's kings show that chivalric principles often gave way.

III THE SPECIAL RESPONSIBILITY OF THE LEADER

Shakespeare concerned himself with the responsibility both of the leader, the king or prince, and of the executioner, the courtier or soldier who carries out orders that are legally or morally wrong. However, the special responsibility of the leader stood at the center of Shakespeare's interests, for it is the leader who carries the heavier obligation.

The case is most effectively made in the *Rape of Lucrece*. Attacked by Tarquinus, the tyrant of Rome, Lucrece pleads with him not to rape her, brilliantly articulating the principle of the special responsibility of leaders: their crimes cannot be covered up; they serve as a model for good or for bad.

> O be remembered, no outrageous thing
> 　From vassal actors can be wiped away;
> 　Then kings' misdeeds cannot be hid in clay.
> . . .
> 　For princes are the glass, the school, the book
> 　Where subjects' eyes do learn, do read, do look.
>
> 'And wilt thou be the school where lust shall learn?
> Must he in thee read lectures of such shame?
> Wilt thou be glass wherein it shall discern
> Authority for sin, warrant for blame,
> To privilege dishonour in thy name?
>
> (607–09, 615–21)

Arguing against the special responsibility of leaders, Cleopatra complains, "Be it known that we, the greatest, are misthought / For things that others do; and when we fall / We answer others' merits in our name, / Are therefore to be pitied' (*Antony and Cleopatra*, V.ii.172–75).

Shakespeare's Henry V resists the attribution to the King of responsibility for the acts, and the fate, of his troops. On the eve of the battle of Agincourt, he is already exhausted and perhaps not entirely satisfied with

---

[27] Frances A. Shirley, Swearing and Perjury in Shakespeare's Plays 80–81 (1979). For the legal arguments invoked by Shakespeare's characters to evade promises against interest, see Meron, *supra* note 21.

his efforts to convince his soldiers Bates and Williams that his war is just
and that he, who combines in his person kingship and mortality,[28] is
therefore not responsible for his soldiers' damnation in such a war.
Whether evading responsibility or engaging simply in self-pity, Henry
states in the famous soliloquy, "Upon the King":

> 'Let us our lives, our souls, our debts, our care-full wives,
> Our children, and our sins, lay on the King.'
> We must bear all. O hard condition,
> Twin-born with greatness: subject to the breath
> Of every fool, whose sense no more can feel
> But his own wringing. What infinite heartsease
> Must kings neglect that private men enjoy?
> And what have kings that privates have not too,
> Save ceremony, save general ceremony?

(Henry V, IV.i.228–36)

Henry also tries to evade responsibility in the scene before the walls of
Harfleur, where he enumerates the dreadful abuses, including rape, that
his troops will commit in the city if it refuses to surrender. He, their
commander, will no longer be able to control them and the leaders of
Harfleur will bear responsibility for the consequences:

> What rein can hold licentious wickedness
> When down the hill he holds his fierce career?
> We may as bootless spend our vain command
> Upon th'enragèd soldiers in their spoil
> As send percepts to the leviathan
> To come ashore. Therefore, you men of Harfleur,
> Take pity of your town and of your people
> Whiles yet my soldiers are in my command.

(Id., III.iii.105–12)

Of course, Shakespeare emphasizes rape and its sheer horror. But his
Henry clearly places the responsibility on Harfleur should it resist his
ultimatum. Although his own ordinances prohibited rape without any
qualification as to situations of siege,[29] Henry washes his hands of the
consequences unless his terms for surrender are promptly accepted.
Given the high incidence of rape in cities taken after siege, the softness
of the rules prohibiting rape,[30] and the difficulty of enforcing the law,

---

[28] *See generally* ERNST H. KANTOROWICZ, THE KING'S TWO BODIES: A STUDY IN MEDIEVAL
POLITICAL THEOLOGY (1957).

[29] MERON, *supra* note 19, ch. 8. For a discussion of modern humanitarian law, see Theodor
Meron, *Rape as a Crime under International Humanitarian Law*, 87 AJIL 424 (1993).

[30] While urging generals to prohibit and prevent rape during the sacking of a city, Vitoria
reluctantly admitted the lawfulness of allowing soldiers to sack a city if "the necessities of
war" required it, or "as a spur to the courage of the troops," even when rape would result.

there is some realism in Henry's statement. In terms of realpolitik, Henry tells Harfleur: "If you do not deal now with me, your one protector able only for a time to maintain discipline among this terrifying force, the force will run amok according to base human nature and I cannot be responsible for the consequences." But such arguments by their very nature are likely to incite illegal conduct by the troops, and these claims of inevitable indiscipline are thus both evasions of the moral responsibility that should continue even into battle, and affirmative encouragement to unrestrained war. Compare Henry's model statement concerning Bardolph:

> We would have all such offenders so cut off, and we here give express charge that in our marches through the country there be nothing compelled from the villages, nothing taken but paid for, none of the French upbraided or abused in disdainful language. For when lenity and cruelty play for a kingdom, the gentler gamester is the soonest winner. (*Id.*, III.vi.108–14)

Surely a leader strong enough to insist that Bardolph be hanged for stealing a pyx from a church, so as to set an example for others and ensure humanitarian treatment of the French population under English occupation; such a leader could have threatened to punish his troops in Harfleur severely if they resorted to rape, so as to ensure the maintenance of discipline.

The ruler's responsibility for waging war is the dominant aspect of *Henry V*. Henry worries about his responsibility for a war that will inevitably cause bloodshed and death. Shakespeare's discussion of Henry's accountability contains an important secular and legal element, found both in Henry's exchange with the Archbishop of Canterbury and in the "little touch of Harry in the night" scene (*id.*, IV.0.47) with the soldiers Bates and Williams, on the eve of Agincourt. Nonetheless, the spiritual dimension dominates, especially in Henry's conversation with Bates and Williams. The two soldiers are clearly more reflective, more doubting and more critical than the self-serving Archbishop, but do not possess the authority to give Henry approval for his recourse to war. Henry has already consulted the Archbishop, the highest spiritual authority in England, for reassurance that the war, with its awesome capacity for the shedding of innocent blood, is just. In this way, Shakespeare highlights spiritual accountability by giving the church, a spiritual authority, the role of declaring the legality and justness of the war (*id.*, I.ii.9–28). Henry then insists further, demanding, "May I with right and conscience make this claim?" (*id.*, 96). In response, Canterbury gives him what for an

---

Franciscus de Victoria, De Indis et de Jure Belli Relectiones 184–85 (52) (Carnegie ed., John Pawley Bate trans. 1917) (1557, posthumous). Gentili categorically rejected the permissibility of rape. Gentili, *supra* note 26, at 257. *See also* Theodor Meron, *Common Rights of Mankind in Gentili, Grotius and Suárez*, 85 AJIL 110, 115–16 (1991).

ecclesiastic is the strongest imaginable stamp of approval, invoking "[t]he sin upon my head, dread sovereign" (*id.*, 97–98).

Shakespeare's Henry probably knows that the church has its own interests in encouraging his involvement in foreign wars (*id.*, I.i), which diminishes the reliability of the Archbishop's assurances. As a result, doubts continue to haunt him. Bates and Williams become a mouthpiece for the common soldier, the subordinate who is ordered to fight in a war whose dynastic justifications are too complicated to understand. Worried, the two soldiers debate their spiritual end should they die fighting in Henry's war. The discussion implicates several related issues, which are not fully explored: the spiritual consequences of dying in war without last rites; the difference with regard to dying without last rites between just and unjust wars (does a soldier who dies in a just war bear spiritual responsibility for unrepented prewar or wartime misdeeds?); the question whether and to what extent the spiritual consequences for the soldiers are assumed by the king; the relationship between the king's responsibility for the spiritual welfare of the soldiers and his general responsibility for their acts; the question whether obedience to the king exonerates soldiers that participate in an unjust war.

In talking to King Henry on the eve of Agincourt, Bates suggests that obedience to the king fighting in a wrong cause "wipes the crime of it out of us" (*id.*, IV.i.131–32). Williams elaborates:

> But if the cause be not good, the King himself hath a heavy reckoning to make, when all those legs and arms and heads chopped off in a battle shall join together at the latter day, and cry all, "We died at such a place." ... I am afeard there are few die well that die in a battle, for how can they charitably dispose of anything, when blood is their argument? Now, if these men do not die well, it will be a black matter for the King that led them to it – who to disobey were against all proportion of subjection.   (*Id.*, 133–45)

Thus is articulated the theory of the king's absolute responsibility for all the acts of his soldiers. By obeying the king, soldiers are absolved of spiritual responsibility not only for killing enemy soldiers in an unjust war, but also for wartime felonies and prewar misdeeds. Henry's rejection of such responsibility includes both secular and spiritual aspects:

> [T]here is no king, be his cause never so spotless, if it come to the arbitrament of swords, can try it out with all unspotted soldiers. Some, peradventure, have on them the guilt of premeditated and contrived murder; some, of beguiling virgins with the broken seals of perjury; some, making the wars their bulwark, that have before gored the gentle bosom of peace with pillage and robbery. Now, if these men have defeated the law and outrun native punishment, though they can outstrip men, they have no wings to fly from God. War is his beadle. War is his vengeance. So that here men are punished for before-breach

of the King's laws, in now the King's quarrel. Where they feared the death, they have borne life away; and where they would be safe, they perish. Then if they die unprovided, no more is the King guilty of their damnation than he was before guilty of those impieties for the which they are now visited. Every subject's duty is the King's, but every subject's soul is his own.   (*Id.*, 157–76)

Since the king, even in a truly just war, cannot solely employ totally virtuous soldiers, he is responsible *only* for the acts of war he ordered ("every subject's duty is the King's"), and not for the soldier's prewar or wartime sins, including pillage during the campaign ("every subject's soul is his own"). In rejecting any responsibility for the spiritual damnation of his soldiers, Henry enunciates the then-prevailing legal doctrine of not holding kings to account for the wrongful private acts of their troops (*respondere non sovereign*, an exception to the general common law rule of *respondeat superior*). Nevertheless, by emphasizing the issue of Henry's accountability, Shakespeare demonstrates that perhaps leaders do have a special responsibility simply because they are in command and have the authority to declare war.

In the Henry-Bates-Williams exchange, Shakespeare raises the question of the moral responsibility of combatants involved in an unjust war.[31] Some moralists argued that a knight who feels the war is unjust need not follow his prince. Others, emphasizing the tradition of absolute obedience to the prince, believed that it was for the prince to determine whether a war was just; the subject, whose duty was to follow, would not endanger his eternal salvation.[32] As early as the fourth century, Saint Augustine argued that the duty of obedience preserved the soldier's innocence.[33] As the justness of war came to depend greatly on whether it was public, that is, declared on the authority of a prince competent to make such a declaration, the dominant view held that the sin of declaring an unjust war was the prince's alone.

According to Christian doctrine, a sinner who dies without receiving communion, without confession and absolution, without a chance to repent, may be doomed to eternal damnation. When the ghost of his father, the king, reveals the circumstances of his murder by Claudius to Hamlet, the ghost expresses particular despair at not having been afforded last rites (*Hamlet*, I.v.78–80). Hamlet finds Claudius praying and is tempted to kill him, but that would be senseless. Claudius killed Hamlet's father without allowing him last rites; if Hamlet kills Claudius

---

[31] Contamine wrote that this question was discussed infrequently in medieval sources. PHILIPPE CONTAMINE, WAR IN THE MIDDLE AGES 287 (1984). It was, however, a significant topic in the Catholic just war tradition.

[32] *Id.* at 288.

[33] *Id.* at 264, 267. SAINT AUGUSTINE, THE CITY OF GOD I(21), I(26) (Henry Bettenson trans., Pelican Books 1972) (1467).

while Claudius is praying, Claudius might go to heaven, surely a travesty of justice. The irony is that Claudius himself recognizes the futility of his prayers (*id.*, III.iii.51–56, 97–98), but Hamlet unknowingly decides to wait for an occasion when Claudius's passage to hell will be assured (*id.*, 73–95).

IV   COMMAND RESPONSIBILITY

I turn to the overlapping issues of responsibility for acts of subordinates and for actions one had the power to prevent. This question, important to the moral and legal responsibility of everyone, not just leaders, arises in the following episode from *Antony and Cleopatra*. The triumvirs of Rome, Mark Antony, Octavius Caesar and Lepidus, are dining and drinking heavily as guests on a boat of their former adversary and competitor, Sextus Pompey. The scene presents an unparalleled opportunity for assassination, and Menas, Pompey's friend, urges him to agree that he kill them:

MENAS   Wilt thou be lord of all the world?
.....
   And, though thou think me poor, I am the man
   Will give thee all the world.
POMPEY   Hast thou drunk well?
MENAS   No, Pompey, I have kept me from the cup.
   Thou art, if thou dar'st be, the earthly Jove.
   Whate'er the ocean pales or sky inclips
   Is thine, if thou wilt ha't.
POMPEY   Show me which way!
MENAS   These three world-sharers, these competitors,
   Are in thy vessel. Let me cut the cable;
   And when we are put off, fall to their throats.
   All there is thine.

(*Antony and Cleopatra*, II.vii.60–72)

Pompey desires nothing more than to remove the triumvirs, provided that his own chivalric honor is not soiled. He may even have considered the possibility of eliminating his competitors for power already. But once Pompey is apprised of the plot, his honor is implicated and he is forced to condemn and thus forbid the assassination:

POMPEY   Ah, this thou shouldst have done
   And not have spoke on't. In me 'tis villainy,
   In thee 't had been good service. Thou must know
   'Tis not my profit that does lead mine honour;

Mine honour, it. Repent that e'er thy tongue
Hath so betrayed thine act. Being done unknown,
I should have found it afterwards well done,
But must condemn it now. Desist, and drink.

(*Id.*, 72–79)

Of course, Menas the pirate was not subtle in his suggestions. The very explicitness of his proposal might have made an indirect and euphemistic reaction more difficult for Pompey.

Shakespeare draws here on both the ideas and the actual language in Plutarch's *Parallel Lives*:

Now, in the midst of the feast ... Menas the pirate came to Pompey, and whispering in his ear, said unto him: "Shall I cut the cables of the anchors, and make thee lord not only of Sicily and Sardinia, but of the whole empire of Rome besides?" Pompey, having paused a while upon it, at length answered him: "Thou shouldest have done it, and never have told it me; but now we must content us with that we have: as for myself, I was never taught to break my faith, nor to be counted a traitor."[34]

Pompey's concept of responsibility is something quite different from the concept of negative responsibility espoused by modern moral philosophy's utilitarian school.[35] At the very minimum, the Pompey episode is analogous to command responsibility, or the *Yamashita* principle, which I discuss further below. The special responsibility of leaders for certain crimes is recognized in modern international law. After the Second World War, only the most senior leaders of Germany and Japan were prosecuted for crimes against peace, or aggression. Responsibility for a war of aggression attached only to the acts of high-ranking officials, not to everyone who fought in such a war. Thus, soldiers fighting in wars of aggression were not prosecuted for that act alone, a policy that was both just and reasonable. In commenting in 1950 on the "Formulation of the Nuernberg Principles," the International Law Commission thus set out

---

[34] Joseph Satin, Shakespeare and His Sources 582 (1966) (quoting Plutarch, Parallel Lives (Thomas North trans. 1579)).

[35] Thomas Nagel, *War and Massacre*, in War and Moral Responsibility 3, 5 (Marshall Cohen, Thomas Nagel & Thomas Scanlon eds., 1974); Bernard Williams, *A Critique of Utilitarianism*, in Utilitarianism: for and against 77, 94–95 (J.J.C. Smart & Bernard Williams eds., 1963).

Because utilitarianism-consequentialism attaches value to states of affairs, a person is as responsible for things that he/she allows or fails to prevent (negative responsibility) as for things that he/she causes (positive responsibility). However, critics of utilitarianism and supporters of the deontological theory of ethics, who stress individual rights and responsibilities in contrast to utilitarianism's emphasis on consequences, accord negative responsibility much weaker significance than positive responsibility. Most nonutilitarians think it would be wrong to fail to throw a life preserver to someone drowning, if this involved little cost. But if the cost of preventing the death of another is substantial, the requirement may disappear, unlike the prohibition against killing.

its interpretation of the understanding of the Nuremberg Tribunal, that the expression "waging of a war of aggression" in Article 6(a) of the Nuremberg Charter[36] referred "only to high-ranking military personnel and high State Officials."[37]

The *Yamashita* principle of modern international law echoes Cleopatra's and Henry's complaints about the burdens and perils of leadership. General Tomuyuki Yamashita, the commander of the Japanese forces in the Philippines in 1944–1945, was charged by the victorious American army with having failed to discharge his duty to control the operations of the persons subject to his command who had violated the laws of war by committing massacres, murder, pillage and rape against civilians and prisoners of war. Yamashita protested that he had not personally either committed or directed the commission of those atrocities. On a petition from a U.S. military commission, the Supreme Court affirmed the conviction and the capital sentence imposed on the general and held that commanders must be responsible for their subordinates.[38] Chief Justice Stone enunciated the doctrine that the law of war imposed an affirmative duty to take such measures to protect prisoners and civilians as were within the commander's power and appropriate in the circumstances.[39] The purpose of the law of war – to protect civilian populations and prisoners from brutality – would largely be defeated if the commander could get away with neglecting to take reasonable measures to that end.

In a powerful dissent, Justice Murphy argued that the United States was not alleging that Yamashita had committed or ordered the commission of atrocities, or that he had had any knowledge of the commission of atrocities by members of his command. The United States had effectively destroyed Yamashita's command and communications and thus his ability to wage war. It was therefore actually charging him with the crime of inefficiency in controlling his troops, which was not recognized in international law.[40] In criticizing the decision, Michael Walzer appears to have agreed with Yamashita's defense lawyers that Chief Justice Stone established a standard of strict liability, a standard inappropriate for criminal justice.[41] However, the Chief Justice and the majority of the Court did not suggest that they were applying such a standard, believing that their standard was one of due diligence.

---

[36] The Nuremberg Charter was adopted by the Agreement for the Prosecution and Punishment of the Major War Criminals of the European Axis, Aug. 8, 1945, 59 Stat. 1544, 82 UNTS 279.

[37] [1950] 2 Y.B. Int'l L. Comm'n 376, UN Doc. A/CN.4/SER.A/1950/Add.1.

[38] *In re* Yamashita, 327 U.S. 1 (1946).   [39] *Id.* at 16.

[40] *Id.* at 34–35 (Murphy, J., dissenting).

[41] Michael Walzer, Just and Unjust Wars 320 (1977).

The exchange between Justices Stone and Murphy foreshadows that in *United States v. Park*[42] between Chief Justice Burger, writing for the majority, and Justice Stewart, writing for the dissenters. In *Park*, which concerned the scope of and limits on the criminal liability of senior corporate managers under the Federal Food and Drug Acts, the Justices voiced strikingly similar arguments. The Acts imposed criminal liability not only on corporate officers who themselves had committed a criminal act, but also on others who by virtue of their positions could be held responsible. The Acts did so by dispensing with the requirement of "consciousness of wrongdoing," declaring instead that failure to act was sufficient when the senior officer had the power to prevent the unlawful conduct.[43] The essentially utilitarian argument of Chief Justice Burger stemmed from his focus on the importance of protecting the health and well-being of the public. In contrast, Justice Stewart emphasized fairness, arguing that the jury had been instructed to find the defendant guilty merely because he had a responsible relation to the situation. Rather, the court below should have instructed the jury that the test for criminality was whether the defendant had engaged in wrongful conduct amounting at least to common-law negligence.[44]

I believe the problem was not the standard set by *Yamashita*. In his criticism of the decision, Walzer recognizes that the majority Justices did not believe they were enforcing the principle of strict liability; international lawyers usually do not read *Yamashita* as introducing strict liability and interpret the standard as requiring an element of *mens rea* through either actual knowledge or the means of knowledge that the commander failed to exercise.[45] The difficulty lies in applying that standard to General Yamashita, which appeared unfair on the facts. In reality, the standard thus edged closer to strict liability. Yamashita was unable to prevent the atrocities, an inability to which U.S. actions heavily contributed. Of course, as Walzer suggests, strict liability is supported by a utilitarian argument: making senior officers automatically responsible for massive violations forces them to do everything possible to avoid such abuse. However, here utilitarianism may clash with justice and fairness to the defendants.[46] Utilitarians might answer that justice and fairness could be achieved by requiring commanders, if they are to avoid liability, to set up effective systems of control of those under their command, but this might not always be possible.

The *Yamashita* doctrine was not incorporated in the Geneva Conventions of 12 August 1949, and Relating to the Protection of Victims of War,

---

[42] 421 U.S. 658 (1974).   [43] *Id.* at 671.   [44] *Id.* at 683 (Stewart, J., dissenting).
[45] *See, e.g.*, William H. Parks, *Command Responsibility for War Crimes*, Mil. L. Rev., Fall 1973, at 1, 37, 40–42, 103.
[46] Walzer, *supra* note 41, at 319–22.

but was codified as what appears to be a due diligence standard in Article 86(2) of Additional Protocol I to the Geneva Conventions ("if they did not take all feasible measures within their power to prevent or repress the breach"),[47] and, in somewhat different language, in the Statutes of the International Criminal Tribunals for the former Yugoslavia and Rwanda.[48] The future case law of these two Tribunals may further clarify the *Yamashita* principle and its place in customary law. I believe that Article 86(2) strikes a fair balance between the utilitarian interests of the community and the interest of justice and fairness to the defendants. A different perspective suggests that there is no conflict between community interests and the interest of justice to the defendants; the latter is also a community interest. The question is therefore one of proper balancing of several community interests.

The *Yamashita* principle was the first authoritative articulation of the modern rule of command responsibility: if a superior did not take all feasible measures to prevent or repress a breach, acts of subordinates would implicate his responsibility if he knew, or had information that should have enabled him to conclude, that the subordinates were about to commit, or had committed, a breach. Under that principle, the commander must enforce the law and make persons subject to his command accountable for compliance with the norms.

If Shakespeare is viewed in this light, we note that the triumvirs are guests on Pompey's boat and that Menas is his friend. Pompey is both the host of his guests and the commander of his troops and the pirates on board. The fact that he is also the host makes his responsibility even more compelling. Since Menas informs Pompey of his criminal intent and in fact asks for Pompey's consent, consent or even acquiescence would make Pompey an accessory to the crime or a party to the conspiracy to commit a crime.

Under the *Yamashita* principle, Pompey's obligations as a commander-host might nevertheless have been violated even if Menas had murdered the triumvirs without Pompey's advance knowledge. However, if they had been murdered elsewhere, by someone else, and without Pompey's involvement in any way as host or commander, the attribution of accountability would be different. In that case, Pompey would regard the murder as his good fortune and not an act triggering his responsibility. Alternatively, he might not hold himself responsible even if he had

---

[47] Protocol Additional to the Geneva Conventions of 12 August 1949, and Relating to the Protection of Victims of International Armed Conflicts, *opened for signature* Dec. 12, 1977, 1125 UNTS 3 [hereinafter Protocol I].

[48] Christopher N. Crowe, *Command Responsibility in the Former Yugoslavia: The Chances for a Successful Prosecution*, 29 U. RICH. L. REV. 191, 229 (1994). It remains to be seen whether the Hague Tribunal will consider Article 7(3) of its Statute to be significantly different from Article 86(2) of Protocol I, *supra* note 47.

learned of such a plot in advance and simply failed to warn the triumvirs. On the assumption that a warning was feasible and that he could therefore have saved them, Pompey would still bear only negative and not positive responsibility for the deaths. As a result, those who do not regard negative responsibility as morally significant would consider him blameless.

Pompey is of course a leader. Most of us believe that, generally speaking, standards of private morality are applicable to public life and public personalities. Public morality thus includes individual private morality. Thomas Nagel posits, however, that public officials could be held to different standards, so that in some respects these standards might be more demanding than those applicable to ordinary people, but in other respects they might allow acts that would be impermissible if measured by the standard of individual morality.[49] To say that standards of private morality are applicable to public personalities does not rule out the possibility that further moral requirements apply to public officials by virtue of their official responsibilities, which derive not from private morality alone but from additional principles of political theory. Yet, even if the public function may modify the moral standards applicable to the leader, as Nagel suggests, when the limits, perhaps the outer limits, imposed by public morality are transgressed, as in the case of judicial murder, the leader must refuse to cross the line.[50] Thus, political killing can never be justified. By preventing Menas from murdering the triumvirs, Pompey meets these standards of morality. In another respect, however, Pompey appears morally wrong. His express willingness to applaud Menas's crime so long as he, Pompey, has not heard about it beforehand is morally objectionable. If Pompey is obligated to prevent the murder, then surely he should be obligated to deplore the crime after the fact.

V   SUPERIOR ORDERS: THE RULER'S ADVISERS AND INTERMEDIARIES

Pompey's obligation in *Antony and Cleopatra* contrasts with that of Sir Robert Brackenbury in *Richard III*. Brackenbury, the Lieutenant of the Tower of London, is given a written order to hand over the imprisoned Duke of Clarence to the hired thugs of Richard, Duke of Gloucester. The two intruders have just entered and accosted Brackenbury:

---

[49] Thomas Nagel, *Ruthlessness in Public Life, in* PUBLIC AND PRIVATE MORALITY 75, 78–79 (Stuart Hampshire ed., 1978).
[50] *Id.* at 90.

BRACKENBURY   What wouldst thou, fellow? And how cam'st thou hither?
SECOND MURDERER   I would speak with Clarence, and I came hither on my legs.
BRACKENBURY   What, so brief?
FIRST MURDERER   'Tis better, sir, than to be tedious. (*To Second Murderer*) Let
   him see our commission, and talk no more.
     (*Brackenbury reads*)
BRACKENBURY   I am in this commanded to deliver
   The noble Duke of Clarence to your hands.
   I will not reason what is meant hereby,
   Because I will be guiltless of the meaning.
   There lies the Duke asleep, and there the keys.
   [*He throws down the keys*]
   I'll to the King and signify to him
   That thus I have resigned to you my charge.
FIRST MURDERER   You may, sir; 'tis a point of wisdom.

                                              (*Richard III*, I.iv.81–95)

Brackenbury represents the submissive collaborator who knows, or at least suspects, the murderous, unarticulated goal of the warrant. He prefers not to think, not to question, even in the privacy of his mind. He collaborates with evil while trying not to sully his hands, or his conscience, by considering what is really involved. Can Brackenbury be compared to the French policeman who follows written orders to round up Jews and deliver them for deportation to the Vel d'Hiv (the roundups in Paris of July 16–17, 1942, pursuant to written directives to the French police from the German High Command)?[51] He does not ask where, why, for what purpose – resettlement, forced labor or worse? Rather, the approach is – do not ask, "be guiltless of the meaning."

The failure of Brackenbury to question the purpose of the order appears morally reprehensible as deliberate self-deception, different from ignorance or lack of awareness.[52] Brackenbury's ignorance, if any, results from his refusal to ask questions because he expects the answer to be unpalatable. I recognize that for some commentators it might not be morally culpable to fail to ask a question when there is nothing the person can do about the answer. In my view, even if there is nothing that Brackenbury could do to save Clarence, he may be guilty of moral negligence by not questioning the morality of what he does.[53]

Legally, both the French policeman and Brackenbury may have a good defense. The order to deliver Jews, in one case, and Clarence, in the other, may not have been manifestly illegal and the agents may not have been sufficiently aware of any illegality. Morally, however, their situation is quite different. The French policeman had far greater latitude to evade the

---

[51] RICHARD H. WEISBERG, VICHY LAW AND THE HOLOCAUST IN FRANCE 65 (1996).
[52] JONATHAN GLOVER, RESPONSIBILITY 176 (1970).   [53] *Id.* at 178.

order. He could have sought out the Jews less diligently, or otherwise sabotaged the order. In contrast, Brackenbury's options were quite limited. He could either obey or refuse, and in the latter case, his own fate would be death. The penal codes of civil law systems, with some exceptions, recognize duress as a complete defense for all crimes. In common law countries, however, duress is not a complete defense for murder. Common law cases, however, typically concerned situations where an accused had a choice between his own life and the life of another, as distinct from cases where the choice was either the death of another or the death of both, as in Erdemović's case, which I discuss below, if his plea were to be believed. Duress, involving lack of moral choice and the risk of death, may provide a moral justification. In modern humanitarian law, such duress provides, at the very least, powerful mitigation and, according to some cases (the case law on the subject is not uniform), complete exoneration. Although the appeals chamber of the International Criminal Tribunal for the former Yugoslavia recently ruled in the *Erdemović* case that duress does not afford a complete defense to a soldier charged with a crime against humanity and/or a war crime involving the killing of innocent human beings, the narrowness of the majority (three to two) and the cogency of Antonio Cassese's dissent may suggest that the jury is still out on this question.[54]

The jurisprudence of the Nuremberg tribunals under Control Council Law No. 10 on the responsibility of senior staff officers of the German army (Wehrmacht) who transferred illegal orders from senior commanders to field units, or who delivered Soviet war prisoners to Nazi authorities such as the Sicherheitsdienst (SD), is not quite clear. Senior commanders who gave clearly illegal orders and the subordinates who carried them out were found responsible. In the *High Command Case*, the Tribunal found that execution of orders to the Wehrmacht to turn over prisoners of war to the Nazi SD, an organization in which all accountability for them would have evaporated, when it was suspected or known that their ultimate fate was extermination, was criminal. On the other hand, tribunals found that, absent command responsibility, staff officers were not responsible for either criminal acts in the command in which they performed staff duties or the mere transfer of commands to the field. But they were responsible if they put the basic idea, which was criminal, into the form of a military order, or took personal action to see that the

---

[54] Prosecutor v. Erdemović, Case No. IT–96–22–A, Appeals Judgment (Oct. 7, 1997), *discussed in* note 57 *infra* [hereinafter Erdemović Appeal]. *See also* Theodor Meron, *The Normative Impact on International Law of the International Tribunal for Former Yugoslavia*, 24 Isr. Y.B. Hum. Rts. 163, 180–82 (1995); Steven R. Ratner & Jason S. Abrams, Accountability for Human Rights Atrocities in International Law: Beyond the Nuremberg Legacy 123 (1997).

order was properly distributed. As regards field commanders, the tribunals held that, to hold such a commander criminally responsible for the transmittal of an order down the chain of command, the order had to be criminal on its face, or one that the commander knew was criminal.[55]

Of course, there are important differences between medieval and modern channels for the communication of commands. Medieval kings often gave orders directly to the executioners. Instructions were frequently delivered in person and usually not in writing. However, in Shakespeare's plays written warrants were frequently invoked. In the German security and extermination apparatus, one could trace at least four stages: from Hitler to Himmler to Heydrich to the camp commanders and finally to the block wardens. Criminal orders such as the Kommandobefehl went through many more command levels in the Wehrmacht, greatly complicating questions of knowledge and responsibility. That order, issued by Hitler on October 18, 1942, provided that enemy troops on commando missions, whether in uniform or not, whether armed or not, and whether in battle or in flight, were to be slaughtered to the last man.[56]

The Wehrmacht officers' latitude for evasion of orders probably exceeded Brackenbury's. By agonizing over his "guiltlessness," Brackenbury reveals that he is aware of the moral dilemma, which the strength of his legal defense cannot resolve. Imagine, however, that Brackenbury definitely knows that Clarence will be murdered. If he delivers Clarence, will Brackenbury become an accessory to the murder, at least on the moral plane? Under the absolutist prong of modern moral philosophy, certain egregious acts such as murder and torture are never allowed, regardless of the benefit they may generate. The prohibition of murder should thus prevail over any other consideration, including a utilitarian conception of consequences. But perhaps the distinction between actual participation in the murder and mere obedience to the order to deliver Clarence to the murderers is significant, especially given the implicit coercion and the absence of any options for evasion. As Thomas Nagel suggested, absolutism forbids doing certain things to people, rather than bringing about certain results through one's own actions.

Whatever his situation under the absolutist theory may be, under a utilitarian view of moral responsibility Brackenbury may be justified in handing over the keys. If he refuses, Clarence will be killed anyway and he will die as well. In a utilitarian-consequentialist sense he is not responsible for Clarence's death, since he cannot do anything to prevent it. Therefore, he should act in such a way that the result will be one death

---

[55] United States v. Von Leeb, 11 Trials of War Criminals before the Nuernberg Military Tribunals under Control Council Law No. 10, at 462, 509–15, 542–49 (1950) [hereinafter Trials]. *See also* United States v. List, *id.* at 757, 1236.

[56] *Von Leeb*, 11 Trials, *supra* note 55, at 525–26.

instead of two. The absolutist-utilitarian controversy was brilliantly illuminated in the appeals chamber of the International Criminal Tribunal for the former Yugoslavia in a recent exchange between President Cassese and Judges McDonald and Vohrah (the *Erdemović* case) pertaining to a soldier who was allegedly coerced by threats of immediate execution into participating as a member of a firing squad in the massacre of a large number of innocent civilians. The utilitarian argument voiced by Cassese was that, because the massacre would have proceeded in any event, Erdemović's refusal to participate in the killings, which would have led to the sacrifice of his life, would have benefited no one and would have simply added one more victim. The law, Cassese argued, could not require Erdemović to forfeit his life, which, apart from setting a heroic example, would be to no avail. The absolutist argument echoed by McDonald and Vohrah rejected any balancing of harms and rested on the categorical prohibition of killing innocent people, even under duress. In addition, however, to the absolutist prohibition of killing innocent people even when the killing results from duress, McDonald and Vohrah invoked the policy consideration of deterring future offenders, thus themselves drawing on a utilitarian argument. Nevertheless, if Cassese's focus was on the facts of Erdemović's case, theirs was on the broader impact of the sentence.[57] Under the McDonald-Vohrah view, Jews in Nazi concentration camps compelled to assist in operating the crematoria would have been denied the defense of duress. Would this be just?

I would like to mention another aspect. There can be cases where a person's refusal to participate in a collective massacre may inspire others to resist orders to kill. When this happens, commanders might find it difficult to carry the massacres out and the absolutist argument could merge with the utilitarian. In the case of Erdemović, prospects of this

---

[57] Erdemović had been sentenced to 10 years' imprisonment, following his guilty plea to one count of a crime against humanity, for participating in the mass execution of a large number of civilian Muslim men in the aftermath of the fall of Srebrenica. Erdemović invoked duress, alleging that when he had at first refused to join in the massacre, he was told that he himself would be shot together with the Muslims. *See further infra* notes 81–86 and corresponding text. Cassese argued that, where the accused has been charged with participation in a collective killing that would have proceeded irrespective of whether the accused was a participant, the defense has been allowed in principle in some cases, and that Erdemović had not enjoyed any real moral choice. Cassese stated the utilitarian argument. Erdemović Appeal, *supra* note 54, Separate and Dissenting Opinion of Judge Cassese, at 58. *See also* note 35 *supra*. The absolutist argument was framed by Judges McDonald and Vohrah. Erdemović Appeal, *supra*, Joint Separate Opinion of Judge McDonald and Judge Vohrah, at 65.

Brackenbury, in contrast to Erdemović, was not required to participate in murder, but only to hand the Duke over. Thomas Nagel's comment on absolutism is apposite to his case: "not everything that happens to others as a result of what one does is something that one has done to them." Nagel, *supra* note 35, at 10.

happening may have been utopian; in the case of Brackenbury's encounter with the two hired murderers, it would have been impossible.

However, Shakespeare provides no evidence that Brackenbury is willing to justify his conduct to himself in a utilitarian way. Presumably, this
means that if he were ordered to kill Clarence himself, he would feel some
reluctance, even if he could not save the Duke by refusing to carry out the
orders. Were Brackenbury thinking only of choosing the lesser evil, he
would not have had to evade full awareness of his role as an active agent
in the murder.

In some ways, Shakespeare is quite kind in his treatment of Brackenbury's failure to prevent Clarence's delivery to his murderers. Perhaps he
sympathizes with Brackenbury's predicament and realizes that there is a
limit to a person's ability to challenge the apparatus of the state in an
environment of terror. Or perhaps the dramatist shows leniency because
he learned from the chroniclers that Brackenbury had resisted an earlier
attempt to kill the two princes (discussed in part VII below).

In *Richard II*, Shakespeare introduces further questions of responsibility. Richard banishes Henry Bolingbroke, the Duke of Hereford and
eldest son of John of Gaunt, the Duke of Lancaster and fourth son of
Edward III. After John's death, Richard decides to confiscate his entire
property, allegedly to finance his Irish campaign, and does so in total
disregard of Bolingbroke's inheritance rights. Richard's uncle, the
Duke of York, warns the King that this lawless confiscation will expose
him to tremendous risks. Richard's rights to the Crown depend on lawful
succession; his encroachment on the legitimate succession rights of the
nobility will inevitably endanger his own rights as well. Thus argues
York:

> Take Hereford's rights away, and take from Time
> His charters and his customary rights:
> Let not tomorrow then ensue today;
> Be not thyself, for how art thou a king
> But by fair sequence and succession?
> Now afore God – God forbid I say true! –
> If you do wrongfully seize Hereford's rights,
> Call in the letters patents that he hath
> By his attorneys general to sue
> His livery, and deny his offered homage,
> You pluck a thousand dangers on your head,
> You lose a thousand well-disposèd hearts.
>
> (*Richard II*, II.i.196–207)

Despite this warning that violation of the law by the King will destroy
the legal foundation on which the King himself rests, the arrogance of
power proves blinding yet again: Richard replies, "Think what you will,

we seize into our hands / His plate, his goods, his money, and his lands"
(*id.*, 210–11).

As York has warned in vain, the confiscation of Bolingbroke's property
arouses the barons' fear that they will suffer a similar fate. They thus
decide to support Bolingbroke against the King.

> Ross   The commons hath he pilled with grievous taxes,
>   And quite lost their hearts. The nobles hath he fined
>   For ancient quarrels, and quite lost their hearts.
> WILLOUGHBY   And daily new exactions are devised,
>   As blanks, benevolences, and I wot not what.
>
> (*Id.*, 246–51)

Clearly, Bolingbroke is not the only victim of the King's excesses; in
fact, the whole population is already suffering from Richard's actions.
Richard's growing unpopularity and prolonged absence while campaign-
ing in Ireland help shift the balance of power to Bolingbroke. The
latter quickly expands his goals so that he not only claims his rightful
inheritance, but also seeks the Crown itself. Richard, though ultimately
forced to abdicate in Henry's favor and imprisoned in Pomfret, is still
regarded as a danger. A deposed monarch, as long as he breathes, and –
as in *Richard III* – his children are a threat to those who deposed and
displaced them, because of the overriding legality of their entitlement to
the Crown. In the end, Richard is assassinated by Exton, one of Henry's
courtiers.

The order to kill Richard is never explicitly stated but is implied by the
courtiers, who transform what they understand as Henry's desire into an
operational order. Sir Piers of Exton interprets the King's words with
chilling clarity. Shakespeare makes Henry's words resemble the statement attributed by oral tradition to Henry II in 1170 before the murder
of Thomas à Becket in the Canterbury Cathedral: "Will no one rid me
from this turbulent priest?"

> EXTON   Didst thou not mark the King, what words he spake?
>   "Have I no friend will rid me of this living fear?"
>   Was it not so?
> [FIRST] MAN   Those were his very words.
> EXTON   "Have I no friend?" quoth he. He spake it twice,
>   And urged it twice together, did he not?
> [SECOND] MAN   He did.
> EXTON   And speaking it, he wishtly looked on me,
>   As who should say "I would thou wert the man
>   That would divorce this terror from my heart",
>   Meaning the King at Pomfret. Come, let's go.
>   I am the King's friend, and will rid his foe.
>
> (*Id.*, V.iv.1–11)

Exton and his men proceed to Pomfret and assassinate Richard. Typically of most of Shakespeare's executioners, remorse comes quickly and the spiritual aspect dominates. Immediately after striking the deadly blow, Exton exclaims, "O, would the deed were good! / For now the devil that told me I did well / Says that this deed is chronicled in hell" (*id.*, V.v.114–16).

The most intriguing aspect of this episode is King Henry's reaction when Exton and his men arrive with Richard's body and Exton claims credit for his deed ("within this coffin I present / Thy buried fear" (*id.*, V.vi.30–31)). Henry disowns the act and punishes the courtier with exile, despite Exton's attempt to exonerate himself by invoking the defense of superior orders.

> KING HENRY   Exton, I thank thee not, for thou hast wrought
>   A deed of slander with thy fatal hand
>   Upon my head and all this famous land.
> EXTON   From your own mouth, my lord, did I this deed.
> KING HENRY   They love not poison that do poison need;
>   Nor do I thee. Though I did wish him dead,
>   I hate the murderer, love him murderèd.
>   The guilt of conscience take thou for thy labour,
>   But neither my good word nor princely favour.
>   With Cain go wander through the shades of night,
>   And never show thy head by day nor light.
>
> (*Id.*, 34–44)

Exton's fate is reminiscent of the complaint voiced by the Second Knight, one of the murderers of Archbishop Thomas à Becket in T. S. Eliot's *Murder in the Cathedral*: "King Henry – God bless him – will have to say, for reasons of state, that he never meant this to happen; and there is going to be an awful row; and at the best we shall have to spend the rest of our lives abroad."[58]

Having banished Exton, Henry remains with his lords and for the first time admits responsibility for Richard's death, offering repentance by making a voyage to the Holy Land.

> Lords, I protest my soul is full of woe
> That blood should sprinkle me to make me grow.
> Come mourn with me for what I do lament,
>   . . .
> I'll make a voyage to the Holy Land
> To wash this blood off from my guilty hand.
> March sadly after.
>
> (*Id.*, 45–51)

---

[58] T. S. ELIOT, MURDER IN THE CATHEDRAL, pt. II, at 77 (1935).

In recounting Henry's wish to have Richard killed and his subsequent murder by Exton, Shakespeare followed Holinshed closely.[59] He also drew on various additional sources.[60] However, the above exchange between Exton and the King, which highlights issues of accountability, is not based on historical sources. This scene, focusing as it does on a ruler's denial of responsibility for an order he did not explicitly issue, may thus have special significance as a reflection of Shakespeare's own attitudes. Obviously, Shakespeare regards Richard as responsible.

Exton's punishment has both a spiritual and a physical component (the "guilt of conscience" and banishment[61]), again highlighting Shakespeare's focus on the spiritual element as an essential complement of accountability.

King John reintroduces the issue of distributing accountability between a leader and his subordinate. In contrast to Richard II, King John takes a

[59] BOSWELL-STONE, *supra* note 5, at 125–26. *See also* EDWARD HALL, HALL'S CHRONICLE 20 (1809) (photo. reprint 1965) (1548); SATIN, *supra* note 34, at 103–04; 3 SOURCES OF SHAKE-SPEARE, *supra* note 4, at 413–14. In both Holinshed and Shakespeare (*Richard II*, V.v.114–16), Exton demonstrates remorse for his actions.

[60] Telling of the start of the episode, Holinshed writes that King Henry said: 'Haue I no "faithful freend which will deliuer me of him, whose life will be my death, and whose death will be the preservation of my life?" This saieng was much noted of them which were present, and especiallie of one called sir Piers of Exton.' BOSWELL-STONE, *supra* note 5, at 125; HALL, *supra* note 59, at 20; 3 SOURCES OF SHAKESPEARE, *supra* note 4, at 413; SATIN, *supra* note 34, at 103. *A Myrroure for Magistrates* (anon. 1559) suggests a more explicit order to Exton, explaining that, '[t]o dash all dowtes [about his reign], he [the king] tooks no farther pause / But sent sir Pierce of Exton a traytrous knight / To Pomfret Castell, with other armed light.' SOURCES OF SHAKESPEARE, *supra*, at 415, 422. In *The First Fowre Books of the Civile Wars* (1595), Samuel Daniel, like Shakespeare, is more subtle. He writes that 'Henry desired Richard's death,' so that

> He knew this time, & yet he would not seeme
> Too quicke to wrath, as if affecting bloud;
> But yet complaines so far, that men might deeme
> He would twere done, & that he thought it good;
> And wisht that some would so his life esteeme
> As rid him of these feares wherein he stood:
> And therewith eies a knight, that then was by,
> Who soone could learne his lesson by his eie.

Id. at 434, 456–57. In a footnote the editor, Bullough, notes that in the margin of the manuscript was written: 'This Knight was Sir Pierce of Exton.' *Id.* at 457 n. 1.

[61] The character of a courtier ready to kill at the mere wink of authority is well described in the 1595 poem by Samuel Daniel, *supra* note 60, which Shakespeare may have read:

> The man he knew was one that willingly
> For one good looke would hazard soule and all,
> An instrument for any villanie,
> That needed no commission more at all:
> A great ease to the king that should hereby
> Not need in this a course of justice call,
> Nor seeme to wil the act, for though what's wrought
> Were his own deed, he grieves should so be thought....

...

more direct and explicit role in ordering a crime. King John is at war with Philip of France, who asserts the claims to the English throne of Prince Arthur, the son of the deceased Geoffrey, John's older brother. During a battle, Arthur is taken prisoner. John entrusts custody of Arthur to Hubert, a courtier, hinting that as long as Arthur is alive, John's entitlement to the Crown of England will not be secure. The obvious conclusion is that Arthur must be killed. Pandolph, the papal envoy, cynically predicts the inevitability of the murder in his conversation with the French King's son, Louis the Dauphin. In his statement (*King John*, III.iv.118, 123–34, 138–67), a marvel of Machiavellian realpolitik, Pandolph also highlights the French gains that will result from the crime. The murder not only will strengthen the Dauphin's claim to England through his wife, Blanche, but also will incite the barons to rebel against John.

By this time, John has enlisted Hubert as Arthur's executioner.

> KING JOHN　Yet I love thee well,
> 　And by my troth, I think thou lov'st me well.
> HUBERT　So well that what you bid me undertake,
> 　Though that my death were adjunct to my act,
> 　By heaven, I would do it.
> KING JOHN　　　　　　　　　Do not I know thou wouldst?
> 　Good Hubert, Hubert, Hubert, throw thine eye
> 　On yon young boy. I'll tell thee what, my friend,
> 　He is a very serpent in my way,
> 　And wheresoe'er this foot of mine doth tread,
> 　He lies before me. Dost thou understand me?
> 　Thou art his keeper.
> HUBERT　　　　　　　And I'll keep him so
> 　That he shall not offend your majesty.
> KING JOHN　Death.
> HUBERT　　　　　My lord.
> KING JOHN　　　　　　　　A grave.
> HUBERT　　　　　　　　　　　　He shall not live.
> KING JOHN　　　　　　　　　　　　　　　Enough.
> 　I could be merry now. Hubert, I love thee.
> 　Well, I'll not say what I intend for thee.
> 　Remember.

(Id., III.iii.54–69)

Despite this atmosphere of terror, legal formalities are not forgotten in *King John*. King John gives Hubert a warrant and the executioner

> This knight, but o why should I call him knight
> To give impiety this reverent stile,
> Title of honour, worth, & vertues right
> Should not be given to a wretch so vile?

Id. at 457.

Hubert finds to carry out the deed insists on seeing it. He says, demonstrating the continued reliance on legal niceties, "I hope your warrant will bear out the deed" (*id.*, IV.i.6). Hubert also shows the warrant to Arthur as a way to justify his bloody mission, asking, "Is it not fair writ?" To which Arthur replies, "Too fairly, Hubert, for so foul effect" (*id.*, 37–38).

Ultimately, when King John disowns the order, Hubert will produce the warrant as formal legal protection from the King's wrath, saying, "Here is your hand and seal for what I did" (*King John*, IV.ii.216).

Although the warrant provides authority and disobedience will be dangerous, Hubert yields to Arthur's pleas for mercy. The executioner is actually pleased with Hubert's decision to spare Arthur. Revealing his distaste for the King's demand and perhaps his sense of morality, he says, "I am best pleased to be from such a deed" (*id.*, 85). Nonetheless, Hubert returns to King John and reports that he has complied with the order, because anything different would entail too much danger.

King John's reaction to the report that Arthur was killed, which he believes to be true, shows the ambivalence between his desire simply to deny responsibility and thus appease the nobles and his twinges of conscience and fear of damnation. King John places the responsibility for the crime on Hubert, bemoaning courtiers who, anxious to please, anticipate their masters' orders and do not hesitate to murder to humor them and win their gratitude. They, like Hubert, certainly do not try to dissuade the leaders from their evil designs, even though they might be able to do so.

Throughout history, the courts of princes and the chanceries of world leaders have been staffed with opportunistic aides and sycophants. How many advisers actually resign to protest egregiously immoral or illegal orders? How many are prepared to tell the leaders that their designs are unethical or illegal? Some have surely resigned, or been demoted or worse, rather than cravenly follow the improprieties of their rulers. Although King John is both self-serving and hypocritical in this exchange with Hubert, his comments about advisers and courtiers still ring true, for many cases. Had Hubert expressed some doubts, or even restated the King's orders in different terms, perhaps John would have rescinded the order.

In her early fifteenth-century *Book of Fayttes of Armes and of Chyvalrye*, translated into English in 1489, Christine de Pisan urged that a prince consult impartial advisers before deciding whether the war under consideration was just. Yet humanists faced a dilemma in becoming their prince's adviser. They aspired to reform the political system through education and could justify their service to the prince as a public obligation. But More's *Utopia* voices a powerful warning that a court expert is bound to lose his independence and tell the prince what he wants to hear. He will sink in sycophancy and tamper with the truth.[62] Although advising on war and warning against crime present different issues, both turn on the integrity of the adviser. As *King John* demonstrates, finding such advisers must have been a difficult task.

> KING JOHN   I had a mighty cause
>   To wish him dead, but thou hadst none to kill him.
> HUBERT   No had, my lord? Why, did you not provoke me?
> KING JOHN   It is the curse of kings to be attended
>   By slaves that take their humours for a warrant
>   To break within the bloody house of life,
>   And on the winking of authority
>   To understand a law, to know the meaning
>   Of dangerous majesty, when perchance it frowns
>   More upon humour than advised respect.
>
> (*King John*, IV.ii.206–15)

Hubert then reminds the King that he had given him the warrant, showing him a piece of paper. John, fearing his own damnation for having issued the order, attempts to shift the blame to the opportunistic courtier, all too willing to commit evil to ingratiate himself with his lord. The King continues:

> Hadst thou but shook thy head or made a pause
> When I spake darkly what I purposèd,
> Or turned an eye of doubt upon my face,
> As bid me tell my tale in express words,
> Deep shame had struck me dumb, made me break off,
> And those thy fears might have wrought fears in me.
> But thou didst understand me by my signs,
> And didst in signs again parley with sin;
>   . . .
> Out of my sight, and never see me more!
> My nobles leave me, and my state is braved,
> Even at my gates, with ranks of foreign powers;
> Nay, in the body of this fleshly land,
> This kingdom, this confine of blood and breath,
> Hostility and civil tumult reigns
> Between my conscience and my cousin's death.
>
> (*Id.*, 232–49)

---

[62] CHRISTINE DE PISAN, BOOK OF FAYTTES OF ARMES AND OF CHYVALRYE 13–14 (William Caxton trans. 1489, A. Byles ed. 1932) (written 1408–09). *See also* MERON, *supra* note 19, at 18–19, 27–28; J. H. HEXTER, THE VISION OF POLITICS ON THE EVE OF THE REFORMATION 82–93 (1973).

Hubert bears a heavy moral responsibility for having failed even to attempt to discourage the King.[63] Furthermore, he cannot benefit from a defense of superior orders. Even if the order to kill or blind Arthur was not illegal on its face – to use a modern law of war term – because it emanated from an absolute monarch, Shakespeare suggests that John had not coerced Hubert into accepting the order.[64] Rather, Hubert's motivation came from his desire to endear himself to the King and to reap the unspecified advantages the King had promised him.

Shakespeare's kings usually do not order murders but, rather, buy promises to kill. In *Richard III*, Buckingham's initial hesitation to become the instrument for killing King Edward's children leads to Richard's anger, creating an immediate threat to Buckingham's survival in the royal court. By this time, his hands are already dirty. But it is Buckingham's decision to join a rebellion that leads, after his defeat and capture, to his execution, not the initial hesitation. As a result, we cannot know if, for Shakespeare, Buckingham's execution has resulted from Richard's desire to get rid of a courtier who can no longer be trusted and who knows too much, or if it is merely a punishment for treason. Perhaps Buckingham could have declined to cooperate earlier on, before his complacent immersion in the evil doings of the tyrannical regime made him too dangerous to be ignored. However, for Richard, though perhaps not for John or other leaders, any refusal may not have been tolerable.

The rest of the episode from *King John* demonstrates the complexities of these issues of responsibility. Although they attribute Arthur's possibly accidental death to John, the barons understand that John is not made of wholly immoral fabric. Salisbury, one of the nobles, recognizes that the King is troubled by his desire to kill Arthur: "The colour of the King doth come and go / Between his purpose and his conscience" (*id.*, 76–77). A modern commentator observed that "Shakespeare's monster [King John] is a terribly human one. . . . [H]e is plagued with all-too-recognizable uncertainties and guilts."[65] His struggles pit his private conscience against his political ambition.

---

[63] Shakespeare's *Richard III* calls attention to a courtier's responsibility to discourage crimes by leaders when King Edward complains bitterly that none of his aides had pleaded against his order to execute the Duke of Clarence (*Richard III*, II.i.107–33).

[64] Writings on the Second World War demonstrate that orders to commit atrocities were often not accompanied by duress, at least, as Michael Walzer pointed out, not to the extent of implicating the risk of death. WALZER, *supra* note 41, at 314. In most cases, reluctance to carry out such orders resulted in a transfer to hardship posts and other harm to one's career. The Nuremberg Tribunal's *High Command Case* discussed the range of options available to German staff officers faced with an illegal order: they could issue orders countermanding the order, resign, or sabotage the order. *Von Leeb*, 11 TRIALS, *supra* note 55, at 511.

[65] MICHAEL MANHEIM, THE WEAK KING DILEMMA IN THE SHAKESPEAREAN HISTORY PLAY 134 (1973).

Nonetheless, it is too late for John to escape responsibility. As in *Richard III*, the barons provide the counterbalance to lawless tyranny. They swear to break their obedience to the King and resort to vengeance. Yet in the end, despite their vows, the barons do not depose John; rather, he dies poisoned by a monk.

Although the rebellious barons do not succeed in their revolt, their fate merits additional comment. Count Melun warns them that, should the French win, they will be delivered to King John to face a traitor's punishment. Consequently, they agree to return and seek John's mercy. Shakespeare's Melun implies that there was a deal between John and the French, saying, "Fly, noble English, you are bought and sold" (*id.*, V.iv.10). But Shakespeare's source, Holinshed, suggests another explanation for this treatment of the seemingly honorable nobles. The French would act on their own in enforcing, even against interest, the international rules of chivalry that condemned as treason and rebellion a knight's disavowal of an oath of allegiance to his sovereign.[66] These chivalric rules certainly did not make rebellion any easier. The party line against rebellions is harshly voiced by the Bastard, who, addressing the English lords, calls them "degenerate," "ingrate revolts," "bloody Neros," "ripping up the womb [o]f your dear mother England" (*id.*, V.ii.151–53). However, perhaps because the nobles rebelled only in reaction to the violation of chivalric rules by the King, Shakespeare attributes their plight to an unsavory deal between John and the French rather than to the normative rules of chivalry. Shakespeare thus refrains from undermining the barons' noble motivation.

The historical basis of the story of Arthur is still shrouded in some mystery.[67] Shakespeare's version of Arthur's disappearance generally incorporates both Holinshed's story and *The Troublesome Raigne of King John*. The moral-ethical discussion of responsibility in Shakespeare, however, tracks the story in *The Troublesome Raigne of King John*, where Hubert initially shows little hesitancy to carry out his warrant and in fact reads it out loud to Arthur. Eventually, he allows his conscience to triumph by accepting Arthur's entreaties, which bear an important resemblance to

---

[66] Boswell-Stone, *supra* note 5, at 72.

[67] Shakespeare's treatment of this episode owes much to Holinshed and to *The Troublesome Raigne of King John*, an anonymous play written in 1591. 4 Sources of Shakespeare, *supra* note 4, at 4, 22. Holinshed's account of the conversation between Hubert and Arthur and his story about Arthur's death originates in a contemporary Essex chronicle of Coggeshall, entitled *The English Chronicle of Radulph of Coggeshall*. F. M. Powicke, Ways of Medieval Life and Thought 27 (1949). *See also* 4 Sources of Shakespeare, *supra*, at 15, 55–60. Holinshed's explanations for Arthur's death are (1) that Arthur died of grief; (2) that he was drowned in attempting to escape from Rouen; or (3) that he was killed by his uncle. Powicke, *supra*, at 32, explains that the main authority for Arthur's disappearance is the annals of Margam, a Cistercian abbey in South Wales. The story Powicke recounts, as described in the chronicle of Margam, suggests that John killed Arthur in a drunken fury. *Id.*

Arthur's pleas for pity in Shakespeare's *King John*. In fact, the sophist-icated discussion of the tension between the moral duty of the individual and the legal obligation of an official in *The Troublesome Raigne of King John* appears to have greatly influenced Shakespeare's treatment of conscience.

At the very beginning of scene xii, Hubert and the three executioners are morally troubled by their assigned task. Hubert shows them the warrant, as he does in *King John*, and explains that the King "threatneth torture for the default."[68] Throughout the scene, Hubert declares his intention to obey his king's command because it is an order, so that "I must not reason why he is your foe, / But doo his charge since he commaunds it so."[69] Echoing Shakespeare's Brackenbury, Hubert thus invokes the need to comply with orders and laws, which is rooted in good order, stability and obedience, saying, "Why then no execution can be lawfull, / If Judges doomes must be reputed doubtfull."[70] Therefore, a subject must comply with superior orders, because "a subject dwelling in the land is tyed to execute the kings commaund."[71]

Arthur argues, however, that illegal orders to commit murder cannot be obeyed and that orders of execution are valid only when in compliance with the substance and form of the law. He states, "no commaund should stand in force to murther. / . . . [W]here in forme of Lawe in place and time, / The offender is convicted of the crime."[72] In the end, Hubert tells Arthur that his "conscience bids desist"[73] and that he will therefore save Arthur. The distinction in *The Troublesome Raigne of King John* between the secular effect of the warrant and its inability to protect the executioner from divine law is echoed by the murderers of Clarence in *Richard III* (I.iv). Hubert says, "My King commaunds, that warrant sets me free: / But God forbids, and he commaundeth Kings."[74] Again, the power of conscience and divine accountability comes to the fore.

The questions raised in *King John* and its sources remain central to modern international law. The Nuremberg Charter provides that the defense of superior orders shall not free a defendant from responsibility, although it may be considered in mitigation of punishment if the Tribunal determines that justice so requires.[75] However, Nuremberg jurisprudence subsequently tempered the severity of this provision.[76] The Nuremberg Charter's approach was followed by the Statutes of the International Criminal Tribunals for the former Yugoslavia and Rwanda.

---

[68] 4 SOURCES OF SHAKESPEARE, *supra* note 4, at 108.

[69] *Id.* at 110.   [70] *Id.*   [71] *Id.*   [72] *Id.*   [73] *Id.* at 111.   [74] *Id.*

[75] Agreement for the Prosecution and Punishment of the Major War Criminals of the European Axis, *supra* note 36, Art. 8.

[76] *See generally* YORAM DINSTEIN, THE DEFENCE OF OBEDIENCE TO SUPERIOR ORDERS IN INTERNATIONAL LAW (1965).

In addressing the criminal liability of East German officials for killing those who tried to escape to the West over the Berlin Wall, German courts have dealt much more harshly with members of the National Defense Council who issued or transmitted orders to shoot pursuant to the laws in force than with border guards who carried out those orders.[77] Guards who initially did not agree to shoot were assigned to inferior maintenance work and reproached for being uncomradely, but they were not threatened with physical harm to themselves or their families.[78] Thus, the defense of duress was not available to the guards.[79] In another case, which involved high officials, the Federal Supreme Court (Bundesgerichtshof) ruled that any justification arising from the statute had to be disregarded by the courts when it implied a patent violation of overriding fundamental principles of justice and humanity. The Court held that the accused officials who drafted, adopted, and saw to the implementation of the orders to eliminate persons attempting to flee from the German Democratic Republic, which permitted the intentional killing of fugitives to prevent them from escaping, had no justification in view of the obvious, intolerable violations of the elemental demands of justice and human rights protected by international law.[80]

Shakespeare's Hubert felt that the King's warrant provided him with a legal justification, but not a moral one. That warrant, however, was only an authorization; given the consensual circumstances in which it was issued, it was not an order. Had Hubert believed that his moral objections tainted the legality of the warrant, he might have invoked the defense of duress, recognizing that disobeying the King's warrant would expose him to danger. In modern international law, however, he would fail since international tribunals do not accept pleas of duress lightly.

The International Criminal Tribunal for the former Yugoslavia recently considered the related questions of superior orders and duress in the sentencing judgment of Dražen Erdemović, a Croat member of the Bosnian Serbian forces. As noted above, Erdemović pleaded guilty to crimes against humanity for having participated in a firing squad during the infamous Srebrenica massacre of July 11, 1995.[81] The defendant argued that, although he had initially refused to carry out the order, he was threatened

---

[77] Hartmuth Horstkotte, *The Role of Criminal Law in Dealing with East Germany's Past: The Mauerschützen Cases, in* DEMOCRACY, MARKET EECONOMY, AND THE LAW 213, 215 (Werner F. Ebke & Detlev Vagts eds., 1995).

[78] *Id.* at 216.

[79] *See, e.g.,* decision of Nov. 3, 1992 (Border Guards Prosecution Case), 100 ILR 366 (Fed. Sup. Ct.).

[80] Horstkotte, *supra* note 77, at 221. For the decision, July 26, 1994, see 1994 NEUE JURISTISCHE WOCHENSCHRIFT 2703. I am grateful to Professors Andreas Lowenfeld and Detlev Vagts for the translation.

[81] Prosecutor v. Erdemović, Case No. IT-96-22-T, Sentencing Judgment (Nov. 29, 1996). *See also supra* note 57.

with instant death and was sure that if he had not obeyed, he would have been killed or his wife and child directly threatened.[82] The trial chamber's review of the Nuremberg jurisprudence suggested that the Nuremberg Tribunals had accepted the defense of superior orders as grounds for mitigating responsibility, showed greater leniency when the accused held a low rank in the military or civilian hierarchy, and recognized the defense of duress as a mitigating circumstance entailing a more lenient sentence.[83] The Tribunals' test for the defense of superior orders was "whether moral choice was in fact possible."[84] However, in the absence of evidence supporting the plea of extreme necessity, the chamber did not accept Erdemović's claim.[85] Sentencing him to a prison term of ten years, the chamber balanced the gravity of the offense against the mitigating circumstances of his youth, low rank and cooperation with the prosecutor's office.[86] Thus, neither the defense of superior orders nor that of duress was ultimately considered in the sentencing calculus. The appeals chamber, as already noted, altogether rejected duress as a defense for crimes against humanity and war crimes involving the killing of innocent persons. On reconsideration, the trial chamber recognized that Erdemović was subjected to duress and reduced his sentence to five years. The case illustrates the reluctance of international tribunals to accept a plea of duress.

VI   RESPONSIBILITY FOR THOUGHT ALONE

Responsibility for thought alone, or imagining evil deeds, is one of the interesting issues to which *2 Henry VI* gives rise. Henry VI exemplifies the good, meek, even saintly, but totally ineffectual, leader,[87] not able or willing to assert his authority to stop the impending crime, the murder of Humphrey, the Duke of Gloucester and the King's Protector. Although the facts surrounding the death of Humphrey remain to be uncovered by historians, and the conflicts and power struggle between him and his opponents at the court are quite complex, Shakespeare presents a clear and simplified version of the episode. For him, the murder of Gloucester is fact and the responsible principal obvious. By portraying Suffolk, whom Shakespeare describes as the Queen's lover, as the main culprit and moving spirit of a plot by Queen Margaret and some of her courtiers,

---

[82] *Id.*, para. 80.   [83] *Id.*, paras. 53–54.

[84] *Id.*, para. 50. For the requirements regarding superior orders as a defense or as a ground for mitigation in U.S. practice, see U.S. DEPARTMENT OF DEFENSE, THE MANUAL FOR COURTS MARTIAL, UNITED STATES, Rules for Court Martial No. 916(b) (1984); U.S. DEPARTMENT OF THE ARMY, LAW OF LAND WARFARE §509 (Field Manual 27–10, 1956).

[85] Case No. IT-96-22-T, *supra* note 81, para. 91.   [86] *Id.*, para. 111.

[87] MANHEIM, *supra* note 65, at 95.

including the Duke of York and Cardinal Beaufort, Shakespeare creates
the necessary elements for the unfolding drama.

Margaret, York and Beaufort are determined to eliminate an honest
man, who, as the young King's Protector and guardian, is close to the
King, by falsely accusing him of treason. Henry protests, but all too
gently, hardly acting like a sovereign:

> [S]hall I speak my conscience?
> Our kinsman Gloucester is as innocent
> From meaning treason to our royal person
> As is the sucking lamb or harmless dove.
> The Duke is virtuous, mild, and too well given
> To dream on evil or to work my downfall.

> *(2 Henry VI,* III.i.68–73)

In denying the trumped-up charges against him, Gloucester alludes to the
chivalric virtue of mercy: "Pity was all the fault that was in me" (*id.*, 125).
As prisoner, Gloucester is entrusted to the Cardinal's custody and the
King capitulates, effectively renouncing his authority: "My lords, what to
your wisdoms seemeth best / Do or undo, as if ourself were here"
(*id.*, 195–96).

Henry does not eliminate his moral responsibility by reiterating his
confidence in Gloucester's innocence, which may be an attempt to
assuage his own conscience. Indeed, his awareness of the certitude of
the impending crime makes his passivity still more reprehensible:

> Ah, uncle Humphrey, in thy face I see
> The map of honour, truth, and loyalty;
> And yet, good Humphrey, is the hour to come
> That e'er I proved thee false, or feared thy faith.
> What louring star now envies thy estate,
> That these great lords and Margaret our Queen
> Do seek subversion of thy harmless life?
> Thou never didst them wrong, nor no man wrong.
> And as the butcher takes away the calf,
> And binds the wretch, and beats it when it strains,
> Bearing it to the bloody slaughterhouse,
> Even so remorseless have they borne him hence.

> *(Id.,* 202–13)

Despite the King's timidity, the anti-Gloucester faction is not confident
that his attitude will endure. Outside Henry's presence, Margaret insists
that, because of the danger that Gloucester represents – "the fear we have of
him" (*id.*, 234) – he must be eliminated quickly. The Cardinal agrees to this
"policy" of eliminating Gloucester. Characteristic of Shakespeare's players
who insist on adhering to the forms of the law, the Cardinal argues that "yet

we want a colour for his death./"Tis meet he be condemned by course of law" (*id.*, 236–37). Suffolk, however, is concerned that the King will "labour" (*id.*, 239), and perhaps even the commons will rise, to save Gloucester. The plotters recognize that Gloucester is innocent, because there is neither evidence nor crime. Although Gloucester may have intended to commit a crime, he has not acted on that intention. Nonetheless, they decide to deprive him of the presumption of innocence and treat him as guilty, perhaps because they fear that a fair trial will reveal his innocence.[88]

Without a legal case, the results of a trial are uncertain, but the plotters decide Gloucester's fate quickly, anyway. Thus, although Gloucester's "purpose is not executed," he must die because "he is a fox," who "[b]y nature proved an enemy to the flock" (*id.*, 256–58). Gloucester is therefore punished for, at most, his intents or thoughts. Even though the plot to kill him is both legally and morally wrong, it is ironically the clergyman, the Cardinal, who agrees to provide the executioner.

Shakespeare demonstrates his opposition to criminalizing thought in other plays. When, for example, in *Richard III*, King Edward learns from Richard of Gloucester that Clarence is dead, having been killed in pursuance of Edward's first order, the King complains:

> Have I a tongue to doom my brother's death,
> And shall that tongue give pardon to a slave?
> My brother slew no man; his fault was thought;
> And yet his punishment was bitter death.

> (*Richard III*, II.i.103–06)

As Herbert Morris argued, the maxim that law is concerned with external conduct while morality is concerned with internal conduct is misleading, because states of mind such as criminal intent and *mens rea* are relevant to law as an element of various crimes, and conduct is relevant to morality.[89] However, Shakespeare's distaste for guilt based on intent alone is not hard to justify. Even if we assume that Gloucester did intend to assassinate English public officials, a thought or intent not accompanied by attempts or any other substantial steps cannot rise to a legal offense. If intent to assassinate public officials, without more, were criminalized through legislation, prosecution would fail for lack of evidence, since only God can know what is in the hearts of men. Morris believed that the legal commentator William Blackstone would not have been troubled by laws making certain mental states criminal and accepting confessions as reliable evidence – note that, although the right not to be penalized for our thoughts alone is now taken for granted, this was not

---

[88] *Id.* at 99.

[89] HERBERT MORRIS, ON GUILT AND INNOCENCE: ESSAYS IN LEGAL PHILOSOPHY AND MORAL PSYCHOLOGY 1–2 (1976).

the case in the Middle Ages, especially in prosecutions for heresy.[90] Modern readers need to be reminded that under the English Treason Act of 1352 imagining and compassing the King's death was treason, as John Bellamy pointed out. Nevertheless, it seems reasonable to believe that, even if Shakespeare's Gloucester confessed his intent to kill public officials, most lawyers would be uncomfortable with a conviction based only on this admission of thought. Despite Shakespeare's apparent antipathy to criminalization of thought, I do not suggest that he had a clear conception of a right to privacy, or that the issues for him and for us are the same. After all, he wrote in an era of developing conceptions of freedom of conscience, which really took form only in the eighteenth century.

Morris correctly argued that laws criminalizing thought alone would certainly trouble the moral philosopher.[91] A person who only intends to commit a crime does not interfere with the liberty of others. No less important, his own liberty to think freely should be protected by law, not prohibited. Our mental processes should enjoy absolute immunity from criminal prosecution even if some future technology (e.g., the "thought police" of George Orwell's *Nineteen Eighty-four*) could reliably bare our thoughts and thus dismantle the evidentiary obstacles. Our inner thoughts must remain at the core of our privacy rights, rights whose protection from the state and others is absolute. This protection is enshrined in modern human rights law, especially in Articles 18 and 19 of the Universal Declaration of Human Rights and Articles 18 and 19 of the International Covenant on Civil and Political Rights, as well as modern constitutions, and must be supported on the moral plane as well.

Shakespeare's King Henry actually does hold a trial. At the trial, he tries to save Gloucester or perhaps establish a favorable historical record. He urges the full application of due process of law: "Proceed no straiter 'gainst our uncle Gloucester / Than from true evidence, of good esteem, / He be approved in practice culpable" (*2 Henry VI*, III.ii.19–22).

Margaret hypocritically supports Henry, saying, "God forbid any malice should prevail / That faultless may condemn a noble man! / Pray God he may acquit him of suspicion!" At this, Henry himself joins in the farce: "I thank thee, Meg. These words content me much" (*id.*, 23–26).

Suffolk then enters the trial chamber to report that Gloucester has been found dead in his bed. Although Shakespeare depicts Suffolk as responsible for ordering the Duke of Gloucester's murder, the chroniclers are less categorical. They emphasize that "hatred and mistrust of [Suffolk] were widely spread."[92] Both Hall and Holinshed describe Gloucester's death

---

[90] HERBERT MORRIS, ON GUILT AND INNOCENCE: ESSAYS IN LEGAL PHILOSOPHY AND MORAL PSYCHOLOGY 1–2 (1976) at 16. *See* H. Ansgar Kelly, *The Right to Remain Silent: Before and After Joan of Arc*, 68 SPECULUM 992 (1993).

[91] MORRIS, *supra* note 89, at 16.   [92] BOSWELL-STONE, *supra* note 5, at 267.

as a murder but do not name the perpetrator. Despite this lack of clear proof, Shakespeare's authority for attributing the responsibility to Suffolk may have been Hall's statement that among the various accusations against Suffolk voiced in the Commons was that he was "the chief procurer of the death of the good duke of Gloucester."[93]

VII   FORMS OF LAW

I have already mentioned the role of a warrant in *King John*. Even in an environment of total terror like Richard III's England, as depicted by Shakespeare, forms of law are not totally ignored. Frequently, it is the executioners or leaders, but sometimes even the victims, that invoke them. Richard, Duke of Gloucester, tries to persuade the Mayor of London that the summary execution of Hastings "against the form of law" was compelled by supreme necessity ("the extreme peril of the case, / The peace of England, and our persons' safety, / Enforced us to this execution" (*Richard III*, III.v.40–44)). The Mayor obligingly promised to "acquaint our duteous citizens / With all your just proceedings in this cause" (*id.*, 63–64).

In an earlier scene, the two murderers hired to kill the Duke of Clarence, who is already incarcerated in the Tower on the orders of King Edward, come to Richard of Gloucester for instructions.

> RICHARD GLOUCESTER   How now, my hardy, stout, resolvèd mates!
>   Are you now going to dispatch this thing?
> A MURDERER   We are, my lord, and come to have the warrant,
>   That we may be admitted where he is.
> RICHARD GLOUCESTER   Well thought upon; I have it here about me.
>   *He gives them the warrant*
>
> (*Id.*, I.iii.338–42)

Despite the warrant, Richard is concerned that the murderers might have second thoughts. He instructs them to hurry and to refrain from any discussion with Clarence (dehumanizing the victim completely, he calls him a "thing"), as the Duke might effectively plead for mercy. Richard is promptly reassured by one of the murderers: "Tut, tut, my lord, we will not stand to prate. / Talkers are no good doers. Be assured, / We go to use our hands, and not our tongues" (*id.*, 344–50).

The murderers produce the warrant ("commission") to persuade the Lieutenant of the Tower, Sir Robert Brackenbury, to give them custody of Clarence. Brackenbury, as already mentioned, prefers to hide behind the language of the commission and not raise questions about its true purpose, so that he can be "guiltless of the meaning" (*Richard III*, I.iv.91).

---

[93] 3 SOURCES OF SHAKESPEARE, *supra* note 4, at 111.

Nevertheless, the warrant does not remedy the problems of account-ability. It may satisfy the demands of human law, but not those of either divine law or conscience. The existence of a warrant also fails to allocate accountability. The Second Murderer hesitates, recognizing the warrant's insufficiency as a means to absolve him of responsibility. His conscience is an obstacle to his bloody designs. The First Murderer urges him on:

> FIRST MURDERER   What, art thou afraid?
> SECOND MURDERER   Not to kill him, having a warrant, but to be damned for killing him, from the which no warrant can defend me.
>
> > (*Id.*, 106–09)

At this point, the origin of the warrant is ambiguous. But the play explains soon thereafter that King Edward had issued it. He thus shares responsi-bility with Richard for the killing.

> FIRST MURDERER   My voice is now the King's; my looks, mine own.
> ....
>   What we will do, we do upon command.
> SECOND MURDERER   And he that hath commanded is our king.
>
> > (*Id.*, 165, 188–89)

In a legal sense, the murderers thus enunciate a defense that, in modern terminology, is the justification of superior orders, reliance on the king's orders.

Although Richard and Edward both incur some blame for the murder, the responsibility is not equally divided. Following Holinshed, Shake-speare recognizes that they share responsibility: On the one hand, the murderers discuss reporting back to Richard and being paid by him (*id.*, 112–13, 125, 269–78). On the other hand, they tell Clarence that King Edward ordered the murder (*id.*, 188–89). But Shakespeare then parts company with Holinshed and more modern historians, portraying Richard as the principal culprit. Shakespeare's Edward reverses the order and Richard arranges through his manipulations that "by [the King's] first order [Clarence] died" (*Richard III*, II.i.87–88). Modern histor-ians usually attribute the entire responsibility for Clarence's death to King Edward. The chroniclers suggest only complicity.[94]

---

[94] The historian Paul Murray Kendall presented King Edward as the architect of Clar-ence's murder and offered no suggestion that could point to Richard as the culprit. Further-more, he described Clarence as a dangerous competitor to Edward and as largely responsible for much of what would befall him in the near future: once the 'Duke of Clarence had grown ripe with secret hopes and private visions,' he began to pose a threat to his brother, the king. PAUL MURRAY KENDALL, RICHARD THE THIRD 122 (1965). After Clarence arranged for the hanging of his former wife's servant, thus arrogating to himself authority he did not have, King Edward accused Clarence of 'subverting the laws of the realm and presuming to take justice into his own hands,' *id.* at 125, and ordered him imprisoned in the Tower.

In presenting Clarence's complaint that he has been deprived of due process of law, since both evidence and conviction are absent, Shakespeare also departs from his sources. According to the chroniclers and historians, Clarence was charged with treason, attainted by Parliament, convicted, and sentenced to death.[95] He was executed a month later, on February 18, 1478.[96] The process therefore followed at least some forms of law. Shakespeare's decision to disregard the chroniclers concerning both the measure of Edward's blame and those forms of law that were in fact followed was deliberate. He must have sensed that the more depraved and evil Richard appeared, the greater the dramatic scope to demonize him in a superb morality tale, and, as already noted, to serve the legitimating purposes of the Tudor court. It was primarily Sir Thomas More's image of the evil Richard, followed by the major chroniclers, that inspired the almost caricatured and ahistorical Richard III of Shakespeare's play.[97] As a matter of fact, the forms of law were as well observed in Richard III's reign as in Edward IV's or Henry VII's.

Even in the terrifying murder scene, Shakespeare's Clarence invokes due process of law. He thus challenges his assassins:

> Are you drawn forth among a world of men
> To slay the innocent? What is my offence?
> Where is the evidence that doth accuse me?
> What lawful quest have given their verdict up
> Unto the frowning judge, or who pronounced
> The bitter sentence of poor Clarence' death?
> Before I be convict by course of law,
> To threaten me with death is most unlawful.

(Id., I.iv.176–83)

Once this invocation of secular law proves unable to deter the assassins, Clarence resorts to religious law, which is equally ineffective:

> Erroneous vassals, the great King of Kings
> Hath in the table of his law commanded
> That thou shalt do no murder. Will you then
> Spurn at his edict, and fulfil a man's?
> Take heed, for he holds vengeance in his hand
> To hurl upon their heads that break his law.

(Id., 190–95)

Unlike the chroniclers, who accused Richard of complicity in the imprisonment and murder of Clarence either indirectly or directly, Kendall described Richard as dismayed by Clarence's fate and recounted how Richard in fact 'pleaded with King Edward for George's life.' *Id.* Jacobs similarly rejected Shakespeare's imputation of responsibility to Richard for the death of Clarence. E. F. Jacob, *The Fifteenth Century: 1399–1485, in* THE OXFORD HISTORY OF ENGLAND 608 (George Clark ed., 1961).

[95] KENDALL, *supra* note 94, at 126. [96] *Id.*
[97] F. J. LEVY, TUDOR HISTORICAL THOUGHT 72 (1967).

The Second Murderer's earlier comment that he is afraid of damnation, from which "no warrant can defend me" (*id.*, 107–09), addresses this notion of spiritual accountability as separate from legal accountability. Thus, although an order by the King can provide a legal defense, for spiritual responsibility the King's order would not constitute a justification.

Shakespeare found some authority for his approach in the chronicles and literary sources and additional authority in the legend of Richard's unlimited evil.[98] When Richard III hires Tyrrell, a "discontented gentleman" whom "corrupting gold / Will tempt unto a close exploit of death" (*Richard III*, IV.ii.35–37), the King tells him that the "bastards in the Tower" are his "sweet sleep disturbers" (*id.*, 74–76) – even in the Tower they are a threat to his aspirations. Tyrrell readily agrees to rid Richard "from the fear of them" (*id.*, 78). Interestingly, like Clarence's assassin, Tyrrell also wants some form of authorization, stating, "Let me have open means to come to them" (*id.*, 77). Richard then gives him a sign of authority, saying, "Go, by this token" (*id.*, 80). Nevertheless, apparently no written document implicates Richard in the murder of the princes, a crime lacking any color of legality, in contrast to the murder of Clarence, for which the first warrant was issued by King Edward.

Holinshed served as the primary historical source for the murder of the princes and for Shakespeare's Richard III. In writing this part of his chronicle, Holinshed drew extensively on Thomas More and Hall, More being the key source for the chroniclers' treatment of Richard.[99] Accord-

---

[98] Shakespeare seems to have drawn inspiration for his story from literary sources, including 'George, Duke of Clarence,' in *A Myrroure for Magistrates*, *supra* note 60, at 301, and the anonymous poem, *The True Tragedy of Richard III* (c. 1594), *in* 3 SOURCES OF SHAKESPEARE, *supra* note 4, at 317. *See also* SATIN, *supra* note 34, at 62–71. The former poem apportions the blame between Richard and King Edward, but places the primary responsibility for the actual murder on Richard. This poem may well have encouraged Shakespeare's desire to depict Richard as the principal culprit. The poet, William Baldwin, discusses Edward's order to imprison the Duke of Clarence in the Tower, and describes Richard's wish to use the opportunity to remove Clarence, a competitor for the Crown, and plot his end. Thus, according to this source, while Edward may have condemned Clarence to death, Richard incited the king, plotted the murder, and actually committed the crime. 'George, Duke of Clarence,' *supra*, at 304–05.

Richard's responsibility is also highlighted in the prologue to *The True Tragedy of Richard III*, in which Truth describes Richard as the person who actually drowned Clarence 'in a butt of wine.' SATIN, *supra*, at 63. In *Richard III*, Clarence decries the lack of legal proceedings and declares his innocence (I.iv.176–87). Shakespeare knew from the chroniclers that Clarence had been tried and convicted by Parliament, but he must have chosen to follow the literary sources to support the historically inaccurate claim of the total absence of judicial process. Thus, Shakespeare may have been echoing poet William Baldwin, who, speaking as the Duke of Clarence, states, 'Take me for one of this wrong punisht sect, / Imprisoned first, accused without cause, / And doen to death, no proces had by lawes.' 'George, Duke of Clarence,' *supra*, at 301.

[99] KENDALL, *supra* note 94, at 398–402. *See also* Jacob, *supra* note 94, at 624; BOSWELL-STONE, *supra* note 5, at 387–94; and SATIN, *supra* note 34, at 1.

ing to the chroniclers, Richard made two attempts to kill the princes. Holinshed, following More, provides a useful description of the first attempt: because the people would not recognize his right to the throne as long as his nephews were alive, Richard sent one John Greene to the Tower's constable, Sir Robert Brackenbury, ordering him to put the princes to death.[100] The most interesting and surprising part of More's story, as reported by Holinshed, is that Brackenbury refused to cooperate with Greene, in contrast to his behavior in Shakespeare's treatment of the murder of Clarence. More explained, "he [Brackenbury] would neuer put them to death."[101] However, this episode is not reflected in Shakespeare's drama. Hall's account of the second attempt, based on More, is different from Shakespeare's. Here Richard gave Tyrrell not only a token, but a letter to Brackenbury; a letter with which Brackenbury complied,[102] much as he did in the murder of Clarence. In Shakespeare's *Richard III*, there is no mention of Brackenbury in the context of the princes' murder, a murder of which we learn through Tyrrell's report to Richard (IV.iii). Shakespeare departs from his sources, perhaps to exonerate Brackenbury from moral and personal responsibility.

VIII   YIELDING TO PRESSURE: THE CARDINAL AND THE SANCTUARY

Shakespeare is at pains to show in his plays how good men yield to pressure. The episode of the sanctuary, which occurs just before the murder of the princes, closely reflects the chronicles that Shakespeare read, providing an interesting example. Queen Elizabeth, afraid that Richard will murder her children, has taken the young Duke of York to a sanctuary under the Lord Cardinal's promise of protection and care (*Richard III*, II.iv.65–72). On his return to London, Prince Edward, the heir to the throne, is informed by Hastings that his brother York is in a sanctuary and therefore cannot welcome him. Edward does not appear to suspect that anything is amiss and wants his brother to come to him.

Buckingham, still Richard's willing accomplice, demands that the Cardinal persuade the Queen to leave the sanctuary and send the Duke of York to his brother. Should persuasion fail, he declares, he will resort to the alternative of brute force: Shakespeare's Hastings would "from her jealous arms pluck him perforce" (*id.*, III.i.36). Hall reports that in the

---

[100] BOSWELL-STONE, *supra* note 5, at 389. For Hall's version of this episode, see 3 SOURCES OF SHAKESPEARE, *supra* note 4, at 277.

[101] BOSWELL-STONE, *supra* note 5, at 389.

[102] 3 SOURCES OF SHAKESPEARE, *supra* note 4, at 278–79.

council, Richard demanded that the prince be forcibly removed if the
Queen refused to surrender him.[103] In both the chronicles and Shakespeare, the Cardinal demurs. He is prepared to try persuasion but would
not dare to violate the holy sanctuary:

> My lord of Buckingham, if my weak oratory
> Can from his mother win the Duke of York,
> Anon expect him. But if she be obdurate
> To mild entreaties, God in heaven forbid
> We should infringe the sacred privilege
> Of blessèd sanctuary. Not for all this land
> Would I be guilty of so deep a sin.

(Id., 37–43)

Insisting on the privileges of sanctuary in a place of religious worship,
Shakespeare's Cardinal thus reflects not only ancient ecclesiastical practice, but also the customs of chivalry and the common law. Shakespeare's
sources, such as Hall,[104] emphasized these normative rules, declaring that
both the secular and the ecclesiastical authorities were obligated to
respect the privileges of sanctuary.

Not satisfied with the Cardinal's response, Buckingham resorts to a
menacing tone. In both Shakespeare and the chronicles, he plays the lead
role in pressuring the Cardinal and invokes legal arguments to support
his claim that York does not qualify for sanctuary. By arguing for the
inapplicability of the rules protecting those accorded sanctuary in this

---

[103] HALL, *supra* note 59, at 352.

[104] Hall wrote:

> Howbeit yf she coulde in no wise be intreated with her good wyll to delyuer hym, then
> thought he and such of the spiritualtie as wer present, that it were not in any wyse too
> bee attempted to take hym out againste her wyll, for it woulde be a thyng that should
> turne to the grudge of all men and high displeasure of God, yf the pryuilege of that
> place should be broken whiche had so many yeres bene kept, whiche bothe Kynges
> and Popes had graunted and confirmed, which ground was sanctifyed by Sainct Peter
> him selfe more then fyue hundreth yeres agone.... [A]nd therefore quod the Arche-
> bishop, God forbid that any manne should for any yearthely enterprise breake the
> immunitie and libertie of that sacred sanctuary that hath bene the safegard of so many
> a good mans life....

Id. Leaving aside canon law, at least in the common law Buckingham's and Holinshed's legal
arguments may be serious. Although the privilege of sanctuary was one that belonged to a
place rather than a person, it was available to felons, including traitors, and even minor
malefactors and debtors. It is unclear, however, whether the common law recognized the
privilege for persons who did not offend against the law and sought protection from other
dangers. *See* J. H. Baker, *The English Law of Sanctuary*, 2 ECCLESIASTICAL L.J. 8 (1990–92); 2 THE
REPORTS OF SIR JOHN SPELMAN 335–39 (Selden Society Pub. No. 94, J. H. Baker ed. 1978).
However, the historian Polydore Vergil, in *De inventoribus rerum* f. 55 (1528), expressed the
view that a sanctuary also protected those who feared an attack. *Id.* at 340 & n. 3. In a criticism
of sanctuaries expressed in his *History of King Richard III* (c. 1513), Thomas More had
Buckingham state that in unsettled times, a sanctuary could have given justifiable protection
to political offenders. *Id.*

case, Buckingham is effectively preparing a justification for the forcible removal of York. He says to the Cardinal:

> You are too senseless-obstinate, my lord,
> Too ceremonious and traditional.
> Weigh it not with the grossness of this age.
> You break not sanctuary in seizing him.
> The benefit thereof is always granted
> To those whose dealings have deserved the place,
> And those who have the wit to claim the place.
> This prince hath neither claimed it nor deserved it,
> And therefore, in my mind, he cannot have it.
> Then taking him from thence that 'longs not there,
> You break thereby no privilege nor charter.
> Oft have I heard of "sanctuary men",
> But "sanctuary children" ne'er till now.

(Id., 44–56)

Again, the chronicles provided a ready source for Shakespeare's treatment of this episode. Buckingham's "legal" arguments, which may have a strong basis in the common law, closely reflect Holinshed's rendition:

> [A]gainst unlawful harms, never pope nor king intended to privilege any one place, for that privilege hath every place. ... But where a man is by lawful means in peril, there needs he the tuition of some special privilege, which is the only ground and cause of all sanctuaries.
>
> From which necessity, this noble prince is far, whose love to his king, nature and kindred proveth; whose innocency to all the world, his tender youth proves; and so sanctuary, as for him, neither none he needs, nor also none can have. ... He must ask it himself that must have it, and reason: since no man has cause to have it but whose conscience of his own fault makes him fain need to require it. ...
>
> And if no body may be taken out of sanctuary, that says he will bide there. ... And verily, I have often heard of sanctuary men, but I never heard erst of sanctuary children.
>
> ... But he can be no sanctuary man that neither has wisdom to desire it nor malice to deserve it; whose life or liberty can by no lawful process stand in jeopardy. And he that takes one out of sanctuary to do him good, I say plainly, that he breaks no sanctuary.[105]

The speed with which Shakespeare's Cardinal, the supreme spiritual authority of England, yields to pressure is shocking. After Buckingham's intimidation, behavior that was a flagrant sin a moment earlier becomes religiously neutral. Shakespeare may have intended here to cast doubts on the moral probity of Catholic clergy or perhaps simply to demonstrate

---

[105] Satin, *supra* note 34, at 16.

that heroes are hard to find in an atmosphere of total terror. Even more important, he may have wanted to show how principles crumble under pressure. Thus, the Cardinal immediately responds to Buckingham's "legal" arguments, "My lord, you shall o'errule my mind for once. – / Come on, Lord Hastings, will you go with me?" And Hastings obediently replies, "I come, my lord" (*id.*, 57–59).

In Hall, the Cardinal's surrender is more subtle.[106] However, as he does throughout his plays, Shakespeare exaggerates his character's actions and behavior to dramatize his goal more effectively.

Shakespeare deliberately does not tell us anything about the pressure the Cardinal exerts on the Queen. He leaves the scene in the sanctuary to our imagination. Nonetheless, Hastings's presence is a clear hint of the alternative means, i.e., brute force, that would be introduced if the Queen were to demur. There is no doubt that the Queen was forced to consent to York's release, so that he would join his older brother and ultimately be murdered in the Tower.[107]

IX   RICHARD III AS MACHIAVELLIAN PRINCE

The landscape of Shakespeare's plays is not filled only with strong and determined villains like Richard III. There are also wanton kings, such as

---

[106] In Hall, the Cardinal says:

> But I trust quod he, we shall not nede it [to use force], but for any maner of nede I would we should not do it, I trust that she with reason shalbe contented and all thing in good maner obteined. And yf it hap that I brynge it not to passe, yet shall I further it to my best power, so that you all shall perceyue my good wyll, diligence, and indeauoure.

HALL, *supra* note 59, at 353.

[107] Nonetheless, Shakespeare was certainly aware of Hall's detailed account of the discussion between the Cardinal and the Queen. The Cardinal cajoles, promises, and repeats Buckingham's legal sophistry, assuring the Queen that no harm will befall the prince, and threatens that, in the absence of her consent, the prince will be forcibly removed: 'they recon no priuilege broken, although they fetch him out of sanctuarie, whiche yf you finally refuse too deliver hym.' *Id.* at 356. In response, the Queen pleads, invoking the prince's poor health, her need to care for him, the jeopardy to which he will be exposed and her right, even in the absence of sanctuary privileges, to be the guardian of her son. Finally, once the exasperated Cardinal pledges the prince's safety with his own body and soul, the Queen yields. However, this is compulsion, not consent. On the immunity of churches in medieval ordinances, see MERON, *supra* note 19, ch. 8.

Although Shakespeare's tale ends here, the chroniclers' story refers to the events following York's removal from sanctuary. Richard III was also concerned about the danger the princesses posed to his monarchical claims. According to the *Croyland Chronicle*, the history of the Croyland Monastery, Richard learned that the king's daughters were told to go abroad so that, 'if any fatal mishap should befall the male children of the late king in the Tower, the kingdom might still, in consequence of the safety of daughters, some day fall again into the hands of the rightful heirs.' CHARLES T. WOOD, THE AGE OF CHIVALRY 188 (1970). Richard responded immediately, apparently with the 'purpose of ending [the] relative freedom of

Richard II and Henry IV; kings who are ruthless, incompetent, inconsistent but essentially humane, such as King John; and good but weak kings, such as Henry VI.[108] Some kings represent a composite of these characteristics. Manheim argued that in Shakespeare's time, under the Tudors, the medieval image of the Christian knightly king was abandoned in favor of the Machiavellian model of a ruthless, calculating, successful king, bent on creating a positive, even if deceptive, image that would appeal to the people. Despite his many virtues, Henry V is almost Machiavellian in effectively manipulating public opinion.[109] But the master of image making is Shakespeare's arch-Machiavellian, Richard III. Consider the scene with the two bishops, staged to persuade the citizens of London of Richard's Christian virtues (Buckingham: "Two props of virtue for a Christian prince, / To stay him from the fall of vanity" (*Richard III*, III.vii.96–97)).

Among the players are also well-meaning but weak princes and, as always, opportunistic courtiers. Each is conscious of what is happening, understands the trend of the events, and foresees the inevitable crime, but lacks either the will or the courage to stand up and resist. Finally, there are the executioners, some only too willing to carry out their orders and others resisting orders, even at risk to their lives.

In part I of this essay, I touched on the role of Machiavelli's *Prince* in inspiring Shakespeare's Richard III. The early sixteenth-century *Prince* (1513) and *The Discourses* were translated into English only in 1640 and 1636, respectively, but Shakespeare most likely had a working knowledge of Italian and may have read these works in the original, or at least may have read about them in secondary sources circulating in England in his time. In any event, as Max Lerner points out, Elizabethan authors made frequent reference to Machiavelli.[110]

In contrast to Erasmus's Christian prince, Machiavelli's Prince is not bound to have, or always to observe, the virtues that are esteemed in people's private lives. To serve his interests, however, he should seem to be endowed with these qualities and thus appear to be merciful, faithful, humane, sincere and religious. Nevertheless, to maintain the state, a prince is often obliged to act against faith, charity, humanity and religion.[111] A prudent ruler should not keep faith when doing so would be against his interest.[112] Interestingly, some of Shakespeare's figures voice

---

action for those in sanctuary,' by appointing men to guard the church of Westminster, setting 'a watch upon all the inlets and outlets of the monastery so that not one of the persons there shut up could go forth, and no one could enter, without his permission.' *Id.* at 189.

[108] MANHEIM, *supra* note 65, at 134.

[109] *Id.* at 4. *See also* David M. White, *Shakespeare and Psychological Warfare*, 12 PUB. OPINION Q. 68 (1948).

[110] Lerner, *supra* note 15, at xxxix–xl.   [111] MACHIAVELLI, *supra* note 15, at 65.

[112] *Id.* at 64.

similar sentiments (as in the discussion of oaths that can be breached for *Staatsraison*). A ruler can always find a colorable excuse for the nonfulfill-ment of a promise.[113] For example, a prince cannot live securely in a state as long as those whom he deposed survive. It is therefore dangerous to deprive a ruler of his kingdom and yet leave him his life, requiring the new leader to resort to violence. New benefits can never cancel old injuries, even less so when the benefits are small in comparison to the injuries inflicted.[114]

Shakespeare's Richard III and the Prince are thus a perfect fit. Richard despises the virtues respected in private life but works hard at appearing to have them. His ascent to the throne and reign are ruthless and devoid of ethical standards, his power, survival and security the only goals. Anyone who is, or could be, a threat must be eliminated. Moreover, references to Machiavelli actually appear several times in Shakespeare's plays. In discussing his plans to obtain the throne of England through killing and scheming, Richard of Gloucester mentions Machiavelli as someone to whom he, Richard, could teach a lesson:

> Torment myself to catch the English crown.
> And from that torment I will free myself,
> Or hew my way out with a bloody axe.
> Why, I can smile, and murder whiles I smile,
> And cry "Content!" to that which grieves my heart,
> And wet my cheeks with artificial tears,
> And frame my face to all occasions.
> I'll drown more sailors than the mermaid shall;
> I'll slay more gazers than the basilisk;
> I'll play the orator as well as Nestor,
> Deceive more slyly than Ulysses could,
> And, like a Sinon, take another Troy.
> I can add colours to the chameleon,
> Change shapes with Proteus for advantages,
> And set the murderous Machiavel to school.
> Can I do this, and cannot get a crown?

> (*3 Henry VI*, III.ii.179–94)

Richard III's defeat at the hands of Henry of Richmond, soon to become Henry VII, is inevitable in Shakespeare's paradigm of the barons rising against bloody tyrants in a just, and therefore winning, cause. Richmond's moving oration to his soldiers before the battle addresses several aspects of Richard's accountability.

> Yet remember this:
> God and our good cause fight upon our side.

---

[113] MACHIAVELLI, *supra* note 15, at 64.   [114] *Id.* at 406–07 (ch. IV of THE DISCOURSES).

The prayers of holy saints and wrongèd souls,
Like high-reared bulwarks, stand before our forces.
Richard except, those whom we fight against
Had rather have us win than him they follow.
For what is he they follow? Truly, friends,
A bloody tyrant and a homicide;
One raised in blood, and one in blood established;
One that made means to come by what he hath,
. . .

Then if you fight against God's enemy,
God will, in justice, ward you as his soldiers.
If you do sweat to put a tyrant down,
You sleep in peace, the tyrant being slain.
If you do fight against your country's foes,
Your country's foison pays your pains the hire.
If you do fight in safeguard of your wives,
Your wives shall welcome home the conquerors.
If you do free your children from the sword,
Your children's children quites it in your age.

(*Richard III*, V.v.193–216)

In effect, Richmond presents strong justification for the right of revolt against a tyrant, especially one that usurped the Crown and is thus an illegitimate monarch. By comparing Richard III to Machiavelli, the counselor of evil, Shakespeare emphasizes that in Elizabethan times Richard was an approved target and a ruler against whom rebellion was, exceptionally, justified.

X ACCOUNTABILITY FOR THE AGINCOURT MASSACRE: HENRY V

Accountability is also the central aspect of *Henry V*. In two important scenes, discussed above, the King consults the Archbishop of Canterbury about the justness of the war (I.ii.9–32) and tries to persuade the skeptical soldiers Bates and Williams, and perhaps reassure himself as well, that the war is just (IV.i).

Henry V is about war with an external enemy, in which, on the whole, the rules applied to the French were the rules of chivalry and the international law of arms, rather than the English law governing treason. As a result, there is less room for tyrannical abuse. Shakespeare's treatment of the laws of war here shows that he was well aware of the difference between internal strife and international wars.[115] Accordingly, the

---

[115] MERON, *supra* note 19, at 201–06.

Southampton plot is described as "dangerous treason" and "high treason" by men who "[j]oined with an enemy proclaimed and fixed" (*Henry
V*, II.ii.183, 145, 164). In contrast, Shakespeare refers to the conflict with
the French as "a fair and lucky war" (*id.*, 181). Similarly, *Richard III*
unambiguously demonstrates Shakespeare's understanding of the difference between domestic and international wars, when King Richard urges,
"March on, march on, since we are up in arms, / If not to fight with
foreign enemies, / Yet to beat down these rebels here at home" (*Richard
III*, IV.iv. 459–61).

The scene at the battle of Agincourt presents a penetrating view
of Henry's accountability for the effects of the war. Henry's order to
kill the French prisoners involves no euphemisms or code words,
perhaps because it is justified as made in reprisal for the killing of the
boys guarding the rear encampment and as impelled by the necessity
of war (Henry fears that the French are regrouping for another attack
and that the multitude of prisoners will rise against their captors in
aid of the attackers). These justifications clearly distinguish the killing
of the prisoners at Agincourt from the obvious crimes of kings
discussed above. However, the plea of necessity for the killing of French
cavalry is weakened when Pistol, who is not a knight, calls it throat
cutting:

> *Alarum*
> KING HARRY   But hark, what new alarum is this same?
> The French have reinforced their scattered men.
> Then every soldier kill his prisoners.
> [*The soldiers kill their prisoners*]
> Give the word through.
> [PISTOL] *Coup' la gorge.*
>
> (*Henry V*, IV.vi.35–39)

Gower's scathing sarcasm further highlights Shakespeare's substantial
doubts about the legality of the order. Gower thus undermines the justification and raises questions of credibility:

> FLUELLEN   Kill the poys and the luggage! 'Tis expressly against the law of
> arms. 'Tis as arrant a piece of knavery, mark you now, as can be offert. In your
> conscience now, is it not?
> GOWER   'Tis certain there's not a boy left alive. And the cowardly rascals that
> ran from the battle ha' done this slaughter. Besides, they have burned and
> carried away all that was in the King's tent; wherefore the King most worthily
> hath caused every soldier to cut his prisoner's throat. O 'tis a gallant king.
>
> (*Id.*, IV.vii.1–10)

I argued elsewhere that the English rear camp constituted a lawful
object of attack and that the French raid was unlikely to have violated

any laws of war.[116] Without a manifest breach of law by the French, Henry could not claim the defense of reprisal, which was then generally permissible. However, because Henry believed that the battle had not been won and danger persisted, and that the captured French prisoners posed a threat to his forces, his order to kill the prisoners probably did not violate medieval legal standards. Nevertheless, it clashed with the views of some of the writers disposed to take a more humanitarian view of the law, including Gentili,[117] an Italian Protestant who took refuge in England and in 1587 became the Regius Professor of Civil Law at Oxford and, later, an adviser to the Crown. In modern humanitarian law, reprisals against prisoners of war are absolutely prohibited.[118]

Those of us who consider Henry's order to be barbaric may need to revisit the law in force during the American Civil War. The well-known Lieber Code, the military law promulgated by President Lincoln and proposed by Francis Lieber of Columbia College Law School, which was generally admired for its humanitarian and enlightened nature, allowed the denial of quarter, on grounds of necessity, to enemy, i.e., Confederate, prisoners: "a commander is permitted to direct his troops to give no quarter, in great straits, when his own salvation makes it impossible to cumber himself with prisoners."[119] This rule, which was law for the United States Army in the mid-nineteenth century, appears almost designed to legitimate the massacre Henry V ordered at Agincourt. Article 62 of the Lieber Code even authorized a savage form of reciprocity, declaring that troops that gave no quarter would receive none in return. Article 66 extended reciprocity and retribution to the period after the battle, when there could no longer be any semblance of necessity. It allowed the killing of enemy prisoners if within three days after the battle it was discovered that they belonged to a corps that gave no quarter.[120]

The tolerance of the Lieber Code for denial of quarter did not long survive in the evolution of modern international humanitarian law. Article 23(d) of the Hague Regulations emphasizes that declaring that no quarter will be granted is particularly forbidden.[121] Today, the denial of

---

[116] *Id*. at 159–60.   [117] *Id*. at 166–69. *See also* GENTILI, *supra* note 24, at 212.

[118] Geneva Convention (No. III) Relative to the Treatment of Prisoners of War, Aug. 12, 1949, Art. 13, 6 UST 3316, 75 UNTS 135.

[119] *See* Instructions for the Government of Armies of the United States in the Field, General Orders No. 100, Art. 60, *reprinted in* THE LAWS OF ARMED CONFLICTS 3 (Dietrich Schindler & Jiří Toman eds., 3d ed. 1988).

[120] Theodor Meron, *Francis Lieber's Code and Principles of Humanity*, 36 COLUM. J. TRANS-NAT'L. L. 269, 273 (1997), *and in* POLITICS, VALUES AND FUNCTIONS: INTERNATIONAL LAW IN THE 21ST CENTURY, ESSAYS IN HONOR OF PROFESSOR LOUIS HENKIN 249, 252–53 (Jonathan I. Charney, Donald K. Anton & Mary Ellen O'Connell eds., 1997).

[121] Convention (No. IV) Respecting the Laws and Customs of War on Land, Oct. 18, 1907, 36 Stat. 2277, 1 Bevans 631.

quarter and killing of captured prisoners of war constitutes one of the most obvious and absolute war crimes.

Shakespeare's Henry V does not try subsequently to disclaim the order, leaving us uncertain about his own feelings as regards the massacre. No less, a look at the sources offers little enlightenment. The real Henry's chronicler, an anonymous chaplain attached to his court who left posterity the only eyewitness account of Agincourt, the wonderful *Gesta Henrici Quinti*, does not even mention the order to kill the prisoners. He describes the killing as almost an act of nature.[122] This may mean that the king was not proud of the order and did not want it to be highlighted. Shakespeare himself probably did not read the *Gesta*, which remained in manuscript form in the sixteenth century.

XI   CONCLUDING OBSERVATIONS

Written during the period of Elizabethan absolutism, Shakespeare's plays advocate a society in which the law should be respected and leaders held to high standards of civilized behavior. In the constant tension between the interests of power and ethical responsibilities, Shakespeare appears to support the latter, even if with occasional equivocation. His condemnation of crimes and euphemisms for crimes is strong. He emphasizes moral duties and the role of conscience as a guide to civilized behavior by the leader and the citizen. Furthermore, suggesting that crimes do not, or at least should not, go unpunished, the dramatist creates a potent image of accountability. However, he also shows that the principle and the ideal occasionally cave in under stress and pressure.

Shakespeare's discussion of accountability gives rise to questions of both legal and moral responsibility. There are several levels of discussion, including the political-secular, the religious-spiritual, and the moral-psychological, each of which reflects the others. Leaders, even kings, who order the killing of innocent victims cannot escape responsibility for their acts. Emphasizing the religious-spiritual dimension, Shakespeare uses conscience as a particularly powerful weapon for ensuring compliance with norms.

Shakespeare's plays convey a message about international humanitarian law and our code of civilized behavior, in civil society as well as in war, that is more poignant, more powerful and more memorable than anything we can read in the language of international treaties or even customary law. Indeed, this message can still serve humankind as a model. To this end, I agree with George Bernard Shaw, who has Queen

---

[122] GESTA HENRICI QUINTI 92–93 (Frank Taylor & John S. Roskell eds., 1975) (1416–17).

Elizabeth acknowledge, in her imaginary exchange with Shakespeare in *The Dark Lady of the Sonnets,* that "the Scottish minstrel hath well said that he that maketh the songs of a nation is mightier than he that maketh its laws."

IV

Common Rights of Mankind in Gentili, Grotius and Suárez*

Students of the concept of *erga omnes*[1] trace its antecedents to the early recognition of the right of humanitarian intervention, which they often attribute to Grotius.[2] Professor Hersch Lauterpacht asserted that Grotius's writings contained "the first authoritative statement of the principle of humanitarian intervention – the principle that exclusiveness of domestic jurisdiction stops when outrage upon humanity begins."[3] However, some of the other principal works on international law before the Peace of Westphalia (1648) reveal that the concept of community interests, and the modern right of humanitarian intervention it spawned, is pre-Grotian,[4] that it appeared in the writings of Suárez and figured prominently in those of its true progenitor, the earlier Gentili.[5]

Whether or not under their influence, the International Court of Justice, in the *Barcelona Traction* case,[6] significantly paralleled concepts articulated by these writers, particularly Gentili. To be sure, the contexts were quite

* I am grateful to Professors Peter Haggenmacher and Louis B. Sohn for their helpful comments.

[1] *See* Charney, *Third State Remedies in International Law*, 10 MICH. J. INT'L L. 57, 61 (1989); T. MERON, HUMAN RIGHTS AND HUMANITARIAN NORMS AS CUSTOMARY LAW 188–90 (1989).

[2] *See, e.g.*, Edwards, *The Law of War in the Thought of Hugo Grotius*, 19 J. PUB. L. 371, 396–97 (1970).

[3] Lauterpacht, *The Grotian Tradition in International Law*, 23 BRIT. Y.B. INT'L L. 1, 46 (1946).

[4] The 1579 *Vindiciae contra tyrannos* asserted that "it is the right and duty of princes to interfere in behalf of neighbouring peoples who are oppressed on account of adherence to the true religion, or by any obvious tyranny." W. DUNNING, A HISTORY OF POLITICAL THEORIES FROM LUTHER TO MONTESQUIEU 55 (1905) (footnote omitted).

[5] 2 A. GENTILI, DE JURE BELLI LIBRI TRES, chs. XVI and XXV (Carnegie ed., J. C. Rolfe trans. 1933). (This is the 1931 translation of the 1612 edition. *Prima commentatio de jure belli* was published in 1588, the second and third parts in 1589. The three books appeared, as a new work, in 1598 under the title *De jure belli libri tres. See* Phillipson, *Introduction* to *id*. at 14a. Regarding Gentili's other writings, see 1 L. OPPENHEIM, INTERNATIONAL LAW 91 (H. Lauterpacht ed. 1955).)

The Grotian scholar Peter Haggenmacher traces the antecedents of the principle of humanitarian intervention even further back, to the "altruistic" 13th-century school of Pope Innocent IV and to the Scholastic writers. Haggenmacher, *Sur un passage obscur de Grotius*, 51 REVUE D'HISTOIRE DU DROIT 295, 301, 304, 313 (1983). Haggenmacher's principal work on Grotius is *Grotius et la doctrine de la guerre juste* (1983).

[6] Barcelona Traction, Light and Power Co., Ltd. (Belg. v. Spain), 1970 ICJ REP. 3 (Judgment of Feb. 5).

different. While the Court implied the right of third states either to make representations to, or to make claims against, a state breaching obligations to the international community as a whole, primarily regarding human rights,[7] the classical writers treated gross abuses of human rights as legitimate grounds for resorting to war – a component of the just war (*bellum justum*) doctrine – or, as modern international lawyers would put it, as a justification for humanitarian intervention.

Hugo Grotius (1583–1645) does not need to be introduced to our readers. In the Prolegomena to his magisterial *De jure belli ac pacis* (1625), Grotius acknowledged, albeit grudgingly, his debt to Gentili[8] but did not mention Suárez. In chapter XXV of book II, entitled "On the Causes of Undertaking War on Behalf of Others," he discussed the right of a state to wage war to aid states allied to it by treaty, or even friendly states without applicable treaty commitments.[9] He then turned to the question "whether there may be a just cause for undertaking war on behalf of the subjects of another ruler, in order to protect them from wrong at his hands."[10] In principle, individuals are subject to the jurisdiction and the power of punishment of their states, and Grotius approvingly

---

[7] *Id.* at 32. *See generally* T. MERON, *supra* note 1, at 191–201.

[8]

The same thing [giving illustrations from history] was attempted on a larger scale, and by referring a great number of examples to some general statements, ... by Alberico Gentili. Knowing that others can derive profit from Gentili's painstaking, as I acknowledge that I have, I leave it to his readers to pass judgment on the shortcomings of his work as regards method of exposition, arrangement of matter, delimitation of inquiries, and distinctions between the various kinds of law. This only I shall say, that in treating controversial questions it is his frequent practice to base his conclusions on a few examples, which are not in all cases worthy of approval, or even to follow the opinions of modern jurists, formulated in arguments of which not a few were accommodated to the special interests of clients, not to the nature of that which is equitable and upright.

... Gentili outlined certain general classes [of just or unjust war], in the manner which seemed to him best; but he did not so much as refer to many topics which have come up in notable and frequent controversies.

2 H. GROTIUS, DE JURE BELLI AC PACIS LIBRI TRES, *Prolegomena*, para. 38 (Carnegie ed., F. Kelsey trans. 1925) (1625). Kelsey translated the 1646 edition rather than the first, 1625, edition of Grotius's work.

Regarding the debt of Grotius to Gentili, Nussbaum, invoking Reiger, observes that the former "even borrowed several of Gentili's miscitations." A. NUSSBAUM, A CONCISE HISTORY OF THE LAW OF NATIONS 108, 331 n. 135 (1954).

Haggenmacher, in his erudite essay *Grotius and Gentili: A Reassessment of Thomas E. Holland's Inaugural Lecture*, in HUGO GROTIUS AND INTERNATIONAL RELATIONS 133, 149–51 (H. Bull, B. Kingsbury & A. Roberts eds. 1990), describes Grotius's frequent repetition of mistakes made by Gentili in quoting classical sources. Haggenmacher observes that "Grotius's" very awareness of the advance he had effected may have induced him to minimize his debt to [his predecessors'] works. This accounts for his marked reservations towards them, no exception being made even for the writer he mentions last in the Prolegomena and values most ...." *Id.* at 175–76.

[9] H. GROTIUS, *supra* note 8, bk. II, ch. XXV, pts. IV–V.   [10] *Id.*, pt. VIII(1).

cited Ambrose's statement that the purpose is "to prevent men from provoking wars by usurping the care for things under the control of others."[11]

Nevertheless, Grotius accepted important qualifications to the principle of non-intervention, which governed only when "subjects are actually in the wrong [i.e., violated their duty towards their ruler], and . . . where the cause is doubtful."[12] If "the wrong is obvious [and some tyrant] should inflict upon his subjects such treatment as no one is warranted in inflicting, the exercise of the right vested in human society is not precluded"[13] and other states may take up arms to help the persecuted. Although he believed that, subject to some significant exceptions,[14] even in case of "extreme necessity" subjects might not rebel against their ruler, Grotius still maintained the lawfulness of intervention by one state on behalf of gravely persecuted citizens of another. He was aware of the ever-present potential for abuse but insisted that occasional abuses did not render the right of intervention invalid:

> Hence, Seneca thinks that I may make war upon one who is not one of my people but oppresses his own, . . . a procedure which is often connected with the protection of innocent persons. We know, it is true, from both ancient and modern history, that the desire for what is another's seeks such pretexts as this for its own ends; but a right does not at once cease to exist in case it is to some extent abused by evil men. Pirates, also, sail the sea; arms are carried also by brigands.[15]

Related to, but broader than, the right of humanitarian intervention is the right to punish the perpetrators of gross violations of human rights committed in another state. Grotius's statement of the latter right, which is implicit in the right to wage war in humanitarian causes, is an important precursor to the recognition in modern international law of universal jurisdiction over such matters as genocide, war crimes and crimes against humanity:

> The fact must also be recognized that kings, and those who possess rights equal to those kings, have the right of demanding punishments not only on account of injuries committed against themselves or their subjects, but also on account of injuries which do not directly affect them but excessively violate the law of nature or of nations in regard to any persons whatsoever . . . .
>
> Truly it is more honourable to avenge the wrongs of others rather than one's own . . . .[16]

---

[11] H. GROTIUS, *supra* note 8, bk. II, ch. XXV, pt. VIII(I).   [12] *Id.*

[13] *Id.*, pt. VIII(2). *See infra* text at note 36.

[14] *See* Edwards, *supra* note 2, at 391–95; Lauterpacht, *supra* note 3, at 45.

[15] H. GROTIUS, *supra* note 8, bk. II, ch. XXV, pt. VIII(4).

[16] *Id.*, ch. XX, pt. XL(1) ("Of Punishments").

Here Grotius's debt to Gentili becomes manifest.[17] However, modern academic standards compelling original writing are considerably stricter than those which guided Renaissance writers.[18]

Francisco Suárez (1548–1617) was a Spanish Jesuit scholar whose well-known *De legibus, ac deo legislatore* (Treatise on Law and God the Legislator) was published in 1612. The law of war was the subject of *De Triplici Virtute Theologica, Fide, Spe, et Charitate* (The Three Theological Virtues, Faith, Hope and Charity), published posthumously in 1621 (four years before Grotius's principal work), in which Suárez was more circumspect than Grotius. In Disputation XIII on War, a part of the latter work, Suárez recognized that the denial by one prince, "without reasonable cause, of the common rights of nations, such as the right of transit over highways, trading in common, &c.,"[19] constituted a cause for a just war. It is far from clear, however, whether Suárez believed it permissible even for a state that was not directly affected to engage in war to uphold "the common rights of nations."

---

[17] E.g., in his reliance on Hercules, who liberated certain lands from "tyrants." *Id.*, pt. XL(2). *Compare* A. GENTILI, *supra* note 5, at 75: "Hercules, the subduer of tyrants and monsters." The resemblance is even more striking in the following reference to Seneca. Grotius: "Says Seneca: 'If a man does not attack my country, but yet is a heavy burden to his own, and although separated from my people he afflicts his own, such debasement of mind nevertheless cuts him off from us.'" H. GROTIUS, *supra*, pt. XL(3). *Compare* A. GENTILI, *supra*:

> Add besides the golden words of Seneca: "Whatever the bond of affection by which any one was united to me, his violation of the common law of mankind has brought it to naught. If such a man does not attack my country, but is troublesome to his own land, and although remote from my nation harasses his own, yet that depravity of mind cuts him off from me none the less ..."

See also infra text at note 36.

[18] Richard Posner has observed that in the classical and medieval periods, "[t]he dominant theory of literary creativity ... was creative imitation: the imitator was free to borrow as long as he added to what he borrowed. The modern equation of creativity to originality is a legacy of the Romantic era, with its cult of individual expression." R. POSNER, LAW AND LITERATURE 346 (1988) (footnotes omitted).

Haggenmacher explains Grotius's predilection for borrowing material from Gentili without acknowledgment:

> Such practices, which today seem surprising and rather questionable, were not then exceptional. Humanist vanity and "elegance" induced scholars to hide their real, direct sources, in order to show only the pure wisdom of antiquity, which was of course supposed to have been drunk at its very spring, not from some intermediary vessel. Moreover, a generally accepted tendency prevailed among lawyers to muster as many references as possible in order to bring home a point; it was therefore understood, and widely practised, that in addition to the real source of a quotation one mentioned all the authors referred to therein, without checking them and without specifying which one was the key to the others. Grotius was both a humanist and a lawyer, so there was nothing unusual about his method, even though his work was obviously far removed from standard legal practice. No doubt Gentili had resorted to similar expedients. It should also be pointed out that the relevant books were sometimes difficult to obtain.

Haggenmacher, *supra* note 8, at 148.

[19] 2 F. SUÁREZ, SELECTIONS FROM THREE WORKS 817 (Carnegie ed., G. Williams, A. Brown & J. Waldron trans. 1944) (1612, 1613, 1621).

Suárez agreed that aid to a friendly country justified resort to war but "only on condition that the friend himself would be justified in waging the war, and consents thereto, either expressly or by implication."[20] Clearly, Suárez contemplated only injuries that created a subjective relationship between two states: "if [the injured party] does not entertain such a wish, no one else may intervene, since he who committed the wrong has made himself subject not to every one indiscriminately, but only to the person who has been wronged."[21] A more permissive regime could trigger abuses and undermine established patterns of territorial jurisdiction; "the assertion made by some writers, that sovereign kings have the power of avenging injuries done in any part of the world, is entirely false, and throws into confusion all the orderly distinctions of jurisdiction."[22]

In one situation, however, Suárez reluctantly accepted the right of the prince to wage war in a cause not his own, without an invitation from the state concerned, i.e., when "a state worshipping the one God inclines toward idolatry through the wickedness of its prince."[23] This reason for waging war would be valid only "if the prince forcibly compelled his [presumably Christian] subjects to practice idolatry; but under any other circumstances, [such a ground] would not be a sufficient cause for war, unless the whole state should demand assistance against its sovereign."[24] Like many modern writers on international law, Suárez felt that to make the right of humanitarian intervention open-ended would invite abuse: "if the reasoning in question [more liberally allowing intervention] were valid, it would always be permissible to declare such a war on the ground of protecting innocent little children."[25]

Alberico Gentili (1552–1608) was an Italian Protestant who took refuge in England and became the Regius Professor of Civil Law at Oxford in 1587. Gentili's vision of the common interests of mankind was not limited to human rights. Consider his striking statements, in *De jure belli libri tres*, in support of the right to wage war to protect the freedom of the seas (which preceded the publication in 1609 of Grotius's *Mare liberum*):[26]

- This [the sea] is by nature open to all men and its use is common to all, like that of the air.
- But there is also a magistracy at sea. Such a magistracy belongs to the law of nations and its jurisdiction also. ... The sovereign himself will bring war

---

[20] 2 F. SUÁREZ, SELECTIONS FROM THREE WORKS 817 (Carnegie ed., G. Williams, A. Brown & J. Waldron trans. 1944) (1612, 1613, 1621).

[21] *Id.*   [22] *Id.*   [23] *Id.* at 824.   [24] *Id.*   [25] *Id.*

[26] A whole section of chapter 12 of Grotius's *De jure praedae*, which became *Mare liberum*, was drawn from Gentili's *De jure belli*. W. KNIGHT, THE LIFE AND WORKS OF HUGO GROTIUS 94 (1925), *cited by* Haggenmacher, *supra* note 8, at 148 & n. 54.

Mare liberum was written in 1604 and published posthumously in 1868. 1 L. OPPENHEIM, *supra* note 5, at 92 & n. 1. For pre-Grotian expressions of support for the freedom of the seas, see E. NYS, LES ORIGINES DU DROIT INTERNATIONAL 381–82 (1894). Nys did not mention Gentili.

upon himself, if he refuses the sea to others; and those will be justified in making war who are refused a privilege of nature.[27]

Gentili opened chapter XXV of book I ("Of an Honourable Reason for waging War") with a discussion of the common interests of mankind (*communi ratione et pro aliis*) as causes of making war:

> There remains now the one question concerning an honourable cause for waging war ... which is undertaken for no private reason of our own, but for the common interest and in behalf of others. Look you, if men clearly sin against the laws of nature and of mankind, I believe that any one whatsoever may check such men by force of arms.[28]

Anticipating the modern distinction between state interests and general, objective, humanitarian causes, Gentili wrote that although "a foreigner may not [has no standing to] conduct a case relating to a road and highway of the state, ... he may do so in a question affecting a man's liberty [human rights] or the like."[29] Resort to wars of religion could not be allowed, unless "a right of humanity is violated [e.g., by the ritual of human sacrifice] at the same time. ... [W]ar is lawful against idolators, if idolatry is joined with the slaughter of innocent victims; for the innocent must be protected."[30] Commenting on the war waged by the Athenians upon the Lacedaemonians, who "contrary to the law of nations ... had taken suppliants from the temples and slain them," Gentili stated that "[t]his is an honourable cause for war and one which is based upon the common sentiments of humanity."[31] Gentili analogized the just causes of waging war on pirates with those underpinning wars for the protection of rights of individuals. "Romans justly took up arms against [pirates] even though those peoples had touched nothing belonging to the Romans, to their allies, or to any one connected with them; for they had violated the common law of nations."[32] For the same reason, wars to protect individuals were justified:

> And if a war against pirates justly calls all men to arms because of love for our neighbour and the desire to live in peace, so also do the *general violation of the common law of humanity and a wrong done to mankind*. Piracy is contrary to the law of nations and the league of human society. Therefore war should be made against pirates by all men, because *in the violation of that law we are all injured*, and individuals in turn can find their personal rights violated ....[33]

---

[27] A. GENTILI, *supra* note 5, at 90, 92. At a later period (1605–1608), however, as advocate for Spain before the English Court of Admiralty, Gentili did not dissent from Venetian and Genovese claims to jurisdiction over a maritime belt extending 100 miles from the coast. *See* A. GENTILI, ADVOCATIO HISPANICA, *discussed by* Abbott, *Alberico Gentili and his Advocatio Hispanica*, 10 AJIL 737, 743–44 (1916).

[28] A. GENTILI, *supra* note 5, at 122.   [29] *Id.*   [30] *Id.* at 123.   [31] *Id.* at 124.
[32] *Id.*   [33] *Id.* (emphasis added).

In thus espousing the right of states to go to war in defense of the common rights of mankind, Gentili mentioned not only such rights as the freedom of the seas, but also human rights. Even more interesting are the comments in chapter XVI of book I ("On defending the Subjects of Another against their Sovereign"), where Gentili espoused the right of humanitarian intervention on behalf of non-citizens (Gentili, just like post-United Nations Charter writers on international law, supported the right of the state to protect ["defend"] its citizens abroad ["whether what is defended is near or at a distance"] as an exercise of "necessary defence"[34]). This chapter contains several passages that are rather similar to those found in Grotius's "On the Causes of Undertaking War on Behalf of Others."[35] Gentili wrote:

> But so far as I am concerned, the subjects of others do not seem to me to be outside of that kinship of nature and the society formed by the whole world. And if you abolish that society, you will also destroy the union of the human race ...[36] And unless we wish to make sovereigns exempt from the law and bound by no statutes and no precedents, there must also of necessity be some one to remind them of their duty and hold them in restraint.[37]

Gentili explained that "if subjects are treated cruelly and unjustly, [the] principle of defending them is approved."[38] He supported Seneca's statement that if another sovereign "remote from my nation harasses his own, ... the duty which I owe to the human race is prior and superior to that which I owe [that sovereign]."[39] A good ruler, Gentili insisted, "will desire to have the power of venting his cruelty upon his subjects taken from him when he is angry ... and he will always bear in mind that kingdoms were not made for kings, but kings for their kingdoms."[40] As to whether "aid may be given to the subjects of another even when they are unjust," Gentili answered yes, provided that the purpose of the intervention ("aid") was to save them "from immoderate cruelty and unmerciful punishment; for it is the part of humanity to do good even to those who have sinned."[41]

---

[34] A. GENTILI, *supra* note 5, at 58 (ch. XIII). *Compare* H. GROTIUS, *supra* note 8, bk. II, ch. XXV, pt. 1.

[35] *See* text at note 9 *supra*. For example: "But the Corinthians spoke in the following unequivocal terms at Athens: 'We openly say that no one ought to be restrained from punishing his own dependents.'" A. GENTILI, *supra* note 5, at 74. Compare Grotius: "In Thucydides the Corinthians find it just that 'each party should punish its own subjects'." H. GROTIUS, *supra* note 8, bk. II, ch. XXV, pt. VIII(1).

"There is also the case of Constantine, who aided the Romans against Maxentius ... We defend sons against fathers who are unjust." A. GENTILI, *supra*, at 75. Compare Grotius: "In conformity with this principle Constantine took up arms against Maxentius." H. GROTIUS, *supra* pt. VIII(2).

[36] *Compare* H. GROTIUS, *supra* text at note 13.
[37] A. GENTILI, *supra* note 5, at 74.
[38] *Id.* at 75.
[39] *Id.*
[40] *Id.* at 76.
[41] *Id.*

Acknowledging that the core of Grotius's thoughts on humanitarian intervention, which include a notion comparable to *actio popularis*, already appeared in the writings of Gentili, Professor Haggenmacher considers Grotius's own contribution principally to be the elaboration of the natural law theory of universal criminal jurisdiction.[42] Yet here, too, Gentili was at the cutting edge of the law as, for example, in his warning to princes who allowed their troops to rape women in occupied territories, with the reluctant imprimatur of some sixteenth-century writers on international law:[43]

> Further, to violate the honour of women will always be held to be unjust. For although it is not contrary to nature to despoil one whom it is honourable to kill, and although where the law of slavery obtains it is permitted according to the laws of war to sell the enemy together with his wives and children, yet it is not lawful for any captive to be visited with insult. ... I make no allowance for retaliation.
>
> At some time the enemy [who allows raping women] will have to render account to [his victims] for his wrong; he will surely render an account to God, and he will render it to the rest of the world, if there is no magistrate here to check and punish the injustice of the victor. He will render an account to those sovereigns who wish to observe honourable causes for war and to maintain the common law of nations and of nature.[44]

Gentili was an original, enlightened[45] – "at least as modern as his Dutch follower"[46] – and eloquent writer who has not been given as much credit as his works clearly deserve. The time has come to acknowledge that we

---

[42] Haggenmacher, *supra* note 5, at 313 & n. 78.

[43] *E.g.*, F. VICTORIA, *The Second Relectio on the Indians, or on the Law of War Made by the Spaniards on the Barbarians*, in DE INDIS ET DE IURE BELLI RELECTIONES 163, 185, para. 52 (Carnegie ed., J. P. Bate trans. 1917) (1557).

[44] A. GENTILI, *supra* note 5, at 257 (emphasis added). Although mentioning the argument for the legality of rape on the ground that "it is not inconsistent with the law of war that everything which belongs to the enemy should be at the disposition of the victor," Grotius reasoned that, being unrelated to either security or punishment, rape "should consequently not go unpunished in war any more than in peace. The latter view is the law not of all nations, but of the better ones." H. GROTIUS, *supra* note 8, bk. III, ch. IV. pt. XIX(1).

[45] Although not without some equivocation, Gentili made a contribution to the emancipation of slaves by arguing that "when a pregnant slave girl is sold, her offspring is not understood to have been sold ... [T]he *foetus* and the mother are in reality two persons, with different rights," which implied that the child of a slave woman would be born free. A. GENTILI, *supra* note 5, at 209. Contrast Grotius (discussing captives):

> Not only do the prisoners of war themselves become slaves, but also their descendants for ever, that is to say those who are born of a slave mother after her enslavement. This is what Marcianus said, that by the law of nations those become our slaves who are born of our slave women ... Tacitus said that [the] womb was subject to slavery.
> ... [T]he effects of this law are unlimited ... There is no suffering which may not be inflicted with impunity upon such slaves ....

H. GROTIUS, *supra* note 8, bk. III, ch. VII, pts. II–III(1).

[46] Haggenmacher, *supra* note 8, at 168.

are indebted to him, more than to any other writer of his era, for the concepts of common rights and interests of humanity and of humanitarian intervention. Perhaps, as Oxford Professor Thomas Erskine Holland argued in his inaugural lecture in 1874, it is only fair that Gentili share with Grotius the latter's reputation as the founder of modern international law.[47]

---

[47] *See id.* at 133, 173–76.

V

Francis Lieber's Code and Principles of Humanity*

Born in Berlin in 1800, Francis Lieber fought against the French in Ligny (close to Waterloo) and was wounded at Namur as a youth of fifteen. Associated with the German liberal movement, Lieber soon encountered difficulties with the Prussian police and went to Greece, where he became involved in the resistance against Turkey. He returned to Berlin in 1823, after a few years in Rome, where he gained the friendship and protection of the Prussian Minister to Rome, the distinguished historian Barthold Georg Niebuhr. As Lieber's difficulties with the authorities continued, he left for London in 1826 and from there went to Boston in 1827. In 1835, he became Professor of History and Political Science at South Carolina College, and, in 1857, was appointed by Columbia College as Professor of History and Political Science. He continued to be associated with Columbia until his death in 1872.[1]

In 1881, two volumes of Lieber's miscellaneous writings were published by the J. B. Lippincott publishing house of Philadelphia. The first volume contains primarily personal reminiscences, academic discourses,

* I acknowledge with thanks the thoughtful help of my research assistant Laurie Rosensweig.

[1] *See generally* Opening Address by Elihu Root at the Seventh Annual Meeting of the American Society of International Law (Apr. 24, 1913), *reprinted in* 7 AM. J. INT'L L. 453 (1913) [hereinafter Opening Address by Elihu Root]; George D. Haimbaugh, Jr., *Introduction to Panel II: Humanitarian Law: The Lincoln-Lieber Initiative*, 13 GA. J. INT'L & COMP. L. 245 (1983); R. R. Baxter, *The First Modern Codification of the Law of War – Francis Lieber and General Orders No. 100*, 3 INT'L. REV. RED CROSS 171 (1963) [hereinafter Baxter I]; R.R. Baxter, *The First Modern Codification of the Law of War – Francis Lieber and General Orders No. 100 (II)*, 3 INT'L. REV. CROSS 234 (1963) [hereinafter Baxter II]; George B. Davis, *Doctor Francis Lieber's Instructions for the Government of Armies in the Field*, 1 AM. J. INT'L L. 13 (1907); Ernest Nys, *Francis Lieber – His Life and His Work*, 5 AM. J. INT'L L. 355 (1911); Michael Harris Hoffman, *The Customary Law of Non-international Armed Conflict: Evidence from the United States Civil War*, 30 INT'L. REV. RED CROSS 322 (No. 277, July-August 1990).

and a few essays.[2] Opening with Dr. J. C. Bluntschli's introduction describing Lieber's service to political science and international law, the second volume reproduces several of his important writings. However, this volume includes neither Lieber's book *Political Ethics* (1838–39), nor his Columbia Law School *Lectures on the Law and Usages of War* (delivered in 1861–62).

The range of Lieber's writings is extraordinary. He made important contributions to U.S. constitutional law, military law, international law, political science, penal law, and educational policy. His essays on international law include the advocacy of both international arbitration and international copyright. He challenged the "fallacies of American Protectionists" and tackled hermeneutics.

Above all, the work that ensured Lieber's lasting fame was his *Instructions for the Government of Armies of the United States in the Field* (1863), originally published as General Orders No. 100, War Department, Adjutant General's Office, on April 24, 1863.[3] The culmination of his long interest in the history and laws of war, Lieber's Code ultimately stemmed from the initiative he voiced persistently to General Halleck, the general in charge of the Union forces and himself a writer on international law. Along with a board of officers approved by President Lincoln, Lieber drafted the Code. This initiative was true to Lieber's character; throughout his career, he was an activist and an advocate, no less than a scholar. In addition, Lieber had personal reasons for his commitment to this project. The American Civil War was much more painful for Lieber than his experience at Waterloo. Three of his sons fought in the war, two on the Union side. His third son, who fought for the South, was killed.

In his opening address as President of the American Society of International Law to the seventh annual meeting, April 24, 1913, which was devoted to Lieber's Code, Elihu Root highlighted the Code's humanitarian content:

> [W]hile the instrument was a practical presentation of what the laws and usages of war were, and not a technical discussion of what the writer thought they ought to be, in all its parts may be discerned an instinctive selection of the best and most humane practice and an assertion of the control of morals to the limit permitted by the dreadful business in which the rules were to be applied.[4]

Root may have overstated the Code's humane nature, however. Lieber's balancing of humanitarian concerns with military necessity did not

---

[2] *See* 1 Francis Lieber, The Miscellaneous Writings of Francis Lieber: Reminiscences, Addresses and Essays (1881).

[3] *See* Instructions for the Government of Armies of the United States in the Field, General Orders No. 100 (Apr. 24, 1863), *reprinted in* The Laws of Armed Conflicts 3 (Dietrich Schindler & Jiří Toman eds., 3d ed. 1988) [hereinafter Lieber's Code].

[4] Opening Address by Elihu Root, *supra* note 1, at 456.

always further the dictates of humanity, suggesting that another assessment would prove both useful and more realistic. In evaluating Lieber's work, Bluntschli, Professor at the University of Heidelberg and the first President of the Institute of International Law, which Lieber helped to found, wrote:

> His legal injunctions rest upon the foundation of moral precepts. The former are not always sharply distinguished from moral injunctions, but nevertheless, through a union with the same, are ennobled and exalted. Everywhere reigns in this body of law the spirit of humanity, which spirit recognizes as fellow-beings, with lawful rights, our very enemies, and which forbids our visiting upon them unnecessary injury, cruelty, or destruction. But at the same time, our legislator remains fully aware that, in time of war, it is absolutely necessary to provide for the safety of armies and for the successful conduct of a campaign; that, to those engaged in it, the harshest measures and most reckless exactions cannot be denied; and that tender-hearted sentimentality is here all the more out of place, because the greater the energy employed in carrying on the war, the sooner will it be brought to an end, and the normal condition of peace restored.[5]

While stressing that the ultimate object of all modern wars is a renewed state of peace, Lieber advocated a harsh and violent war on the theory that the harsher the war, the shorter it would be: "[t]he more vigorously wars are pursued, the better it is for humanity. Sharp wars are brief."[6] To this end, the law of war should impose certain limitations on the basic "principles of justice, faith, and honor."[7]

His concern for not unduly limiting the military's discretion or curtailing its ability to win a victory swiftly led Lieber to articulate a number of principles that appear quite harsh to the modern commentator. Thus, he allows an army "to starve the hostile belligerent," whether "armed or unarmed," in order to effect "the speedier subjection of the enemy."[8] The Hague Regulations do not mention resort to starvation, but article 54(1) of Additional Protocol I to the Geneva Conventions outlaws the "[s]tarvation of civilians as a method of warfare."[9] Furthermore, Lieber allows the besieging army, albeit as an extreme measure, to drive non-combatants back into a besieged city that is short of provisions, "so as to hasten on the surrender."[10]

His rules addressing the treatment of classical works of art, libraries, collections, or instruments belonging to a hostile nation exemplify

---

[5] J. C. Bluntschli, *Introduction: Lieber's Service to Political Science and International Law, in* 2 FRANCIS LIEBER, THE MISCELLANEOUS WRITINGS OF FRANCIS LIEBER: CONTRIBUTIONS TO POLITICAL SCIENCE 12–13 (1881).

[6] Lieber's Code, *supra* note 3, art. 29.   [7] *Id*. art. 30.   [8] *Id*. art. 17.

[9] Protocol Additional to the Geneva Conventions of 12 August 1949, and Relating to the Protection of Victims of International Armed Conflicts (Protocol I), *opened for signature* Dec. 12, 1977, art. 54(1), 16 I.L.M. 1391 (1977); 1125 U.N.T.S. 3 [hereinafter Protocol I].

[10] Lieber's Code, *supra* note 3, art. 18.

Lieber's acceptance of the spoils of war at the cost of the protection of cultural property. The Code states that "[i]f such works ... can be removed without injury, the ruler of the conquering state or nation may order them to be seized and removed for the benefit of the said nation. The ultimate ownership is to be settled by the ensuing treaty of peace."[11] If such a rule had been recognized as valid during the Second World War, for example, Germany would have had legal authority for removing the treasures of the Louvre to Berlin. Fortunately, article 56 of the Hague Regulations establishes quite a different principle: "[t]he property of municipalities, that of institutions dedicated to religion, charity and education, the arts and sciences, even when State property, shall be treated as private property"[12] and is therefore protected under articles 46 and 50, which preserve private property.

One area in which Lieber's balancing act shocks even the most unsentimental modern commentators lies in his discussion of the principle of quarter. Lieber makes this otherwise supreme principle of granting mercy and quarter subject to both necessity and reprisals. Although the Code's general rule starts by prohibiting the denial of quarter, it quickly slides to allow the exception of military necessity:

> It is against the usage of modern war to resolve, in hatred and revenge, to give no quarter. No body of troops has the right to declare that it will not give, and therefore will not expect, quarter; but a commander is permitted to direct his troops to give no quarter, in great straits, when his own salvation makes it *impossible* to cumber himself with prisoners.[13]

The barbaric rule stated in this proviso almost appears designed to legitimate the massacre Henry V ordered of his French prisoners at Agincourt.[14] Although article 71 of the Code prohibits the killing of or infliction of additional wounds on enemies already disabled, several other articles imply the residual legality of the denial of quarter, going still further than article 60. For example, article 61 protects persons *hors de combat* and prisoners of war, but nonetheless presupposes the permissibility of the denial of quarter to other combatants: "[t]roops that give no quarter have no right to kill enemies already disabled on the ground, or prisoners captured by other troops."[15] Article 62 then authorizes a savage form of reciprocity, declaring that "[a]ll troops of the enemy known or discovered to give no quarter in general, or to any portion of the army,

---

[11] Lieber's Code, *supra* note 3, art. 36.

[12] Convention (IV) Respecting the Laws and Customs of War on Land, *signed at* The Hague, October 18, 1907, art. 56, 36 Stat. 2277, T.S. No. 539; 1 Bevans 631, *reprinted in* THE LAWS OF ARMED CONFLICTS, *supra* note 3, at 63 [hereinafter Hague Convention (IV)].

[13] Lieber's Code, *supra* note 3, art. 60.

[14] *See* THEODOR MERON, HENRY'S WARS AND SHAKESPEARE'S LAWS 154–71 (1993).

[15] Lieber's Code, *supra* note 3, art. 61.

receive none."[16] Finally, article 66 extends reciprocity and retribution to the period after the battle, when there clearly can no longer be any semblance of a claim of necessity:

> Quarter having been given to an enemy by American troops, under a misapprehension of his true character, he may, nevertheless, be ordered to suffer death if, within three days after the battle, it be discovered that he belongs to a corps which gives no quarter.[17]

Not surprisingly, Lieber's tolerance for the denial of quarter did not long survive in the evolution of modern international humanitarian law. Article 23(d) of the Hague Regulations emphasizes that "declar[ing] that no quarter will be given" is particularly forbidden.[18] Today, the denial of quarter constitutes one of the most obvious war crimes. International humanitarian law has quickly discarded the few instances in which Lieber departed from humanitarian principles. They should not detract attention, however, from the overall humanitarian spirit that imbues the Code and appears in most of its provisions. Rather than any one technical or detailed rule, the Lieber Code's foundation in broad humanitarian principles explains its tremendous impact both on later multilateral treaties codifying the law of war and on the development of customary law.

Thus, in addressing the issue of martial law, the Code requires that "it is incumbent upon those who administer it to be strictly guided by the principles of justice, honor, and humanity – virtues adorning a soldier even more than other men, for the very reason that he possesses the power of his arms against the unarmed."[19] The Code proclaims that the law of war "disclaim[s] all cruelty and bad faith concerning engagements concluded with the enemy during the war," as well as those contracted before the war with the intent that they should remain in effect in case of war.[20] Although the Code defines military necessity broadly, it balances the powers justified by the invocation of military necessity with a reminder of our common humanity and the fact that "[m]en who take up arms against one another in public war do not cease on this account to be moral beings, responsible to one another and to God."[21] Furthermore, "[m]ilitary necessity does not admit of cruelty – that is, the infliction of suffering for the sake of suffering or for revenge, nor of maiming or wounding except in fight, nor of torture to extort confessions [or] ... of the use of poison [or] ... of the wanton devastation of a district."[22]

The distinction between combatants and non-combatants, and the grant of the broadest protection to the latter, are important themes of the Code, themes that also occupy an important place in modern international

---

[16] *Id*. art. 62.   [17] *Id*. art. 66.   [18] Hague Convention (IV), *supra* note 12, art. 23(d).
[19] Lieber's Code, *supra* note 3, art. 4.   [20] *Id*. art. 11.
[21] *Id*. art. 15.   [22] *Id*. art. 16.

humanitarian law. While asserting that a citizen of a hostile country is an enemy,[23] the Code recognizes that as civilization has progressed, the distinction between the state and its army on the one hand, and the private individual on the other hand, has solidified. As a result, the "principle has been more and more acknowledged that the unarmed citizen is to be spared in person, property, and honor as much as the exigencies of war will admit."[24] In contrast to the mores of earlier times,[25] the Code proclaims that "[i]n modern regular wars of the Europeans, and their descendants in other portions of the globe, protection of the inoffensive citizen of the hostile country is the rule; privation and disturbance of private relations are the exceptions."[26] In a provision anticipating the Fourth Geneva Convention's provisions prohibiting deportations,[27] the Code declares that "[p]rivate citizens are no longer murdered, enslaved, or carried off to distant parts, and the inoffensive individual is as little disturbed in his private relations as the commander of the hostile troops can afford to grant in the overruling demands of a vigorous war."[28]

The Code enunciates detailed rules regarding the protection of private persons and private property in language that the Hague Regulations closely imitate. Private property can only be seized because of military necessity, and a receipt is required to enable the owner to obtain indemnity.[29] In occupied territories, the governing power has an obligation to protect religion, private property, the person of the inhabitants, especially of women, and domestic relations. Some types of property may, however, be appropriated for "temporary and military uses," and soldiers may be billeted.[30] Property belonging to churches, hospitals, or other institutions of charitable character, educational and scientific institutions, schools, universities, and museums may not be considered public property and thus receives greater immunity from wartime destruction.[31] In several respects, including in the explicit prohibition of rape, the Code's protection of occupied territories is even more advanced than that provided by the Hague Regulations:

> All wanton violence committed against persons in the invaded country, all destruction of property not commanded by the authorized officer, all robbery, all pillage or sacking, even after taking a place by main force, all rape, wounding, maiming, or killing of such inhabitants, are prohibited under the penalty of death, or such other severe punishment as may seem adequate for the gravity of the offense.[32]

---

[23] *See* Lieber's Code, *supra* note 3, art. 21.   [24] *Id*. art. 22.
[25] *See id*. art. 24.   [26] *Id*. art. 25.
[27] *See* Convention (IV) Relative to the Protection of Civilian Persons in Time of War (Geneva Convention No. IV), *opened for signature* Aug. 12, 1949, art. 49, 6 U.S.T. 3516, 75 U.N.T.S. 287.
[28] Lieber's Code, *supra* note 3, art. 23.   [29] *See id*. art. 38.   [30] *Id*. art. 37.
[31] *See id*. art. 34.   [32] *Id*. art. 44.

Similarly, the Code also states that:

> [c]rimes punishable by all penal codes, such as arson, murder, maiming, assaults, highway robbery, theft, burglary, fraud, forgery, and rape, if committed by an American soldier in a hostile country against its inhabitants, are not only punishable as at home, but in all cases in which death is not inflicted, the severer punishment shall be preferred.[33]

Slavery in the South, which Lieber opposed, and deep anti-black sentiments triggered several principles that reflected the spirit of emancipation. The first proclaimed that slavery could only exist according to municipal law; neither the law of nature nor the law of nations has ever acknowledged the legitimacy of slavery.[34]

> Therefore, in a war between the United States and a belligerent which admits of slavery, if a person held in bondage by that belligerent be captured by or come as a fugitive under the protection of the military forces of the United States, such person is immediately entitled to the rights and privileges of a freeman. To return such person into slavery would amount to enslaving a free person ... Moreover, a person so made free by the law of war is under the shield of the law of nations ....[35]

Yet another principle prohibited discrimination between combatants, declaring that "[n]o belligerent has a right to declare that enemies of a certain class, color, or condition, when properly organized as soldiers, will not be treated by him as public enemies."[36] Furthermore, Lieber stated that the law of nations admits no distinctions based on color.[37] The continuing importance of this prohibition, designed to protect black soldiers of the Union army who might fall into the hands of the Confederate army, and later incorporated into article 16 of the Third Geneva Convention,[38] became apparent in World War II, when the Nazis denied the privileges granted to prisoners of war to Jews in the Polish and Soviet armies and to blacks in the French army.

Two other provisions address matters of continuing importance in modern international humanitarian law. First, the Code excludes the use of poison from modern warfare by unconditionally prohibiting its use in any form, such that whoever uses it "puts himself out of the pale of the law and usages of war."[39] Secondly, it proclaims a categorical prohibition on the assassination of enemies:

> [t]he law of war does not allow proclaiming either an individual belonging to a hostile army, or a citizen, or a subject of the hostile government, an outlaw, who

---

[33] *Id.* art. 47.   [34] *See id.* art. 42.   [35] *Id.* art. 43.   [36] *Id.* art. 57.
[37] *See id.* art. 58.
[38] *See* Convention (III) Relative to the Treatment of Prisoners of War (Geneva Convention No. III), *opened for signature* Aug. 12, 1949, 6 U.S.T. 3316, 75 U.N.T.S. 135.
[39] Lieber's Code, *supra* note 3, art. 70.

may be slain without trial by any captor, any more than the modern law of peace allows such intentional outlawry; on the contrary, it abhors such outrage. The sternest retaliation should follow the murder committed in consequence of such proclamation, made by whatever authority. Civilized nations look with horror upon offers of rewards for the assassination of enemies as relapses into barbarism.[40]

As was perhaps inevitable in the mid-nineteenth century, the Code recognizes a right of retaliation, but only as "the sternest feature of war," and only when there are no other means of preventing the "repetition of barbarous outrage."[41] Retaliation is only allowed as "a means of protective retribution" and after a careful inquiry, not for purposes of revenge.[42] "Unjust or inconsiderate retaliation removes the belligerents farther and farther from the mitigating rules of regular war, and by rapid steps leads them nearer to the internecine wars of savages."[43]

Although the Civil War sparked the drafting of the Code, only 9 of the 157 articles appear under the heading "Insurrection – Civil War – Rebellion."[44] Lieber added this section reluctantly, only at the urging of General Halleck, because he wanted to avoid the impression that the Code was applicable to civil rather than to international wars. Nonetheless, the sections on civil war are extraordinarily enlightened for their era.

Even now, central governments faced with an insurrection generally deny that international humanitarian law is applicable to the rebels on the ground that according the rebels the privileges of humanitarian law would be tantamount to granting them political and legal recognition. To encourage governments to apply humanitarian law to such conflicts, common article 3 of the Geneva Conventions therefore provides that its application "shall not affect the legal status of the Parties to the conflict."[45] In the same vein, article 4 of Additional Protocol I to the Geneva Convention, which applies as well to wars of national liberation, states that "[t]he application of the Conventions and of this Protocol, as well as the conclusion of the agreements provided for therein, shall not affect the legal status of the Parties to the conflict."[46]

The Code, which similarly encourages the applicability of humanitarian rules and the minimization of harsh treatment of rebels, states that "[w]hen humanity induces the adoption of the rules of regular war toward rebels, whether the adoption is partial or entire, it does in no way whatever imply a partial or complete acknowledgement of their government …"[47] Treating captured rebels as prisoners of war, exchanging them, or engaging in any other practice sanctioned or demanded by the law and

---

[40] Lieber's Code, *supra* note 3, art. 148.   [41] *Id*. art. 27.   [42] *Id*. art. 28.
[43] *Id*.   [44] *See id*. § X, arts. 149–57.
[45] Common article 3 of the Geneva Conventions of August 12, 1949.
[46] Protocol I, *supra* note 9, art. 4.   [47] Lieber's Code, *supra* note 3, art. 152.

usages of public law between sovereign belligerents, "neither proves nor establishes an acknowledgment of the rebellious people, or of the government which they may have erected, as a public or sovereign power."[48]

The Code preserves the government's right to try the leaders of the rebellion for high treason, but only the leaders: "[t]reating, in the field, the rebellious enemy according to the law and usages of war has never prevented the legitimate government from trying the leaders of the rebellion or chief rebels for high treason. . .unless they are included in a general amnesty."[49] This right of a central government to treat rebels as traitors has survived even in modern humanitarian law.

Both the Code's high quality and its timing, written when no other significant compilations of laws and customs of war were available, can explain its tremendous impact on the codification of international humanitarian law. For example, the Prussian army adapted the Code into the regulations it issued for its war in France in 1870.[50] Lieber's friendship with Bluntschli, who was greatly interested in the codification of the law of nations, also helped guarantee the widespread influence of the Code. When Emperor Alexander II of Russia convened a conference in Brussels in 1874 for the purpose of discussing the practicality of the codification of laws and customs of war on land,[51] he invited Bluntschli to prepare a compilation of laws and customs of war. Bluntschli himself fully acknowledged his indebtedness to Lieber; he in effect paraphrased Lieber's Code.[52] The Lieber Code and the Brussels Declaration[53] in turn influenced the Oxford manual adopted in 1880 by the Institute of International Law.

The Brussels declaration was also the principal source of the 1899 and 1907 regulations annexed to The Hague Convention (No. IV) on the Laws and Customs of War on Land, as Frédéric de Martens, the Russian jurist-diplomat and one of the great architects of The Hague Convention, fully recognized.[54] The statement in the Judgment of the International Military Tribunal for the Trial of German Major War Criminals (Nuremberg 1946) that "by 1939 these rules [Hague Regulations] laid down in the Convention were recognised by all civilised nations [sic], and were regarded as being declaratory of the laws and customs of war,"[55] effectively granted

---

[48] *Id.* art. 153.   [49] *Id.* art. 154.

[50] *See* Richard Shelly Hartigan, Lieber's Code and the Law of War 22 (1983).

[51] *See* Davis, *supra* note 1, at 22.   [52] *See* Bluntschli, *supra* note 5, at 13.

[53] *See* Final Protocol and Project of an International Declaration Concerning the Laws and Customs of War, Aug. 27, 1874, *reprinted in* The Laws of Armed Conflict, *supra* note 3, at 25.

[54] *See* Davis, *supra* note 1, at 23. For a chart comparing the Hague Regulations of the Hague Convention of 1899 with Lieber's Code, see Appendix, 7 Am. J. Int'l L. 466 app. (1913).

[55] *Trial of German Major War Criminals*, 1946, Cmd. 6964, Misc. No. 12, at 65; *see also* Theodor Meron, Human Rights and Humanitarian Norms as Customary Law 38–39 (1989).

the highest judicial imprimatur to the Lieber Code's status as customary law. Still relevant nearly one hundred years after its writing, the Code influenced the Geneva Conventions of 1949 as well.

In detailing his sources, Lieber wrote that he found no guide or text-book, but drew principally on "[u]sage, history, reason, and conscientiousness, a sincere love of truth, justice, and civilization."[56] Lieber did incorporate a number of General Orders already promulgated during the Civil War, drew on a treatise of international law published by General Halleck in 1861, and consulted general and classical texts of international law, but he hardly used any specialized and technical sources of the law of war.[57] He did draw on his own works, however, including *Political Ethics* (1838–39), in which he considered the conduct of war, and, particularly, his Columbia Law School *Lectures on the Law and Usages of War* (1861–62).[58] Since there were few writings on the technical rules of war and reliance on custom was considered central, Lieber drafted his Code in terms of broad principles. This very generality of language, perhaps more than anything else, explains the Code's lasting influence, especially as a statement of customary law.

Despite his great learning, Francis Lieber was probably not aware of the important medieval and Renaissance ordinances of war that codified both military discipline and principles of humanity.[59] These included the famous ordinances of war made by Richard II of England at Durham (1385),[60] by Henry V of England at Mantes (1419)[61] and by Charles VII of France at Orléans (1439),[62] among many others. In particular, given his support for the denial of quarter, it is especially regretable that Lieber was unaware of Scotland's *Articles and Ordinances of War for the Present Expedition of the Army of the Kingdom of Scotland*.[63] These ordinances contained an enlighted prohibition of murder in time of war: "[m]urder is no less unlawful and intollerable in the time of war, than in the time of peace, and is to be punished with death."[64] More important for the present discussion, they also prohibited the denial of quarter: "[i]f it shall come

---

[56] Baxter I, *supra* note 1, at 184.

[57] *See id*. at 186–89; *see* Baxter II, *supra* note 1, at 234–35.

[58] *See* Baxter I, *supra* note 1, at 174–78.

[59] *See* MERON, *supra* note 14, at 142–53.

[60] *See* THE BLACK BOOK OF THE ADMIRALTY, *reprinted in* I MONUMENTA JURIDICA 453 (Travers Twiss ed. 1871).

[61] *See id*. at 459. *See also* EXCERPTA HISTORICA 30 (Samuel Bentley ed., 1831).

[62] *See* ORDONNANCES DES ROIS DE FRANCE DE LA TROISIÈME RACE viii, 306 (Louis Guillaume de Vilevault & Louis G.O.F. Bréquigny eds., 1782).

[63] ARTICLES AND ORDINANCES OF WARRE FOR THE PRESENT EXPEDITION OF THE ARMY OF THE KINGDOME OF SCOTLAND BY THE COMMITTEE OF ESTATES AND HIS EXCELLENCE THE LORD GENERAL OF THE ARMY (Early English Books Series 1641–1700, Edinburgh, Scotland, Evan Tyler, 1644).

[64] *Id*. art. VIII, at 6.

to pass, that the enemy shall force us to battle, and the lord shall give us victory, none shall kill a yielding enemy..."[65] Finally, these ordinances concluded with an important statement in anticipation of the Martens clause, whose object is to substitute principles of humanity for the unlimited discretion of the military commander:

> matters, that are clear by the light and law of nature, are presupposed; things unnecessary are passed over in silence; and other things may be judged by the common customs and constitutions of war; or may upon new mergents, be expressed afterward.[66]

Of course, Lieber did not have the research facilities that modern scholars have. Indeed, he produced his Code in times of war, when various pressures served to emphasize those norms important to the Union. Francis Lieber unquestionably deserves our gratitude for his Code and especially for those provisions that draw on broad principles of humanity.

---

[65] *Id.* art. XV, at 9.
[66] *Id.* at 10; *see also* ON CUSTOM AND THE ANTECEDENTS OF THE MARTENS CLAUSE IN MEDIEVAL AND RENAISSANCE ORDINANCES OF WAR 173 (Rudolf Bernhardt Festschrift 1995).

VI

Deportation of Civilians as a War Crime under Customary Law

Asbjørn Eide's strong interest in human rights, humanitarian law, and their interrelationship is demonstrated not only by his writings but also by his organizing in Oslo (1987), and co-organizing in Turku\Åbo (1990), conferences to develop and to promote the acceptance by the international community of a declaration on internal strife (the Turku Declaration of Minimum Humanitarian Standards). It is, therefore, appropriate, in a collection of essays in his honour, to focus on an important humanitarian law question, namely, whether deportations of civilians by an occupying power in the context of an armed conflict of an international character constitute violations of customary international law, or war crimes. Although deportations carried out in violation of Article 49 of the Fourth Geneva Convention[1] constitute grave breaches of the Convention (Article 147), the question whether that prohibition is not only conventional but customary in nature is important both for those states that are not as yet parties to the Geneva Conventions and for those that maintain that the Convention *qua* convention is not applicable in the territories they occupy.

The object of this article is to demonstrate, largely through an analysis of the Nuremberg jurisprudence, that deportations from occupied territories had been prohibited under customary international law already prior to the adoption of the Geneva Conventions. Since the adoption of the Fourth Geneva Convention on August 12, 1949 there have been many expressions of support for its customary law nature (*opinio juris*). However, the practice of states demonstrating the Convention's customary law character has been limited. It is for this reason that I shall focus on the situation preceding the adoption of the Convention. Although the prohibition of deportations by a number of major human rights instruments is of relevance to the issue under consideration, the article will be limited to questions of humanitarian law.

Deportation of civilians was already prohibited by Article 23 of Lieber's Code, which states that '[p]rivate citizens are no longer murdered,

---

[1] Convention Relative to the Protection of Civilian Persons in Time of War (Geneva Convention No. IV), Aug. 12, 1949, 6 UST 3516, TIAS No. 3365, 75 UNTS 287.

enslaved, or carried off to distant parts. ...' [2] This Code has had a major influence on national statutes and regulations pertaining to the law of war and on such treaties as the Convention Respecting the Laws and Customs of War on Land, with Annex of Regulations (Hague Convention No. IV)[3] – which is generally recognized as customary law.[4] Also largely influenced were the Geneva Conventions and, of course, the formation of customary law.

It is of course true that the Hague Regulations did not explicitly mention deportations from occupied territories. The failure of the Hague Regulations to explicitly proscribe deportation of civilians must be explained, however, not by any erosion of the customary law prohibition of deportations, but by the fact that deportation of civilians was no longer practiced, certainly not on a large scale, at the beginning of the Twentieth Century. Nazi Germany's resort to the large scale deportation of civilians for slave labour and extermination during the Second World War led the drafters to restate in Article 49 of the Fourth Geneva Convention an absolute prohibition of '[i]ndividual or mass forcible transfers [and] deportations of protected persons from occupied territory to the territory of the Occupying Power or to that of any other country ... regardless of motive.' Persons protected by the Convention are defined (Article 2) as those who 'find themselves ... in the hands of the party to the conflict or Occupying Power of which they are not nationals', with the exception of nationals of a neutral state and nationals of a co-belligerent state if their state of nationality has normal diplomatic representation in the state in whose hands they are.

In its authoritative Commentary on the Fourth Convention,[5] the International Committee of the Red Cross (ICRC) explains the silence of the Hague Regulations on the question of deportations, while insisting that their prohibition was already a norm of existing international law. The Commentary states:

> The Hague Regulations do not refer to the question of deportation; this was probably because the practice of deporting persons was regarded at the beginning of this century as having fallen into abeyance. The events of the last few

---

[2] Lieber, F., 'Instructions for the Government of Armies of the United States in the Field (1863)', originally published as 'General Orders No. 100, War Department, Adjutant General's Office, Apr. 24, 1863' (reprinted in Hartigan, R.S., *Lieber's Code and the Law of War* (1983), pp. 45–71).

[3] 36 Stat. 2277; TS 539; 1 *Bevans* 631.

[4] Roberts, A., 'Prolonged Military Occupation: The Israeli-Occupied Territories Since 1967', *American Journal of International Law*, vol. 84 (1990), p. 44, at p. 53; Meron, T., *Human Rights and Humanitarian Norms as Customary Law* (1992), pp. 37–41.

[5] Uhler, O.M. and Coursier, H. (eds.), *Commentary on the Geneva Conventions of 12 August 1949; Geneva Convention Relative to the Protection of Civilian Persons in Time of War* (1958), p. 279.

years have, however, made it necessary to make more detailed provisions on this point *which may be regarded to-day as having been embodied in international law.* (emphasis added)

In a footnote, the ICRC states that a similar view is reflected in Articles 6(b) and 6(c) of the Nuremberg Charter, in the judgment of the (Nuremberg) International Military Tribunal, and in '[a] great many other decisions by other courts which have had to deal with this question [and] which have also stated that the *deportation of inhabitants of occupied territory is contrary to the laws and customs of war.*' (emphasis added)[6]

The same point is made by the Official Notes prepared by the staff of the United Nations War Crimes Commission on the case of *Heinrich Gerike (the Velpke Children's Home Case)* decided by the British Military Court in Brunswick (1946), which concerned the conviction of a number of German defendants for the killing by wilful neglect of a number of Polish children, in violation of the laws and usages of war. The prosecution based its case on Article 46 of the Hague Regulations, which stated that '[f]amily honour and rights, individual life, and private property, as well as religious convictions and worship, must be respected.'[7] It pointed out:

> that under international law it was forbidden in time of war to kill the innocent and defenceless population of any country overrun, 'either in their own country or in the country of the occupying power'. [It added that] [I]t was unlawful for an occupying power to deport slave labour from the occupied country to its own territory, in the first place.[8]

The Notes on the case observed that:

> *Article 46 of the Hague Convention No. IV of 1907, which was drafted at a time when deportations for forced labour on the scale carried out by Nazi Germany could not have been contemplated,* strictly speaking applies only to the behaviour of the occupying Power *within occupied territory.* Nevertheless, it is clear that the general rule laid down therein must be followed also in respect of inhabitants of occupied territory who have been sent into the country of the occupant for forced labour, as had the mothers of the children who were sent to the Velpke home, and to children born to them in captivity. (emphases added)[9]

---

[6] Uhler, O.M. and Coursier, H. (eds.), *Commentary on the Geneva Conventions of 12 August 1949; Geneva Convention Relative to the Protection of Civilian Persons in Time of War* (1958), p. 279, at n. 3.

[7] *7 Law Reports of Trials of War Criminals* 78 (1948). This series of reports was prepared by the United Nations War Crimes Commission.

[8] *Ibid.*

[9] *7 Law Reports of Trials of War Criminals, supra* n. 7, p. 80. (See also, *Krupp* case, *infra*). The prosecution cited also Lassa Oppenheim in Lauterpacht, Hersh (ed.), *International Law* (6th edition) (hereafter *Oppenheim-Lauterpacht*), pp. 345–346:

> There is no right to deport inhabitants to the country of the occupant, for the purpose of compelling them to work there. When during the World War the Germans deported to Germany several thousands of Belgian and French men and women, and compelled

The judgment in the case of the *United States of America v. Milch* mentions the attempt by the German Supreme Command, pursuant to an order of October 3, 1916, to deport Belgian vagrants and idlers to Germany for work while specifying that such labour was not to be used in connection with operations of war. The order 'resulted in such a storm of protest that it was at once abandoned by the German authorities.'[10] The judgment cites the German manual for war on land[11] which recognized that the 'inhabitants of an invaded territory are persons endowed with rights [and who live] as in time of peace, under the protection of the laws.'[12]

In the case of *United States v. Alfred Krupp*, the Tribunal emphasized that the German order of October 3, 1916 triggered 'protests . . . so wide spread and vigorous that the Kaiser was forced to retreat'. These protests were based upon either the general principles of international law or humanity or specifically upon the Hague Regulations. For instance, the United States Department of State protests 'against this action which is in contravention of all precedent and of those humane principles of international practice which have long been accepted and followed by civilized nations in their treatment of noncombatants in conquered territory.'[13] The Tribunal stated:

> The protest of the Netherlands Government pointed out the incompatibility of the deportations with the precise stipulations of Article 52 of the Hague Regulations. It was pointed out by Professor James W. Garner . . . that if 'a belligerent were allowed to deport civilians from occupied territory, in order to force them to work in his industries and thereby to free his own workers for military service, this would make illusory the prohibition to compel enemy citizens to participate in operations of war against their own country. The measures must be pronounced as an act of tyranny, contrary to all notions of humanity, and one entirely without precedent in the history of civilized warfare.'[14]

The above mentioned United States protest (Nov. 29, 1916), addressed through the U.S. Chargé d'Affaires in Germany to the Chancellor of Germany, read as follows:

them to work there, the whole civilized world stigmatized this cruel practice as an outrage.

This work was published in 1944 and thus prior to the Nuremberg Charter: It should be observed that *Oppenheim-Lauterpacht* discusses events that occurred during the First World War.

[10] 2 *Trials of War Criminals before the Nuernberg Military Tribunals under Control Council Law No. 10*, (hereafter *Nuernberg Trials*) (1949), p. 790.

[11] *Kriegsbrauch im Landkriege* (1902 edition).

[12] 2 *Nuernberg Trials, supra* n. 10, pp. 789–90.

[13] 9 *Trials of War Criminals before the Nuernberg Military Tribunals under Control Council Law No. 10* (1950), p. 1430 (footnotes omitted).

[14] *Ibid.*

The Government of the United States has learned with the greatest concern and regret of the policy of the German Government to deport from Belgium a portion of the civilian population for the purpose of forcing them to labor in Germany, and is constrained to protest in a friendly spirit, but most solemnly, against this action, which is in contravention of all precedent and of those principles of international practice which have long been accepted and followed by civilized nations in their treatment of non-combatants in conquered territory.[15]

The norms stated in Article 46 of the Geneva Convention can be regarded as encompassing the prohibition of deportations for purposes of slave labour and *a fortiori* for extermination. Also, deportations breach other Hague Regulations. The International Military Tribunal for the Trial of German Major War Criminals regarded the statement contained in Article 6(b) of the Nuremberg Charter that ill-treatment or deportation for slave labour, or for any other purpose, of civilian population of or in occupied territory constitutes a war crime, as rooted in Hague Regulation 52, concerning requisitions in kind and services.[16]

Count Three of the Indictment against the German major war criminals submitted by the United States, France, the United Kingdom and the Soviet Union stated that murder and ill-treatment of the civilian populations of occupied territories committed by the defendants was contrary

> to International Conventions, in particular to Article 46 of the Hague Regulations, 1907, the laws and customs of war, the general principles of criminal law as derived from the criminal laws of all civilized nations, the internal penal laws of the countries in which such crimes were committed, and to Article 6(b) of the Charter.[17]

Lauterpacht, referring to Article 46 of the Hague Regulations and to the extermination in concentration camps of Jews deported from occupied territories, pointed out that most of the accused in the trial of the major

[15] Hackworth, G.H., 6 *Digest of International Law* (1943), p. 399.

[16] See 'International Military Tribunal (Nuremberg), Judgment and Sentences' (hereafter Nuremberg Judgment), *American Journal of International Law*, vol. 41 (1947), p. 172, at p. 239. Other relevant Hague Regulations include Article 47 (prohibition of pillage), Article 49 (which provides that the only money contributions lawfully collected by the occupant are those for the needs of the army or the administration of the territory in question), and Article 50 (prohibiting the imposition upon the population of collective punishment ('no general penalty').

[17] See *Trial of the Major War Criminals before the International Military Tribunal* (1947), p. 44. The Indictment used the same language in establishing the war crimes character of deportation of 'able bodied citizens from ... occupied countries to Germany and to other occupied countries for the purpose of slave labor upon defense works, in factories, and in other tasks connected with the German war effort.' *Ibid.*, at 51. The judgment of the International Military Tribunal treated deportation for slave labour as a war crime. 2 Oppenheim, L.F.L., *International Law* (Lauterpacht, H.(ed.) (7th edition) (1952), p. 412; Judgment, *supra*, n. 16, pp. 239–43.

German War Criminals before the International Military Tribunal were sentenced for war crimes connected with military occupation.[18] It will be demonstrated that other war crimes tribunals also condemned the practice of deportations as illegal and criminal.

The indictment in the *Milch* case (*supra*) charged the accused with the war crimes of deportation to slave labour of the civilian population of, *inter alia*, Czechoslovakia, 'in the course of which millions of persons were enslaved, deported, ill-treated, terrorized, tortured, and murdered.'[19] The judgment found the defendant guilty of these 'war crimes,'

> to wit, that he was a principal in, accessory to, ordered, abetted, took a consenting part in and was connected with, plans and enterprises involving slave labor and deportation to slave labor of the civilian populations of countries and territories occupied by the German armed forces, and in the enslavement, deportation, ill-treatment and terrorization of such persons ....[20]

That the Council Control Law No. 10 reflects already existing customary law in treating deportations as a war crime is highlighted by the concurring opinion of Judge Michael A. Musmanno:

> In the first place, it is not Control Council Law No. 10 which makes abuse of civilian populations an international crime, nor even the decision of the International Military Tribunal, which in turn derived its power from the London Charter which had as its antecedent the Moscow Declaration of 1943. International law is not a body of codes and statutes, but the gradual expression, case by case, of the moral judgments of the civilized world, and no international law textbook of the last century ever sanctioned the deportation of a civilian population for labor. Although under Article 52 of the Hague Regulations, the inhabitants of occupied countries may be used for the needs of the occupying army, such civilians may be utilized only in proportion to the resources of the country, and they may not under any circumstances be required to take part in military operations against their own country.[21]

In another concurring opinion in this case, Judge Fitzroy D. Phillips discusses the conditions under which deportations become a war crime under customary international law. The existence of any one of these conditions, severally, taints a deportation with the character of a war crime. The first condition arises when the displacement is carried out without a legal title recognized by the Hague Regulations:

> International law has enunciated certain conditions under which the fact of deportation of civilians from one nation to another during times of war becomes

---

[18] See *Oppenheim-Lauterpacht, op. cit.*, n. 17, pp. 449–50.

[19] 2 *Nuernberg Trials, supra*, n. 10, p. 360.   [20] *Ibid.*, p. 790.

[21] *Ibid.*, p. 849. Oppenheim states flatly that there is no right to deport inhabitants to the country of the occupant for the purpose of compelling them to work there. See *Oppenheim-Lauterpacht, op. cit.*, n. 9, p. 345.

a crime. If the transfer is carried out without a legal title, as in the case where people are deported from a country occupied by an invader while the occupied enemy still has an army in the field and is still resisting, the deportation is contrary to international law. The rationale of this rule lies in the supposition that the occupying power has temporarily prevented the rightful sovereign from exercising its power over its citizens. Articles 43, 46, 49, 52, 55, and 56, Hague Regulations, which limit the rights of the belligerent occupant, do not expressly specify as crime the deportation of civilians from an occupied territory. Article 52 states the following provisions and conditions under which services may be demanded from the inhabitants of occupied countries. . . .

Insofar as this section limits the conscription of labor to that required for the needs of the army of occupation, it is manifestly clear that the use of labor from occupied territories outside of the area of occupation is forbidden by the Hague Regulations.[22]

It may also be observed that Judge Phillips mentions Article 46 of the Hague Regulations, which was undoubtedly violated by these deportations.

Judge Phillips' 'second condition under which deportation becomes a crime occurs when the purpose of the displacement is illegal, such as deportation for the purpose of compelling the deportees to manufacture weapons for use against their homeland or to be assimilated in the working economy of the occupying country.'[23] The third and final condition, under which deportation becomes illegal, occurs 'whenever generally recognized standards of decency and humanity are disregarded.'[24]

In the case of the *United States of America v. Alfred Krupp (supra)*, the Tribunal 'regard[ed] Judge Phillips' statement [in the *Milch* case] of the applicable law [with respect to deportations from occupied territory] as sound and accordingly adopt[ed] it.'[25] The indictment accused the defendants of

war crimes and crimes against humanity as defined in Article II of Control Council Law No. 10, in that they participated in atrocities and offenses against persons, including murder, extermination, enslavement, deportation, imprisonment, torture, abuse, and other inhumane acts committed against civilian populations of countries and territories under the belligerent occupation of, or otherwise controlled by, the Third Reich. . . .[26]

The statement of the prosecution in this case cogently addresses the customary law character of the prohibition of deportations, exploitation and abuse of slave labour:

Foreign civilians in or from occupied territories and prisoners of war are both protected by the Hague Conventions of 1907, to which Germany was a party.

---

[22] 2 *Nuernberg Trials, supra*, n. 10, p. 865.   [23] *Ibid.*   [24] *Ibid.*, p. 866.
[25] 9 *Nuernberg Trials, supra*, n. 13, p. 1432.   [26] *Ibid.*, p. 29.

They represent a codification of the determination of civilized man to value human life and dignity and to lessen suffering; so far as possible even during war. The Conventions did not foresee these recent reversions to barbarism, nor spell out the prohibitions against the crimes which the Third Reich and these defendants devised. Nevertheless, the Convention does prohibit such excesses of occupying military forces [in Articles 46 and 52].[27]

The prosecution went on to explain how the cluster of norms stated in Articles 46 and 52 was applicable to the deportation and enslavement of inhabitants of occupied territories:

It is clear that deportation, enslavement, and exploitation in Germany were impositions of services upon the inhabitants of an occupied country which were neither for the needs of the army of occupation, nor in proportion to the resources of the country. When married persons or children were so treated the rights of the family were certainly violated.

Law No. 10 and the Hague Conventions are, of course, only a part of the law which prescribed the crimes here charged. Deportation, enslavement, and brutal mistreatment are crimes under the general principles of international law and under the domestic laws of all civilized nations.[28]

The most important case for demonstrating the customary law character of the Hague Regulations is, of course, that of *United States of America v. von Leeb* (the *High Command* case).[29] The case is of importance also as a clear statement of the prohibition of deportations as customary law. The Tribunal treated 'the compulsory recruitment ["and compulsory requisitioning"] from the population of an occupied country for labor in the Reich [as] illegal' under Hague Regulations 43, 46, 47, 49, 50, 52, and 53.[30] In its discussion of deportation and enslavement of civilians, the Tribunal highlighted the fact that the norms prohibiting such practices are grounded in general international law:

At the outset of our consideration of this subject, it should be said that there is no international law that permits the deportation or the use of civilians against their will for other than on reasonable requisitions for the needs of the army, either within the area of the army or after deportation to rear areas or to the homeland of the occupying power. This is the holding of the IMT judgment and this consistently has been the holding of all of the Nuernberg Tribunals. It is necessary then only to determine factually whether with the knowledge, consent, or approval of the defendant the deportation and enslavement occurred.[31]

---

[27] *Ibid.*, pp. 113–114.   [28] *Ibid.*, p. 114.
[29] 11 *Trials of War Criminals before the Nuernberg Military Tribunals under Control Council Law No. 10* (1950), p. 462, discussed in Meron, T., *op. cit.*, n. 4, pp. 39–40.
[30] *Ibid.*, p. 540.   [31] *Ibid.*, p. 603.

In the *Rusha* case, the indictment, which led to the conviction of a number of defendants, stated that the defendants committed war crimes, as defined by Control Council Law No. 10, and were members of organizations or groups 'connected with atrocities and offenses against persons and property constituting violations of laws and customs of war, including ... murder, extermination, enslavement, deportation. ...' These acts 'constitute violations of international conventions, including the Articles of the Hague Regulations, 1907 ... of the laws and customs of war, of the general principles of criminal law as derived from the criminal laws of all civilized nations, of the internal penal laws of the countries in which such crimes were committed, and of Article II of Control Council Law No. 10.'[32] The judgment declared that

> The acts and conduct set forth in this judgment, and as substantially alleged in the indictment, also constitute war crimes, as defined in Article II(b) of Control Council Law No. 10, and are violative of international conventions, and particularly of Articles 23, 45, 46, 47, 52, and 56 of the Hague Regulations (1907), and are violative of the general principles of criminal law as derived from the criminal laws of all civilized nations and of the internal penal laws of the countries in which such crimes were committed.[33]

In the *Ministries* case, the indictment, which led to convictions, charged the defendants with participation in various war crimes, 'including murder, extermination, enslavement, deportation. ...'[34] The judgment rejected the defendants' claims of ignorance of the final solution and of the purpose of the deportation of Jews to the East:

> Knowing as they did what happened to the Jews when they came under the control of the SS, Gestapo, and police, we find ourselves unable to believe that these defendants had any idea that these deportations ended in anything but the death of these deportees through exhaustion from overwork, starvation, or mistreatment, and by mass murder. The defendants are not men of only ordinary intelligence and understanding. They are educated and trained to official life and experienced in the evaluation of policy, and the motives and acts of parties.[35]

Deportation and slave labour were also included in the indictments in the *Farben* case.[36] The prosecution stated that the crimes involved were

[32] 4 *Trials of War Criminals before the Nuernberg Military Tribunals under Control Council Law No. 10* (1946–1949), pp. 617–618.

[33] 5 *Trials of War Criminals before the Nuernberg Military Tribunals under Control Council Law No. 10* (1950), p. 153.

[34] 12 *Trials of War Criminals before the Nuernberg Military Tribunals under Control Council Law No. 10* (1946–1949), p. 44.

[35] 14 *Trials of War Criminals before the Nuernberg Military Tribunals under Control Council Law No. 10* (1946–1949), p. 473.

[36] 7 *Trials of War Criminals before the Nuernberg Military Tribunals under Control Council Law No. 10* (1953), pp. 51 and 189.

'recognized as such not only under international law, but by the ordinary penal laws of all civilized nations ... [and] Hague and Geneva Conventions ...'[37]

'Enslavement and deportation to slave labor on a gigantic scale of members of the civilian populations of countries and territories *under the belligerent occupation of, or otherwise controlled by Germany*' (emphasis added) was included among the war crimes charged in the indictment in the *Flick* case.[38] The prosecution emphasized that these war crimes were recognized as crimes under international law long before the enactment of Control Council Law No. 10:

> That the slave-labor program was criminal, is beyond doubt. The international Military Tribunal has so found. The relevant provisions of Control Council Law No. 10 are clear. ... Article 52 of the Hague Convention [annex] as to the use of labor in occupied territories, and the provisions of the Geneva Convention as to the employment of prisoners of war, had, long before the enactment of Law No. 10, established principles of international law which condemned such practices. Indeed, an attempt by Germany in World War I to deport labor forcibly from Belgium met such an outcry of world opinion that the plan was attacked even in the Reichstag, and subsequently abandoned.[39]

In the *Josef Altstotter* case (*Justice* case), the defendants were accused of implementation of the *Nacht und Nebel* decree. The Night and Fog program was instituted for the deportation to Germany of many thousands of inhabitants of occupied territories for the purpose of making them disappear without trace and so that their subsequent fate remained secret.[40] The United States Military Tribunal pointed out in its judgment that deportation of civilians was included upon the list of crimes drawn up in the Paris Conference of 1919 and recognized by the Versailles Treaty.[41] The Tribunal referred also to the recognition by the International Military Tribunal of deportation of inhabitants of occupied territories for the purpose of efficient and enduring intimidation as a violation of the laws and customs of war.[42] The Tribunal elaborated on the customary law antecedents of 'Control Council Law No. 10 which makes deportation of the civilian population for any purpose an offense':[43]

> The international law of war has for a long period of time protected the civilian population of any territory or country occupied by an enemy war force. This law finds its source in the unwritten international law as established by the customs and usages of the civilised nations of the world. Under international

---

[37] *Ibid.*, p. 189.
[38] 6 *Trials of War Criminals before the Nuernberg Military Tribunals under Control Council Law No. 10* (1952), p. 13.
[39] *Ibid.*, p. 53.   [40] 6 *Law Reports of Trials of War Criminals* (1948), p. 56.
[41] *Ibid.*   [42] *Ibid.*, pp. 56–57.   [43] *Ibid.*, p. 58.

law the inhabitants of an occupied area or territory are entitled to certain rights which must be respected by the invader occupant.

This law of military occupation has been in existence for a long period of time. It was officially interpreted and applied nearly a half-century ago by the President of the United States of America during the war with Spain in 1898. By General Order No. 101, 18th July 1898, *Foreign Relations of the United States*, 783, the President declared that the inhabitants of the occupied territory 'are entitled to the security of their person and property and in all their private rights and religions.' ... The President referred to the fact that these humane standards of warfare had previously been established by the laws and customs of war, which were later codified by the Hague Conventions of 1899 and 1907, and which constituted the effort of the civilised participating nations to diminish the evils of war by the limitation of the power of the invading occupant over the people and by placing the inhabitants of the occupied area or territory 'under the protection and rules of principles of law of nations as they result from usage established among the civilised peoples from the laws of humanity and the dictates of public conscience'.[44]

Deportations from occupied territories have been treated as war crimes under international customary law not only in international but also in national tribunals. Thus, in the case of *Jean-Pierre Lex* decided by the Permanent Military Tribunal of Nancy (France), the defendant, a German citizen, was accused of violations of French law and of the war crime of deportations. The official Notes on the case address the customary law nature of this war crime:

> It should, however, be stressed that the acts for which the accused was con-demned are also punishable under the laws and customs of war. The accused took part in the deportation of inhabitants of an occupied territory, and such deportations are recognized as a war crime. They are expressly included in the definition of war crimes in Art. 6(b) of the Nuremberg Charter, as well as in Art. II, 1(b) of Law No. 10 of the Allied Control Council for Germany. They were also recognized as such by the United Nations War Crimes Commission in connec-tion with numerous cases reported to it by member governments, in dealing with which the Commission had in mind the Preamble of the 4th Hague Convention concerning the Laws and Customs of War on Land, which covers violations not explicitly prohibited in the various provisions of the Convention.[45]

The official 'Notes on the [*Milch*] Case' refer to the attitude taken by certain other laws and courts to the question of deportation as a war crime. They mention a Norwegian case (*Wagner case*), where the court ruled that 'the deportation of 531 Norwegian Jews was a war crime at variance with

---

[44] 6 *Law Reports of Trials of War Criminals* (1948), p. 58.
[45] 7 *Law Reports of Trials of War Criminals*, *supra*, n. 7, p. 75.

the laws of humanity and the laws and customs of war.'[46] The Norwegian court also found that the accused knew that the victims faced slavery and many of them death. The Notes add that the laws of France, Australia, China and Yugoslavia treated deportation as a war crime.

In the Polish case of *Koch*, the defendant has been accused of war crimes committed by his participation in the deportation of Jews to the concentration camps as part of the 'final solution.'[47] The Court stated that

> Hague Convention No. IV, which is a law still in force, was accordingly applied by Polish courts when they decided on the compatibility of the activities of the German Occupant in Polish territory with that Convention and with the substantive criminal law of the land in force.
>
> ...
>
> Hague Convention No. IV of 1907 contains legal rules with penal sanctions and therefore there is no room for objection based on the principle *nulla poena sine lege*. For the purposes of the present trial it should be observed that Article 6(b) of the Charter of the International Military Tribunal at Nuremberg specifies as war crimes violations of the laws or customs of war. ...[48]

Finally, the case of *Attorney-General v. Adolf Eichmann* may be mentioned. Here, suffice it to observe that Eichmann was convicted, *inter alia*, of count 8 which concerned war crimes. The Jerusalem District court stated:

> In the eighth Count, the accused is charged with a war crime in that during the Second World War in Germany and other Axis States and in areas occupied by them, he, together with others, caused the ill-treatment, deportation and murder of the Jewish inhabitants of the States occupied by Germany and the other Axis States. All acts of persecution, deportation and murder in which the accused took part, as we have found in discussing crimes against the Jewish people and crimes against humanity, are *ipso facto* also war crimes within the meaning of ... the [Israeli] Law, as far as they were committed during the Second World War and the Jews who fell victim to these acts belonged to the population of the countries conquered by Germany and the other Axis States.[49]

The preceding discussion reviewed the Nuremberg jurisprudence and legal literature on the question whether deportation of civilians in time of war reflected, already during the Second World War, a customary law norm. That discussion merits, I believe, the conclusion that even prior to the adoption of the Geneva Conventions for the Protection of Victims of War on 12 August 1949, deportation of civilians constituted, in many circumstances, a violation of international customary law.

---

[46] *Ibid.*, p. 55.   [47] *International Law Reports*, vol. 30 (1966), p. 502.
[48] *Ibid.*, pp. 503–504.
[49] *International Law Reports*, vol. 36 (1968), p. 243; see, also, *ibid.*, p. 275.

VII

Geneva Conventions as Customary Law

The few international judicial decisions on international humanitarian law reveal little, if any, inquiry into the process by which particular instruments have been transformed into customary law. The leading case on the Hague Regulations of 1907 is the judgment of the International Military Tribunal (IMT) for the *Trial of German Major War Criminals* (Nuremberg, 1946). The argument was raised that Hague Convention No. IV did not apply because of the general participation (*si omnes*) clause – several of the belligerents not being parties to the Convention. In response, the IMT apparently acknowledged that at the time the Regulations were adopted the participating states believed that they were making new law: '[b]ut by 1939 these rules laid down in the Convention were recognised by all civilised nations, and were regarded as being declaratory of the laws and customs of war'.[1] The IMT did not even discuss the process by which the Hague Regulations had metamorphosed from conventional into customary law. The Tribunal's language (the use of the word 'regarded') suggests that the Tribunal may have looked primarily at the *opinio juris*, rather than at the actual practice of states.

Similarly, although more cautiously, the International Military Tribunal for the Far East (1948) characterized Hague Convention No. IV 'as good evidence of the customary law of nations, to be considered by the Tribunal along with all other available evidence in determining the customary law to be applied in any given situation'.[2] This Tribunal, in contrast to the IMT, did not view the entirety of the Hague Regulations as necessarily an accurate mirror of customary law.

The most interesting case on the relationship between custom and treaty in the context of the Geneva Conventions is *United States v. von Leeb* ('The High Command Case').[3] The IMT judgment focused on the

---

[1] *Trial of German Major War Criminals*, 1946, Cmd. 6964, Cmd. 6964, Misc. No. 12, at 65.

[2] *In re Hirota*, 15 Ann. Dig. 356, 366. The Tribunal stated that 'acts of inhumanity to prisoners which are forbidden by the customary law of nations as well as by conventions are to be prevented by the Government having responsibility for the prisoners.' Ibid.

[3] 11 Trials of War Criminals before the Nuernberg Military Tribunals under Control Council Law No. 10, at 462 (1948) (hereinafter cited as Trials of War Criminals).

significance of the *si omnes* clause in Hague Convention No. IV 32 years after its adoption. In contrast, *von Leeb* principally concerned whether and to what extent the 1929 Geneva Prisoners of War Convention could be binding on Nazi Germany *vis-à-vis* the Soviet Union, which was not a party to the Convention, regarding actions stemming from the Nazi invasion of the USSR only 12 years after the convention was adopted.

In *von Leeb*, the Nuremberg Tribunal endorsed the principle applied by the IMT with regard to the Hague Regulation extrapolating from that principle to the 1929 Convention. The Tribunal noted:

> [I]t would appear that the IMT ... followed the same lines of thought with regard to the Geneva Convention as with respect to the Hague Convention to the effect that they were binding insofar as they were in substance an expression of international law as accepted by the civilized nations of the world, and this Tribunal adopts this viewpoint ...
>
> Most of the provisions of the Hague and Geneva Conventions, considered in substance, are clearly an expression of the accepted views of civilized nations and binding upon Germany and the defendants on trial before us in the conduct of the war against Russia.[4]

While admitting that 'certain detailed provisions pertaining to the care and treatment of prisoners of war' could be binding only as conventional law,[5] the Tribunal cited as customary law five provisions of the 1907 Hague Regulations and nineteen provisions of the 1929 Geneva Convention, even including a provision, Article 9, requiring that '[p]risoners captured in unhealthful regions or where the climate is injurious for persons coming from temperate regions, shall be transported, as soon as possible, to a more favourable climate.' Some of the provisions of the Geneva Convention listed by the Tribunal ranged far beyond the few short principles stated in the Hague Regulations. The Tribunal did not address the process by which those provisions of the Geneva Convention that did not echo the provisions of the Hague Regulations had been transformed in just a few years into customary law.

The Tribunal was similarly silent concerning the rationale for determining which provisions were part of customary law. Baxter observed that '[a] rough-and-ready distinction may be discerned between those

---

[4] Ibid. at 534–5. The Nuremberg Tribunal cited with approval Admiral Canaris's remarkable protest against the German regulations for the treatment of Soviet prisoners of war. His protest stated that the regulations were based on a 'fundamentally different viewpoint' from that underlying the principles of international law: 'Since the 18th century these have gradually been established along the lines that war captivity is neither revenge nor punishment, but solely protective custody, the only purpose of which is to prevent the prisoners of war from further participation in the war.' The admiral concluded that while the Geneva Convention was not binding on Germany *vis-à-vis* the Soviet Union, the principles of international law on the treatment of prisoners were. Ibid. at 533.

[5] Ibid. at 535.

safeguards that are essential to the survival of the prisoner, on the one hand, and those protections that are not basic or which give depth to or implement the essential principles.'[6] He acknowledged, however, that that line is not rigorously observed. The Tribunal did refer to the Soviet Union's practice of using German POWs to construct fortifications during the war as 'evidence given to the interpretation of what constituted accepted use of prisoners of war under international law'.[7]

In another case, involving the defence of superior orders and thus unrelated to the Geneva Convention, the Tribunal noted that the recognition by states of such a defence in their manuals of military law was not a competent source of international law but might have evidentiary value.[8] This position appears to have been supported by an understandable reluctance to accept the defence of superior orders from German officers. Generally, however, given the difficulty of ascertaining significant state practice in periods of hostilities, manuals of military law and national legislation providing for the implementation of humanitarian law norms as internal law should be accepted as among the best types of evidence of such practice, and sometimes as statements of *opinio juris* as well. This is especially so because military manuals frequently not only state government policy but establish obligations binding on members of the armed forces, violations of which are punishable under military penal codes. For states, manuals create mutual expectations of compliance and many of the rules stated therein are good evidence of customary law.[9] Of course, the practice of states is also reflected in the adoption of such international instruments as normative declarations and, especially, in the multilateral treaty, which 'constitutes an expression of their attitude toward customary international law, to be weighed together with all other

---

[6] Baxter, *Multilateral Treaties as Evidence of Customary International Law*, 41 Brit. YB Int'l L. 275, 282 (1965–6).

[7] *Von Leeb*, above n. 3, at 534. The Tribunal concluded that because of the 'uncertainty of international law...orders providing for ... use [of prisoners of war in the construction of fortifications outside of] dangerous areas, were not criminal upon their face ...'. Ibid.

[8] 'We point out that army regulations are not a competent source of international law. They are neither legislative nor judicial pronouncements ... [But] it is possible ... that such regulations, as they bear upon a question of custom and practice in the conduct of war, might have evidentiary value, particularly if the applicable portions had been put into general practice. It will be observed that the determination, whether a custom or practice exists, is a question of fact.' *United States* v. *List*, above n. 3, at 1230, 1237.

US Dep't of the Army, The Law of Land Warfare 3 (Field Manual No. 27–10, 1956) (referring to the black-letter text), states that its purpose 'is to provide authoritative guidance to military personnel on the customary and treaty law applicable to the conduct of warfare on land and to relationships between belligerents and neutral States'. I agree with Baxter that such manuals provide 'telling evidence' of the practice of states. Baxter, above n. 6, at 283.

[9] Gasser, *Customary Law and Additional Protocol I to the Geneva Conventions for the Protection of War Victims: Future Directions in Light of the U.S. Decision not to Ratify*, 81 ASIL PROC. 31, 33 (1989).

consistent and inconsistent evidence of the state of customary international law'.[10]

Only a few international judicial decisions discuss the customary law nature of international humanitarian law instruments. These decisions nevertheless highlight certain trends in this area, including the tendencies to ignore, for the most part, the availability of evidence concerning state practice scant as it may have been, and to assume that humanitarian principles deserving recognition as the positive law of the international community have in fact been recognized as such by states. The 'ought' merges with the 'is', the *lex ferenda* with the *lex lata*. The teleological desire to solidify the humanizing content of the humanitarian norms clearly affects the judicial attitudes underlying the 'legislative' character of the judicial process. Given the scarcity of actual practice, it may well be that tribunals have been guided, and may continue to be guided, by the degree to which certain acts are offensive to human dignity. The more heinous the act, the more willing the tribunal will be to assume that it violates not only a moral principle of humanity but also a positive norm of customary law.

Although the Court in the *Nicaragua* case did not discuss the formation of customary law in the direct context of the Geneva Conventions, the method adopted there cannot but influence future consideration of customary law in various fields of international law, including the Geneva Conventions. Having posed all the traditional, correct questions regarding the existence of actual practice and the *opinio juris*, the Court made only perfunctory and conclusory references to the practice of states. Despite the variety of reasons which impel states to adopt their respective positions in international fora, the Court found *opinio juris* in verbal statements of governmental representatives to international organizations, in the content of resolutions, declarations, and other normative instruments adopted by such organizations, and in the consent of states to such instruments. This approach, which has important antecedents,[11] is

---

[10] Baxter, *Treaties and Custom*, 129 Recueil des cours 27, 52 (1970–I). For other evidence of state practice, see also the US field manual, above n. 8, at 6.

[11] 1896 ICJ Rep. at 98–108. The Court's approach has significant antecedents in earlier cases. See *Legal Consequences for States of the Continued Presence of South Africa in Namibia (South West Africa) Notwithstanding Security Council Resolution 276 (1970)*, 1971 ICJ Rep. 16, 31–2 (Advisory Opinion of 21 June); *Western Sahara*, 1975 ICJ Rep. 12, 30–7 (Advisory Opinion of 16 Oct.).

In discussing the Court's view (expressed in the *Nicaragua* case) that 'voting for a norm-declaring resolution is an exercise in *opinio juris*', Professor Franck warns that '[t]he effect of this enlarged concept of the lawmaking force of General Assembly resolutions may well be to caution states to vote against "aspirational" instruments if they do not intend to embrace them totally and at once, regardless of circumstance. That would be unfortunate. Aspirational resolutions have long occupied, however uncomfortably, a twilight zone between 'hard' treaty law and the normative void.' Franck, *Some Observations on the ICJ's Procedural and Substantive Innovations*, 81 AJIL 116, 119 (1987).

not without doctrinal support. A scholar as respected as Judge Baxter has argued that

> [t]he actual conduct of States in their relations with other nations is only a subsidiary means whereby the rules which guide the conduct of States are ascertained. The firm statement by the State of what it considers to be the rule is far better evidence of its position than what can be pieced together from the actions of that country at different times and in a variety of contexts.[12]

Despite perplexity over the reasoning and, at times, the conclusions of a tribunal, both states and scholarly opinion in general will accept judicial decisions confirming the customary law character of some of the provisions of the Geneva Conventions as authoritative statements of the law. Eventually, the focus of attention will shift from the inquiry into whether certain provisions reflect customary law to the conclusions of judicial decisions establishing that status.

As far as law-making is concerned, the starting-point is, of course, the practice of states. Yet in non-codifying multilateral treaties even outside the humanitarian law field, norms and values that differ from the actual practice of states are commonly asserted. For human rights or humanitarian conventions – i.e. conventions whose object is to humanize the behaviour of states, groups, and persons – the gap between the norms stated and actual practice tends to be especially wide.

The law-making process does not merely 'photograph' or declare the current state of international practice. Far from it. Rather, the law-making process attempts to articulate and emphasize norms and values that, in the judgment of some states, deserve promotion and acceptance by all states, in order to establish a code for the better conduct

---

A tendency similar to that of the ICJ can be found also in decisions of national courts on the customary law of human rights: e.g. in the emphasis by Judge Kaufman on international and domestic normative instruments prohibiting torture, on government statements, and on scholarly opinion, in *Filartiga* v. *Peña-Irala*, 630 F. 2d 876 (2d Cir. 1980), in the focus on normative instruments to determine the prohibition in international customary law of arbitrary detention, *Rodriguez-Fernandez* v. *Wilkinson*, 505 F. Supp. 787, 796–800 (D. Kan. 1980), *aff'd on other grounds*, 654 F. 2d 1382 (10th Cir. 1981), and in the discussion of the principle of diplomatic immunity (in the case of Raoul Wallenberg), *Von Dardel* v. *Union of Soviet Socialist Republics*, 623 F. Supp. 246, 261 (DDC 1985). Cf. Schachter's list of types of evidence adduced to support a finding that a particular human right is a part of customary law, *International Law in Theory and Practice*, 178 Recueil des cours 11, 334–5 (1982–V). See also Schrader, *Custom and General Principles as Sources of International Law in American Federal Courts*, 82 Colum. L. Rev. 751, 762–8 (1982). On practice creating customary human rights, see also Restatement of the Law Third, Restatement of the Foreign Relations Law of the United States §701, Reporters' note 2 (1987). See also Gerstel and Segall, *Conference Report: Human Rights in American Courts*, 1 Am. U. J. Int'l L. & Pol. 137, 162 and nn. 79–80 (1986). For a critique of *Filartiga* and *Rodriguez-Fernandez*, see Oliver, *Problems of Cognition and Interpretation in Applying Norms of Customary International Law of Human Rights in United States Courts*, 4 Hous. J. Int'l L. 59, 60 (1981).

[12] Baxter, above n. 6, at 300.

of nations.[13] This applies in particular to instruments designed to human-ize the behaviour of states in armed conflict, which is characterized by violence and violations, by the necessity of committing acts frequently not preceded by careful deliberation, by exceptional conditions, by limited third-party access to the theatre of operations, and by the parties' con-flicting factual and legal justifications for their conduct. Because of these circumstances, humanitarian conventions may have lesser prospects for actual compliance than other multilateral treaties, even though they enjoy stronger moral support. Consequently, in the violent situations addressed by the humanitarian conventions, the gulf between the more enlightened norms and the actual practice of states may, to some extent, be expected to remain formidable. With regard to humanitarian instruments, the inter-national community expects neither strict nor immediate compliance with the stated norms. Because of the requirements or perceptions of security, states are willing to accept gradual and partial compliance as fulfilling the requirements for the formation of customary law.

Far from codifying the actual behaviour of states or the mores of the international community, law-making conferences try to promulgate more protective rules of conduct,[14] stretching the consensus of the nego-tiating states as widely as possible. As a mixture of actual and desired practice, humanitarian instruments may thus reflect deliberate ambiguity, designed to encourage broader compliance with the stated norms and to promote the greatest possible acceptance of the norms as the general law of the international community. In the creation of international human-itarian law, the teleological component of *lex ferenda* is especially import-ant, though often deliberately downplayed. The sound judgment of the 'legislators' and the distance between the 'is' and the 'ought to be' deter-mine whether a particular instrument will raise the expectations of the international community, will be accepted in practice as the living, bind-ing general law of the international community, or will become marginal or even fall eventually into desuetude.

In discussing the customary law character of the Geneva Conventions, two questions merit consideration. The first pertains to the status of the Conventions as declaratory of customary law at the time of their

---

[13] Meron, *The Meaning and Reach of the International Convention on the Elimination of All Forms of Racial Discrimination*, 79 AJIL 283, 317–18 (1985).

[14] The Preamble to Hague Convention No. IV expresses this approach with rare candor:

'Animated by the desire to serve, even in this extreme case, the interests of humanity and the ever progressive needs of civilization;

Thinking it important, with this object, to revise the general laws and customs of war . . . confining them within such limits as would contain their severity as far as possible;

[I]nspired by the desire to diminish the evils of war, as far as military requirements permit . . . .'

adoption, the second to the subsequent passage into customary law of norms stated in the Conventions.

As regards the first question, a further distinction is perhaps necessary. Most of the substantive provisions of Conventions Nos. I, II, and III are based on earlier Geneva Conventions, and thus have a strong claim to customary law status. Geneva Convention No. IV, in contrast, was the first Geneva Convention ever to be addressed to the protection of civilians. A product of the universal condemnation of the Nazis' treatment of civilians in occupied Europe during the Second World War, the Convention is rooted only in the few provisions on the treatment of civilians in combat zones and occupied territories found in Articles 23, 25, 27, 28, 42–56 of the Hague Regulations. The ICRC *Commentary* on Article 154 of Geneva Convention No. IV demonstrates, however, that the Convention repeats the bulk of the Hague Regulations relating to the protection of civilian persons.[15] Although in their range and depth, some of the provisions in the Geneva Convention No. IV retain only an attenuated link with the brief and fairly primitive Hague Regulations, I believe that the Hague Regulations can provide the foundation for building the customary law content of this Convention. Those involving procedures and implementation lack any such antecedents.

Nevertheless, because some provisions of Conventions Nos. I–III formed new, conventional law, and some provisions of Convention No. IV reflected customary law (e.g. the principle of protection of the physical and mental integrity of civilians, and of sick and wounded), the significant difference between the former Conventions and Convention No. IV is quantitative, not qualitative. The Conventions contain a core of principles (e.g. the Martens clause)[16] that express customary law. Of course, the identification of the various provisions as customary or conventional law presents the greatest difficulties. Neither international practice nor scholarly studies provide a comprehensive foundation for identifying

---

[15] Commentary on the Geneva Conventions of 12 August 1949: Geneva Convention Relative to the Protection of Civilian Persons in Time of War 620 (O. Uhler and H. Coursier eds. 1958). Regarding the antecedents of Geneva Conventions Nos. I–II, see Dinstein, *Human Rights in Armed Conflict: International Humanitarian Law*, in 2 Human Rights in International Law: Legal and Policy Issues 345, 346 (T. Meron ed. 1984).

However, as regards protection of private property, the Hague Regulations provide the basic principles, while Geneva Convention No. IV states a number of supplementary rules.

[16] See Strebel, *Martens' Clause*, [Instalment] 3 Encyclopedia of Public International Law 252 (R. Bernhardt ed. 1982); F. Kalshoven, Constraints on the Waging of War 14–15 (1987). The Martens clause reads as follows: 'Until a more complete code of the laws of war has been issued, the High Contracting Parties deem it expedient to declare that, in cases not included in the Regulations adopted by them, the inhabitants and the belligerents remain under the protection and the rule of the principles of the law of nations, as they result from the usages established among civilized peoples, from the laws of humanity, and the dictates of the public conscience.'

those rules in Geneva Convention No. IV which are declaratory of pre-existing customary law. Only an overconfident commentator would try to identify all the customary norms embodied in Geneva Convention No. IV. Nevertheless, a tentative attempt to identify some examples of such rules may be worthwhile. The relationship of the provisions of the Geneva Conventions to the Hague Regulations provides a rational guideline for such a survey.

In my opinion, the following partial list of Geneva Convention No. IV provisions exemplifies norms of which the cores, although not necessarily the specific language and details, embody customary law: The prohibition of destruction of property, set forth in Article 53, which originates in Hague Regulations 23(g) and 46 and which may be related to the prohibition of collective penalties in Hague Regulation 50; the prohibition of enlistment and of certain types of labour of protected persons which are in conflict with their allegiance to the ousted sovereign, stated in Article 51, which is grounded in Hague Regulations 23(h) and 52; the prohibition of coercion stated in Article 31 which is derived from Hague Regulation 44 and Hague Regulation 23(h); the prohibition of murder, torture, corporal punishment, mutilation, and other measures of brutality, stated in Article 32, which is implicit in Hague Regulation 46[17] and reflects reaction to treatment of civilians by Nazi authorities during World War II; the right of protected persons to enjoy respect for their persons, honour, family rights, religious convictions and practices stated in Article 27, which is clearly derived from the Hague Regulation 46; the protection of civilian hospitals and of their personnel, set forth in Articles 18 and 20, which is

---

The Martens clause appears also, in modified form, in the common Article on the denunciation of Geneva Conventions (63/62/142/158); in Art. 1(2) of the Protocol Additional to the Geneva Conventions at 12 August 1949, and Relating to the Protection of Victims of International Armed Conflicts (Protocol I), opened for signature 12 Dec. 1977, 1125 UNTS 3; in the Preamble to the Protocol Additional to the Geneva Conventions of 12 August 1949, and Relating to the Protection of Victims of Non-International Armed Conflicts (Protocol II), opened for signature 12 Dec. 1977, 1125 UNTS 609; and in the Preamble to the Convention on Prohibitions or Restrictions on the the Use of Certain Conventional Weapons which may be Deemed to be Excessively Injurious or to Have Indiscriminate Effects, opened for signature 10 Apr. 1981, UN Doc. A/CONF.95/15 (1980), reprinted in 19 ILM 1524 (1980).

In 'the *Krupp Case*', the Martens clause was described as much more than a pious declaration:

'It is a general clause, making the usages established among civilized nations, the laws of humanity, and the dictates of public conscience into the legal yardstick to be applied if and when the specific provisions of the Convention and the Regulations annexed to it do not cover specific cases occurring in warfare, or concomitant to warfare.' *United States* v. *Krupp von Bohlen und Halbach* (Case 10, Military Tribunal III), 9 Trials of War Criminals at 1341.

Professor Dinstein highlights the 'innovations' in Art. 118 of the Geneva Convention No. III. Dinstein, *The Release of Prisoners of War*, in Studies and Essays on International Humanitarian Law and Red Cross Principles in Honour of Jean Pictet 37, 44 (C. Swinarski ed. 1984).

[17] Art. 46 reads as follows: '[f]amily honour and rights, the lives of persons, and private property, as well as religious convictions and practice, must be respected ...'.

rooted in the Hague Regulation 27; the prohibition of pillage, stated in Article 33, which is based on the Hague Regulations 28 and 47; the prohibitions of collective punishment, intimidation, and terrorism, and of reprisals against protected persons and their property set forth in Article 33, which have their roots in Hague Regulation 46 and Hague Regulation 50 and the principle of individual responsibility which Regulation 50 articulates; the absolute prohibition of the taking of hostages, stated in Article 34, which may be related to the prohibition of collective penalties stated in Hague Regulation 50 and the principle of individual responsibility which underlies it. In addition to the prohibition upon the taking of hostages in international humanitarian law instruments (e.g. common Article 3 of the Geneva Conventions, Article 75(2)(c) of Protocol I and Article 4(2)(c) of Protocol II), the taking of hostages has been solemnly prohibited by the International Convention Against the Taking of Hostages, which was adopted by the UN General Assembly on 17 December 1979, and by other authoritative statements, such as treaties criminalizing hijacking of aircraft and resolutions condemning hostage-taking. I would, therefore, submit that the norm tracking the prohibition stated in Article 1 of the Convention of 17 December 1979 is maturing into customary humanitarian and human rights law. More directly, the prohibition of hostage-taking is a result of the international community's revulsion over the Nazi practice of taking and killing hostages and the crystallization, by the time the Geneva Conventions were adopted, and since then under the influence of the evolving human rights law, of a universal *opinio juris* assessing this inhuman practice as unlawful. Hostage-taking is clearly contrary to the natural right of the human person not to be made responsible for acts which he or she did not commit.[18]

Article 49 of Geneva Convention No. IV, which prohibits, among other things, '[i]ndividual or mass forcible transfers [and] deportations of protected persons from occupied territory to the territory of the Occupying Power or to that of any other country . . . regardless of their motive', has no antecedents in the Hague Regulations. Nevertheless, the ICRC *Commentary* to that Convention argues, on the basis of post-World War II trials of German war criminals, that the prohibition of deportations has been 'embodied in international law.'[19] I believe that at least the central elements of Article 49(1), such as the absolute prohibitions of forcible mass

---

[18] *Commentary* on Geneva Convention No. IV, above n. 15, at 231. The UN Commission on Human Rights affirmed that the taking of hostages constitutes a grave violation of human rights and censured 'the actions of all persons responsible'. Res. 1988/38, UN ESCOR Supp. (No. 2) 97–8, UN Doc. E/1988/12, E/CN.4/1988/88. See also the International Convention against the Taking of Hostages, GA Res. 345/146, 34 UN GAOR Supp. (No. 46) at 245, UN Doc. A/34/46 (1980).

[19] *Commentary* on Geneva Convention No. IV, above n. 15, at 279 and n. 3.

and individual transfers and deportations of protected persons from occupied territories stated in Article 49(1), are declaratory of customary law even when the object and setting of the deportations differ from those underlying German World War II practices which led to the rule set forth in Article 49.[20] Although it is less clear that individual deportation was

[20] Justice H. Cohn's dissenting opinion in *Kawasme v. Minister of Defence*, 35(1) Piskei Din 617, summarized in 11 Isr. YB Hum. Rts. 349, 352–4 (1981), and Dinstein, *Expulsion of Mayors from Judea*, 8 Tel Aviv U. L. Rev. 158 (Hebrew, 1981), discuss the controversy concerning the customary law content of Art. 49. In several decisions (most recently in High Court of Justice Dec. 785/87, 845/87, 27/88, of 10 Apr. 1988) the Israel Supreme Court asserted that Art. 49 was not intended to prohibit deportation of individuals on security grounds from occupied territories and that it does not embody principles of customary law. In the decision of 4 Apr. 1988 (High Court of Justice Dec. 785/87, 845/87, 27/88), Mr Meir Shamgar, the President of the Supreme Court, supported by the majority of the Court, asserted that, as a matter of treaty interpretation, Art. 49 prohibited only such, especially collective, deportations as are carried out for purposes similar to those underlying the deportations carried out by the Nazi authorities during World War II. He stated that individual, security-motivated deportations were not prohibited by Art. 49. For an incisive criticism of this decision, see Dinstein, *Deportation from Administered Territories*, 13 Tel Aviv U. L. Rev. 403 (1988).

This interpretation of Art. 49 is, in my judgment, contrary to the rules of treaty-interpretation stated in the Vienna Convention on the Law of Treaties. Art. 31(1) of the Vienna Convention requires that a treaty be interpreted in good faith in accordance with the ordinary meaning to be given to its terms, etc. The language of Art. 49 is clear and categorical. It prohibits both individual and collective deportations, regardless of their motive. Recourse to supplementary means of interpretation (Article 32 of the Vienna Convention) was, therefore, not justified. In any event, the object and purpose of Geneva Convention No. IV, a humanitarian instrument *par excellence*, was not only to protect civilian populations against Nazi-type atrocities, but to provide the broadest possible humanitarian protection for civilian victims of future wars and occupations, with their ever-changing circumstances.

The opinion accepting the prohibition stated in Art. 49(1) as customary law finds further support in the virtually universal condemnation by the international community, reflecting *opinio juris*, of deportations from occupied territories and in the proscription of deportations of a citizen from his or her own country stated in international human rights instruments. See e.g. Arts. 12–13 of the Political Covenant and Art. 12 of the African Charter on Human and Peoples' Rights (which clearly imply such a prohibition); and Art. 3(1) of Protocol 4 to the European Convention and Art. 22(5) of the American Convention (which contain explicit prohibitions of such deportations).

Deportation is already prohibited by Art. 23 of Lieber's Code ('[p]rivate citizens are no longer murdered, enslaved, or carried off to distant parts...'). F. Lieber, Instructions for the Government of Armies of the United States in the Field (1863), originally published as General Orders No. 100, War Department, Adjutant General's Office, 24 Apr. 1863; reprinted in R. Hartigan, Lieber's Code and the Law of War 45–71 (1983). This Code has had a major influence on the drafting of national statutes and regulations pertaining to the law of war and of such treaties as Hague Convention No. IV and the Geneva Conventions and, of course, on the formation of customary law. The ICRC explains the silence of the Hague Regulations on the question of deportations by 'the practice of deporting persons ... at the beginning of this century ... having fallen into abeyance'. *Commentary* on Geneva Convention No. IV, above n. 15, at 279. It adds that the prohibition of deportations 'may be regarded to-day as having been embodied in international law.' (footnote omitted). Ibid. In *United States v. von Leeb*, above n. 3, at 603, the Tribunal observed that 'there is no international law that permits the deportation or the use of civilians against their will for other than on reasonable requisitions for the needs of the army, either within the area of the army or after deportation to rear areas or to the homeland of the occupying power.'

already prohibited in 1949, I believe that this prohibition has by now come to reflect customary law.

Additionally, the core of the due process guarantees stated in Geneva Convention No. IV embodies norms constituting general principles of law. Thus, the principle *nullum crimen, nulla poena sine lege* (Article 65), the requirement that courts apply only those provisions of the applicable law 'which are in accordance with general principles of law, in particular the principle that the penalty shall be proportionate to the offence' (Article 67), and the rule stating that '[n]o sentence shall be pronounced by the competent courts of the Occupying Power except after a regular trial' (Article 71) are among provisions which the authoritative ICRC *Commentary* to these Articles of Geneva Convention No. IV considers as reflecting universally recognized legal principles and fundamental notions of justice recognized by all civilized nations. These due process provisions therefore exemplify norms binding on states not only as treaty obligations but also as general principles of law (Article 38(1)(c) of the Statute of the ICJ).

Discussion of the second question, the development of the law of the Geneva Conventions since their adoption in 1949, should begin by noting their unparalleled success, as manifested by their acceptance as treaties by the entire international community. Because practically all the potential participants in creating customary law have become parties to the treaty, little evidence is available demonstrating that non-parties behave in accordance with the norms of the Conventions, and thereby create concordant customary law. The 'Baxter paradox' (Judge Baxter himself coined the term 'paradox' in this context) is in full blossom: 'As the number of parties to a treaty increases, it becomes more difficult to demonstrate what is the state of customary international law dehors the treaty ... As the express acceptance of the treaty increases, the number of States not parties whose practice is relevant diminishes. There will be less scope for the development of international law dehors the treaty....'[21] In Baxter's opinion, the Geneva Conventions typify this phenomenon:

> Now that an extremely large number of States have become parties to the Geneva Conventions ... who can say what the legal obligations of combatants would be in the absence of the treaties? And if little or no customary international practice is generated by the non-parties, it becomes virtually impossible

---

[21] Baxter, above n. 10, at 64, 73. Charney points out: 'In cases where ... widespread adherence to the agreement exists, substantial evidence of state actions taken in circumstances where the agreement is not directly applicable may be hard to obtain. As a consequence, support for new rules of customary law will have to be found in the agreement and in secondary evidence derived from writers, and perhaps in self-serving official state policy statements.' Charney, *International Agreements and the Development of Customary International Law*, 61 Wash. L. Rev. 971, 990 (1986).

to determine whether the treaty has indeed passed into customary international law.[22]

Does this suggest necessarily that the door is now closed to further creation of customary law regarding matters governed by the Geneva Conventions? I do not believe it does. In confronting this problem, it should be noted that Baxter's approach is supported principally by the judgment in the *North Sea Continental Shelf Cases*. The Court's denial that the practice of parties to a convention has evidentiary weight in the creation of customary law is striking in its brevity and categorical nature:

> [O]ver half the States concerned, whether acting unilaterally or conjointly, were or shortly became parties to the Geneva Convention [on the Continental Shelf], and were therefore presumably...acting actually or potentially in the application of the Convention. From their action no inference could legitimately be drawn as to the existence of a rule of customary international law in favour of the equidistance principle.[23]

It is far from certain that the Court intended, in this context, to refer to universally accepted conventions, especially those of humanitarian character whose object is not so much the reciprocal exchange of rights and obligations among a limited number of states, as the protection of the human rights of individuals.[24] Significantly, the Court did allude briefly to the possibility of transforming widely accepted conventions into general law:

> With respect to the other elements usually regarded as necessary before a conventional rule can be considered to have become a general rule of international law, it might be that, even without the passage of any considerable period of time, a very widespread and representative participation in the convention might suffice of itself, provided it included that of States whose interests were specially affected.[25]

[22] Baxter, above n. 10, at 96. In the same vein, Judge Jennings observed in the *Nicaragua* case that 'there are obvious difficulties about extracting even a scintilla of relevant "practice" ... from the behaviour of those few States which are not parties to the Charter; and the behaviour of all the rest, and the *opinio juris* which it might otherwise evidence, is surely explained by their being bound by the Charter itself.' 1986 ICJ Rep. at 531 (Jennings J. dissenting).

[23] 1969 ICJ Rep. at 43.

[24] See *The Effect of Reservations on the Entry into Force of the American Convention (Arts. 74 and 75)*, Advisory Opinion OC-2/82 of 24 Sept. 1982, Inter-American Court of Human Rights. Ser. A. Judgments and Opinions, No. 2, at 19–22 (1982); *Ireland v. United Kingdom*, 25 Eur. Ct. HR (Ser. A), para. 239 (1978); *Reservations to the Convention on Genocide*, 1951 ICJ Rep. 15, 23 (Advisory Opinion of 28 May); T. Meron, Human Rights Law-Making in the United Nations: A Critique of Instruments and Process 146–7 (1986).

[25] 1969 ICJ Rep. at 42. More recently, the Court stated that '[i]t is of course axiomatic that the material of customary international law is to be looked for primarily in the actual practice and *opinio juris* of States, even though multilateral conventions may have an important role to play in recording and defining rules deriving from custom, or indeed in developing them ... [I]t cannot be denied that the 1982 Convention [United Nations Convention on the Law of the

It is unfortunate that the Court did not elaborate on this statement, which acknowledges that a widespread participation in a multilateral convention is a form of practice. This statement suggests, perhaps, why the 'Baxter paradox' does not present an unsurmountable obstacle to the maturation into customary law of rules stated in the universally ratified Geneva Conventions. It lends additional support to the conclusions of the Court in the *Nicaragua* case concerning the customary law character of the norms embodied in common Articles 1 and 3 of the Geneva Conventions.

Commenting on this statement, Sinclair observed that 'the Court has in terms recognised the possibility that customary international law may be generated by treaty. But it has carefully qualified this recognition by establishing a series of conditions which, in the instant case, it was found had not been fulfilled.'[26] Moreover, in the statement quoted,[27] the Court did not address the question of practice by non-parties. In a trenchant dissenting opinion, Judge Lachs pointedly referred to the practice of States that were 'both parties and not parties to the Convention'[28] (in delimiting the continental shelf on the basis of the equidistance rule.) However, even the Court's statement 'that no inference could legitimately be drawn' from the action of states parties to a convention does not necessarily suggest a priori that such action can *never* be taken into account for the formation of customary international law.

Acts concordant with the treaty obviously are indistinguishable from acts 'in the application of the Convention'. If it could be demonstrated, however, that in acting in a particular way parties to a convention believed and recognized that their duty to conform to a particular norm was required not only by their contractual obligations but by customary or general international law as well (or, in the case of the Geneva

Sea, which has not yet entered into force] is of major importance, having been adopted by an overwhelming majority of States; hence it is clearly the duty of the Court, even independently of the references made to the Convention by the Parties, to consider in what degree any of its relevant provisions are binding upon the Parties [before the Court] as a rule of customary international law.' *Continental Shelf* (Libyan Arab Jamahiriya/Malta), 1985 ICJ Rep. 13, 29–30 (Judgment of 3 June). The Court's explicit defence of the importance of practice and *opinio juris* to the establishment of customary law is not necessarily followed by a genuine effort to identify the relevant practice. Charney thus observes that the Court fails to identify 'the actual evidence of state practice upon which [it] purport[s] to rely'. Charney, above n. 21, at 995.

A recent study notes the diminishing investigation by the ICJ of the existence of practice and of *opinio juris* in the formation of customary law. Haggenmacher, *La Doctrine des deux éléments du droit coutumier dans la pratique de la Cour internationale*, 90 Rev. gén. droit int'l pub. 5, 111–14 (1986). See also Art. 38 of the Vienna Covention on the Law of Treaties; Marek, *Le Problème des sources du droit international dans l'arrêt sur le plateau continental de la mer du Nord*, Revue belge de droit international 44, 57 (1970).

[26] I. Sinclair, The Vienna Convention on the Law of Treaties 23 (2nd edn. 1984) (referring, primarily, to the statement by the Court to be found in 1969 ICJ Rep. at 41–2).

[27] See above text accompanying n. 25.

[28] 1969 ICJ Rep. at 228 (Lachs J. dissenting).

Conventions, by binding and compelling principles of humanity), such an
opinio juris should be given probative weight for the formation of customary law. Such a distinction between an *opinio juris generalis* and an *opinio
obligationis conventionalis* has already been suggested by Professor
Cheng.[29]

Opinio Juris is thus critical for the transformation of treaties into general
law.[30] To be sure, it is difficult to demonstrate an *opinio juris*,[31] but this
poses a problem of proof rather than of principle. The possibility that a
party to the Geneva Conventions may be motivated by the belief that a
particular course of conduct is required not only contractually but by the
underlying principles of humanity is not far fetched.

In any event, the 'real issue', as Sinclair stated in his discussion of
Professor D'Amato's arguments, appears

> to be whether treaties, considered as elements of State practice ... need to be
> accompanied by *opinio juris* in the traditional sense in order to be regarded as
> being expressive of or as generating rules of customary international law; and, if
> so, how this requirement of *opinio juris* can be satisfied.[32]

How does one assess the weight of such *opinio juris*, which is not
accompanied by practice of non-parties *vis-à-vis* non-parties? In the
absence of practice extrinsic to the treaty, non-parties are unlikely to
accept being bound by principles which the parties may consider to be
custom grafted on to the treaty. On the other hand, parties to normative
treaties embodying deeply felt community values have a strong interest in
ensuring concordant behaviour by non-parties and, thus, in promoting
the customary character of the treaty. It is well known that states and nongovernmental organizations invoke provisions of human rights and
humanitarian treaties characterized as customary or as general law
against non-party states guilty of egregious violations of important values
of the international community.

---

[29] Cheng, *Custom: The Future of General State Practice in a Divided World*, in The Structure
and Process of International Law 513, 532–3 (R. Macdonald and D. Johnston eds. 1983). In a
different context (concerning the adoption of a treaty at an international conference), Professor Sohn speaks of *opinio juris* in the sense that the provisions of a convention 'are
generally acceptable'. Sohn, *'Generally Accepted' International Rules*, 61 Wash. L. Rev. 1073,
1078 (1986). He considers a multilateral convention 'not only as a treaty among the parties to
it, but as a record of the consensus of experts as to what the law is or should be'. Sohn,
Unratified Treaties as a Source of Customary International Law, in Realism in Law-Making:
Essays on International Law in Honor of Willem Riphagen 231, 239 (A. Bos and H. Siblesz
eds. 1986). On customary law applicable between parties to agreements, see Bos, *The
Identification of Custom in International Law*, 25 Ger. YB Int'l L. 9, 25 (1982).

[30] 1969 ICJ Rep. at 41.

[31] Professor D'Amato alludes to this difficulty in his article, *The Concept of Human Rights in
International Law*, 82 Colum. L. Rev. 1110, 1141 (1982).

[32] I. Sinclair, above n. 26, at 256.

The effectiveness of this invocation may thus depend on the proof of acquiescence in the norm stated in the treaty by non-parties. The parties, striving to impose the treaty norm on non-parties,[33] may urge a lower burden of proof. Obviously, a tension exists between community interests which seek to impose the treaty norms upon third states and the sovereignty of third states. Public opinion tends to view provisions of widely ratified humanitarian and human rights treaties as authoritative statements of values binding on all states (*erga omnes*), without much concern for legal niceties. However, this question is moot with regard to the Geneva Conventions, because all the potential actors are already parties to them.

In the *Nicaragua* case, the Court held that the Charter does not subsume or supervene customary international law and that 'customary international law continues to exist and to apply, separately from international treaty law, even where the two categories of law have an identical content.'[34] In contrast to the brevity and the high level of abstraction of the principles of the Charter, the provisions of the Geneva Conventions are characterized by their extensive detail. The accretion of a significant corpus of customary law alongside the Conventions is therefore even more hampered, especially when the Conventions are applied only infrequently in the field.[35]

---

[33] On acquiescence, see Baxter, above n. 10, at 73. See also Sohn, *'Generally Accepted' International Rules*, above n. 29, at 1074–5. On a critique of contemporary tendencies to impose conventional rules on non-parties, see Weil, *Towards Relative Normativity in International Law?*, 77 AJIL 413, 439 (1983). Professor Weil expresses the classical view: 'It has never been denied that a provision in a convention, though binding as such only on states parties thereto, could play a role in the formation of a customary rule that would also be binding on third states (provided they had not manifested any objection to it). Even so, it would still be necessary for that provision to have been corroborated by state practice, whether before or after its enactment.' Ibid. at 434. Weil's view, that state conduct is an essential element in the formation of customary rule, may be contrasted with that of Professor Bernhardt, who states that '[i]f ... the community of States unequivocally and without any dissent considers certain acts, which have not been known before, to be illegal, the *opinio juris* might suffice even if no practice could evolve.' Bernhardt, *Customary International Law*, [Instalment] 7 Encyclopedia of Public International Law 65 (R. Bernhardt ed. 1984).

[34] 1986 ICJ Rep. at 96. See also ibid. at 93–5.

[35] Professor Dinstein argues that because Geneva Convention No. IV had not been applied between its adoption in 1949 and the Six Day War (1967), there was no practice that could have been relied upon for the transformation of the Convention's norms into customary law. Dinstein, above n. 20, at 167–8. But see generally Roberts's discussion of the application in practice of the rules of the Convention even by states not acknowledging its applicability. Roberts, *What Is a Military Occupation?*, 55 Brit. YB Int'l L. 249 (1984). Consider also the Convention's application in the case of Falklands (Malvinas), ICRC Annual Report 1982, at 30 (1983); 53 Brit. YB Int'l L. 523–5 (1982). Concerning the controversy between Argentina and the United Kingdom as to whether the islands 'were occupied' by Argentina and as to the 'strict applicability' of Geneva Convention No. IV, see S. Stoyanka-Junod. Protection of the Victims of Armed Conflict Falkland-Malvinas Islands (1982) at 34 (1984).

However, the sparse application of the Conventions by the states directly concerned is balanced, at least up to a point, by other forms of practice. Such forms include the universal acceptance of the Conventions as treaties, ICRC's and Security Council's appeals to parties to conflicts to apply the Geneva Conventions,[36] as well as Security Council resolutions stating that Geneva Convention No. IV applies to the territories occupied by Israel and requesting Israel to abide by its obligations under that Convention.[37] The Secretary-General of the United Nations recently stated that 'even though Israel does not accept the *de jure* applicability of the Fourth Geneva Convention, the *opinio juris* of the world community is that it must be applied.'[38] Yet another type of supporting practice is to be found in the repetition of many of the humanitarian provisions of the Geneva Conventions, including Geneva Convention No. IV, and the Hague Regulations in Additional Protocol I, parts of which are widely recognized as embodying customary law.

The possibility of accretion of a significant corpus of customary law alongside the Conventions should not be discounted altogether, especially with regard to practice not adequately or explicitly regulated by the Conventions, e.g. in situations of prolonged belligerent occupation, where Geneva Convention No. IV leaves some questions unanswered, or internal strife falling short of non-international armed conflict.[39] Such development of customary law in the interstices of a treaty, however, does not suggest that the treaty itself would necessarily become customary law.

Practice by states that modifies the original provisions of the Conventions may also spawn new rules of customary law. But it may prove difficult to distinguish such rules from additional layers of treaty law

---

[36] For ICRC's invocation of Geneva Conventions Nos. III and IV in the Iran-Iraq conflict, see International Committee of the Red Cross, Annual Report 1986 at 66–8 (1987). For ICRC's invocation of Geneva Convention No. IV in the case of territories occupied by Israel, see ibid. at 71–2. ICRC Press Release No. 1559 (13 Jan. 1988) contains ICRC's reaction to the recent expulsions of a number of individuals from those territories.

See also Security Council Resolution 598 which deplored the violation, in the conflict between Iran and Iraq, of international humanitarian law and other laws of armed conflict and urged the release and repatriation of prisoners of war in accordance with Geneva Convention No. III. UN Doc. S/RES/598 (1987).

[37] See e.g. Security Council Resolutions 605, 607, and 608, UN Docs. S/RES/605 (1987), S/RES/607 (1988), S/RES/608 (1988). Other Security Council Resolutions on this subject are listed in UN Doc. S/19443, at 8 (21 Jan. 1988). Regarding the invocation of Geneva Convention No. III by the European Commission of Human Rights, see T. Meron, above n. 24, at 217.

[38] UN Doc. S/19443, above n. 37, at 9 (1988).

[39] Meron, *On the Inadequate Reach of Humanitarian and Human Rights Law and the Need for a New Instrument*, 77 AJIL 589 (1983) (hereinafter cited as *Inadequate Reach*); Meron, *Towards a Humanitarian Declaration on Internal Strife*, 78 AJIL 859 (1984).

created by the parties through interpretation or modification as a result of practice.[40]

In addition, the emergence of customary law in other fields of international law may have an impact on the transformation of the parallel norms of the Geneva Conventions (i.e. those with an identical content) into customary norms. Consider, for instance, the developments in the human rights field that led to the recognition of the prohibitions of the arbitrary taking of life and of torture as norms of customary law.[41] The recognition as customary of norms rooted in international human rights instruments will probably affect, through a kind of osmosis, or application by analogy, the interpretation, and eventually perhaps even the status, of the parallel norms in instruments of international humanitarian law, including the Geneva Conventions. Through a similar process, humanitarian norms will affect human rights. If governments, the scholarly community and the informed public opinion learn to regard as customary a particular human rights norm which has a parallel norm with an identical content in humanitarian law, in the perception of the decision-makers the latter norm will also be regarded as an embodiment of customary rules, even when not supported by significant state practice. Professor Schachter discusses a somewhat similar phenomenon which has occurred in the field of law-making:

> Officials who ... have to ascertain ... law naturally look to the product of the process in which they or their colleagues took part. ... Practical and bureaucratic factors help to increase the use made of the adopted texts. ... The consequences over time are two-fold: (1) the instrument generally accumulates more authority as declaratory of customary law and (2) in cases where the declaratory nature of a particular provision is shown to be contrary to the understanding of the drafters ... the tendency to apply that provision will in time result in custom 'grafted' upon the treaty.[42]

Finally, as suggested by the preceding discussion of the *North Sea Continental Shelf Cases*, observance of the provisions of the Conventions, especially if accompanied by verbal affirmations supporting the binding, even *erga omnes*, character of the humanitarian principles stated in the Conventions, may evince *opinio juris* facilitating the gradual metamorphosis of those conventional norms into customary law.

Both scholarly and judicial sources have shown reluctance to reject conventional norms whose content merits customary law status as can-

---

[40] See Vienna Convention on the Law of Treaties, opened for signature 23 May 1969, Arts. 31 and 41, 1155 UNTS 331, reprinted in 63 AJIL 875 (1969), 8 ILM 679 (1969). See also I. Sinclair, above n. 26, at 138.

[41] See e.g., Restatement, above n. 11, at §702(c)–(d).

[42] Schachter, above n. 11, at 97–8.

didates for that status, or to deprive those norms of customary law character because of contrary practice. This reluctance may reflect the strength of moral claims for the application and observance of the norms in instruments relating to international human rights and humanitarian law,[43] and of other norms which express basic community values and are essential for the preservation of an international public order,[44] as well as the differences in the kinds of evidence of state practice involved.[45] Nevertheless, contrary practice or violations of a norm may be so rampant and sweeping that it becomes unclear whether the 'norm' or the violations represent the true reflection of the policy and practice of states. A distinction should therefore be made between episodic breaches of the rule that do not nullify the rule's legal force, and massive, grave, and persistent violations of the rule, which amount to '"State practice" that nullifies the legal force of [a] right'.[46] In the same vein, an official publication of the US Navy states as follows:

> Occasional violations do not substantially affect the validity of a rule of law, provided routine compliance, observance, and enforcement continue to be the norm. However, repeated violations not responded to by protests, reprisals, or other enforcement actions may, over time, indicate that a particular rule of warfare is no longer regarded by belligerents as valid.[47]

Other norms which are frequently violated, such as the prohibition of torture, concern practices contrary both to national law and the official state policy. Their endurance as legal norms, despite frequent breaches, can also be explained by a deeply felt belief in the norms' importance. Lamenting the continuing incidence of torture, the UN Human Rights Commission's Special Rapporteur on Torture and Other Cruel, Inhuman or Degrading Treatment or Punishment notes that

> allegations of torture have continued to come in; their number does not show a tendency to decrease. ... How can this remarkable discrepancy between legal opinion (*opinio juris*) and practice be explained, a discrepancy which is not unknown in the field of human rights in general but is all the more remarkable

---

[43] See Baxter, above n. 6, at 286.

[44] Schachter, *In Defense of International Rules on the Use of Force*, 53 U. Chi. L. Rev. 113, 131 (1986).

[45] See Schachter, above n. 11, at 334–5. Schachter observes that 'value-judgments are always implicit in the recognition of practice as law'. Ibid. at 96.

[46] Ibid. at 336. Professor Schachter observes that some norms 'are so widely disregarded in practice as a matter of state policy as to be more the norm than the exception'. Ibid.

See also the exchange between Watson and Sohn on the significance of the discrepancy between human rights and the reality of state practice in Watson, *Legal Theory, Efficacy and Validity in the Development of Human Rights Norms in International Law*, 1979 U. Ill. LF 609, 626–35; and Sohn, *The International Law of Human Rights: A Reply to Recent Criticisms*, 9 Hofstra L. Rev. 347, 350–1 (1981).

[47] Department of the Navy, the Commander's Handbook on the Law of Naval Operations NWP 9, at 6.1 (1987).

with respect to torture, since here the practice is never justified by those who are alleged to have practised it but is flatly denied.[48]

As a yardstick for differentiating episodic breaches from breaches which reflect state policy, Professor Schachter proposes assessing the 'intensity and depth of the attitudes of condemnation'[49] by third parties. This criterion emphasizes the reactions of others to a particular breach rather than the statements of the actor state. In the *Nicaragua* case the Court focused on the statements of the actor state:

> The Court does not consider that, for a rule to be established as customary, the corresponding practice must be in absolutely rigorous conformity with the rule. In order to deduce the existence of customary rules, the Court deems it sufficient that the conduct of States should, in general, be consistent with such rules, and that instances of State conduct inconsistent with a given rule should generally have been treated as breaches of that rule, not as indications of the recognition of a new rule. If a State acts in a way prima facie incompatible with a recognized rule, but defends its conduct by appealing to exceptions or justifications contained within the rule itself, then whether or not the State's conduct is in fact justifiable on that basis, the significance of the attitude is to confirm rather than to weaken the rule.[50]

Elsewhere, the Court elaborated on this statement by considering third-party responses to a particular state's claim: 'Reliance by a State on a novel right or an unprecedented exception to the principle might, if shared in principle by other states, tend towards a modification of customary international law.'[51]

The earlier statement by the Court should be understood in light of the latter statement. Statements which states make to justify alleged breaches of international law have considerable weight in assessing the significance of the breach for the continued vitality of the customary norm in question. Account must, however, be taken of the fact that states bent on evading compliance with international law commonly resort to factual or legal exceptions or justifications contained in the rule itself and in the relationship of their particular case or situation to that rule. Obviously, states normally shield themselves with self-serving justifications, calculated to minimize international censure of their course of action. In infrequent situations, a state may want to challenge frontally the existence of a rule of law, but as Professor Charney observes, 'States will rarely, if ever, admit that they have violated customary international law, even in order to change it. Rather, they will argue that their behaviour is consistent with the traditional law, or that the law has already changed.[52] Why should

---

[48] UN Doc. E/CN.4/1988/17, at 23 (1988).   [49] Schachter, above n. 11, at 336.
[50] 1986 ICJ Rep. at 98.   [51] Ibid. at 109.
[52] Charney, *The Power of the Executive Branch of the United States Government to Violate Customary International Law*, 80 AJIL 913, 916 (1986). See also Akehurst, *Custom as a Source of*

states challenge a rule head on, if less provocative conduct would better serve them?[53] Of course, because of its legitimate interest in safeguarding the stability of customary law, the international community tends to view violations as mere episodic breaches which do not directly challenge the binding character of a recognized norm.

If states fail to observe the provisions of the Geneva Conventions in conflicts or resort to numerous reservations[54] having a significant adverse impact on the actual observance of the norms in the Conventions, naturally the claims of the Conventions' provisions to customary law status will be weakened. To illustrate, the fact that, in most cases, states fail either to prosecute or to extradite perpetrators of grave breaches of the Geneva Conventions weakens the claim of the obligations to prosecute or to extradite perpetrators of grave breaches to customary law status. Cumulatively, frequent evasions of the Conventions' norms by states through reliance on the specific circumstances of particular situations (*sui generis* claims) may erode the position of the Conventions as crucial instruments of humanitarian law and as claimants to customary, and *a fortiori* to *jus cogens*, status. Concordant practice is, of course, the best indicator of expectations about binding prescriptions on state behaviour. It must, however, be made clear that the requirement of concordant

---

International Law, 47 Brit. YB Int'l L. 1, 8 (1974–5): '[A]s an alternative to changing customary law by breaking it, States can change it by repeatedly declaring that the old rule no longer exists...'

[53] With some exceptions, e.g. Iran's claim that Iraqi POWs should be treated according to the dictates of the Koran, which claim implies the subordination to the Koran of Geneva Convention No. III (see UN Doc. S/16962, at 38, 42 (1985)), states tend to avoid a frontal challenge to the Conventions, preferring instead to justify their discordant practices on differences between the conflicts presently encountered and those for which these instruments were originally adopted. Aldrich, *Human Rights and Armed Conflict: Conflicting Views*, 67 ASIL PROC. 141, 142 (1973); Roberts, above n. 35, at 279–83.

Professor Henkin has cogently observed that to reduce the 'cost' of violating the law, states will often stress ambiguities about the facts and their proper characterization, as well as uncertainties about the applicable norm. See L. Henkin, How Nations Behave 70 (1968).

The recent resolution on Respect for International Humanitarian Law in Armed Conflicts and Action by the ICRC for Persons Protected by the Geneva Conventions highlighted violations of the Geneva Conventions and 'a disturbing decline in the respect of international humanitarian law' and acknowledged that 'disputes about the legal classification of conflicts too often hinder the implementation of international humanitarian law ...' 25th International Conference of the Red Cross, Doc. P.2/CI, Ann. 1 (1986).

ICRC President Alexandre Hay has recently complained that '[n]ot only are conflicts increasing in number and length, but practices prohibited by international humanitarian law are becoming more and more common ...'. Hay, *Respect for International Humanitarian Law: ICRC Report on its Activities*, Int'l Rev. Red Cross, No. 256, Jan.-Feb. 1987, at 60, 61. See also Tavernier, *La Guerre du Golfe: Quelques Aspects de l'application du droit des conflits armés et du droit humanitaire*, 30 Annuaire français de droit international 43 (1984).

[54] I am addressing here the question of the number and the extent of the reservations actually made rather than the question of whether a particular reservation is compatible with the purpose and object of the Convention or is prohibited. See generally Baxter, above n. 6, at 285; Baxter, above n. 10, at 48–52.

practice must not be interpreted to mean that the practice must be totally uniform. As the *Nicaragua* Court observed in the statement discussed above, it is only required that the conduct of states should, in general, be consistent with such rules.

Violations are, of course, much more visible than practice demonstrating respect for a norm. To balance the greater visibility of violations, it is therefore necessary that any inquiry into international practice should focus on cases of conduct consistent with a norm. The characteristic compliance by states with, for example, Geneva Convention No. III must be taken into account no less than the much more publicized violations of that Convention. Because the Geneva Conventions are meant to apply in exceptional situations only, in which violations abound, it is particularly difficult to quantify cases of conduct concordant with the Conventions. It is considerably easier to take into account practice consistent with human rights instruments which apply to day-to-day life.

The decisive factor is whether or not states observe the Geneva Conventions. As with other widely ratified treaties, if states parties comply with the Geneva Conventions in actual practice, verbally affirm their vital normative value, and accept them in *opinio juris*, both states and tribunals will be reluctant to advance or to accept the argument that the law of Geneva is solely,[55] or even primarily, conventional. Such observance by the parties will eventually lead, in the perception of governments and scholars, to the blurring of the distinction between norms of the Conventions that are already recognized as customary law and other humanitarian provisions of the Conventions that have not yet achieved that status. In the final analysis, movement in this direction depends on whether states realize that, in the long run, bona fide compliance with the Geneva Conventions serves their best interests.

---

[55] Such a position has been asserted by the Supreme Court of Israel with regard to Geneva Convention No. IV. See above n. 20. *Contra Mauritius Transport Case* (Supreme Court of West Berlin) (1967): 'Although the Geneva . . . Convention concerning the protection of Civilians in Wartime was enacted on 12 August 1949, its provisions reflect only what had already been recognized previously by civilized nations. . . .' 60 Int'l L. Rep. 208, 215 (1981).

VIII

The Time Has Come for the United States to Ratify Geneva Protocol I*

At the conclusion of a diplomatic conference convened by Switzerland as depositary of the four Geneva Conventions of 12 August 1949 for the protection of war victims, which met in Geneva in four sessions from 1974 to 1977, two Protocols Additional to the Geneva Conventions (together with the Charter of the United Nations, the most widely ratified treaties) were adopted. The first Protocol concerned international wars;[1] the second addressed civil wars.[2] The U.S. delegation (in which the Department of Defense was strongly represented), under the able leadership of Ambassador George Aldrich, played an important role in the negotiations. The United States signed both Protocols. In the belief that any problems could be corrected by understandings or reservations, it proceeded to negotiate statements of understanding and reservations with its NATO allies.

However, because of fears that Protocol I would legitimize the claims of the Palestine Liberation Organization to prisoner-of-war privileges for its combatants and promote various liberation movements to state or quasi-state status, the Protocol attracted vigorous opposition in the United States and Israel. In a 1987 letter to the Senate, President Reagan censured Protocol I and asked the Senate to give its advice and consent to the ratification of Protocol II alone.[3] Largely because of this perception of Protocol I as proterrorist and also because of military objections by the Joint Chiefs of Staff, the President concluded that the Protocol was

---

* I was consultant to a symposium of the Council on Foreign Relations (Enid Schoettle was the program director and Rita Hauser the chair) on whether the United States should ratify Additional Protocol I, but the views expressed here are my own. I am grateful to my research assistant Audrey Schaus for her help.

[1] Protocol Additional to the Geneva Conventions of 12 August 1949, and Relating to the Protection of Victims of International Armed Conflicts, *opened for signature* Dec. 12, 1977, 1125 UNTS 3, *reprinted in* 16 ILM 1391 (1977) [hereinafter Protocol I].

[2] Protocol Additional to the Geneva Conventions of 12 August 1949, and Relating to the Protection of Victims of Non-International Armed Conflicts, *opened for signature* Dec. 12, 1977, 1125 UNTS 609, *reprinted in* 16 ILM at 1442 [Protocol II].

[3] Letter of Transmittal from President Ronald Reagan, PROTOCOL II ADDITIONAL TO THE 1949 GENEVA CONVENTIONS, AND RELATING TO THE PROTECTION OF VICTIMS OF NONINTERNATIONAL ARMED CONFLICTS, S. TREATY DOC. No. 2, 100th Cong., 1st Sess., at III (1987), *reprinted in* 81 AJIL 910 (1987).

"fundamentally and irreconcilably flawed"[4] and that its weaknesses could not be remedied through reservations.

The decision not to recommend ratification provoked an acrimonious debate on the political, military and legal implications of Protocol I. No action was taken on Protocol II in the Senate; the Protocols' supporters felt, perhaps, that ratifying Protocol II alone would destroy any prospects there might be for Protocol I.

President Clinton's Defense Department is now involved in a review of Protocol I.[5] What does the Protocol achieve? Is it so fundamentally flawed that, as President Reagan asserted, its weaknesses could not be remedied through reservations? What prompted the new review? And what should the U.S. position be?

The principal object of Protocol I was to bring up to date in a single treaty both the 1949 Geneva Conventions for the protection of war victims (Geneva law) and the 1907 Hague Convention (No. IV) on the Laws and Customs of War on Land (Hague law or the law governing means and methods of conducting war). The focus of the Protocol was greater protection for victims of war. The Protocol created a new regime for the protection of medical aircraft; developed rules protecting medical personnel and governing relief efforts for the civilian population; and, in reaction to the Vietnam War, codified norms for recovering the missing

---

[4] Letter of Transmittal from President Ronald Reagan, PROTOCOL II ADDITIONAL TO THE 1949 GENEVA CONVENTIONS, AND RELATING TO THE PROTECTION OF VICTIMS OF NONINTERNATIONAL ARMED CONFLICTS, S. TREATY DOC. No. 2, 100th Cong., 1st Sess., at III, 81 AJIL at 911.

[5] In addition to provisions of Protocol I on liberation movements, privileges of irregular combatants and reprisals, other issues involved in the military review include: (1) which provisions codify existing customary law and which are new law, and whether the latter are militarily acceptable; (2) the problems posed by the codification of the rules on the conduct of hostilities, such as those limiting permissible collateral damage, and whether these problems can be effectively addressed through military manuals, statements of understanding or reservations; (3) whether the ambiguity regarding the application of the Protocol to nuclear warfare (most of the participants in the diplomatic conference had intended to limit it to conventional warfare but did not spell it out in the Protocol's text) might weaken nuclear deterrence, since military experts believe that it would not be possible to conform the use of nuclear weapons to the provisions on proportionality and collateral damage to civilians; and whether this problem can be remedied by an understanding or a reservation (to be sure, the question of the legality of the use of nuclear weapons arises also under the customary law of war, apart from Protocol I); (4) what in practical terms is involved by the apparently increased obligation for armed forces to care for all sick and wounded regardless of the availability of civilian medical facilities; (5) the practical effect of the new regime on the operation of medical aircraft and the implementation problems in light of modern technology; (6) the practicality and military acceptability of the newly revised annex on identification of medical and religious personnel, involving the use of distinctive protective emblems and signals to facilitate identification of medical aircraft, vessels and facilities; and (7) the seriousness of the ambiguity built into several provisions of the Protocol and the possibility of its leading to contradictory, and sometimes extreme, interpretations.

and the dead and disposing of the remains of the dead. It strengthened civil defense and the protection of women and children and elaborated a list of fundamental guarantees and human rights for persons affected by an international armed conflict who are in the power of a party to the conflict and are not otherwise entitled to more favorable treatment. With regard to enforcement, it created an international fact-finding commission to examine violations of the laws of war.

By its definitions of "attacks," "civilian[s]," "military objectives" and proportionality, the Protocol narrowed the parameters of permissible collateral damage to civilians resulting from attacks on military objectives and totally prohibited reprisals against any civilian population even in case of persistent violations by one belligerent of the laws of war protecting civilians.

The Protocol encroached upon two politically sensitive topics. First, in response to pressure from the PLO, South African liberation movements and – more broadly – developing states, the diplomatic conference upgraded to international wars "armed conflicts in which peoples are fighting against colonial domination and alien occupation and against racist régimes in the exercise of their right of self-determination" (Art. 1(4)). Second, the Protocol (Arts. 43–44) departed from customary law, and the law of the 1949 Geneva POW Convention, by conferring POW status, or at least equivalent treatment, on irregular fighters who were not able, because of the military situation (occupation, wars of liberation), to comply with the traditional requirements for combatants and prisoners of war (carrying arms openly, wearing a fixed sign that would make them clearly distinguishable from the civilian population, complying with the laws and customs of war).

Critics argued that the Protocol's humanitarian tilt would thwart quick victories in war and would pose additional dangers to members of the armed forces. They charged that diplomatic compromises had created deliberate ambiguity resulting in the possibility of contradictory interpretations, especially of the rules governing warfare and the protection of irregular combatants. These fears were heightened in response to the experience in Korea and Vietnam, where spurious charges of war crimes were invoked to deny POW protections to members of the U.S. armed forces. Opponents claimed that the more relaxed rules defining privileges of irregular fighters might endanger civilians, who would no longer be clearly distinguishable from combatants. Article 1(4), they argued, introduced political and ideological considerations into what had previously been politically neutral law of war.[6]

---

[6] For a discussion of the background of Article 1(4) and explanation of the ineffectiveness of that article, see George H. Aldrich, *Prospects for United States Ratification of Additional Protocol I to the 1949 Geneva Conventions*, 85 AJIL 1, 4–7 (1991).

OTHER STATES' REACTION TO THE PROTOCOL

When the Reagan administration announced its opposition to Protocol I, relatively few states, and even fewer major military powers, were parties to it. The U.S. decision to stay out and discourage our allies from ratifying the Protocol may have made some sense as long as the United States was not the odd man out. At the same time, the administration tried to identify those provisions of the Protocol that reflect customary law and are therefore binding on the United States and other countries; those provisions that are beneficial and constitute emergent customary law (these categories comprise most of the Protocol's provisions); and finally, those provisions that are neither customary nor beneficial and are therefore unacceptable to the United States.[7] Taking a position somewhat like its policy on the United Nations Convention on the Law of the Sea, the Reagan administration hoped that it could benefit from the Protocol's clearer articulation of customary law and desirable new developments, while rejecting the rest of the package. Interestingly, international reality and a fresh view of U.S. interests have compelled rethinking of the U.S. attitudes on both of these instruments.[8]

Despite the fact that the U.S. policy of discouraging other states from joining the Protocol proved a failure – eventually all the other members of NATO but France and Turkey decided to ratify – our efforts to establish common rules with our allies and create a sort of NATO-based approach were beneficial in one important respect. They produced, on behalf of most of America's allies, a fairly consistent body of interpretive statements and reservations, reflecting some of the U.S. concerns, on both military and political issues. For example, these efforts confirmed the unwritten understanding of most of the conference's participants that the Protocol was inapplicable to nuclear weapons, a narrow interpretation of Article 1(4) on liberation wars, a construction strengthening the requirements for irregular fighters to carry weapons openly in deployment preparatory to attack, the right to resort to reprisals in response to violations of the Protocol's provisions pertaining to the protection of civilians, and so on.

Clearly, the international community has judged the Protocol far less harshly than the Reagan administration did. As of the date of writing, 135 states have ratified the Protocol (making it, already, one of the most widely ratified international treaties), including two permanent members

[7] Theodor Meron, Human Rights and Humanitarian Norms as Customary Law 62–70, 74–78 (1989).

[8] For some U.S. views on the Law of the Sea Convention, see *Law of the Sea Forum: The 1994 Agreement on Implementation of the Seabed Provisions of the Convention on the Law of the Sea*, 88 AJIL 687 (1994).

of the Security Council (China and Russia). Another permanent member, the United Kingdom, announced that it would ratify as soon as the implementing legislation is adopted by Parliament. In addition to most members of NATO, the parties to the Protocol include such major states and military powers as Argentina, Australia, Brazil, Belarus, Canada, Chile, Egypt, Mexico, Nigeria, Sweden, Syria and Ukraine. The number and the quality of the ratifying states enhance the character of the Protocol as an instrument largely declaratory of customary law. In addition, nearly forty states have made declarations recognizing the competence of the International Fact-Finding Commission. Some thirty states have made interpretive statements and reservations. Thus, even NATO members that shared some of the American concerns felt that the weaknesses of the Protocol could be remedied through interpretations or reservations and that the Protocol was therefore not fundamentally flawed.

PROTOCOL I AND THE PRACTICE OF WAR

Almost from its adoption, Protocol I entered the mainstream of humanitarian law concepts, terminology and scholarship. Today discussion of any subject of humanitarian law without recognition of the Protocol is unimaginable. Military manuals of major powers such as Germany are based on the Protocol, and even the U.S. Air Force and Navy commanders' handbooks commonly use its language. The Protocol is frequently invoked in various conflicts by governments, UN rapporteurs, the International Committee of the Red Cross (ICRC) and nongovernmental organizations. As public opinion has become aware of its humanitarian principles, there has been a growing expectation of compliance. The formation of additional layers of customary law in response to the Protocol has clearly begun.

Despite the U.S. attitude, the Protocol had an impact on the conduct of the Persian Gulf war. Although the Pentagon's final report to Congress on the conduct of the Persian Gulf war of April 1992 stated that Protocol I was not in effect during that war because neither the United States nor Iraq was a party, this is true only in the formal sense.[9] As a matter of policy on the conduct of hostilities, America's coalition partners, most of which were parties to the Protocol, followed most of its provisions. To a considerable extent, the United States did so as well because of the need to coordinate rules of engagement within the coalition and because, as the

---

[9] U.S. Dep't of Defense, Conduct of the Persian Gulf War: Final Report to Congress, Pursuant to Title V of the Persian Gulf Conflict Supplemental Authorization and Personnel Benefits Act of 1991, App. O, at O–13 (1992).

Defense Department's report observed, several provisions of the Protocol are "generally regarded as a codification of the customary practice of nations, and therefore [as] binding on all."[10] In response to a memorandum of the ICRC of December 1990, which contained its version of the applicable rules, the Joint Chiefs of Staff prepared and the Department circulated to the ICRC and the coalition partners of the United States the U.S. interpretation and restatement of the applicable rules.[11] One thing was clear: even the greatest superpower could not ignore the Protocol in a multinational war.

PROTOCOL I AND THE CREATION OF CUSTOMARY LAW

What is particularly worrisome about the past U.S. posture is that the United States may already have wasted much of its vast potential for shaping the customary law of war. Ultimately, we may find ourselves bound by rules that may not best serve U.S. national interests. By clearly articulating interpretations, declarations and even reservations as part of the ratification process, the United States, because of its preeminence as a military power, can greatly enhance its influence on the creation of customary law. U.S. statements made in the context of ratification could serve as a model for those states which have not yet ratified the Protocol and, to the extent that the parties to the Protocol do not object to U.S. reservations or statements of understandings, the latter may yet induce a large measure of agreement on the interpretation of the Protocol, even in states that have already become parties.

But there is not much time left. By remaining aloof, the United States may be abdicating its historical leadership in the shaping of the law of war. Occasional dissents from the Protocol might not be clear and blunt enough to keep the country out of the customary law regime being created by the Protocol. A new and clear statement of U.S. interpretations and reservations is necessary. The process of negotiating and consulting with friendly states, which resulted in useful NATO interpretations and reservations, has run its course. Unless the United States ratifies with reservations and interpretations, it will be left with the choice of generalized resistance to the rules it does not acquiesce in or accept. However, as the Protocol is increasingly regarded as a guide by a great number of

---

[10] U.S. Dep't of Defense, Conduct of the Persian Gulf War: Final Report to Congress, Pursuant to Title V of the Persian Gulf Conflict Supplemental Authorization and Personnel Benefits Act of 1991, App. O, at O–13 (1992).

[11] U.S. Dep't of Defense, message (unpublished) (on file with author).

states (even for nonparties it defines the parameters of discussion on means and methods of warfare), generalized resistance would be ineffective. Acquiescence would simply hasten the crystallization as customary law of rules the United States does not regard as beneficial. Future discourse in the United States on Protocol I must therefore weigh the effects of ratification against the effects of nonratification. If the principal military concerns of the United States can be accommodated by qualifying its acceptance of the Protocol, the shaping of the customary law of war would be best served by ratification accompanied by clear interpretations and reservations, such as those already made by Canada and Germany and soon to be made by the United Kingdom.

CHANGED CIRCUMSTANCES

The massive ratification of the Protocol, its centrality in military manuals, its role in the coordination of rules of engagement, and, of course, the beginning of a new administration are among the factors that triggered the U.S. review. An obvious question was how an instrument regarded as fundamentally flawed could be ratified by so many responsible and friendly states. Nevertheless, the review was also facilitated by changed international circumstances.

Past discourse was based on worst-case scenarios derived from Articles 1(4) (on national liberation wars) and 96 (allowing peoples engaged in conflicts listed in Article 1(4) to make unilateral declarations undertaking to apply – and thus bring into force – the Geneva Conventions and the Protocol), and intensified by the specter of the PLO, the African National Congress and countless others both terrorizing civilian populations and successfully claiming combatant and POW privileges. Article 1(4) was an immensely controversial provision, but it reflected both the majority view in Geneva and the then-prevailing United Nations doctrine.

Oliver Wendell Holmes wrote that "[t]he life of the law has not been logic: it has been experience."[12] The scenarios drawn by the Protocol's critics have been proven wrong. No liberation movement has seriously attempted to make the required declaration under Article 96, perhaps because it would have had difficulty accepting and carrying out all the obligations stated in the Protocol[13] and could thus expose its members to

---

[12] OLIVER WENDELL HOLMES, THE COMMON LAW 1 (Boston, Little, Brown 1881).

[13] Aldrich, *supra* note 6, at 7, observes:

If it were feasible to apply the Geneva Conventions and Protocol I to the armed conflicts for which that provision [Art. 1(4)] was designed, compliance with these treaties would bring significant humanitarian benefits. Such application and compliance have not been

war crimes prosecutions. There is no recorded case of combatant and POW privileges being granted to members of such movements as a result of the Protocol. In some cases, American criminal groups have unsuccessfully invoked the Protocol's provisions on liberation movements in U.S. courts. In the future, criminal elements or insurgents facing prosecution or extradition might rely on the Protocol in U.S. courts to plead the protection of Articles 1(4) and 43–44, but they would surely fail, as the courts would take the advice of the executive branch on such matters.

Although the language of Article 1(4) is broad, the legislative history (of course, the Vienna Convention on the Law of Treaties limits resort to legislative history) demonstrates that the diplomatic conference targeted only three specific situations involving the following states: Portugal, because of its African colonies; South Africa, because of apartheid; and Israel, because of the occupied territories. Since the target states naturally refused to ratify, the article has never been applied.

In any event, time has passed Article 1(4) by. Portugal no longer has colonies, apartheid in South Africa has been dismantled, and Israel and the PLO have recognized each other and – despite various setbacks – are moving toward an end to the occupation. Moreover, should hostilities later erupt between Israel's army and the security or police forces of the Palestinian Authority, both parties may have an interest in extending POW privileges to each other. Article 1(4) may still have a certain symbolic and political significance. But in view of its limited scope, the changed circumstances and the improbability of its ever being given effect, could not U.S. concerns be remedied by appropriate interpretations or reservations? Are the U.S. concerns unique?

Such reservations and interpretations would not make the U.S. ratification hollow. Although some reservations could be quite important, it is not expected that reservations or understandings will touch on more than a few provisions of the Protocol.

The ICRC has met one of the U.S. concerns regarding possible abuse of the Protocol by terrorists and irregular combatants; its official commentary interpreted Articles 43–44 as meaning that a liberation movement's armed forces must comply with the international law applicable in armed conflicts at the risk of disqualification. This is a constitutive condition for the recognition of such forces. Noncompliance leads to forfeiture of their members' combatant and POW privileges.[14] Nevertheless, some reservations to or interpretations of Articles 1(4) and 43–44 are inevitable,

---

feasible and seem unlikely to become feasible for a multitude of reasons, both political and practical. In effect, the provision is a dead letter.

[14] COMMENTARY ON THE ADDITIONAL PROTOCOLS OF 8 JUNE 1977 TO THE GENEVA CONVENTION OF 12 August 1949, at 522–25 (Yves Sandoz, Christophe Swinarski & Bruno Zimmermann eds., 1987).

perhaps along the lines of the ICRC's Commentary. Another probable reservation concerns reprisals. Although the idea of reprisals against any civilian population, and thus innocent bystanders, is abhorrent, it is unlikely that the United States would entirely abandon the right to take reprisals in the event of a serious and systematic attack on either its own civilian population or that of Western Europe. A reservation of the right to reprisals in very limited circumstances might be appropriate. Statements of understanding might suffice to deal with any other problems.

Changed circumstances in the United Nations and the elimination of the bipolar characteristics of international relations also enhance the possibility of ratification. The former position of the United States was driven by our Vietnam experience, the paralysis of the Security Council and the perception that the reprisal option must be kept alive. The revitalization of the United Nations and the improvement in U.S. relations with Russia open the possibility for such measures as the operation of the fact-finding machinery under Article 90 of the Protocol; they even make it possible for the Security Council to establish special criminal tribunals to be used as alternative remedies, as in the case of the former Yugoslavia, or, perhaps eventually, for states to establish a treaty-based permanent international criminal court as proposed by the International Law Commission. The explicit preservation of the nuclear option has lost some of its cogency.

The demonization of the Protocol has given way to healthy pragmatism. Thus, although the statute of the Yugoslav Tribunal does not mention the Protocol among the Tribunal's sources of law, in the Security Council U.S. Ambassador Madeleine Albright interpreted those sources as encompassing international humanitarian law that was applicable in the former Yugoslavia, including Protocol I.[15] That construction was important because atrocities committed in Yugoslavia clearly constituted war crimes and grave breaches under the Protocol. The United States regarded as particularly useful the Protocol's provisions on humanitarian relief, which represent a real improvement on the 1949 Geneva Conventions.

THE LAW OF WAR TREATIES AND LEGISLATIVE PRIORITIES

It may have been inevitable that, with the proliferation of tragic armed conflicts around the world, ratification of law of war treaties would be an

---

[15] UN Doc. S/PV. 3217, at 15 (May 25, 1993).

important item on the legislative agenda of the new administration. The Convention on Prohibitions or Restrictions on the Use of Certain Conventional Weapons Which May Be Deemed to Be Excessively Injurious or to Have Indiscriminate Effects (the Conventional Weapons Convention) of 1980, with its three Protocols (Protocol I, on nondetectable fragments; Protocol II, on prohibitions or restrictions on the use of mines, booby traps and other devices; and Protocol III, on prohibitions or restrictions on the use of incendiary weapons),[16] has aroused great interest in Congress as a result of the widespread use of land mines in various conflicts and the countless civilian casualties. The United States has proposed a moratorium on the export of land mines and has been involved in efforts to strengthen the Convention's Protocol II on land mines. On May 12, 1994, the President transmitted this Convention and the first two Protocols to the Senate for its advice and consent.[17] Protocol III, on incendiary weapons, presented some military concerns and was held back for further examination. The Conventional Weapons Convention is thus among the first of several law of war conventions recommended for the Senate's advice and consent by the Clinton administration. The next treaty likely to be recommended for ratification is the 1954 Hague Convention for the Protection of Cultural Property in the Event of Armed Conflict.[18] In 1958 the United States decided not to ratify, but this decision appears to have been reversed, possibly in response to requests from the Senate prompted by the deliberate targeting of cultural property in Yugoslavia.

The ratification of these two treaties would pave the way for a possible decision, at the end of the military review, to recommend the 1977 Protocols for the Senate's advice and consent. The first step, of course, will be the conclusion of the military review. The Protocol certainly is a most complicated instrument, and the list of issues involved is, not surprisingly, so broad and complex that, without political guidance, the review could come out either way. Should the recommendation be favorable and be accepted by the President, it would probably trigger thorough, and perhaps arduous, hearings in both the Foreign Relations Committee and the Armed Services Committee.

---

[16] UN Doc. A/CONF.95/15, Apps. A-D (1980), *opened for signature* Apr. 10, 1981, *reprinted in* 19 ILM 1524 (1980), and S. TREATY Doc. No. 25, 103d Cong., 2d Sess. (1994). *See* Contemporary Practice of the United States Relating to International Law, 88 AJIL 748 (1994).

[17] Letter of Transmittal from President William J. Clinton, S. TREATY Doc. No. 25, *supra* note 16. President Clinton had previously, on November 23, 1993, submitted the Convention on the Prohibition of the Development, Production, Stockpiling and Use of Chemical Weapons to the Senate for advice and consent to ratification. For that Convention, *opened for signature* Jan. 13, 1993, see 32 ILM 800 (1993), S. TREATY Doc. No. 21, 103d Cong., 1st Sess. (1993).

[18] May 14, 1954, 249 UNTS 240.

HUMANITARIANISM AND UNIVERSALITY

Some critics of the Protocol suggest that its rules on warfare tilt toward humanitarianism at the expense of military considerations; that the latter require that wars be ended as quickly as possible by the massive use of force; and that the net effect of complying with the Protocol would be to prolong wars and, over time, increase civilian casualties and the danger to U.S. military personnel. Supporters of the Protocol answer that it strikes a reasonable balance between humanitarian and military considerations and that its application would not prolong wars or increase American casualties.

Obviously, an objective and credible military review is necessary and desirable and, indeed, is a condition for favorable consideration by the President and the Senate. The security of U.S. military personnel must, of course, be a primary concern. But U.S. national interests are not limited to situations in which the United States is militarily involved. In most conflicts there is no direct American military presence, but the United States is usually otherwise involved, through peacekeeping, diplomacy, economic aid, humanitarian relief, and so on. Since the Protocol will contribute, at least in some measure, to the humanization of conflicts, reduction of bloodshed and protection of relief operations, it would serve U.S. national interests by, for example, diminishing pressure for the United States to intervene. A broad interpretation of factors entering into the calculus of U.S. interests is therefore needed. That calculus should take into account all armed conflicts around the world, not only those in which the United States is militarily involved.

The existence of the Protocol is not, in and of itself, a guarantee that it will be respected by belligerent parties. But invocation of the chapter and verse of the Protocol by third states and humanitarian organizations, especially the ICRC, and concerted pressure for compliance with its provisions are clearly preferable to reliance on sometimes-vague and often-disputable principles of customary law. More frequently than not, U.S. interests coincide with those of victims of armed conflicts. As the media relay reports and images of the terrible abuses perpetrated in wars, the United States is forced to consider popular demands for intervention. By contributing to the process of humanizing conflicts, the United States would reduce both internal and external pressure on it to play the world's policeman, a role the nation neither desires nor can afford.

Perhaps the United States could invoke the Protocol, especially its customary parts, even without ratifying it. The credibility of such efforts, however, would be suspect. Parties to armed conflicts cannot be expected to show much sympathy for the invocation of a treaty by a state that considers it unworthy of ratification. U.S. ratification would change this situation completely. The President's statement to the Senate regarding the Conventional Weapons Convention is relevant to Protocol I as well: "by becoming Party, we will encourage the observance by other countries of restrictions on landmines and other weapons that U.S. Armed Forces and those of our allies already observe as a matter of humanity, common sense, and sound military doctrine."[19]

As the preeminent military power, the United States has an interest in clear and universal rules of warfare. By ratifying the Protocol with unambiguous interpretations and reservations, the United States would influence both the universality and the shape of the law of war. Japan is likely to follow the U.S. example and, sooner or later, perhaps even France and such other states as India, Indonesia and Pakistan. Protocol I is undoubtedly a prime humanitarian instrument that may have a significant humanizing influence on warfare. Fostering humanitarian rules is consistent with the ever-present humanistic strand in U.S. foreign policy. Power implies responsibility and invites leadership. By ratifying the Protocol, we would be recognizing the former and accepting the latter. I urge ratification.

---

[19] Letter of Transmittal from President William J. Clinton, *supra* note 17, at IV.

IX

The Case for War Crimes Trials in Yugoslavia

THE NEED TO ASSERT INTERNATIONAL LAW

THE CREDIBILITY of international humanitarian law demands a war crimes tribunal to hold accountable those responsible for gross violations in the former Yugoslavia. Opponents in the bitter ethnic and religious conflict have subjected civilians to summary execution, torture, rape, mass internment, deportation, destruction or confiscation of property and other violations of their rights. Many thousands have died.

A war crimes tribunal, sought by the U.N. Security Council, would be the first since the Nuremberg and Far East trials following World War II. The Security Council's decision, embodied in U.N. Resolution 808, derives its binding authority from the U.N. Charter's Chapter VII provisions regarding threats to peace, breaches of peace and acts of aggression. The Security Council's determination that violations of international humanitarian law constitute a threat to international peace and security and that the establishment of the tribunal would contribute to the restoration and the maintenance of peace is of ground-breaking importance. Considered from a different perspective, the Security Council's decision to establish a war crimes tribunal reflects the failure of the Security Council's primary mission to end the conflict and the atrocities.

Reaffirming the Nuremberg tenets and the principle of accountability should deter those in Yugoslavia and elsewhere who envisage "final solutions" to their conflicts with ethnic and religious minorities. A war crimes tribunal could also educate the general public not to accept egregious violations of human rights and humanitarian norms. Above all, there is a moral imperative to rigorously prosecute the offenders, given the deliberate, systematic and outrageous nature of the violations in the former Yugoslavia.

WAR CRIMES HISTORY

THERE IS NOTHING new, of course, in prosecuting offenders against the laws and customs of war as reflected in national military codes. For centuries military commanders – from Henry V of England, under his famous ordinances of war in 1419, to the American military prosecutions of soldiers involved in the My Lai massacre under the U.S. Code of Military Justice – have enforced such laws against violators. In other cases, states have brought to trial captured prisoners of war for offenses committed against the customary laws of war. Thus both the accused's own state and the captor state have standing to prosecute. Neither system, however, has functioned with any degree of efficiency. Except in the case of a total defeat or subjugation – for example, Germany after World War II – prosecutions of enemy personnel accused of war crimes have been both rare and difficult. National prosecutions have also been rare because of nationalistic, patriotic or propagandistic considerations.

The Versailles Treaty after World War I illustrates the case of a defeated but not wholly occupied state. Germany was obligated to hand over to the allies for trial about 900 persons accused of violating the laws of war. But even a weak and defeated country such as Germany was able to effectively resist compliance. The allies eventually agreed to trials by German national courts of a significantly reduced number of Germans. The sentences were both few and clement. The Versailles model proved to be clearly disappointing.

On the other hand, after the four principal victorious and occupying powers established an international military tribunal (IMT) following World War II, several thousand Nazi war criminals were tried either by national courts under Allied Control Council Law No. 10 or by various states under national decrees. Nuremberg's IMT, before which about 20 major offenders were tried, and the national courts functioned reasonably well; the Allies had supreme authority over Germany and thus could often find and arrest the accused, obtain evidence and make arrangements for extradition.

Despite the revolutionary development of human rights in the U.N. era, no attempts have been made to bring to justice such gross perpetrators of crimes against humanity or genocide as Pol Pot, Idi Amin or Saddam Hussein, perhaps because the atrocities in Cambodia, Uganda and Iraq (against the Kurds) did not occur in the context of international wars. Internal strife and even civil wars are still largely outside the parameters of war crimes and the grave breaches provisions of the Geneva conventions.

The Persian Gulf War, as an international war, provided a classic environment for the vindication of the laws of war so grossly violated by Iraq by its plunder of Kuwait, its barbaric treatment of Kuwait's civilian population, its mistreatment of Kuwaiti and allied prisoners of war and during the sad chapter of the U.S. and other hostages. Although the Security Council had invoked the threat of prosecutions of Iraqi violators of international humanitarian law, the ceasefire resolution did not contain a single word regarding criminal responsibility. Instead, the U.N. resolution promulgated a system of war reparations and established numerous obligations for Iraq in areas ranging from disarmament to boundary demarcation.

This result is not surprising, for the U.N. coalition's war objectives were limited, and there was an obvious tension between negotiating a ceasefire with Saddam Hussein and demanding his arrest and trial as a war criminal. A historic opportunity was missed to breathe new life into the critically important concept of individual criminal responsibility for the laws of war violations. At the very least, the Security Council should have issued a warning that Saddam and other responsible Iraqis would be subject to arrest and prosecution under the grave breaches provisions of the Geneva conventions whenever they set foot abroad.

NORMS OF DUE PROCESS

TO BE CREDIBLE, an ad hoc tribunal for the former Yugoslavia must respect impeccable legality and fairness. For better or worse, the precedent of such a tribunal will be invoked in future situations. The tribunal must comply with the basic norms of due process, including the right of the defendants to counsel, to cross-examine witnesses, to present evidence and, going beyond the procedural guarantees of Nuremberg, to appeal to an appeals court. The defendants' right to participate in their own defense should preclude *in absentia* trials, which are inherently vulnerable to abuse.

The rejection of *in absentia* trials need not, however, lead to the conclusion that nothing should be done. An independent and credible prosecuting authority, acting under the Security Council's mandate, could request arrest warrants from the new tribunal for suspected offenders and call on all states to hand over those persons for trial. Such warrants could clash with the accused's claims of diplomatic or sovereign immunity. Security Council resolutions adopted under Chapter VII must, of course, trump such claims.

Atrocities have been committed by all parties. Fairness and credibility require that the Serbs, although reportedly responsible for most violations, not be the only group prosecuted. Muslims and Croatians who have committed war crimes – or anyone else for that matter – should thus be equally investigated and prosecuted.

The marshaling of evidence strong enough to support convictions in criminal cases will prove difficult, especially as regards senior ranks. The

U.N. Kalshoven Commission of experts charged with providing evidence of violations has negligible resources, consisting of only two lawyers and no investigators of its own. Fortunately Canada and the Physicians for Human Rights provided some investigators, but this is hardly enough. In contrast, the prosecution at Nuremberg employed hundreds of lawyers and investigators.

The Kalshoven interim report states that, while grave breaches have indeed been committed, tangible evidence has yet to be obtained. There is a world of difference between reliable reports on the events and evidence establishing individual guilt. The Kalshoven database contains information on places, dates, times, victims, types of violations and the identity of the militia involved, but rarely does it include the identity of perpetrators. Weaving together the Kalshoven information with data known to U.N. peacekeeping forces would help, but not overcome the underlying weaknesses. Moreover, proof of command responsibility will be very difficult. In many cases, different and at times obscure militias reporting to unknown or little-known authorities have been involved in successive stages of fighting and violations. In several areas there has been not just one, but several, conflicts between different groups.

In the absence of cooperation by those in control of areas where offenses have been committed, and because the International Committee of the Red Cross (ICRC) cannot disclose information incriminating individuals, gathering evidence will remain extremely difficult. If it is not already too late – for evidence might not be preserved much longer – the United Nations and member states must provide the Kalshoven Commission with the necessary resources, and evidence already obtained by other bodies must be fed into the system.

Critics of the Nuremberg trials censured as retroactive the rules of international humanitarian law that formed the basis for the prosecutions. However, the principle of individual responsibility of persons committing or ordering grave breaches of humanitarian law is now generally accepted, as is the list of treaty and customary provisions defining war crimes. In addition, both Nuremberg jurisprudence and the post-Nuremberg international law clearly reject the act of state defense and, except as possibly mitigating circumstances, the defense of superior orders. It is equally evident that the complaint that Nuremberg was a case of victors' justice is irrelevant to the new tribunal.

Although the definition of war crimes is now well developed, the same is not true of the penalties provided for the various crimes. The Geneva conventions define offenses but let the contracting states determine the penal sanctions. Under the conventions' universal jurisdiction system, all offenders already are subject to both the jurisdiction and the system of penalties of any state having custody of the offender. The terms of imprisonment imposed by the tribunal should not exceed the penalties stated in national laws implementing the Geneva conventions, especially those of the former Yugoslavia, with which the accused would be familiar. The accused, therefore, could not persuasively argue that they are being subjected to retroactive penal sanctions.

Warnings of war crimes trials have been unsuccessful deterrents in past wars and may prove no more effective in the case of the former Yugoslavia. The precedent and moral considerations for the establishment of the tribunal require action in any event. Furthermore, several factors may yet strengthen deterrence. First, modern media ensures that all actors in the former Yugoslavia know of the steps being taken to establish the tribunal. Second, the tribunal will probably be established while the war is still being waged. Even the worst war criminals involved in the present conflict know that their countries will eventually want to emerge from isolation and be reintegrated into the international community. Moreover, they themselves will want to travel abroad. Normalization of relations and travel would depend on compliance with warrants of arrest. A successful tribunal for Yugoslavia will enhance deterrence in future cases; failure may doom it.

THE LAW TO BE APPLIED

THE 1907 FOURTH Hague Convention, which codified the principal laws of war on land and provided the normative core for the post-World War II war crimes prosecutions, applies to international wars only. Likewise, the other principal prong of the penal laws of war, the Geneva conventions' and Protocol I's grave breaches provisions, is directed toward international wars. Violations of Common Article 3 of the Geneva conventions, which concerns internal wars, do not constitute grave breaches giving rise to universal criminal jurisdiction. Were any part of the former Yugoslav conflict deemed internal rather than international, the perpetrators of even the worst atrocities could not be prosecuted for grave breaches or war crimes but only for the crime of genocide, which is much more difficult to establish, and for crimes against humanity.[1]

Although the war in the former Yugoslavia has been both internal and international, broad consensus outside the region views the fighting to be an international armed conflict to which the totality of the laws of war is applicable, including, of course, the rules governing war crimes. This

---

[1] This may be of particular importance in Kosovo, which is still seen as an internal affair, should conditions there deteriorate further.

conclusion is shared by the Kalshoven Commission and by the U.N. secretary general. It is entirely possible, however, that should any trials be held, an individual defendant might try to argue that the conflict was internal and that he or she could not be accused of war crimes under international law.

The first international tribunal established by the international community since World War II should apply only those provisions of international law that are clear and generally accepted and establish the individual criminal liability of persons, not just the civil responsibility of the state. The tribunal's charter should be patterned on Nuremberg, supplemented as necessary by the law developed since. The Nuremberg charter listed three classes of offenses: crimes against peace (which are not relevant here), war crimes and crimes against humanity.

Nuremberg's charter defined war crimes as violations of the laws and customs of war by soldiers and civilians. They included murder; ill-treatment or deportation of a civilian population for slave labor or any other purpose; murder or ill-treatment of prisoners of war or persons on the seas; killing of hostages; plunder of public or private property; wanton destruction of cities, towns or villages; and devastation not justified by military necessity. The Nuremberg tribunal decided that these acts had already been recognized as crimes prior to World War II under customary international law, which was codified in the Fourth Hague Convention and the Geneva Prisoners of War Convention of 1929.

The 1949 Geneva conventions further codified war crimes by listing violations of certain fundamental norms as "grave breaches," subject to the universal jurisdiction of each contracting party. The conventions contemplate trials by national courts but do not preclude trials before an international tribunal.

Article 147 of the Fourth Geneva Convention, which is of special importance to the prosecution of crimes committed in Bosnia and Herzegovina, lists as grave breaches willful killing, torture or inhuman treatment, willfully causing great suffering or serious injury to body or health, unlawful deportation or transfer, unlawful confinement, depriving a protected person of the right of a fair and regular trial, the taking of hostages, and extensive destruction and appropriation of property not justified by military necessity and carried out unlawfully and wantonly.

Croatia and Serbia, in the pact concluded on November 27, 1991, and all the parties involved in the Bosnia and Herzegovina conflict, in an accord reached on May 22, 1992, agreed to apply most of the protective provisions of Additional Protocol I, except those concerning grave breaches. Both agreements specified a limited number of applicable articles of the Fourth Geneva Convention, again excluding those listing grave breaches. For the most part, however, the Fourth Geneva Convention concerns customary law and, in many respects, even peremptory norms that cannot be excluded by agreements. The case for applying the grave breaches provisions to the Yugoslav conflict is strengthened by the fact that all states involved have agreed to honor the obligations of the former Yugoslavia under the Geneva conventions. All states have also accepted the "Statement of Principles" approved by the London Conference on Yugoslavia on August 26, 1992, concerning compliance with international humanitarian law and personal responsibility for violations of the conventions.

Crimes against humanity were defined in the Nuremberg charter as murder, extermination, enslavement, deportation and other inhumane acts committed against any civilian population, before or during the war, or persecutions on political, racial or religious grounds. Control Council law No. 10, adopted by the occupying powers as a charter for war crimes trials by their national courts, expanded the list to include rape. A possible option for the Security Council would be to adapt the Nuremberg or Control Council concept of crimes against humanity to the circumstances of Yugoslavia.

The Nuremberg jurisprudence suggested that war crimes, if committed in a widespread, systematic manner on political, racial or religious grounds, may also amount to crimes against humanity. Proof of systematic governmental planning of alleged acts was a necessary element of crimes against humanity. There is no such requirement for war crimes; crimes against humanity are therefore more difficult to establish. The character and systematic nature of some of the atrocities, especially mass murder and ethnic cleansing, make it imperative that appropriate prosecution be based on crimes against humanity and that a precedent be established.

The U.N. Convention on the Prevention or Punishment of the Crime of Genocide defines it to include "killing members of the group," "causing serious bodily or mental harm to members of the group" and "deliberately inflicting on the group conditions of life calculated to bring about its physical destruction in whole or in part." The convention requires proving intent to destroy, in whole or in part, a national, ethnic, racial or religious group as such. The violence in the former Yugoslavia targeted against religious or ethnic groups, especially in cases of mass killing and ethnic cleansing, gives rise to a strong case for genocide.[2] The crime of genocide is not based on a link to war and is thus equally applicable in

---

[2] On March 20, 1993, Bosnia and Herzegovina instituted (civil) proceedings in the International Court of Justice against Serbia and Montenegro for violating the Genocide Convention. On April 8, 1993, the ICJ issued an order calling upon Yugoslavia (Serbia and Montenegro) to "take all measures within its powers to prevent commission of the crime of genocide" and to ensure that any armed units, organizations and persons that may be subject to its control, direction or influence do not commit any acts of genocide.

times of peace. It is not necessary to demonstrate that the perpetrator was acting on behalf of a state.

In its advisory opinion of May 28, 1951, the International Court of Justice stated that the principles underlying the Genocide Convention were "recognized as binding on states even without any conventional obligation." The former Yugoslavia is in fact a party to the Genocide Convention, but the convention's norms applicability can in any case be derived from its customary or peremptory law character. The invocation of the crime of genocide by the international penal tribunal would have importance transcending the case of the former Yugoslavia. Because genocide is not limited to international wars, prosecuting this crime could become a significant deterrent to future atrocities.

DO THE VIOLATIONS FIT THE LAW?

SUMMARY EXECUTIONS, TORTURE, arbitrary mass internment, deportation and displacement, taking of hostages, inhuman treatment of prisoners and destruction or confiscation of private property not justified by military necessity would all be covered by war crimes under customary international law and by the grave breaches provisions of the Geneva conventions. When committed on a mass scale, such violations would also give rise to charges of crimes against humanity and of genocide, provided that the Genocide Convention's requirements are met, and should be prosecuted as such.

Under the weight of the horrifying reports of abuse against women, readiness to clarify the status of rape as a crime under international law has rapidly formed. Despite the fact that rape is not listed among the grave breaches of the Fourth Geneva Convention or Additional Protocol I, it is explicitly prohibited by both. The ICRC and the U.S. government have thus stated that rape can amount to a grave breach of the convention and to a war crime under customary law. A recent ICRC aide-mémoire discussing the systematic abuses committed against the civilian population in Bosnia and Herzegovina stated that the grave breach of "willfully causing great suffering or serious injury to body or health" obviously covers rape. There is no reason why rape should not be seen as torture or inhuman treatment under the Geneva conventions as well. Because of the mass and systematic practice of rape as an instrument of ethnic cleansing, it can also be prosecuted as a crime against humanity.[3]

---

[3] The draft charters of the tribunal proposed by the United States, Italy and the Organization of the Islamic Conference, as well as the Statute of the International Tribunal proposed by the U.N. secretary general on May 3, 1993, consider rape a crime against humanity.

Ethnic cleansing consists of harassment, discrimination, beatings, torture, summary executions, expulsions, forced crossing of the lines between combatants, intimidation, destruction of secular and religious property, mass and systematic rape, arbitrary arrests and executions, deliberate military attacks on civilians and civilian property, uses of siege and cutting off essential supplies destined for civilian populations. Many of these methods, considered in isolation, constitute a war crime or a grave breach. Considered as a cluster of violations, these practices also constitute crimes against humanity and perhaps also crimes under the Genocide Convention.

THE NECESSITY AND UTILITY OF A TRIBUNAL

THE INTERNATIONAL COMMUNITY'S response to alleged war crimes in the former Yugoslavia must include the establishment by the Security Council of an ad hoc international criminal tribunal. The risks and difficulties of establishing such a tribunal require that the international community be cautious to avoid unrealistic expectations.

Despite its desirability, it is probable that the tribunal will not be very effective. This stark assessment is based on several considerations. First, as the situation now stands, there is insufficient evidence for prosecutions to begin. A major source for gathering evidence thus far has been nongovernmental organizations (NGOs), which do not always have expertise in marshaling evidence for criminal proceedings. In fact, the information normally gathered by NGOs and the evidence necessary to secure a criminal conviction are significantly different. The Kalshoven Commission has tried to gather information but has been frustrated by a lack of funding and personnel. NGOs, the Kalshoven Commission and other U.N. organizations, the European Community and the Conference on Security and Cooperation in Europe are all handicapped by the fact that the rules of evidence that will be applied by the future tribunal have yet to be established. Further problems will arise because, without the cooperation of the authorities, physical evidence cannot be properly preserved.

A second complication relates to the issue of custody. It is recognized that persuading states and authorities to carry out arrest warrants will be difficult and compliance will be negligible unless compelled by the international community. Further, in contrast to Nuremberg, the ad hoc tribunal for the former Yugoslavia will probably not enjoy the cooperation of the authorities controlling the territory in which the crimes were committed. Also, in contrast to the German practices in World War II, there is not likely to be a paper trail clearly linking the perpetrators to the crimes. Furthermore, the effectiveness of deterrence and the prospects of prosecutions are weakened by the need to negotiate with alleged perpetrators who may insist on assurances of immunity as part of a future agreement. If more of Bosnia and Herzegovina falls into Serbian hands, the international community's will to vindicate international law will be severely tested, especially since continued Russian cooperation in the Security Council remains uncertain.

Despite these obstacles, the establishment of an ad hoc tribunal is a laudable and necessary goal. The Security Council has already established the Kalshoven Commission to gather facts. By U.N. Resolution 808 the Council decided in principle on the establishment of the tribunal and requested the U.N. secretary general to submit proposals for implementation. Accordingly, there are already fairly high expectations in the international community in this regard. Abandoning the tribunal now would have a negative impact on the behavior of the parties to the conflict as well as adverse repercussions on general principles. On the ground, those committing war crimes would infer that regardless of their past or future violations they will not be held criminally accountable by the international community. As a matter of principle, abandoning the ad hoc tribunal would erode the values of Nuremberg. Additionally, it is important to try individuals responsible for crimes if there is to be any real hope of defusing ethnic tensions in this region. Blame should not rest on an entire nation but should be assigned to individual perpetrators of crimes and the responsible leaders. Confirmation of the principle of accountability might also discourage those in the former Yugoslavia and elsewhere who envisage "final solutions" to resolve conflicts within their countries, and would serve to promote justice and the effectiveness of international law.

Given the desirability of establishing an ad hoc tribunal, serious efforts are necessary to reduce the risks involved. There should be an energetic collection of information and evidence by both the international community and by states acting separately. Specifically, the budget and staff of the Kalshoven Commission should be drastically augmented to achieve this goal, and the prosecutorial arm of the future tribunal should be given all the required resources. Acting under Chapter VII, the Security Council could specify a system of measures requiring states to cooperate with the enforcement of arrest warrants. It should request that those involved in the conflict arrest and hand over for trial any of the accused whose arrest is sought by the tribunal and that all claims of immunity be denied. The offenders would be placed on an international "most wanted" list and would be subject to arrest the moment they enter a foreign country. Further, the international community must condition the resumption of normal relations with the states concerned on the handing over of suspects for trial before the tribunal. Finally, sanctions must be continued at least partially until those countries concerned comply with warrants of arrest. The Security Council should require other states, under Articles 48 and 49 of the U.N. Charter, to provide all necessary assistance to the tribunal.

States have been reluctant to exercise the universal jurisdiction granted them by the 1949 Geneva conventions in large part because of the perceived political price of prosecution. It is possible that the added factor of a Security Council demand for cooperation could provide the impetus needed to prosecute these crimes in national tribunals. This would serve to link the process in national tribunals to the continued development and revitalization of humanitarian law as a result of the work of the international tribunal.

The establishment of an ad hoc tribunal should not stand alone, however, as a sole or adequate solution. The world has failed to prosecute those responsible for egregious violations of international humanitarian law and human rights in Uganda, Iraq and Cambodia. To avoid charges of Eurocentrism this ad hoc tribunal for the former Yugoslavia should be a step toward the creation of a permanent criminal tribunal with general jurisdiction. The drafting of a treaty on a permanent tribunal, on which work has begun by the U.N. International Law Commission, should be expedited, providing an opportunity to supplement the substantive development of international law by an institutional process.

Though the risks attendant upon an ad hoc tribunal are substantial, they are outweighed by the detrimental effects that would result from abandoning this prospect. The Security Council and the international community must now accept the challenge and create the precedent for a more rigorous enforcement of humanitarian law. This step does not diminish the primary task of the Security Council, thus far unrealized, to bring about a conclusion of the conflict and to diminish the level of violence and atrocities while the conflict endures.

X

From Nuremberg to The Hague*

I am grateful to John Norton Moore and Robinson O. Everett for inviting me to this important conference on Nuremberg and the Rule of Law: A Fifty-Year Verdict. Both the establishment of the Nuremberg Tribunals and of the ad hoc Tribunals for the Former Yugoslavia and Rwanda were of major, perhaps even monumental importance for the establishment of the rule of law in the international community. My task as a commentator has been made easy by the comprehensive and thoughtful paper of my friend Graham Blewitt.

The time could not be more suitable for such a conference, and especially for some reflections on ad hoc Tribunals half a century after Nuremberg. The subject is vast and I have selected a few themes as a focus for my remarks comparing the two ad hoc Tribunals established by the Security Council to Nuremberg.

We often describe the ad hoc Tribunals as the first international criminal tribunals since Nuremberg. The institutional settings are quite different, however. Nuremberg was the first multinational criminal tribunal. I hesitate to repeat the commonly used term "victors' court" because this would imply an arbitrary, perhaps unjust tribunal. Yet, despite certain shortcomings of due process rules of Nuremberg, which I shall mention, Nuremberg was neither arbitrary nor unjust. It tempered the Charter's harsh rules to protect the accused, it assessed evidence according to accepted and fair legal standards, and was even ready to acquit outright some defendants. Although *tu quoque* arguments were not addressed directly, they were important as the underpinnings of the proceedings. Because of them, some offences were not prosecuted (e.g., the bombing of Coventry) and some charges were rejected on the ground that similar practices of the Allies demonstrated that certain norms did not harden into clear prohibitory rules (Doenitz, von Raeder, and unrestricted submarine warfare).

That victors sat in judgment did not corrupt the essential fairness of the proceedings. Some German critics of Nuremberg acknowledged that

* Address presented 17 November 1995 during "Nuremberg and the Rule of Law: A Fifty-Year Verdict," a Conference co-sponsored by The Center for National Security Law, University of Virginia, The Center of Law, Ethics and National Security, Duke University School of Law, and The Center for Law and Military Operations, The Judge Advocate General's School, United States Army. The Conference was held in the Decker Auditorium, The Judge Advocate General's School, United States Army, Charlottesville, Virginia, November 17–18, 1995.

defendants before that Tribunal enjoyed more due process protections than they would have before occupation courts and other courts of the Allies. While rejecting the ex post facto arguments advanced by the defence against: charges of aggressive war; conspiracy to wage it; crimes against humanity; and organized criminality, the Tribunal mitigated the severity of the controversial provisions on criminality of belonging to certain organizations, so as to criminalize only the voluntary joining of such organizations with knowledge. The Tribunal mitigated the Charter's arguably novel provisions on conspiracy to wage aggressive war by limiting liability to those leaders directly involved in the formulation or implementation of a plan to wage the war of aggression. It liberally allowed the defendants to raise a superior orders defence in mitigation of punishment.

This is not to excuse due process defects, including a certain lack of equality under the Nuremberg procedures between prosecution and defence. For American lawyers it is particularly difficult to comprehend that witnesses and defendants could and sometimes were questioned by the judges; that there was no specific recognition in the Charter of the presumption of innocence and no discussion of burden of proof; that defendants were not allowed an opening statement; that trials *in absentia* were permitted; that the judgments could not be appealed to higher judicial instances; and that defendants could not challenge the Tribunal. We should, however, remember that the Charter and the procedure of the Tribunal reflected a compromise which reflected civil law traditions that recognize, for example, *in absentia* judgments.

The two ad hoc Tribunals are the first truly international criminal courts, having been established by the United Nations Security Council, and also through the approval of the budget and the election of the judges by the most representative organ of the United Nations, the General Assembly.

The statutes of the ad hoc Tribunals are an epitome of the most advanced United Nations human rights standards. The statutes, the judges, and the prosecution are extremely sensitive to due process rights of the accused.

There are obvious differences between Nuremberg and the new Tribunals. In Germany, the Allies had full police powers, almost sovereign authority, and most defendants were to be found within the territories controlled by the Allies. The ad hoc Tribunals only have the still largely untested powers delegated from Chapter VII of the United Nations Charter. Despite the potential penalties for states and authorities for refusing to cooperate with the Tribunals, that cooperation has not been forthcoming in important cases. Persuading states and authorities to carry out arrest warrants has proved extremely difficult, just as the readiness of the international community to compel compliance has been disappointing.

In Nuremberg, the Allies had the practically unlimited resources of the victorious states. The Hague tries to make ends meet with ridiculously limited means.

In Nuremberg, we had the luxury of a paper trail clearly linking the perpetrators to the crimes. At The Hague, there is no paper link and often no access to the scene of crimes.

Both Nuremberg and The Hague are largely the result of United States initiative and support. This is well known as regards The Hague, but the discussions leading to Nuremberg may require special mention. The British initially were hostile to trials, favoring, as the oral history of Herbert Wechsler suggests, an execution list to be carried out on identification. In Yalta, in February 1945, Stalin is supposed to have mentioned the need to kill some 50,000 Nazis. The Morgenthau Plan proposed a sort of "scorched earth" policy for postwar Germany which would have been accompanied by the identification and shooting of major war criminals. It was not until Potsdam and Truman in July and August 1945, that the agreement in London on the Nuremberg Charter was essentially reached and the United States historical respect for due process reasserted itself.

The alternative to Nuremberg could well have been a blood bath, in which populations long victim to Nazi atrocities would have resorted to lynching, summary executions, and massacres of Germans. The Allies' intentions to render justice through courts and the Tribunals prevented such acts.

I mention this aspect of Nuremberg to address the continuing debate about the tension between the achievement of peace and the rendering of justice in the Yugoslav context. Were it not for the existence of the two Tribunals, not only would the inclination to individual and collective vengeance, private or unofficial violence, be even stronger, but future reconciliation would be impeded because blame would rest on entire peoples instead of being assigned to individual perpetrators of crimes and responsible leaders.

Tension between justice and peace will become more apparent as the negotiations advance. Short-sighted diplomatic goals should not obscure what closing of the Tribunals would mean to prospects of reconciliation and stability of international law.

The scale of atrocities, unthinkable in Nuremberg, terrible in Yugoslavia and Rwanda, make the very idea of immunity or pardon difficult to contemplate.

The Hague was established to put an end to the crimes which were being committed, presumably through deterrence, to vindicate justice, and to contribute to the restoration and maintenance of peace. Nuremberg was established to bring Nazi war criminals to justice. Both The Hague and Nuremberg had additional normative goals, but I would like to focus for a moment on the problem of deterrence.

During the Second World War, especially through the highly publicized and broadcast Moscow Declaration of 1943, severe warnings of punishment of those committing atrocities were issued and widely publicized. Like the warnings issued by the Security Council with regard to crimes committed in the former Yugoslavia, there is no empirical evidence of effective deterrence in either case. Why have we failed?

Deterrence is often ineffective to prevent crimes, even in nation states with their law enforcement apparatus. The effect of deterrence on the international plane is further reduced by such factors as religious hatred, xenophobia, fanatic patriotism, discipline, superior orders, expectations of victory, and, if need be, of martyrdom.

But I do not believe that the failure of deterrence is inevitable. It is because prosecutions for war crimes on both national and international planes are so exceptional that criminals do not believe that they are likely to be prosecuted and punished. Were war crime trials made a consistent reality, deterrence would be taken more seriously. Instead of despairing over the prospects of deterrence, the international community should enhance the probability of punishment by encouraging prosecutions before the national courts, especially of third states, by making ad hoc Tribunals effective, and by establishing a vigorous, standing international criminal court.

Although punishment was the primary articulated justification for Nuremberg, a less obvious, but nonetheless important, goal was to attain respect for international law, to give a new vitality to that law, and to signal to the German people that the rule of law had returned. For the very first time, international law was applied to war criminals in actual cases leading to punishment, even capital. The principle of individual criminal responsibility was vindicated. For the first time the diffuse body of customary law coalesced in a multinational context into criminal law applied in a real Tribunal to defendants in the dock.

It is in the context of the significance of Nuremberg and The Hague for the development of international law that I turn to for a brief discussion of their subject matter jurisdictions. It is here, in the confirmation and the development of international humanitarian law and its essentially customary character through the Charter, statutes, and the case law, that these Tribunals made a historic contribution to the rule of law. In addition to restating war crimes, the Nuremberg Charter attempted to define, for the first time, crimes against humanity and crimes against peace. The former were unfortunately limited by the linkage with other crimes within the jurisdiction of the Tribunal, thus effectively reducing them to wartime atrocities.

The statutes of the ad hoc Tribunals represent a tremendous advance over the Charter of Nuremberg. First, grave breaches of the Geneva Conventions and the crime of genocide have been given the central place. Crimes against humanity have been recognized for noninternational armed conflicts (not only for international wars) in the Yugoslavia Statute and arguably even for peacetime in the Rwanda Statute. Thus, the trend suggested by *Control Council Law Number 10* is being followed. Rape has been criminalized as a crime against humanity. Most importantly, by recognizing the criminality of violations of common Article 3 and of Additional Protocol II to the Geneva Conventions, the Statute for Rwanda constitutes an extremely positive statement of international humanitarian law with regard to internal atrocities.

In Nuremberg and, despite progress since then, also at The Hague, the defence unsuccessfully raised ex post facto challenges with respect to subject-matter jurisdiction. At The Hague these challenges have now been resolved by the Appeals Chamber in the Tadić case. But they are likely to reappear in subsequent proceedings and other cases. Both the prosecution and the Tribunal should approach this matter with prudence. Whether justice has been rendered will, in the long run, be decided in the courts of public opinion and in the halls of academia.

On the other hand, are we not witnessing a certain erosion of Nuremberg's concept of crimes against peace? These crimes had a considerable foundation in normative statements prohibiting aggressive war as national policy and defining aggressive war as a crime. After World War I, serious consideration was given to prosecuting Kaiser Wilhelm.

In a recent statement on the proposed international criminal court, the United States expressed many caveats about the crime of aggression as a crime for which responsibility attaches to individuals. It described aggression as essentially a crime of states, which is ill-defined, and liable to be politicized. The crime of aggression, despite its recognition in ILC draft codes, was not invoked by the Security Council even in such an obvious case as Iraq's invasion of Kuwait and it is seldom invoked in international practice. Yet, it was the United States, and especially Justice Jackson, who insisted on criminalizing war of aggression in the Nuremberg Charter and subsequent proceedings, clearly viewing this crime as one for which responsibility attaches to individuals.

Let me conclude. Under the pressure of atrocities in the Former Yugoslavia and Rwanda we have seen a rapid adjustment of law, process, and institutions. The moral importance of attaching guilt to individuals has been reaffirmed. The establishment of a permanent criminal court has been given a tremendous impetus. Is the cycle of impunity slowly closing?

The possible fear by states that international Tribunals might preempt national prosecutions also may have the beneficial effect of spurring prosecutions before national courts for serious violations of humanitarian law. No matter how many cases the ad hoc Tribunals try, their very existence sends a powerful message supporting the paramountcy of international law even for the most egregious violators and reaffirming the rule of law.

XI

Rape as a Crime Under International Humanitarian Law

It is a pity that calamitous circumstances are needed to shock the public conscience into focusing on important, but neglected, areas of law, process and institutions. The more offensive the occurrence, the greater the pressure for rapid adjustment. Nazi atrocities, for example, led to the establishment of the Nuremberg Tribunal;[1] the evolution of the concepts of crimes against peace, crimes against humanity and the crime of genocide; the shaping of the fourth Geneva Convention;[2] and the birth of the human rights movement. The starvation of Somali children prompted the Security Council to apply chapter VII of the UN Charter to an essentially internal situation, bringing about a revolutionary change in our conception of the authority of the United Nations to enforce peace in such situations. There is nothing new in atrocities or starvation. What is new is the role of the media. Instant reporting from the field has resulted in rapid sensitization of public opinion, greatly reducing the time lapse between the perpetration of such tragedies and responses to them.

It took the repeated and massive atrocities in former Yugoslavia, especially in Bosnia-Hercegovina, to persuade the Security Council that the commission of those atrocities constitutes a threat to international peace, and that the creation of an ad hoc international criminal tribunal would contribute to the restoration of peace. The Security Council therefore decided to establish such a tribunal under chapter VII (Resolutions 808 and 827).[3] For the first time since the founding of the United Nations, the Security Council has become, at least for the moment,[4] a major force for ensuring respect for international humanitarian law.

---

[1] *See* Agreement for the Prosecution and Punishment of the Major War Criminals of the European Axis, Aug. 8, 1945, 59 Stat. 1544, 82 UNTS 279 [London Agreement].

[2] Convention Relative to the Protection of Civilian Persons in Time of War, Aug. 12, 1949, 6 UST 3516, 75 UNTS 287 [Geneva Convention No. IV].

[3] SC Res. 808 (Feb. 22, 1993); SC Res. 827 (May 25, 1993). For a discussion of the prospects for and difficulties concerning the tribunal, see Theodor Meron, *The Case for War Crimes Trials in Yugoslavia*, FOREIGN AFF., Summer 1993, at 122. There has been a broad consensus outside Yugoslavia to consider the conflicts there as international.

[4] The continued cooperation of Russia with regard to the conflict in former Yugoslavia is still uncertain.

Today, in contrast to the past, the rapid dissemination of knowledge about the continuing abuses combined with the public's broader sensitivity to human rights to strengthen political will and make some kind of action a moral imperative. Because the international community has failed in the central task of ending the bloodshed and atrocities, the establishment of the tribunal has become the preferred means to promote justice and effectiveness of international law.[5] This editorial considers only one example of the egregious violations of human dignity in former Yugoslavia – rape.

That the practice of rape has been deliberate, massive and egregious, particularly in Bosnia-Hercegovina, is amply demonstrated in reports of the United Nations, the European Community, the Conference on Security and Cooperation in Europe and various nongovernmental organizations. The special rapporteur appointed by the UN Commission on Human Rights, Tadeusz Mazowiecki, highlighted the role of rape both as an attack on the individual victim and as a method of "ethnic cleansing" "intended to humiliate, shame, degrade and terrify the entire ethnic group."[6] Indescribable abuse of thousands of women in the territory of former Yugoslavia was needed to shock the international community into rethinking the prohibition of rape as a crime under the laws of war.[7] Important as the decision to establish the tribunal is, institutional process must work in tandem with substantive development of international law. What, then, is the current status of rape as a crime under international humanitarian law?

Rape by soldiers has of course been prohibited by the law of war for centuries, and violators have been subjected to capital punishment under

---

[5] In the statute of the international tribunal prepared by the UN Secretary-General and submitted to the Security Council in his Report pursuant to paragraph 2 of Security Council resolution 808 (1993), the Secretary-General proposed that the *ratione materiae* competence of the tribunal encompass grave breaches of the Geneva Conventions, violations of the laws and customs of war, genocide and crimes against humanity. UN Doc. S/25704, Annex, Arts. 2–5 (1993). In selecting these particular categories of crimes, the Secretary-General was guided by this consideration: "the application of the principle *nullum crimen sine lege* requires that the international tribunal should apply rules of international humanitarian law so that the problem of adherence of some but not all States to specific conventions does not arise." UN Doc. S/25704, *supra*, at 9, para. 34. The above categories of crimes constituted "beyond doubt ... part of international customary law ... applicable in armed conflict." *Id.*, para. 35.

[6] Tadeusz Mazowiecki, Report on the situation of human rights in the territory of the former Yugoslavia, UN Doc. A/48/92–S/25341, Annex, at 20, 57 (1993).

[7] There has already been considerable recognition that custodial rape, or rape in circumstances for which a government is liable under the law of state responsibility, violates the prohibitions of torture or inhuman treatment in international human rights. The reports of Peter Kooijmans, special rapporteur of the UN Commission on Human Rights, have greatly contributed to this development. *See also* European Commission of Human Rights, Cyprus v. Turkey, Applications Nos. 6780/74 and 6950/75 (1976); Andrew Byrnes, *The Committee against Torture, in* THE UNITED NATIONS AND HUMAN RIGHTS 509, 519 & n. 38 (Philip Alston ed., 1992).

national military codes, such as those of Richard II (1385) and Henry V (1419).[8] Of more immediate influence on the modern law of war was the prohibition of rape as a capital crime by the Lieber Instructions (1863).[9] Indeed, rape committed on an individual soldier's initiative has frequently been prosecuted in national courts. In many cases, however, rape has been given license, either as an encouragement for soldiers or as an instrument of policy.[10] Nazi and Japanese practices of forced prostitution and rape on a large scale are among the egregious examples of such policies.[11]

Under a broad construction, Article 46 of the Hague Regulations can be considered to cover rape,[12] but in practice it has seldom been so interpreted. Rape was neither mentioned in the Nuremberg Charter nor prosecuted in Nuremberg as a war crime under customary international law.[13] But it was prosecuted in Tokyo as a war crime.[14]

Another seed for future normative development was sown in Control Council Law No. 10,[15] adopted by the four occupying powers in Germany as a charter for war crimes trials by their own courts in Germany. It

---

[8] THEODOR MERON, HENRY'S WARS AND SHAKESPEARE'S LAWS, chs. 6, 8 (1993).

[9] Francis Lieber, Instructions for the Government of Armies of the United States in the Field, Art. 44, originally published as U.S. WAR DEPARTMENT, ADJUSTANT GENERAL'S OFFICE, GENERAL ORDERS No. 100 (Apr. 24, 1863), *reprinted in* THE LAWS OF ARMED CONFLICTS 3 (Dietrich Schindler & Jiří Toman eds., 3d rev. ed. 1988).

[10] MERON, *supra* note 8, ch. 6; *see also* Theodor Meron, *Common Rights of Mankind in Gentili, Grotius and Suárez*, 85 AJIL 110, 115–16 (1991).

[11] For another example, see Walter Kälin, Report on the Situation of Human Rights in Kuwait under Iraqi Occupation, UN Doc. E/CN.4/1992/26, at 47–48.

[12] "Family honour and rights, the lives of persons, and private property, as well as religious convictions and practice must be respected." Convention Respecting the Laws and Customs of War on Land, with Annex of Regulations, Oct. 18, 1907, 36 Stat. 2277, 1 Bevans 631 [Hague Convention No. IV].

[13] In some cases, enforced prostitution was prosecuted in national courts outside Germany. 15 UNITED NATIONS WAR CRIMES COMMISSION, LAW REPORTS OF TRIALS OF WAR CRIMINALS 121 (1949). A Netherlands court in Batavia, for example, found some Japanese persons responsible for forced prostitution guilty of violating the laws and usages of war. PHILIP R. PICCIGALLO, THE JAPANESE ON TRIAL 179–80 (1979).

[14] Charter of the International Military Tribunal for the Far East, Jan. 19, 1946, *amended* Apr. 26, 1946, TIAS No. 1589, 4 Bevans 20. The International Military Tribunal in Tokyo found some Japanese military and civilian officials guilty of war crimes, including rape, because they failed to carry out their duty to ensure that their subordinates complied with international law. *See* JOHN ALAN APPLEMAN, MILITARY TRIBUNALS AND INTERNATIONAL CRIMES 259 (1971). 2 THE TOKYO JUDGMENT: THE INTERNATIONAL MILITARY TRIBUNAL FOR THE FAR EAST 965, 971–72, 988–89 (B. V. A. Röling & C. F. Ruter eds., 1977); 1 *id.* at 385; Gordon Ireland, *Uncommon Law in Martial Tokyo, in* 4 WORLD AFF. Y.B. 54, 61 & n. 14 (1950). Regarding the case of Admiral Toyoda, who was charged with violating laws and customs of war by tolerating various abuses, including rape (he was acquitted of all charges), see William H. Parks, *Command Responsibility for War Crimes*, MIL. L. REV., Fall 1973, at 1, 69–73.

[15] CONTROL COUNCIL FOR GERMANY, OFFICIAL GAZETTE, Jan. 31, 1946, at 50, *reprinted in* NAVAL WAR COLLEGE, DOCUMENTS ON PRISONERS OF WAR 304 (International Law Studies vol. 60, Howard S. Levie ed., 1979).

expanded the list of crimes against humanity found in the Nuremberg Charter to include rape. Nevertheless, although both the fourth Geneva Convention[16] and the Additional Protocols[17] explicitly and categorically prohibit rape, these instruments did not follow the precedent of Control Council Law No. 10 and do not list rape among the grave breaches subject to universal jurisdiction.[18]

It is time for a change. Indeed, under the weight of the events in former Yugoslavia, the hesitation to recognize that rape can be a war crime[19] or a grave breach has already begun to dissipate. The International Committee of the Red Cross (ICRC) and various states aided this development by adopting a broad construction of existing law. The ICRC declared that the grave breach of "wilfully causing great suffering or serious injury to body or health" (Article 147 of the fourth Geneva Convention) covers rape.[20] If so, surely rape – in certain circumstances – can also rise to the level of such other grave breaches as torture or inhuman treatment.[21] Moreover, the massive and systematic practice of rape and its use as a "national" instrument of "ethnic cleansing" qualify it to be defined and prosecuted as a crime against humanity.

Independently of the ICRC aide-mémoire and soon after it was issued, the U.S. Department of State unequivocally stated that rape already was a war crime or a grave breach under customary international law and the Geneva Conventions and could be prosecuted as such.[22]

---

[16] *Supra* note 2, Art. 27.

[17] Protocol Additional to the Geneva Conventions of 12 August 1949, and Relating to the Protection of Victims of International Armed Conflicts, *opened for signature* Dec. 12, 1977, Arts. 76(1) and 85, 1125 UNTS 3, 16 ILM 1391 (1977) [Protocol I]; Protocol Additional to the Geneva Conventions of 12 August 1949, and Relating to the Protection of Victims of Non-International Armed Conflicts, *opened for signature* Dec. 12, 1977, Art. 4(2)(e), 1125 UNTS 609, 16 ILM 1442 (1977) [Protocol II].

[18] *See generally* Françoise Krill, *The Protection of Women in International Humanitarian Law*, 25 INT'L REV. RED CROSS 337, 341 (1985).

[19] War crimes are crimes against the conventional or customary law of war that are committed by persons "belonging" to one party to the conflict against persons or property of the other side. The perpetrator, as the Nuremberg jurisprudence makes clear, need not necessarily be a soldier. Attacks committed by persons against other persons belonging to the same side are not considered war crimes.

[20] ICRC, Aide-Mémoire (Dec. 3, 1992).

[21] As early as 1958, the ICRC Commentary on the fourth Geneva Convention recognized that the grave breach of "inhuman treatment" (Art. 147) should be interpreted in the context of Article 27, which also prohibits rape. COMMENTARY ON THE GENEVA CONVENTIONS OF 12 AUGUST 1949; GENEVA CONVENTION RELATIVE TO THE PROTECTION OF CIVILIAN PERSONS IN TIME OF WAR 598 (Oscar M. Uhler & Henri Coursier eds., 1958).

[22] The Department stated:

> We believe that there is no need to amend the Geneva Conventions to accomplish the objectives stated in your letter, however, because the legal basis for prosecuting troops for rape is well established under the Geneva Conventions and customary international law. As stated in the authoritative Department of the Army Law of War Manual, any

This evolution in the approach of the ICRC and the United States is paralleled by the positions and draft charters submitted by several states to the UN Secretary-General pursuant to Security Council Resolution 808. France, in defining the crimes within the jurisdiction of the tribunal under its draft charter, lists "[o]utrages upon personal dignity, in particular humiliating and degrading treatment, rape, forced prostitution and indecent assault."[23] This language draws on Articles 75(2)(b) and 76(1) of Additional Protocol I and upgrades its prohibition of rape – which is not specifically mentioned as a grave breach of the Protocol – to a crime punishable by the tribunal, provided, however, that rape (as well as the other crimes mentioned in Article VI(1)(b)) is "mass and systematic." The United States proposal adapts the definition of crimes against humanity in Control Council Law No. 10 to the Yugoslav circumstances, and lists rape among the punishable crimes.[24] Documents submitted by seven states on behalf of the Organization of the Islamic Conference and by Italy also define rape as a crime against humanity.[25] Most important, the statute of the international tribunal proposed by the UN Secretary-General lists rape among crimes against humanity.[26]

> violation of the Geneva Conventions is a war crime (FM 27–10, para. 499.). Article 27 of the Geneva Convention Relative to the Protection of Civilian Persons in Time of War provides that women shall be "especially protected ... against rape." Article 13 of the Geneva Convention Relative to the Treatment of Prisoners of War provides that prisoners "must at all times be protected, particularly against acts of violence"; article 14 requires that women "be treated with all the regard due to their sex." Both Conventions list grave breaches, including willful killing, torture or inhuman treatment, and (with regard to civilians) willfully causing great suffering or serious injury to body or health. Under the Geneva Conventions and customary international law, all parties to an international conflict (including all parties to the conflict in the former Yugoslavia) are required either to try persons alleged to have committed grave breaches or to extradite them to a party that will.
>
> In our reports to the United Nations on human rights violations in the former Yugoslavia, we have reported sexual assaults as grave breaches. We will continue to do so and will continue to press the international community to respond to the terrible sexual atrocities in the former Yugoslavia.

Letter from Robert A. Bradtke, Acting Assistant Secretary for Legislative Affairs, to Senator Arlen Specter (Jan. 27, 1993).

---

[23] UN Doc. S/25266, Ann. V, Art. VI(1)(b)(iv) (1993).

[24] "Acts of murder, torture, extrajudicial and summary execution, illegal detention, and rape that are part of a campaign or attack against any civilian population in the former Yugoslavia on national, racial, ethnic, or religious grounds." UN Doc. S/25575, Ann. II, Art. 10(b)(i) (1993). This article does not use the term *crimes against humanity*.

[25] The formulation of the Islamic Conference reads: "*Crimes against humanity*, as defined in articles 6(c) and 5(c) of the London and Tokyo Charters, respectively and as further developed by customary international law, which includes: murder, torture, mutilation, rape ...." UN Doc. A/47/920–S/25512, Annex, Art. II(1)(c) (1993). For the wording in the charter proposed by Italy, see UN Doc. S/25300, Ann. I, Art. 4(c) (1993).

[26] UN Doc. S/25704, *supra* note 5. Annex, Art. 5. This statute was approved by SC Res. 827, *supra* note 3.

The crimes against humanity specified in the London Agreement were only those committed "against any civilian population," not against individual civilians. Nuremberg case law suggests that war crimes committed in a widespread and systematic manner on political, racial or religious grounds may rise to the level of crimes against humanity. Proof of systematic governmental planning has been considered a necessary element of crimes against humanity,[27] in contrast to war crimes. Crimes against humanity are therefore more difficult to establish. The acquisition of facts supporting policy planning, mass character and command responsibility may present evidentiary hurdles to possible prosecutions.

Confirmation of the principle stated in Control Council Law No. 10, that rape can constitute a crime against humanity, is, both morally and legally, of ground-breaking importance. Nevertheless, the possibility of prosecuting the far more frequent cases of rape that are regarded as the "lesser" crimes of war crimes or grave breaches should not be neglected. The references to war crimes and grave breaches in the proposed charters, together with the recognition that rape can be a war crime or a grave breach, provide a basis for such prosecutions.

Although, formally, the law stated by the Security Council under chapter VII is necessarily contextual and applicable only to former Yugoslavia, the tribunal's charter, like that of Nuremberg, is likely quickly to become a fundamental normative instrument of the general law of war. The approval by the Security Council (Res. 827), acting under chapter VII of the UN Charter, of the tribunal's charter recognizing rape as a punishable offense under international humanitarian law validates this important normative development and, it is hoped, may expedite the recognition of rape, in some circumstances, as torture or inhuman treatment in the international law of human rights as well.[28] Meaningful progress in combating rape can only be made by more vigorous enforcement of the law. The recognition of rape as a crime under international law punishable by the future war crimes tribunal for former Yugoslavia is a step in that direction.

---

[27] 15 UNITED NATIONS WAR CRIMES COMMISSION, *supra* note 13, at 134–36.

[28] The pernicious phenomenon of rape continues unabated in war as in peace. *See e.g.*, MAJORITY STAFF OF THE SENATE JUDICIARY COMMITTEE, 102D CONG., 2D SESS., VIOLENCE AGAINST WOMEN: A WEEK IN THE LIFE OF AMERICA (1992); AMERICAS WATCH, UNTOLD TERROR: VIOLENCE AGAINST WOMEN IN PERU'S ARMED CONFLICT (1992); MIDDLE EAST WATCH, PUNISHING THE VICTIM: RAPE AND MISTREATMENT OF ASIAN MAIDS IN KUWAIT (1992); AMERICAS WATCH, CRIMINAL INJUSTICE: VIOLENCE AGAINST WOMEN IN BRAZIL (1991). For efforts by the Committee on the Elimination of Discrimination to combat violence against women, see CEDAW General Recommendation No. 19: Violence against Women, *in* COMPILATION OF GENERAL COMMENTS AND GENERAL RECOMMENDATIONS ADOPTED BY HUMAN RIGHTS TREATY BODIES, UN Doc. HRI/GEN/1, at 74 (1992).

XII

The Normative Impact on International Law of the International Tribunal for Former Yugoslavia

In a discussion of ethnic cleansing, Cornelio Sommaruga, President of the International Committee of the Red Cross [hereinafter: ICRC], lamented that the practices that were believed to belong to the museum of horrors of the Second World War have become routine in the territory of the former Yugoslavia. In a series of public statements, the ICRC – usually so discreet – has spoken out on the failure to respect the rights of the civilian population, which has been subjected to systematic abuses including summary execution, torture, rape, mass internment, deportation and displacement in the process of which thousands may have died, intimidation, taking of hostages, ill-treatment and confiscation of private property. The most basic principles of international humanitarian law – and of course of human rights – have been and are being violated.

Whether or not one accepts the comparison to World War II's atrocities, those being committed in the former Yugoslavia every day before our very eyes exceed even those abuses perpetrated in Kuwait by Saddam Hussein's occupation forces. Our sense of justice cannot accept the impunity enjoyed by the offenders. Because we were unable, or unwilling to prevent the atrocities as they were unfolding, the prosecution of the perpetrators must be undertaken, at the very least. Without action, humanitarian law would be in danger of being swept aside entirely, and losing whatever credibility it still has.

Whatever the practical achievements of the International Tribunal for Yugoslavia may prove to be, the United Nations Security Council has established the first truly international criminal tribunal[1] for the prosecution of persons responsible for serious violations of international humanitarian law. Its creation portends at least some deterrence to future violations and gives a new lease on life to that part of international criminal law which applies to violations of humanitarian law. These are

---

[1] The post-World War II Nuremberg and Tokyo Tribunals are regarded by some commentators as victors' courts.

major, though obvious, achievements.[2] However, the tragic and massive abuses in the former Yugoslavia have also triggered additional institutional and normative developments, which are the subject of this article.

The first noteworthy development is the ground-breaking determination by the Security Council that the commission of atrocities in the former Yugoslavia, particularly in Bosnia-Herzegovina, constituted a threat to international peace, and that the creation of an *ad hoc* international criminal tribunal would contribute to the restoration of peace. It was on this basis, pursuant to Chapter VII of the UN Charter, that the Security Council decided in Resolutions 808 and 827 to establish such a tribunal.[3] The singling out of violations of humanitarian law as a major factor in the determination of a threat to the peace creates an important precedent, and the establishment of the tribunal as an enforcement measure under the binding authority of Chapter VII, rather than through a treaty creating an international criminal court whose jurisdiction would be subject to the consent of the States concerned, may foreshadow more effective international responses to violations of humanitarian law.[4]

The factual basis for the Security Council's conclusions was ample. The expulsion of great numbers of inhabitants, the creation of a major refugee problem spilling over frontiers, and the possibility of the conflicts expanding into Kosovo, Macedonia, and triggering even a broader Balkan conflagration, provided strong rationales for the Security Council. Furthermore, under the Charter, the Security Council has broad discretion to take enforcement measures involving even sanctions and the use of force; thus *a fortiori* it may take such lesser measures as the establishment of a tribunal for the prosecution of perpetrators of atrocities.[5]

Second, the Statute of the tribunal contributes significantly to affirming certain major components of international humanitarian law as

---

[2] *See generally* C. O'Brien, "The International Tribunal for Violations of International Humanitarian Law in the Former Yugoslavia", 87 *Am. J. Int'l L.* 639 (1993); T. Meron, The Case for War Crimes Trials in Yugoslavia, 72 *Foreign Aff.* 123 (1993). For criticism of the tribunal, *see* P. Rubin, "International Crime and Punishment," *Nat'l Interest* 73 (1993). No attempt has been made to prosecute those responsible for egregious violations of humanitarian law and human rights in Uganda, Iraq, Cambodia and occupied Kuwait. The credibility of the international system of justice requires prosecutions for atrocities everywhere, not only those committed in the former Yugoslavia. *See also infra* note 4.

[3] For the statute of the tribunal, *see* Report of the Secretary-General pursuant to para. 2 of UN S.C. Res. 808 (1993), UN Doc. S/25704 (hereinafter: Commentary) and Annex (3 May 1993), reprinted *in* 32 *I.L.M.* 1159, 1192 (1993).

[4] On a permanent international criminal court, *see* Report of the Working Group on the draft statute for an international criminal court, Annex to Report of the International Law Commission on the work of its Forty-fifth session, 48 UN *GAOR*. Supp. (No. 10), at 255, UN Doc. A/48/10 (1993); J. Crawford, "The ILC's Draft Statute for an International Criminal Tribunal," *88 Am. J. Int'l L.* 140 (1994).

[5] O'Brien, *supra* note 2, at 640, 643.

customary law.[6] In his commentary on the Statute approved by the Security Council, the UN Secretary-General emphasized that the principle *nullum crimen sine lege* requires that "the international tribunal should apply rules of international humanitarian law which are beyond any doubt part of customary law so that the problem of adherence of some but not all States to specific conventions does not arise."[7] That "part of conventional international humanitarian law which has beyond doubt become part of international customary law", according to the Secretary-General, is the law of armed conflict embodied in the Geneva Convention for the Protection of War Victims of 12 August 1949; the Hague Convention (No. IV) Respecting the Laws and Customs of War on Land and annexed Regulations of 18 October 1907; the Convention on the Prevention and Punishment of the Crime of Genocide of 9 December 1948; and the Charter of the International Military Tribunal of 8 August 1945.[8] The Geneva Conventions constitute "the core of the customary law applicable in international armed conflicts".[9]

These statements will undoubtedly be quoted often to support the characterization of the Geneva Conventions as declaratory of customary law.[10] However, the Secretary-General's list of unquestionably customary instruments does not include the 1977 Protocol Additional to the Geneva Conventions Relating to the Protection of Victims of International Armed Conflicts (Protocol I). Although its norms are largely customary,[11] Protocol I also contains some provisions that are not, as yet, customary law. Perhaps the Secretary-General thought it would be unwise to list only those provisions of the Protocol that have undoubtedly acquired the status of customary law.

For purposes of the *ad hoc* Tribunal's jurisdiction – though not for the elaboration of customary law – this omission was somewhat remedied by the robust interpretation of the US representative, Ambassador Madeleine K. Albright, immediately after the tribunal's Statute was adopted in the Security Council. In the view of the United States, the application of the law of the former Yugoslavia, which incorporated Protocol I, satisfies the principle *nullum crimen sine lege*. Hence, Ambassador Albright said: "it is understood that the 'laws or customs of war' referred to in Article 3 include all obligations under humanitarian law agreements in force in the territory of the former Yugoslavia at the time

---

[6] See generally T. Meron, *Human Rights and Humanitarian Norms as Customary Law* (1989).
[7] Commentary, 1170, para. 34.
[8] *Ibid.*, para. 35 (footnotes omitted).   [9] *Ibid.*, para. 37.
[10] See, e.g., Task Force of the American Bar Association Section of International Law and Practice, Report on the International Tribunal to Adjudicate War Crimes Committed in the Former Yugoslavia 12–13 (1993) (hereinafter: ABA Report).
[11] Meron, *supra* note 6, at 62–70, 74–78.

the acts were committed, including ... the 1977 Additional Protocols to these Conventions".[12]

The tribunal may have an opportunity to develop and further clarify customary law by interpreting and applying the provisions of the Statute on jurisdiction, especially Article 3, which provides only an illustrative list of laws and customs of war. Fulfilment of this function, however, will depend both on effective and vigorous use of the tribunal and on the cases presented to it.

The third development of note is the concerted and successful effort to treat the conflicts in the territory of the former Yugoslavia as international armed conflicts, which triggers the applicability of the entire body of international humanitarian law, including provisions of Hague law and Geneva law (grave breaches) establishing the personal responsibility of the perpetrators.

Whether the conflicts in the former Yugoslavia are characterized as internal or international is critically important. The Fourth Hague Convention of 1907, which codified the principal laws of war and served as the normative core for the post-World War II war crimes prosecutions, applies to international wars only. The other principal prong of the penal laws of war, the grave breaches provisions of the Geneva Conventions and Protocol 1, is also directed to international wars. Violations of common Article 3 of the Geneva Conventions, which concerns internal wars, do not constitute grave breaches giving rise to universal criminal jurisdiction.[13] Were any part of the conflict deemed internal rather than international, the perpetrators of even the worst atrocities might try to challenge prosecutions for war crimes or grave breaches, but not for genocide or crimes against humanity. Should the situation in Kosovo, which is still considered an internal situation, deteriorate further, rules on war crimes and grave breaches might not necessarily be applicable. Crimes against humanity, and perhaps genocide, might then provide the main applicable international criminal law bases for prosecutions.

In the *Nicaragua* case, the International Court of Justice contrasted the conflict between the contras and the Sandinista Government with that between the United States and Nicaragua. The first, as internal, was governed by common Article 3 only; the second, as international, fell

---

[12] UN Doc. S/PV. 3217, at 15 (25 May 1993).

[13] The International Law Commission has made Article 22 of its Draft Code of Crimes against the Peace and Security of Mankind, entitled "Exceptionally serious war crimes", applicable to both international and internal armed conflicts. However, Art. 22 has yet to take root as a norm of international law. Report of the International Law Commission on the Work of its Forty-third Session, 46 UN *GAOR*, Supp. (No. 10), at 270, UN Doc. A/46/10 (1991).

under the rules on international conflicts.[14] I am not suggesting any parallels between the parties to the conflict in Nicaragua and in the former Yugoslavia and would simply submit that any attempt to apply the *Nicaragua* Court's distinctions to the conflict in Yugoslavia would result in Byzantine complexity, making prosecutions difficult and often impossible.

The black letter of international humanitarian law still adheres, at least in theory, to a categorical (though often artificial) distinction between internal and international conflicts. Because of the involvement of foreign actors, most internal conflicts are in fact mixed internal-international conflicts. The conflicts in Yugoslavia, and especially Bosnia-Herzegovina, are prime examples. Yet despite their concurrent or successive character as internal, mixed or international, there are valid reasons to consider the entire conflict as international, and therefore subject to the rules on international wars. The relevant factors in the transition of the Yugoslav conflicts from internal to international were the recognition by foreign States of Slovenia, Croatia and Bosnia and Herzegovina; the admission of these States to the United Nations; and the agreements concluded between the parties to the conflicts under the auspices of the ICRC, which provide for the application of the Geneva Conventions, in whole or in part. Notwithstanding these agreements, the parties' position on the nature of the conflict remains unclear. The unacknowledged, but clear, intervention in the Bosnian conflict by Belgrade on behalf of the Serbs, and against the government of Bosnia-Herzegovina, could transform the conflict from internal to international, even under classic principles of international law.

The various proposals submitted to the Security Council treat all the aspects of the conflict as international, ensuring the possibility of prosecutions for classic war crimes and grave breaches of the Geneva Conventions. The UN War Crimes Commission shares the view that the conflicts in the former Yugoslavia are international and thus that all the laws of war, including, of course, the rules governing war crimes, are

[14] Military and Paramilitary Activities in and against Nicaragua (Nicar. v. U.S.), Merits, [1986] *I.C.J Rep.* 14, 114 (Judgment of June 27). The Court considered common Art. 3 as reflecting a customary norm ("laws of humanity"), *ibid.*, 113–14, and as a minimum yardstick applicable not only to noninternational armed conflicts but also to international armed conflicts, *ibid.*, 114. Invoking this I.C.J. pronouncement, the ABA Task Force recommended that certain provisions of common Art. 3 be incorporated into Art. 5 of the statute, which enumerates crimes against humanity. The Task Force noted that

> such modifications would also confirm that these crimes will be within the Tribunal's subject-matter jurisdiction even if it should determine that they were committed in a *non-international* armed conflict, and thus were not covered by parallel provisions in Art. 2 of the Statute, which address only grave breaches of the Conventions committed in *international* armed conflict.

ABA Report, 15 (footnotes omitted).

applicable.[15] The Secretary-General's proposals on the tribunal's subject matter jurisdiction, particularly those pertaining to war crimes and grave breaches of the Geneva Conventions,[16] are clearly based on the assumption that the conflicts are international. Moreover, as we have seen, in the report approved by the Security Council as a basis for its action, the Secretary-General emphasized that the tribunal should apply only those rules of international customary law applicable in international armed conflicts.[17] It is fair to conclude, I submit, that the Statute of the tribunal constitutes a determination that the conflicts in the former Yugoslavia are international in character.

This characterization should not prevent individual defendants from arguing that they fought in an internal war and therefore could not be accused of grave breaches of the Geneva Conventions or war crimes under the Hague Regulations. In contrast to the Nuremberg Charter,[18] the Statute of the *ad hoc* tribunal does not preclude challenges of its authority by defendants. The tribunal may rule on challenges concerning the international character of the conflicts and, indeed, other jurisdictional matters. Whether the tribunal will be ready assertively to question the Security Council resolutions under which it was established, or its constitutive Charter, the Statute, is another matter. Be that as it may, by internationalizing the conflicts, the United Nations enhances and expands the applicability of humanitarian and criminal international law.

Fourth, there has been a movement toward international criminalization of the offences under common Article 3 of the Geneva Conventions committed in noninternational armed conflicts. As a basis for criminal prosecutions, common Article 3 does not fit the black letter law of either the Hague Regulations or of the grave breaches provisions of the Geneva Conventions. However, Article 3 of the Statute of the tribunal, which lists violations of the laws and customs of war, is merely illustrative ("Such violations shall include, but not be limited to . . ."). Again, the interpretative statement of Ambassador Albright is relevant; she pointed out that

---

[15] The Commission stated that

> the character and complexity of the armed conflicts concerned, combined with the web of agreements on humanitarian issues the parties have concluded among themselves, justify an approach whereby it applies the law applicable in international armed conflicts to the entirety of the armed conflicts in the territory of the former Yugoslavia.

Interim Report of the Commission of Experts Established Pursuant to Security Council Resolution 780 (1992), UN Doc. S/25274, Annex I, para. 45 (1993) (hereinafter: UN War Crimes Commission).

[16] Commentary, 1170, para. 35.   [17] *Ibid.*, paras. 33–37 and text at *supra* note 6.
[18] *See* Agreement for the Prosecution and Punishment of the Major War Criminals of the European Axis, Charter of the International Military Tribunal, 8 August 1945, Art. 3, 59 *Stat.* 1544, 82 *U.N.T.S.* 279, *reprinted in* 39 *Am. J. Int'l L.* 257 (1945) (hereinafter: Nuremberg Charter or London Agreement).

the "laws or customs of war" referred to in Article 3 of the tribunal's Statute cover the entire body of humanitarian law "in force in the territory of the former Yugoslavia at the time the acts were committed, including common Article 3 of the 1949 Geneva Conventions".[19] Thus, in the view of the United States, because Article 3 could be a basis for criminal prosecutions in the law of the former Yugoslavia, it could form such a basis for those before the tribunal as well. The British representative, Sir David Hannay, apparently agreed: "it would be our view that the reference to the laws or customs of war in Article 3 is broad enough to include applicable international conventions."[20] The French representative, Ambassador Jean-Bernard Merimée, approached the matter from the perspective of Yugoslav law: the "expression 'laws or customs of war' used in Article 3 of the Statute covers specifically, in the opinion of France, all the obligations that flow from the humanitarian law agreements in force in the territory of the former Yugoslavia at the time when the offences were committed."[21]

I agree with James O'Brien that,

> [w]hether or not it is well-established international law that common Article 3 gives rise to individual criminal responsibility, the prohibitions in that article are part of the law of the former Yugoslavia, and the tribunal can therefore rely on it without fear of invoking criminal law of which the defendants did not know.[22]

It remains to be seen if the tribunal will regard the above interpretative statements as authoritative. This possibility is weakened by the fact that in his proposals the Secretary-General stressed that reference to the domestic practice of Yugoslavia will be limited to the matter of penalties.[23] Article 24 of the new statute limits the penalty that may be imposed by the new tribunal to that of imprisonment. Departing both from the law and practice of Nuremberg and from the law of the former Yugoslavia, the statute thus adopts an abolitionist policy.

It should be understood that common Article 3 clearly imposes several important prohibitions on the behaviour of parties to noninternational armed conflicts, norms that were recognized as customary in the *Nicaragua* case. That these prohibitions are not listed among the grave breaches provisions of the Geneva Conventions does not detract from their normative character, as these provisions pertain to universal jurisdiction, not substantive law.[24] Jurisdictional obligations can be otherwise created, for

---

[19] UN Doc. S/PV. 3217, at 15 (25 May 1993).   [20] *Ibid.*, 19.   [21] *Ibid.*, 11.
[22] O'Brien, *supra* note 2, at 647.   [23] Commentary, 1170, para. 36.
[24] Art. 146(3) of the Geneva Convention (IV) obligates all State parties to "take measures necessary for the suppression of all acts contrary to the provisions of the present Convention other than the grave breaches defined in the following Article". Geneva Convention (IV) Relative to the Protection of Civilian Persons in Time of War, 1949, 6 *U.S.T.* 3516, 75 *U.N.T.S.*

example by national law,[25] or, exceptionally, by mandatory resolutions of the Security Council.

Perpetrators of atrocities in internal wars should not be treated more leniently than those engaged in international wars. Whether or not the indictments and convictions are based on common Article 3, the extension of the concept of war crimes under international law to abuses perpetrated in noninternational armed conflicts is a welcome, though still tentative, development.

The fifth normative development worth mentioning is the abolitionist position taken by the Statute. Article 27 of the Nuremberg Charter gave the Tribunal "the right to impose upon a defendant, on conviction, death or such other punishment as shall be determined by it to be just". Similarly, the Control Council Law No. 10 allowed, under Article II(3)(a), the imposition of death sentences. The death penalty was, moreover, a penalty in Yugoslav law implementing international humanitarian treaties.[26] Nevertheless, and without explanation in the Commentary, Article 24 of the new Statute limits the penalty that may be imposed by the Tribunal to that of imprisonment. This reflects, it is believed, opposition to capital punishment expressed by countries that have strongly supported abolitionist instruments such as the Second Optional Protocol to the International Covenant on Civil and Political Rights, Aiming at the Abolition of the Death Penalty; and the Sixth Protocol to the [European] Convention for the Protection of Human Rights and Fundamental Freedoms Concerning the Abolition of the Death Penalty.

The sixth significant development is that the due process protections in the Statute exceed those in the Charters of the Nuremberg and Tokyo Tribunals. Articles 20 and 21 of the Statute are exemplary in this regard, based as they are[27] on the extensive catalogue in Article 14 of the International Covenant on Civil and Political Rights. In contrast to the

---

287. Suppression involves punishment. 4 *Commentary on the Geneva Conventions of 12 August 1949: Geneva Convention Relative to the Protection of Civilian Persons in Time of War* 594 (O. M. Uhler & H. Coursier eds., 1958).

[25] As pointed out above, common Art. 3 was incorporated in the law of the former Yugoslavia. The United States Army appears to regard violations of that article as encompassed by the notion of war crimes and would prosecute for war crimes captured military personnel accused of breaches of Art. 3. US Department of The Army, *The Law of Land Warfare*, para. 499 (Field Manual No. 27–10, 1956); Uniform Code of Military Justice, 10 *U.S.C.* §§802, 818 (1988). These texts mention neither common Art. 3 nor other provisions of the Geneva Conventions. US military personnel accused of violating common Art. 3 would be prosecuted for the substantive offences listed in the UCMJ (Uniform Code [of] Military Justice). I am grateful to Mr. George Peirce and to Major William Hudson for the information on which this note is based.

[26] O'Brien, *supra* note 2, at 655.

[27] The Secretary-General emphasizes this point in his Report. *See* Commentary, 1184, 1185, paras. 101, 106.

International Law Commission's proposal for a permanent criminal tribunal, the tribunal's Statute appears not to allow trials *in absentia* because,
in the words of the Secretary-General, "[t]here is a widespread perception
that ... this would not be consistent with Article 14 of the International
Covenant on Civil and Political Rights, which provides that the accused
shall be entitled to be tried in his presence".[28] Thus, the Secretary-General
and the Security Council interpret Article 14 as pro-defendant, contrast-
ing with the I.L.C. proposal for a permanent criminal tribunal. While
certain I.L.C. members felt that *in absentia* trials were entirely unacceptable from the point of view of the rights of the accused as well as due to the
fact that "judgments by the Court without the actual possibility of implementing them might lead to a progressive loss of its authority and effectiveness in the eyes of public opinion",[29] other members, were in favour
of *in absentia* trials, subject to certain distinctions. In particular, three
situations were distinguished:

(a) the accused has been indicted but is totally unaware of the proceedings;
(b) the accused has been duly notified but chooses not to appear before the
    Court;
(c) the accused has already been arrested but escapes before the trial is com-
    pleted.[30]

The general inclination of the I.L.C. vis-à-vis these three situations was to
consider that while in situation (a), *in absentia* proceedings should not take
place, an *in absentia* trial would be appropriate in situation (b) or (c), as
"otherwise, the Court's jurisdiction would, in fact, be subject to the veto of
the accused".[31] Further arguments proffered in favour of *in absentia* trials
were that a judgment *in absentia* would "in itself constitute a kind of moral
sanction which could contribute to the isolation of the accused wherever
located and, possibly, to eventual capture",[32] that an expeditious trial
would allow evidence to be preserved that might otherwise be lost were
proceedings to be delayed until the accused could appear before the
Court,[33] and finally that disruption of the trial for security reasons or
due to ill health of the accused could be avoided.[34]

Scholars will often disagree on whether or not *in absentia* trials
should be allowed, as provided in Article 12 of the Nuremberg
Charter. I come out against such trials, which, particularly in the circumstances of the former Yugoslavia, are inherently vulnerable to error or
abuse.

---

[28] The Secretary-General emphasizes this point in his Report. *See* Commentary, 1184, para.
101 (footnote omitted).
[29] Report of the International Law Commission on the Work of its Forty-fifth Session, 48
UN *GAOR* Supp. (No. 10), at 305, UN Doc. A/48/10 (1993) (Art. 44(1) (h)).
[30] *Ibid.*   [31] *Ibid.*, 306.   [32] *Ibid.*   [33] *Ibid.*   [34] *Ibid.*

It may be of interest to note that it was Israel that proposed to add to Article 14(3)(d) of the Covenant the reference to the right of the accused to be tried in his presence.[35] In explaining his amendment, the representative of Israel emphasized that because this right constituted an essential condition of equitable administration of justice, it had to be stated explicitly.[36] He did not mention any qualifications whatsoever as to the exercise and scope of that right.

The controversy concerning the exclusion of *in absentia* trials has continued even after the adoption of the tribunal's Statute. France, reflecting perhaps the greater allowance of *in absentia* judgments in civil law countries, has thus argued that "[t]he Statute of the Tribunal does not explicitly exclude the possibility of judgment in the defendant's absence, but does not actually provide for it"[37] and that

> it would be appropriate for the rules of procedure of the Tribunal, which are designed to clarify the provisions of the Statute, to eliminate any possible ambiguities and to fill any gaps, should provide for the possibility of judgment in the absence of the accused in cases where the latter refuses to appear (and cannot be compelled to do so) and cannot be contacted after a certain period of time.[38]

Does such a proposal go beyond interpretation and amount to a revision of the Charter?

Of course, as in the criminal procedure of the United States and many other countries, there are certain rules against abuse by the accused of the right to be tried in his presence. The US draft Rules of Procedure and Evidence for the International Tribunal for the Prosecution of Persons Responsible for Serious Violations of International Humanitarian Law Committed in the Former Yugoslavia[39] provide that

> the accused shall be considered to have waived the right to be present whenever:
>
> (A) the accused is voluntarily absent after his or her initial appearance; or
> (B) having been warned by the Trial Chamber that disruptive conduct will cause the accused to be removed from the courtroom, persists in conduct which justifies exclusion from the courtroom.[40]

---

[35] M. J. Bossuyt, *Guide to the "Travaux Préparatoires" of the International Covenant on Civil and Political Rights* 298–300 (1987).

[36] UN Doc. 14 *GAOR* A/C.3 SR 961, para. 13 (19 November 1959).

[37] Note No. 803 from the Permanent Mission of France to the United Nations, para. 4 (28 October 1993).

[38] *Ibid.*, para 6. It may be noted that in its "General Comment" No. 13 (1984?), the Human Rights Committee did not entirely exclude the possibility of *in absentia* trials ("[W]hen for exceptionally justified reasons trials *in absentia* are held, strict observance of the rights of the defence is all the more necessary".), UN Doc. HRI/GEI/I at 15 (1992).

[39] Presented by letter dated 18 November 1993 from the United States Embassy at the Hague to the Secretary-General of the United Nations for transmission to the judges of the Tribunal.

[40] *Ibid.*, Rule 21.

Again, on the basis of Article 14, the right of appeal to a chamber of the tribunal was incorporated in the Statute,[41] which goes beyond Nuremberg.[42] The incorporation of the norms under Article 14 of the Covenant in the Statute of the first international criminal court since the post-World War II tribunals stands as a significant precedent that enhances the importance of these norms *per se* and in the context of international criminal tribunals.

Seventh, again going beyond the Nuremberg Charter, the new Statute follows Control Council Law No. 10, adopted by the four occupying powers as a charter for war crimes trials by their national courts in Germany, by providing that rape can constitute a crime against humanity.[43] Both morally and legally, the importance of this provision cannot be overstated. Nevertheless, the possibility of prosecuting the far more frequent cases of rape that are regarded as "lesser" war crimes or grave breaches should not be neglected. The references to war crimes and grave breaches in the charters proposed for the *ad hoc* tribunal, together with the recognition by the United States and the ICRC that rape can be a war crime or a grave breach, strengthen the case for such prosecutions.[44]

My eighth point pertains to the nexus between crimes against humanity and war. Crimes against humanity were defined in the Nuremberg Charter as murder, extermination, enslavement, deportation and other inhumane acts committed against any civilian population, before or during the war, or persecutions on political, racial or religious grounds in execution of, or in connection with, any crime within the jurisdiction of the Tribunal, i.e., crimes against peace and war crimes, and whether or not in violation of the domestic law of the country where perpetrated.[45] Control Council Law No. 10[46] deleted the jurisdictional nexus between war crimes and crimes against peace. Although largely because of an amending Protocol to the Charter the Nuremberg Tribunal did not consider crimes committed before the war to be crimes against humanity,[47] it may have been guided by jurisdictional considerations and not necessarily by a conceptually narrow definition of crimes against humanity.

Most crimes against humanity listed in the London Agreement, for instance violations of the law of belligerent occupation, were also war

---

[41] Commentary, 1187, para. 116 & Art. 25.

[42] Meron, *supra* note 2, at 125; O'Brien, *supra* note 2, at 655.

[43] Control Council Law No. 10 expanded the formulation of crimes against humanity by including rape among the prohibitions listed in Art. II(1)(c). Control Council for Germany, Official Gazette, 31 January 1946, at 50, *reprinted in 60 International Law States* 304 (60 International Law Studies (H.S. Levie ed., 1979)) (hereinafter: Control Council Law No. 10).

[44] T. Meron, "Rape as a Crime under International Humanitarian Law", 87 *Am. J. Int'l L.* 424, 428 (1993).

[45] Nuremberg Charter, Art. 6(c).   [46] Control Council Law No. 10.

[47] Oppenheim, 2 *International Law* 579 n. 5 (H. Lauterpacht ed., 7th ed., 1952).

crimes under customary international law, and therefore could not, then or now, be seen as *ex post facto*. In the trials of lesser war criminals by US occupation courts, war crimes were often merged with crimes against humanity.

An innovative feature of the Nuremberg Charter was that certain crimes against the perpetrator's own citizens were considered crimes against humanity. Today, however, because of the intervening development of international law and the recognition, through human rights law and otherwise, of the central status of the individual as a subject of international law, this facet of the London Agreement would not be regarded as innovative. Many human rights conventions, e.g., on the prohibition of torture, render certain types of behaviour between citizens of the same State as internationally criminal, regardless of their commission in wartime. The tangled meshing of crimes against humanity and human rights militates against requiring a link with war for the former. The better opinion today, it is submitted, is that crimes against humanity exist independently of war. The recent edition of Oppenheim's treatise by Jennings and Watts, for example, considers crimes against humanity "as a self-contained category, without the need for any formal link with war crimes".[48] The International Law Commission expressed the view that crimes against humanity may be committed before a war,[49] and in the *Barbie* case the French *Cour de Cassation* appeared to regard the nexus with war as unnecessary ("In fact, in contrast to crimes against humanity, war crimes are directly connected with the existence of a situation of hostilities.").[50] Nevertheless, neither in the literature nor in the work of the ILC can one find consistent positions on the nexus requirement.[51]

---

[48] Oppenheim's 1 *International Law* 996 (R. Y. Jennings & A. Watts eds., 9th ed., 1992).

[49] [1950] II *Y.B. Int'l L. Comm'n* 377, para. 120, UN Doc. A/CN.4/SER.A/1950/Add. 1.

[50] Fédération Nationale des Déportés et Internes Resistants et Patriotes v. Barbie, 78 *I.L.R.* 125, 136 (Fr. Cass. crim. 1985).

[51] In the definition of crimes against humanity (Principle VI(c)) in its 1950 Report on the formulation of the Nuremberg principles, the International Law Commission retained the nexus with crimes against peace and war crimes. [1950] II *Y.B. Int'l L. Comm'n, supra* note 49, at 377. The nexus with other crimes was eliminated from the definition of crimes against humanity (Art. 2(11)) in the 1954 Draft Code of Offences against the Peace and Security of Mankind, [1954] II *Y.B. Int'l L. Comm'n* 150, UN Doc. A/CN.4/SER.A/1954/Add. 1, and today the I.L.C. considers the autonomy of crimes against humanity to be absolute, [1986] II *Y.B. Int'l L. Comm'n* 56, UN Doc. A/CN.4/SER.A/1986/Add. 1. *See also* D. Thiam, Seventh Report on the Draft Code of Crimes against the Peace and Security of Mankind, [1989] II *Y.B. Int'l L. Comm'n* 86, UN Doc. A/CN.4/SER.A/1989/Add. 1 (pt.1). ("First linked to a state of belligerency ... the concept of crimes against humanity gradually came to be viewed as autonomous and is today quite separate from that of war crimes'. And "[C]rimes against humanity may be committed in time of war or in time of peace; war crimes can be committed only in time of war", *ibid.*, 87). The draft articles of the Draft Code of Crimes against the Peace and Security of Mankind provisionally adopted by the I.L.C. on first reading abandon the "distinction between crimes against peace, war crimes, and crimes against humanity". Report of the International Law Commission on the Work of its Forty-third Session, 46 UN

Although crimes against humanity were undoubtedly committed in the former Yugoslavia in wartime (the tribunal's temporal jurisdiction begins on 1 January 1991), rendering the Nuremberg limitation largely irrelevant to the new tribunal's jurisdiction, the views of States, expert bodies and other organizations on the nexus question will evidently affect both the construction of the Statute[52] and the development of customary law. The UN War Crimes Commission clearly rejected the nexus with war and defined crimes against humanity as being "irrespective of war".[53] Italy's proposal for the Statute of the tribunal considered "the reference to 'crimes against mankind" in the wording of the Nuremberg Tribunal statute [to be] obsolete, in that it envisaged a link with a war crime, thus largely restricting the scope of action of the Court to be set up".[54] The proposals by France, the United States and the Organization of the Islamic Conference did not refer to any such requirement. The ABA Task Force ably led by Monroe Leigh stated that, "[w]hile the Statute follows the Nuremberg precedent in asserting jurisdiction over crimes against humanity that are 'committed in armed conflict", the [ABA] Task Force recognizes that, as a general principle, there are compelling reasons to punish crimes against humanity having no nexus to armed conflict".[55] In its suggestions to the United Nations concerning the Statute, the ICRC affirmed that, "unlike [war crimes], [crimes against humanity] can be committed independently of an armed conflict and, even when committed during a conflict, are not necessarily related to it".[56] O'Brien notes that most governments' comments on the proposed Statute did not connect crimes against humanity to other crimes or to an armed conflict.[57]

GAOR, Supp. (No. 10), at 259, UN Doc.A/46/10 (1991). By combining in a single article (draft Art. 21, entitled "Systematic or mass violations of human rights") some violations of human rights with elements previously considered crimes against humanity, the I.L.C. appears to support the latter's autonomy from war. *Ibid.*, 265.

D.F. Orentlicher sums up the evolution of the nexus requirement by observing that "while post-Nuremberg developments have tended to free crimes against humanity from a wartime context, the trend has been inconclusive." Orentlicher, "Settling Accounts: The Duty to Prosecute Human Rights Violations of a Prior Regime", 100 *Yale L.J.* 2537, 2539 (1991). *See also* M. Ch. Bassiouni, *Crimes Against Humanity in International Criminal Law* 257 (1992); Y. Dinstein, "International Criminal Law", 20 *Is. L. Rev.* 206, 211 (1985); E. Schwelb, "Crimes Against Humanity," 23 *Brit. Y.B. Int'l L.* 178, 193–97, 205–206 (1946).

[52] In any event, the task of the *ad hoc* tribunal will be largely to interpret its Statute, rather than to resort to the customary law of crimes against humanity. O'Brien, *supra* note 2, at 649 n. 44.

[53] UN War Crimes Commission, para. 49.

[54] UN Doc. S/25300, at 11 (17 February 1993).   [55] ABA Report 16 n. 53.

[56] Some Preliminary Remarks by the *I.C.R.C.* on the Setting-up of an International Tribunal for the Prosecution of Persons Responsible for Serious Violations of International Humanitarian Law Committed in the Territory of the Former Yugoslavia 8 (25 March 1993).

[57] O'Brien, *supra* note 2, at 649 & n. 45.

Article 5 of the Statute, dealing with crimes against humanity, gives the tribunal competence regarding such crimes "when committed in armed conflict, whether international or internal in character, and directed against any civilian population". The interpretative statements of the United States[58] and of the United Kingdom[59] suggest that the words "in armed conflict" can be understood as meaning "during armed conflict", regardless of a substantive link with either another crime within the jurisdiction of the tribunal or the state of war. O'Brien comments that, "[o]n its face, the Yugoslav statute requires only a connection between crimes against humanity and armed conflict, which is not itself a crime under the statute; it thus marks a modest advance over the Nuremberg Charter by expressly removing the requirement of connection to another crime under international law".[60] The US draft Rules of Procedure and Evidence[61] confirm this trend. Rule 2(2) (D) states that the subject matter jurisdiction of the Tribunal extends to

> crimes against humanity as enumerated in Article 5 of the Statute when committed contrary to law as part of a widespread or systematic campaign against any civilian population on national, political, ethnic, racial, gender, or religious grounds, during a period of armed conflict, whether internal or international in character, including all acts committed in the territory of the former Yugoslavia during the time of armed conflict, whether or not in execution of or in connection with that armed conflict, all acts committed in preparation of such armed conflict, and all acts committed not during such armed conflict but in execution of or in connection with (as interpreted by tribunals applying the Charter of the International Military Tribunal at Nuremberg or Control Council Law No. 10) that armed conflict.

Maintenance of even such a reduced nexus to war, however, is disappointing. It may have been triggered by the drafters' concern that some members of the Security Council would be opposed to the criminalization of peacetime human rights abuses.

While the black letter of the Statute confers jurisdiction on the tribunal only for crimes against humanity committed in armed conflict, the Secretary-General's commentary appears to provide a different and much wider definition of such crimes, specifying that they are prohibited "regardless of whether they are committed in an armed conflict,

---

[58] The US representative stated:

> [I]t is understood that Article 5 applies to all acts listed in that article, when committed contrary to law during a period of armed conflict in the territory of the former Yugoslavia, as part of a widespread or systematic attack against any civilian population on national, political, ethnic, racial, gender, or religious grounds.

UN Doc. S/PV. 3217, at 16 (25 May 1993).

[59] "Article 5 covers acts committed in time of armed conflict." *Ibid.*, 19.

[60] O'Brien, *supra* note 2, at 650.   [61] *Supra* note 39.

international or internal in character".[62] Thus, the restrictive approach to crimes against humanity adopted in the Statute of the *ad hoc* tribunal will be tempered by the wider definition in the commentary, which effectively discards any nexus with war. This tempering may have important consequences on the future development of customary law in this field.

The reaction of the international community to the appalling abuses in the former Yugoslavia has brought about certain advances – some of them of considerable importance – in international criminal and humanitarian law. One may hope that these institutional and normative developments will enhance prospects for firm responses to future atrocities.

Not in all cases did the drafters of the Statute avail themselves of this unique opportunity to advance the frontiers of international law. In the matter of the defence of superior orders, for example, the Statute reflects the black letter of the Nuremberg Charter without taking into account the more nuanced approach adopted by the post-World War II war crimes tribunals, literature[63] and manuals of military law. Like the Nuremberg Charter, the Statute of the International Tribunal rejects the defence of superior orders,[64] except for purposes of mitigation of punishment, in terms nearly identical to those employed by the Nuremberg Charter.[65] It remains to be seen whether this deficiency will be remedied by the case law of the Tribunal, which by taking into account developments subsequent to the Nuremberg Charter could temper the rigidity of the categorical rejection of the defence of superior orders. Of course, as Professor Dinstein emphasized, the Nuremberg Statute amounted to a necessary repudiation of the doctrine of *respondeat superior*.[66]

In the proceedings under Control Council Law No. 10,[67] the defence of superior orders was found to be admissible in certain circumstances. In the *von Leeb* case, the tribunal did not reject that defence as regards transmittal of orders to the extent that the order was not manifestly illegal

---

[62] Commentary, 1173, para. 47.

[63] *See particularly* the seminal work of Y. Dinstein, *The Defence of "Obedience to Superior Orders" in International Law* (1965).

[64] Art. 7(4) of the Statute reads:

> The fact that an accused person acted pursuant to an order of a Government or of a superior shall not relieve him of criminal responsibility, but may be considered in mitigation of punishment if the International Tribunal determines that justice so requires.

For its text *see supra* note 3.

[65] Art. 8 of the Nuremberg Charter:

> The fact that the Defendant acted pursuant to order of his Government or of a superior shall not free him from responsibility, but may be considered in mitigation of punishment if the Tribunal determines that justice so requires.

Supra note 18.

[66] Dinstein, *supra* note 63, at 156.   [67] *Supra* note 43.

or when the accused was not aware that the order was unlawful.[68] The
Ohlendorf case emphasizes that "[t]o plead superior orders one must show
an excusable ignorance of their illegality",[69] and a later Austrian case used
the test of factual illegality.[70] The "manifest illegality principle"[71] or, as
defined by Dinstein, the "personal knowledge principle",[72] are present in
the post-war military manuals of the US Army.[73] The Manual for Courts

[68] [A] distinction must be drawn as to the nature of a criminal order itself. Orders are the
basis upon which any army operates. It is basic to the discipline of an army that orders
are issued to be carried out. Its discipline is built upon this principle. Without it, no
army can be effective and it is certainly not incumbent upon a soldier in a subordinate
position to screen the orders of superiors for questionable points of legality. Within
certain limitations, he has the right to assume that the orders of his superiors and the
state which he serves and which are issued to him are in conformity with international
law. Many of the defendants here were field commanders and were charged with heavy
responsibilities in active combat. Their legal facilities were limited. They were soldiers –
not lawyers. Military commanders in the field with far reaching military responsibilities
cannot be charged under international law with criminal participation in issuing orders
which are not obviously criminal or which they are not shown to have known to be
criminal under international law. Such a commander cannot be expected to draw fine
distinctions and conclusions as to legality in connection with orders issued by his
superiors. He has the right to presume, in the absence of specific knowledge to the
contrary, that the legality of such orders has been properly determined before their
issuance. He cannot be held criminally responsible for a mere error in judgment as to
disputable legal questions.
It is therefore considered that to find a field commander criminally responsible for the
transmittal of such an order, he must have passed the order to the chain of command
and the order must be one that is criminal upon its face, or one which he is shown to
have known was criminal.

United States v. von Leeb, 11 *Trials of War Criminals before the Nuernberg Military Tribunals
under Control Council Law No.* 10, at 510–11 (1950).

[69] United States v. Ohlendorf, 4 *Trials of War Criminals before the Nuernberg Military
Tribunals under Control Council Law No.* 10, at 473.
The tribunal went on to reject the likelihood of the applicability of the defence to the cases
being considered by querying: "What SS man could say that he was unaware of the attitude
of Hitler toward Jewry?" *Ibid.*

[70] [o]rders to kill, given without previous proceedings, in respect of individual or groups
of inmates of this labour camp could not even as a matter of form have any legal
justification. They were therefore straightaway recognizable as illegal.
Public Prosecutor v. Leopold L. Austrian Supreme Court 1967, 47 *I.L.R.* 464, 466 (1974).

[71] [A] subordinate should incur responsibility for his act if he commits a crime pursuant to
a manifestly illegal order, whereas he ought to be absolved of guilt if he commits an
offence in compliance with an order whose illegality is not palpable. Clearly the
manifest illegality test is objective in character, and based on the intelligence of the
reasonable man.
Dinstein, *supra* note 63, at 26–27.

[72] [A]n accused should not be held responsible, under international law, for a criminal act
executed in obedience to a superior order if he committed the act without being aware of its
illegality.
Ibid., 30. Dinstein goes on to suggest that if the order was manifestly illegal, the defendant is
presumed to have been aware of this illegality, and perhaps will not even be allowed to
present proof in rebuttal of the presumption. *Ibid.*

[73] The Department of the Army Field Manual: *Law of Land Warfare* 27–10, Sec. 509 (1956)
reads:

Martial, United States 1984, is even clearer in recognizing as a defence "to any offense that the accused was acting pursuant to orders unless the accused knew the orders to be unlawful or a person of ordinary sense and understanding would have known the orders to be unlawful".[74] These documents clearly temper the rigidity of Nuremberg's black letter law. A position reflecting contemporary concepts was taken with regard to the Statute for the new tribunal by the United States representative to the Security Council, Ambassador Albright,[75] and by the ABA Task Force on War Crimes in Former Yugoslavia.[76] The ABA Task Force agrees that the defence of superior orders should provide a mitigating circumstance in cases of duress only.[77] Even more recently, the US draft Rules of Procedure and Evidence[78] suggest that the Statute's rigid rejection of the defence of superior orders should be mitigated. Rule 25(14)(A) thus provides that

    a. the fact that the law of war has been violated pursuant to an order of a superior authority, whether military or civil, does not deprive the act in question of its character of a war crime, nor does it constitute a defense in the trial of an accused individual, unless he did not know and could not reasonably have been expected to know that the act ordered was unlawful. In all cases where the order is held not to constitute a defense to an allegation of war crime, the fact that the individual was acting pursuant to orders may be considered in mitigation of punishment.

    b. In considering the question whether a superior order constitutes a valid defense, the court shall take into consideration the fact that obedience to lawful military orders is the duty of every member of the armed forces; that the latter cannot be expected, in conditions of war discipline, to weigh scrupulously the legal merits of the orders received; that certain rules of warfare may be controversial; or that an act otherwise amounting to a war crime may be done in obedience to orders conceived as a measure of reprisal. At the same time it must be borne in mind that members of the armed forces are bound to obey only lawful orders.

[74] *Rules for Courts Martial* (hereinafter: *R.C.M.*) 916(b).

[75] It is, of course, a defence that the accused was acting pursuant to orders where he or she did not know the orders were unlawful and a person of ordinary sense and understanding would not have known the orders to be unlawful. UN Doc. S/PV.3217 at 16 (25 May 1993).

[76] The Task Force does not support what appears to be an unqualified rejection of the defence of superior orders reflected in the language of Art. 7(4). Such a position does not give adequate consideration to the exigencies of military discipline in combat and the circumstance where a defendant acting under such conditions did not know and could not reasonably have been expected to now [*sic*] that the orders he carried out were unlawful.

ABA Report, *supra* note 10, at 37–38.

The Task Force recommends that Art. 7(4) either be revised or interpreted to recognize the defence of superior orders where a military defendant subject to superior orders in armed conflict did not know the orders to be unlawful and a person of ordinary sense and understanding would not have known the orders to be unlawful.

Ibid., 40.

[77] [I]f the defense of superior orders is rejected because the defendant knew or should have known that the order was unlawful, then mitigation of punishment is not appropriate based on superior orders unless execution of the unlawful orders was compelled by duress.

Ibid., 40.

[78] *Supra* note 39.

[i]t is a defense to any offense that the accused was acting pursuant to orders unless the accused knew the orders to be unlawful or a person of ordinary sense and understanding would have known the orders to be unlawful.

And Rule 25(14)(B), which concerns duress or coercion states that

[i]t is a defense to any offense, except any crime involving killing, that the accused's participation in the offense was caused by a reasonable apprehension that the accused or another innocent person would be immediately killed or would immediately suffer serious bodily injury as a result of the accused's refusal to commit the act. The Trial Chamber may consider as a matter of mitigation in offenses involving killing the extent to which the accused was compelled by duress to commit the crime.

The plea of duress, it may be noted, was recognized in such Nuremberg judgments under Control Council Law No. 10 as the *von Leeb*[79] and the *Ohlendorf*[80] cases.[81] The Secretary-General's Commentary recognizes that the Tribunal "may consider the factor of superior orders in connection with other defences such as coercion or lack of moral choice",[82] but this, it is submitted, does not go far enough in reflecting the post-Nuremberg law.[83]

It is, of course, only too easy to criticize or second guess the drafters. There is no question that despite the extremely short time available to the drafters, the Statute is a remarkable document that will have an important impact on the development of international law.

---

[79] The defendants in this case who received obviously criminal orders were placed in a difficult position, but servile compliance with orders clearly criminal for fear of some disadvantage or punishment not immediately threatened cannot be recognized as a defence. To establish the defence of coercion or necessity in the face of danger, there must be a showing of circumstances such that a reasonable man would apprehend that he was in such imminent physical peril as to deprive him of freedom to choose the right and refrain from the wrong.

Supra note 58, at 509.

[80] [I]t is stated that in military law even if the subordinate realizes that the act he is called upon to perform is a crime, he may not refuse its execution without incurring serious consequences, and that this, therefore, constitutes duress.... The test to be applied is whether the subordinate acted under coercion or whether he himself approved of the principle involved in the order.

Supra note 69, at 480.

If one claims duress in the execution of an illegal order it must be shown that the harm caused by obeying the illegal order is not disproportionally greater than the harm which would result from not obeying the illegal order.

Ibid., 471.

[81] *See also* Dinstein, *supra* note 63, at 149.   [82] Commentary, 1175, para. 57.

[83] *Compare* O'Brien, *supra* note 2, at 654:

[t]he defense's evidence should be evaluated in the light of, among other things, the exigency of the situation, the requirements of military discipline, whether the accused could have had subjective or objective knowledge of the order's lawfulness, and whether the rule of law at issue was controversial.

XIII

International Criminalization of
Internal Atrocities*

For half a century, the Nuremberg and Tokyo trials and national prosecutions of World War II cases remained the major instances of criminal prosecution of offenders against fundamental norms of international humanitarian law. The heinous activities of the Pol Pot regime in Cambodia and the use of poison gas by Iraq against its Kurdish population are among the many atrocities left unpunished by either international or national courts. Some treaties were adopted that provide for national prosecution of offenses of international concern and, in many cases, for universal jurisdiction; but, with a few exceptions, these treaties were not observed. Notwithstanding the absence of significant prosecutions, an international consensus on the legitimacy of the Nuremberg Principles, the applicability of universal jurisdiction to international crimes, and the need to punish those responsible for egregious violations of international humanitarian law slowly solidified. The International Law Commission, veterans of the Nuremberg and Tokyo proceedings, individuals such as Rafael Lemkin (who advocated the adoption of the Genocide Convention) and a handful of academics (most notably M. Cherif Bassiouni), among others, helped keep alive the heritage of Nuremberg and the promise of future prosecutions of serious violators of international humanitarian law.

Recent atrocities in the former Yugoslavia and Rwanda shocked the conscience of people everywhere, triggering, within a short span of time, several major legal developments: the promulgation by the Security Council, acting under chapter VII of the United Nations Charter, of the Statutes of the international criminal Tribunals for the former Yugoslavia and Rwanda, and the adoption by the International Law Commission of a treaty-based statute for an international criminal court. These developments warrant a fresh examination of the present state and future direction of the criminal aspects of international humanitarian law applicable to noninternational armed conflicts, conflicts that occur with far greater frequency than international armed conflicts.

* I should like to express my thanks to Professors George Aldrich, Georges Abi-Saab, Antonio Cassese and Andreas Lowenfeld for their suggestions and, in particular, to Luigi Condorelli for his very important contribution.

The sovereignty of states and their insistence on maintaining maximum discretion in dealing with those who threaten their "sovereign authority" have combined to limit the reach of international humanitarian law applicable to noninternational armed conflicts.[1] Governments have been determined to deal with rebels harshly and to deny them legal recognition and political status. They have refused to be reassured by treaty language, such as Article 3(2) common to the Geneva Conventions for the Protection of Victims of War,[2] which explicitly states that application of listed protective norms will not affect the legal status of the parties. This trend has been attenuated only in part by the heightened impact of human rights law and acceptance of the principle that human rights are a matter of international concern.

International lawmaking and various diplomatic conferences, for example, the conference that adopted the Additional Protocols to the Geneva Conventions in 1977, have, on the whole, been unsympathetic toward extending the protective rules applicable to international wars to civil wars – an attitude that has dampened prospects for redress through orderly treaty making. Because conferences often make decisions by consensus and try to fashion generally acceptable texts, even a few recalcitrant governments may prevent the adoption of more enlightened provisions.

However, the Security Council's Statutes for the criminal Tribunals for the former Yugoslavia and Rwanda have contributed significantly to the development of international humanitarian law and its extension to noninternational armed conflicts.[3] This advance can be explained by the

---

[1] This applies even more to situations of lower-intensity internal strife. For a discussion of the norms applicable in noninternational armed conflicts and internal strife and the problem of characterizing conflicts, see generally Theodor Meron, *On the Inadequate Reach of Humanitarian and Human Rights Law and the Need for a New Instrument*, 77 AJIL 589 (1983); Theodor Meron & Allan Rosas, *A Declaration of Minimum Humanitarian Standards*, 85 AJIL 375 (1991); Asbjørn Eide, Allan Rosas & Theodor Meron, *Combating Lawlessness in Gray Zone Conflicts through Minimum Humanitarian Standards*, 89 AJIL 215 (1995).

For description of noninternational armed conflicts, see common Article 3 of the Geneva Conventions, *infra* note 2, and Article 1 of Additional Protocol II to the Geneva Conventions, *infra* note 20.

[2] Convention for the Amelioration of the Condition of the Wounded and Sick in Armed Forces in the Field (Geneva Convention No. I), Aug. 12, 1949, 6 UST 3114, 75 UNTS 31; Convention for the Amelioration of the Condition of Wounded, Sick, and Shipwrecked Members of Armed Forces at Sea (Geneva Convention No. II), Aug. 12, 1949, 6 UST 3217, 75 UNTS 85; Convention Relative to the Treatment of Prisoners of War (Geneva Convention No. III), Aug. 12, 1949, 6 UST 3316, 75 UNTS 135; Convention Relative to the Protection of Civilian Persons in Time of War (Geneva Convention No. IV), Aug. 12, 1949, 6 UST 3516, 75 UNTS 287.

See also Hague Convention on the Protection of Cultural Property, May 14, 1954, Art. 19(4), 249 UNTS 240; Protocol Additional to the Geneva Conventions of 12 August 1949, and Relating to the Protection of Victims of International Armed Conflicts, *opened for signature* Dec. 12, 1977, Art. 4, 1125 UNTS 3, *reprinted in* 16 ILM 1391 (1977) [hereinafter Protocol I].

[3] *See* James C. O'Brien, *The International Tribunal for Violations of International Humanitarian Law in the Former Yugoslavia*, 87 AJIL 639 (1993); Theodor Meron, *War Crimes in Yugoslavia and the Development of International Law*, 88 AJIL 78 (1994).

pressure, in the face of atrocities, for a rapid adjustment of law, process and institutions.[4] No matter how many atrocities cases these international tribunals may eventually try, their very existence sends a powerful message. Their statutes, rules of procedure and evidence, and practice stimulate the development of the law. The possible fear by states that the activities of such tribunals might preempt national prosecutions could also have the beneficial effect of spurring prosecutions before national courts for serious violations of humanitarian law.

While supporting the Security Council's establishment of international tribunals for Yugoslavia,[5] where consent to a treaty creating such a tribunal could not be obtained, and Rwanda, I am concerned about the selectivity involved in a system where the establishment of a tribunal for a given conflict situation depends on whether consensus to apply chapter VII of the UN Charter can be obtained. What is needed is a uniform and definite corpus of international humanitarian law that can be applied apolitically to internal atrocities everywhere, and that recognizes the role of all states in the vindication of such law.[6]

The enforcement of international humanitarian law cannot depend on international tribunals alone. They will never be a substitute for national courts. National systems of justice have a vital, indeed, the principal, role to play here. The Draft Statute for an International Criminal Court adopted by the International Law Commission, if generally accepted, may eliminate some need for establishing more ad hoc tribunals, but the problem of the scope of the substantive international criminal law would remain. Because of the uncertainties surrounding the prospects for an international criminal court, doubts about establishing additional ad hoc criminal tribunals for violations committed in specific countries, and the recognition that the role of international tribunals will always be complementary to that played by national justice systems, the function of national courts cannot be ignored.

To be sure, the record of national prosecutions of violators of such international norms as the grave breaches of the Geneva Conventions is disappointing, even when the obligation to prosecute or extradite violators is unequivocal. A lack of resources, evidence and, above all, political will has stood in the way. International criminal law, of course, is just one element in the life of the society. Addressed in isolation, it will not eliminate abuses. However, greater reliance on that law by national prosecutors and judges would be a move in the right direction. We

---

[4] Theodor Meron, *Rape as a Crime under International Humanitarian Law*, 87 AJIL 424 (1993).
[5] Theodor Meron, *The Case for War Crimes Trials in Yugoslavia*, FOREIGN AFF., Summer 1993, at 122.
[6] *See* James Crawford, *The ILC Adopts a Statute for an International Criminal Court*, 89 AJIL 404, 416 (1995).

must therefore rethink the traditional concepts regarding the norms of international law that are applicable to noninternational armed conflicts. We should take a new look at the penal and jurisdictional elements of international humanitarian law, especially universal jurisdiction. In this article, I shall try to develop a broad, principled approach to the prosecution of perpetrators of atrocities committed in civil wars or noninternational armed conflicts (but not in civil strife or situations involving violence of lower intensity), focused not only on the role of international tribunals but also on that of national courts.

THE YUGOSLAVIA AND RWANDA STATUTES AND INTERNAL ATROCITIES

Acting both on the basis of chapter VII of the UN Charter and in pursuance of a request of the Government of Rwanda, the Security Council recently adopted a Statute for the International Tribunal for Rwanda.[7] The new Statute constitutes an extremely important development of international humanitarian law with regard to the criminal character of internal atrocities in Rwanda, and, one may hope, in other conflicts as well. In contrast to the Statute of the International Criminal Tribunal for the Former Yugoslavia, which appears to treat the conflicts in the former Yugoslavia as international,[8] the Statute for Rwanda is predicated on the assumption that the conflict in Rwanda is a noninternational armed conflict.

The offenses listed in Articles 2 and 3 of the Yugoslavia Statute (grave breaches of the Geneva Conventions and violations of the laws or customs of war) indicate that the Security Council considered the armed conflicts in Yugoslavia as international. The facts on the ground and the applicable rules of international law strongly support this conclusion.[9] Treating the conflicts in Yugoslavia as international armed conflicts enhances the corpus of the applicable international humanitarian law and fully respects the principle of *nullum crimen sine lege*.

Subject matter jurisdiction under the Rwanda Statute encompasses three principal offenses. First, like the Yugoslavia Statute, the Rwanda Statute grants the Tribunal the power to prosecute persons who have committed genocide.[10] Of course, the criminal nature of genocide

---

[7] UN Doc. S/RES/955, annex (1994) [hereinafter Rwanda Statute].

[8] UN Doc. S/25704, annex (1993) [hereinafter Yugoslavia Statute]. Note, however, that the first annual report of the Yugoslav Tribunal states that the Tribunal is empowered to adjudicate cases of crimes committed in both interstate wars and internal strife. UN Doc. A/49/342–S/1994/1007, para. 19 (1994). For the practice of the Tribunal see *infra* ch. XIV.

[9] O'Brien, *supra* note 3, at 647; Meron, *supra* note 3, at 80–81.

[10] SC Res. 995 (1994), UN Doc. S/RES/995, *supra* note 7, Art. 2.

committed in internal conflicts has never been doubted; the customary law character of the peremptory prohibitions stated in the Convention on the Prevention and Punishment of the Crime of Genocide[11] was affirmed long ago by the International Court of Justice,[12] and the possible prosecution of the perpetrators before an international penal tribunal is envisaged by Article VI of the Convention.

Second, the Rwanda Statute – following the example set by the Yugoslavia Statute – confers on the Tribunal the power to prosecute persons who have committed crimes against humanity. Apart from the Nuremberg Charter, where they first appeared, no treaty has defined crimes against humanity and, perhaps inevitably, they have not always been viewed in an identical fashion.

The tangled meshing of crimes against humanity and human rights violations militates against requiring that the former be linked with war.[13] Thus, the UN Secretary-General's commentary to Article 5 of the Yugoslavia Statute properly suggests that crimes against humanity can be committed even outside international or internal armed conflicts.[14] Nevertheless, the black letter of the Statute itself gives the Tribunal competence over such crimes only when committed in international or internal armed conflicts.[15] By making no allusion to the international or noninternational character of the conflict, the broad language of Article 3 of the Rwanda Statute (entitled "Crimes against humanity") both strengthens the precedent set by the commentary to the Yugoslavia Statute and enhances the possibility of arguing in the future that crimes against humanity (in addition to genocide) can be committed even in peacetime.[16]

---

[11] Dec. 9, 1948, 78 UNTS 277 [hereinafter Genocide Convention].

[12] Reservations to the Convention on the Prevention and Punishment of the Crime of Genocide, 1951 ICJ Rep. 15, 23 (Advisory Opinion of May 28), *discussed in* Theodor Meron, Human Rights and Humanitarian Norms as Customary Law 10–11 (1989).

[13] For further discussion, see Meron, *supra* note 3, at 85.

[14] Report of the Secretary-General pursuant to paragraph 2 of Security Council Resolution 808, UN Doc. S/25704, para. 47 (1993) [hereinafter Report of the Secretary-General].

[15] "[W]hen committed in armed conflict, whether international or internal in character, and directed against any civilian population ..." *Id.*, para. 49; Yugoslavia Statute, *supra* note 8, Art. 5.

[16] The Charter of the International Military Tribunal, 82 UNTS 280, Art. 6(c), defined crimes against humanity as crimes including "murder, extermination, enslavement, deportation, and other inhumane acts committed against any civilian population, before or during the war, or persecutions on political, racial or religious grounds in execution of or in connection with any crime within the jurisdiction of the Tribunal." Article 3 of the Rwanda Statute defines crimes against humanity in accordance with paragraph 48 of the commentary to Article 5 of the Yugoslavia Statute (Report of the Secretary-General, *supra* note 14). The ILC's commentary on Article 20 of the Draft Statute for an International Criminal Court reflects the same trend:

> It is the understanding of the Commission that the definition of crimes against humanity encompasses inhumane acts of a very serious character involving widespread or systematic violations aimed at the civilian population in whole or part. The hallmarks of

This positive element, however, is balanced by a somewhat more complicated definition of crimes against humanity. Thus, in contrast to the Nuremberg definition, the Rwanda Statute requires proof that such crimes were committed "as part of a widespread or systematic attack against any civilian population on national, political, ethnic, racial or religious grounds" (Article 3, chapeau).[17] While Article 3(h) is based on the Nuremberg Charter ("[p]ersecutions on political, racial and religious grounds"), the chapeau draws on the Secretary-General's commentary to Article 5 of the Yugoslavia Statute.

To prosecute crimes against humanity under Article 5 of the Yugoslavia Statute, it is required to show only that the crimes listed in that article were "directed" against any civilian population. Although the requirement of establishing the large-scale, systematic nature of attacks against a civilian population appears in the jurisprudence of Nuremberg,[18] there was no need to include it in the statutory definition. One may ask whether, by stating all these requirements in the text of the Rwanda Statute, the Security Council has not inadvertently made the burden of proving crimes against humanity more difficult to meet.

Clearly, crimes against humanity overlap to a considerable extent with the crime of genocide. Indeed, the latter can be regarded as a species and particular progeny of the broader genus of crimes against humanity. Crimes against humanity are crimes under customary law. Genocide is a crime under both customary law and a treaty. The core prohibitions of crimes against humanity and the crime of genocide constitute *jus cogens* norms.

> such crimes lie in their large-scale and systematic nature. The particular forms of unlawful act ... are less crucial to the definition than the factors of scale and deliberate policy, as well as in their being targeted against the civilian population in whole or in part.... The term "directed against any civilian population" should be taken to refer to acts committed as part of a widespread and systematic attack against a civilian population on national, political, ethnic, racial or religious grounds. The particular acts referred to in the definition are acts deliberately committed as part of such an attack.

Report of the International Law Commission on the work of its forty-sixth session, UN GAOR, 49th Sess., Supp. No. 10, at 76, UN Doc. A/49/10 (1994). The black-letter law of Article 20 tracks the definition of crimes against humanity that appears in the Yugoslavia Statute.

The Final Report of the Commission of Experts on Rwanda complicates the matter further by defining crimes against humanity as "gross violations of fundamental rules of humanitarian and human rights law committed by persons demonstrably linked to a party to the armed conflict, as part of an official policy based on discrimination against an identifiable group of persons, irrespective of war and the nationality of the victim." UN Doc. S/1994/1405, annex, para. 135 (1994).

[17] Rwanda Statute, *supra* note 7, Art. 3.

[18] Meron, *supra* note 5, at 130; 15 LAW REPORTS OF TRIALS OF WAR CRIMINALS 135–36 (1949).

The crime of genocide requires a particularly heavy burden of proof. There is a distinct advantage in being able to prosecute offenders for the crime of genocide or other crimes against humanity, or even both. The departure from the simpler Nuremberg model of crimes against humanity and the drift toward merging these two offenses are unfortunate.

In the circumstances of Rwanda, the crime of genocide and crimes against humanity appear to cover most of the murders that have been committed. Genocide, as we know, requires evidence of "intent to destroy, in whole or in part, a national, ethnical, racial or religious group, as such."[19] Some killings and other violations might fall outside the specific offenses of the crime of genocide and crimes against humanity because of either definitional difficulties or a failure to satisfy the burden of proof. Proof of systematic and deliberate planning, however, is not required to establish the violation of common Article 3 or Additional Protocol II.[20]

In this case, Article 4 of the Statute provides a safety net that is the Statute's greatest innovation. Under Article 4, the Tribunal may prosecute persons who have committed serious violations of common Article 3 of the Geneva Conventions and of Additional Protocol II.[21] A recent report by the UN Secretary-General recognizes that

> the Security Council has elected to take a more expansive approach to the choice of the applicable law than the one underlying the statute of the Yugoslav Tribunal, and included within the subject-matter jurisdiction of the Rwanda Tribunal international instruments regardless of whether they were considered

---

[19] Genocide Convention, *supra* note 11, Art. 2. *See also* Rwanda Statute, *supra* note 7, Art. 2.

[20] Protocol Additional to the Geneva Conventions of 12 August 1949, and Relating to the Protection of Victims of Non-International Armed Conflicts, *opened for signature* Dec. 12, 1977, 1125 UNTS 609, *reprinted in* 16 ILM at 1442 [hereinafter Protocol II].

[21] Article 4 of the Rwanda Statute, *supra* note 7, reads:

> The International Tribunal for Rwanda shall have the power to prosecute persons committing or ordering to be committed serious violations of Article 3 common to the Geneva Conventions of 12 August 1949 for the Protection of War Victims, and of Additional Protocol II thereto of 8 June 1977. These violations shall include, but shall not be limited to:
>
> (a) Violence to life, health and physical or mental well-being of persons, in particular murder as well as cruel treatment such as torture, mutilation or any form of corporal punishment;
> (b) Collective punishments;
> (c) Taking of hostages;
> (d) Acts of terrorism;
> (e) Outrages upon personal dignity, in particular humiliating and degrading treatment, rape, enforced prostitution and any form of indecent assault;
> (f) Pillage;
> (g) The passing of sentences and the carrying out of executions without previous judgement pronounced by a regularly constituted court, affording all the judicial guarantees which are recognized as indispensable by civilized peoples;
> (h) Threats to commit any of the foregoing acts.

part of customary international law or whether they have customarily entailed the individual criminal responsibility of the perpetrator of the crime. Article 4 of the statute, accordingly, includes violations of Additional Protocol II, which, as a whole, has not yet been universally recognized as part of customary international law, and for the first time criminalizes common Article 3 ...[22]

The listed violations draw on both Article 4 of Protocol II ("Fundamental guarantees" clause) and common Article 3. Because the list of violations in Article 4 of the Statute is illustrative and not exclusive, the Tribunal is empowered to apply other provisions of Protocol II as well.

Article 4 of the Rwanda Statute stands in sharp contrast to the Yugoslavia Statute. Apart from crimes against humanity and the crime of genocide, the Yugoslavia Tribunal's subject matter jurisdiction under the Statute covers rules of international humanitarian law that are applicable to international armed conflicts (discussed in the next section) and are declaratory of customary law. The jurisdiction of the Tribunal under Article 4 of the Rwanda Statute also derives from instruments governing noninternational armed conflicts (common Article 3 and Additional Protocol II). Whatever the Tribunal does in practice, this development has enormous normative importance.

CRIMINALITY OF HUMANITARIAN LAW

Until very recently, the accepted wisdom was that neither common Article 3 (which is not among the grave breaches provisions of the Geneva Conventions) nor Protocol II (which contains no provisions on grave breaches) provided a basis for universal jurisdiction, and that they constituted, at least on the international plane, an uncertain basis for individual criminal responsibility.[23] Moreover, it has been asserted that the normative customary law rules applicable in noninternational armed conflicts do not encompass the criminal element of war crimes. In its comments on the proposed draft statute for the Yugoslavia tribunal, the International Committee of the Red Cross thus "underline[d] the fact that, according to International Humanitarian Law as it stands today, the notion of war crimes is limited to situations of international armed

---

[22] UN Doc. S/1995/134, para. 12 (1995).

[23] One of the legal advisers of the International Committee of the Red Cross thus wrote: "IHL applicable to non-international armed conflicts does not provide for international penal responsibility of persons guilty of violations." Denise Plattner, *The Penal Repression of Violations of International Humanitarian Law Applicable in Non-international Armed Conflicts*, 30 INT'L REV. RED CROSS 409, 414 (1990).

The chapter on execution of the Convention in each of the 1949 Geneva Conventions contains provisions on penal sanctions. For example, for the grave breaches provisions of the Fourth Geneva Convention, *supra* note 2, see Articles 129–30.

conflict."[24] In its final report, the United Nations War Crimes Commission (for Yugoslavia) was equally categorical.[25]

The International Law Commission also excluded Additional Protocol II from the subject matter jurisdiction of the proposed international criminal court. Its criteria for listing treaties that state crimes within the jurisdiction of that court are:

> (a) that the crimes are themselves defined by the treaty so that an international criminal court could apply that treaty as law in relation to the crime, subject to the *nullum crimen* guarantee contained in article 39;
>
> (b) that the treaty created either a system of universal jurisdiction based on the principle *aut dedere aut judicare* or the possibility for an international criminal court to try the crime, or both, thus recognizing clearly the principle of international concern.[26]

As to why Additional Protocol II is not included in the list of treaties stating crimes within the court's jurisdiction, the ILC explained that it excluded treaties "which merely regulate conduct, or which prohibit conduct but only on an inter-State basis,"[27] and that "Protocol II prohibits certain conduct but contains no clause dealing with grave breaches, nor any equivalent enforcement provision."[28]

The ILC's attitude was too restrictive. Respect for the fundamental guarantees of Protocol II does involve individual conduct and, obviously, is a matter of "international concern." An international tribunal could thus apply the provisions of Protocol II as criminal law.

Nevertheless, one should not attribute too much general doctrinal importance to the Commission's list of treaties establishing crimes over which the tribunal will have jurisdiction. As the ILC itself explained, "article 20(a)–(d) is not intended as an exhaustive list of crimes under general international law. It is limited to those crimes under general international law which the Commission believes should be within the jurisdiction of the Court at this state ..."[29] The ILC was thus

---

[24] Unpublished comments (Mar. 25, 1993).

[25] "[T]he content of customary law applicable to internal armed conflict is debatable. As a result, in general ... the only offences committed in internal armed conflict for which universal jurisdiction exists are 'crimes against humanity' and genocide, which apply irrespective of the conflicts' classification." UN Doc. S/1994/674, annex, para. 42 (1994).

"[T]here does not appear to be a customary international law applicable to internal armed conflicts which includes the concept of war crimes." *Id.*, para. 52.

"It must be observed that the violations of the laws or customs of war referred to in article 3 of the statute of the International Tribunal [for the Former Yugoslavia] are offences when committed in international, but not in internal armed conflicts." *Id.*, para. 54.

[26] Report of the International Law Commission on the work of its forty-sixth session, *supra* note 16, at 78 (commentary to Art. 20).

[27] *Id.*, commentary to annex, at 142.   [28] *Id.* at 145.

[29] Report of the International Law Commission on the work of its forty-sixth session, *supra* note 16, at 77–78.

concerned with the prospects for states to accept the proposed statute rather than with the broader question of criminality of offenses committed in internal conflicts. As the preamble to the statute states: the "court is intended to exercise jurisdiction only over the most serious crimes of concern to the international community as a whole."[30] The Commission acknowledged that it would be difficult to draw a distinction between treaty crimes and crimes under general international law,[31] that the statute is primarily "adjectival and procedural,"[32] and that it was not its function "authoritatively to codify crimes under general international law."[33]

As early as the discussions of the Yugoslavia Statute, however, voices urging international criminalization of violations of common Article 3 and Additional Protocol II had been heard. In the Security Council, Ambassador Albright explained the U.S. understanding that the "laws or customs of war" in Article 3 of the Statute (which is illustrative and not exclusive) "include all obligations under humanitarian law agreements in force in the territory of the former Yugoslavia at the time the acts were committed, including common article 3 of the 1949 Geneva Conventions, and the 1977 Additional Protocols to these Conventions."[34]

An additional basis for considering that common Article 3 is applicable to the Yugoslav conflicts despite their international character can be mentioned. This is the *Nicaragua* Court's dictum that Article 3 contains rules that "constitute a minimum yardstick,"[35] or a normative floor, for international conflicts.

The U.S. Joint Chiefs of Staff proposed defining "other inhumane acts" referred to in Article 5 of the Yugoslavia Statute (crimes against humanity) as encompassing various offenses stated in common Article 3 of the Geneva Conventions, which "are part of customary international law and, therefore, [are] consistent with the principle of *nullum crimen sine lege*."[36]

---

[30] *Id.* at 44. [31] *Id.* at 66. [32] *Id.* at 71. [33] *Id.*

[34] UN Doc. S/PV.3217, at 15 (May 25, 1993). The prosecution at the Yugoslavia Tribunal has followed this approach in treating forcible sexual intercourse as cruel treatment in violation of common Article 3(1)(a). *See* note 59 *infra*. The prosecution appears to believe that it may bring actions for violations of common Article 3 as if they were violations of the laws or customs of war. Thus, Indictment No. 1 against Nicolic (Nov. 7, 1994) states at paragraph 16.2 that Nicolic "violated the Laws or Customs of War, contrary to Article 3(1)(a) of the [Fourth] Geneva Convention" by participating in cruel treatment of certain victims. More generally, the indictment charges the accused with "[v]iolations of the Laws and Customs of War including those recognized by Article 3 of the Fourth Geneva Convention." On common Article 3 in the Yugoslavia Statute, see also O'Brien, *supra* note 3, at 646.

[35] Military and Paramilitary Activities in and against Nicaragua (Nicar. v. U.S.), Merits, 1986 ICJ REP. 14, 114 (June 27).

[36] Office of the Chairman, Joint Chiefs of Staff, Memorandum for the DOD General Counsel, appendix (June 25, 1993) (unpublished, in the author's files).

The International Law Section of the American Bar Association took a similar position.[37]

There is no moral justification, and no truly persuasive legal reason, for treating perpetrators of atrocities in internal conflicts more leniently than those engaged in international wars. Ambassador Albright's statement was therefore a welcome attempt to extend the concept of crimes under international law to abuses committed in noninternational armed conflicts.

The trend toward regarding common Article 3 and Additional Protocol II as bases for individual criminal responsibility was accentuated in reports concerning atrocities in Rwanda.[38] Having determined that the conflict in Rwanda constitutes a noninternational armed conflict, the Independent Commission of Experts on Rwanda asserted that common Article 3 and Additional Protocol II,[39] and the principle of individual criminal responsibility in international law,[40] are applicable.

In contrast to the Yugoslavia Statute, on which there is abundant contemporaneous documentation, the Statute for Rwanda is lacking in documented legislative history. However, one thing is clear, though surprising. Perhaps because it was realized that the crime of genocide and crimes against humanity might not adequately cover the field and that, for practical reasons, the safety net of common Article 3 and Protocol II was needed, there was no opposition in the Security Council to treating violations of common Article 3 and Additional Protocol II as bases for the individual criminal responsibility of the perpetrators. Objections to the subject matter jurisdiction of the Tribunal based on the arguably *ex post facto* character of Article 4 of the Statute have not been raised either. For Rwanda, at least, one of the most important weaknesses of international humanitarian law was remedied.

In his commentary on the Yugoslavia Statute, the Secretary-General stated that the principle of *nullum crimen sine lege* requires that the Tribunal "apply rules of international humanitarian law which are beyond any doubt part of customary law so that the problem of adherence of some but not all States to specific conventions does not arise."[41] Because Rwanda is a party to both the Geneva Conventions and the Additional Protocols, the customary law character of common Article 3, which has been explicitly

---

[37] Task Force of the ABA Section of International Law and Practice, Report on the International Tribunal to Adjudicate War Crimes Committed in the Former Yugoslavia 15 (1993).

[38] René Degni-Séqui, Report on the Situation of Human Rights in Rwanda, UN Doc. E/CN.4/1995/7, para. 54 (1994). *See also infra* text at notes 39–40.

[39] UN Doc. S/1994/1125, annex, paras. 90–93 (1994). Rwanda has been a party to Protocol II since 1984.

[40] *Id.*, paras. 125–28.

[41] Report of the Secretary-General, *supra* note 14, para. 34.

recognized by the International Court of Justice,[42] and Protocol II is not an issue here. Rather, the question is whether these treaty provisions, which prohibit certain enumerated acts, establish the individual criminal responsibility of the perpetrators, that is, whether the proscriptions applicable to noninternational armed conflicts are criminal in character.

Those who reject common Article 3 and Additional Protocol II as a basis for individual criminal responsibility tend to confuse criminality with jurisdiction and penalties. The question of what actions constitute crimes must be distinguished from the question of jurisdiction to try those crimes. Failure to distinguish between substantive criminality and jurisdiction[43] has weakened the penal aspects of the law of war. Treaties typically obligate contracting states to enforce their norms and punish those who commit listed offenses.[44] A treaty may specify the state or states competent to exercise jurisdiction. When it does not, it may be necessary to resort to interpretation to ascertain whether certain states only, third states or all states parties to the treaty are permitted to exercise jurisdiction over the offense.

Since the readiness of the Nuremberg Tribunals to proceed against violations of the Convention Respecting the Laws and Customs of War on Land[45] and the (Geneva) Convention Relative to the Treatment of Prisoners of War,[46] neither of which contains provisions on punishment of breaches or penalties, it has not been seriously questioned that some acts of individuals that are prohibited by international law constitute criminal offenses, even when there is no accompanying provision for the establishment of the jurisdiction of particular courts or a scale of penalties.

Whether international law creates individual criminal responsibility depends on such considerations as whether the prohibitory norm in question, which may be conventional or customary, is directed to individuals, states, groups or other authorities, and/or to all of these.[47] The extent to which the prohibition is addressed to individuals, whether the prohibition is unequivocal in character, the gravity of the act, and the interests of the international community are all relevant factors in determining the criminality of various acts.

---

[42] Military and Paramilitary Activities in and against Nicaragua, *supra* note 35, 1986 ICJ Rep. at 114. The Court also decided that the obligation of states under common Article 1 to respect and to ensure respect for the Geneva Conventions applies to common Article 3.

[43] G. I. A. D. Draper, *The Modern Pattern of War Criminality*, 6 Isr. Y.B. Hum. Rts. 9, 22 (1976).

[44] Yoram Dinstein, *International Criminal Law*, 20 Isr. L. Rev. 206, 221–22 (1985).

[45] Oct. 18, 1907, 36 Stat. 2277, 118 LNTS 343 [hereinafter Hague Convention No. IV].

[46] *Opened for signature* July 27, 1929, 47 Stat. 2021 (1932).

[47] *See generally* Nguyen Quoc Dinh, Droit International Public 621 (Patrick Daillier & Alain Pellet eds., 5th ed. 1994); Meron, *supra* note 12, at 208–15.

That an obligation is addressed to governments is not dispositive of the penal responsibility of individuals, if individuals clearly must carry out that obligation. The Nuremberg Tribunals thus considered as binding not only on Germany, but also on individual defendants those provisions of the 1929 Geneva Convention and the fourth 1907 Hague Convention that were addressed to "belligerents," the "occupant" or "an army of occupation."[48] In light of this jurisprudence and the rudimentary nature of instruments of international humanitarian law as penal law, I find unpersuasive the view of commentators who contest the criminality of common Article 3 on the ground that it speaks of the obligations of "each Party to the conflict." As the International Military Tribunal so eloquently stated, "Crimes against international law are committed by men, not by abstract entities, and only by punishing individuals who commit such crimes can the provisions of international law be enforced."[49]

Typically, norms of international law have been addressed to states. Enforced by individuals acting as agents of the state, they have engaged, in case of violation, the international responsibility of the state.[50] With increasing frequency, however, international law, and especially the law of war, has directed its proscriptions both to states and to individuals and groups. Modern international humanitarian law imposes, and is perceived as imposing, criminal responsibility on individuals, often in addition to the state's international responsibility. International conventions that proscribe certain activities of international concern without creating international tribunals to try the violators characteristically obligate states to prohibit those activities and to punish the natural and legal persons under their jurisdiction for violations according to national law.[51]

The fact that international rules are normally enforced by national institutions and national courts applying municipal law does not in any way diminish the status of the violations as international crimes. Moreover, the evolution of individual criminal responsibility must not erode the vital concepts of state responsibility for the violation of international norms.

---

[48] United States v. von Leeb, 11 TRIALS OF WAR CRIMINALS BEFORE THE NUERNBERG MILITARY TRIBUNALS UNDER CONTROL COUNCIL LAW No. 10, at 462, 537, 539–40 (1948) (*"The High Command Case"*) [hereinafter TRIALS].

[49] TRIAL OF THE MAJOR WAR CRIMINALS BEFORE THE INTERNATIONAL MILITARY TRIBUNAL, NUREMBERG, 14 NOVEMBER 1945–1 OCTOBER 1946, 1 OFFICIAL DOCUMENTS 223 (1947) [hereinafter TRIAL DOCUMENTS].

[50] Cf. crimes of state in the meaning of Article 19 of the ILC's draft articles on state responsibility (part one), adopted by the ILC on first reading. [1976] 2 Y.B. Int'l L. Comm'n, pt. 2, at 73, 95–96, UN Doc. A/CN.4/SER.A/1976/Add.1 (pt. 2). *See generally* MERON, *supra* note 12, at 208–15.

[51] *E.g.*, Convention on the Prohibition of the Development, Production, Stockpiling and Use of Chemical Weapons and on Their Destruction, Jan. 13, 1993, Art. VII, 32 ILM 800, 810 (1993).

It is often difficult to determine which of the acts prohibited under international law are offenses. As noted above, the penal element of international humanitarian law is still rudimentary. Its development has been nourished by such broad ideas as the Martens clause,[52] general principles of law recognized by civilized nations, and general principles of penal law.[53] When treaties fail to clearly define the criminality of prohibited acts, the underlying assumption has been that customary law and internal penal law would supply the missing links.

The development of penal aspects of international humanitarian law has shifted back and forth between a preference for more or less comprehensive lists of crimes and brief references to the laws and customs of war. The first approach was attempted in the report of the commission established by the Preliminary Peace Conference in 1919, which adopted a formal list of thirty-two different crimes.[54] This approach was also taken in the lists of grave breaches in the 1949 Geneva Conventions, and in the expanded list of grave breaches in Additional Protocol I to the Geneva Conventions. In Article 228 of the Treaty of Versailles, however, the German Government recognized the right of the Allied and Associated Powers to bring persons before military tribunals who were accused of having committed acts in violation of the laws and customs of war *tout court*.[55]

The fourth Hague Convention, which contains a normative statement in the "Regulations respecting the laws and customs of war on land, annexed to the present Convention," was silent regarding penal responsibility. The early Geneva Conventions contain no penal provisions whatsoever. Nor does the 1929 POW Convention[56] (except with respect to

---

[52] Hersch Lauterpacht, *The Law of Nations and the Punishment of War Crimes*, 21 Brit. Y.B. Int'l L. 58, 65 (1944). *See also* Lord Wright, *War Crimes under International Law*, 62 L. Q. Rev. 40, 42 (1946). The Martens clause reads as follows:

> Until a more complete code of the laws of war has been issued, the High Contracting Parties deem it expedient to declare that, in cases not included in the Regulations adopted by them [and annexed to the Convention], the inhabitants and the belligerents remain under the protection and the rule of the principles of the law of nations, as they result from the usages established among civilized peoples, from the laws of humanity, and the dictates of the public conscience.

Hague Convention No. IV, *supra* note 45, Preamble.

[53] Draper, *supra* note 43, at 18.

[54] United Nations War Crimes Commission, History of the United Nations War Crimes Commission and the Development of the Laws of War 34–35 (1948).

[55] Treaty of Peace with Germany, June 28, 1919, 2 Bevans 43, 11 Martens Nouveau Recueil (ser. 3) 323. *See also* Commission on the Responsibility of the Authors of the War and on Enforcement of Penalties, *Report Presented to the Preliminary Peace Conference, reprinted in* 14 AJIL 95, 112–15 (1920) and Carnegie Endowment for International Peace, Division of International Law, Pamphlet No. 32, Violation of the Laws and Customs of War 16–19 (1919). The Commission recommended prosecuting all those guilty of offenses "against the laws and customs of war or the *laws of humanity*." 14 AJIL at 117 (emphasis added).

[56] *Supra* note 46.

penal and disciplinary measures against POWs), which so prominently figured in the Nuremberg trials as a basis for the prosecution and conviction of offenders. However, the other Geneva Convention of the same date, the Convention for the Amelioration of the Condition of the Wounded and Sick in the Field, contained a weak provision requiring governments to "propose to their legislatures should their penal laws be inadequate, the necessary measures for the repression in time of war of any act contrary to the provisions of the present Convention" (Article 29).[57]

The Nuremberg Tribunals appear to have taken it for granted that violations of the substantive provisions of the Hague and Geneva Conventions were criminal. These Tribunals considered those provisions of the two treaties that were declaratory of customary law as having created an adequate basis for individual criminal responsibility. Establishing the customary law character of these provisions was compelled because the Hague Convention was not formally applicable as a result of the *si omnes* clause (some belligerents were not parties), and because the Soviet Union was not a party to the Geneva Convention.[58] Thus, although neither the Geneva Conventions that preceded those of 1949 nor the fourth Hague Convention contained explicit penal provisions, they were accepted as a basis for prosecutions and convictions in the post-World War II Tribunals.

The grave breaches system was introduced by the Geneva Conventions of August 12, 1949. The penal system of the Conventions requires the states parties to criminalize certain acts, and to prosecute or extradite the perpetrators. The advantage of this approach is its clarity and transparency, which is so important for criminal law. The disadvantage is the creation of the category of "other" breaches, which involves the violation of all the remaining provisions of the Conventions, which are arguably less categorically penal. Of course, the introduction of the system of grave breaches cannot alter the possibility that the other breaches may be considered war crimes under the customary law of war. Moreover, the list of grave breaches may always be expanded through interpretation and various types of conduct may be treated as war crimes.[59]

---

[57] 118 LNTS 303.   [58] MERON, *supra* note 12, at 37–41.

[59] As happened in the case of rape, *see* Meron, *supra* note 4, at 426–47 (concerning the readiness of the International Committee of the Red Cross and the U.S. Government to regard rape as a grave breach or war crime). It may be noted that the indictments presented by the Prosecutor against Meakić and others (Indictment No. 2, paras. 22.8–22.10 (Feb. 13, 1995)), and against Tadić and others (Indictment No. 3, paras. 4.2–4.4 (Feb. 13, 1995)) to the International Criminal Tribunal for the Former Yugoslavia treat "forcible sexual intercourse" as "cruel treatment" in violation of the laws or customs of war recognized by Article 3 of its Statute and common Article 3(1)(a) of the Geneva Conventions, and also as a grave breach of the Conventions of causing "great suffering" under Article 2(c) of its Statute. "Rape" is treated as a crime against humanity recognized by Article 5(g) of the Statute of the Tribunal.

The creation of the penal system of the Geneva Conventions led some commentators to conclude that jurisdiction was limited to the courts of the detaining powers and that international courts, such as the Nuremberg and Tokyo Tribunals, would have no competence in respect of grave breaches of the Conventions and Protocol I.[60] I disagree. Although international trials are not contemplated by the Conventions, which envisage a national and cooperative system of penal enforcement, neither do they exclude the possibility of establishing international criminal tribunals and granting them jurisdiction over breaches of the Geneva Conventions[61] or Protocols, as the Security Council did in the Statutes of the ad hoc Tribunals for Yugoslavia and Rwanda. Surely, states can do jointly what they may do severally, especially when such joint action is undertaken through the Security Council.

Mandatory prosecution (or extradition) of perpetrators of grave breaches of the Geneva Conventions and discretionary prosecution for other (nongrave) breaches are left to the penal courts of the detaining power, as are, subject to certain broad principles stated in the Conventions, the law of evidence, procedural rules and the system of penalties.

Treating violations of common Article 3 as a basis for individual criminal responsibility is affirmed by some national military manuals or laws (discussed below). The U.S. Department of the Army's Field Manual, for example, lists common Article 3[62] together with other provisions of the Geneva Conventions and the Hague Convention Respecting the Laws and Customs of War on Land and, without any exception for that article, proclaims that "[e]very violation of the law of war is a war crime."[63] The U.S. Army thus regards violations of Article 3 as encompassed by the notion of war crimes and it could prosecute captured military personnel for war crimes if they were accused of breaches of Article 3.[64] The recent

---

[60] G. I. A. D. Draper, *The Implementation and Enforcement of the Geneva Conventions of 1949 and of the Two Additional Protocols of 1977*, 164 Recueil des Cours 1, 38 (1979 III).

[61] Theodor Meron, *Prisoners of War, Civilians and Diplomats in the Gulf Crisis*, 85 AJIL 104, 106 (1991).

The Commentary on the Geneva Conventions of 12 August 1949: [No. IV] Geneva Convention Relative to the Protection of Civilian Persons in Time of War 593 (Oscar M. Uhler & Henri Coursier eds., 1958) observes that Article 146(2) of the Fourth Geneva Convention "does not exclude handing over the accused to an international criminal court whose competence has been recognized by the Contracting Parties."

[62] U.S. Dep't of the Army, The Law of Land Warfare, para. 11 (Field Manual No. 27–10, 1956).

[63] *Id.*, para. 499. The British Military Manual states that "all other violations of the Conventions not amounting to 'grave breaches', are also war crimes." UK War Office, The Law of War on Land, being Part III of the Manual of Military Law, para. 626 (1958).

[64] Regarding the exercise of jurisdiction over war crimes, see U.S. Dep't of the Army, *supra* note 62, para. 505(d). Regarding the law to be applied, see *id.*, para. 505(e). *See also* 10 U.S.C. §802(a) (9)–(10) (1988) (the following persons, among others, are subject to the U.C.M.J.: prisoners of war in custody of the armed forces and, in time of war, persons

German Military Manual actually describes some violations of common Article 3 and Protocol II as "[g]rave breaches of international humanitarian law."[65] The draft Canadian Forces manual takes a different approach but agrees that violations of common Article 3 and Protocol II should be prosecuted. "While non-application [of common Article 3] would appear to render those responsible to trial for war crimes, trials would be held under national criminal law, since no 'war' would be in existence."[66] As for breaches of Protocol II in noninternational armed conflicts, the Canadian manual requires that "both the governmental and rebel authority should treat them as breaches of the national criminal law, since the law concerning war crimes relates to international armed conflicts."[67] Although this manual may not support the proposition that violations of common Article 3 and Protocol II are a matter for universal jurisdiction, it supplies additional evidence of the growing recognition of the criminality of violations of common Article 3.

EX POST FACTO?

Future defendants may well challenge Article 4 of the Rwanda Statute as contrary to the principle prohibiting retroactive penal measures. The prohibition of retroactive penal measures is a fundamental principle of criminal justice and a customary, even peremptory, norm of international law that must be observed in all circumstances by national and international tribunals. The Security Council could not have intended in Resolution 955 to oblige the Tribunal to act counter to this fundamental principle. The prospects of such a challenge must therefore be assessed.

The ILC's recent discussion of the principle of legality (*nullum crimen sine lege*) in the Draft Statute for an International Criminal Court (Article 39) is illuminating. With regard to crimes under general international law (Article 20(a)-(d) of the statute), Article 39 requires that the accused not be held guilty unless the act or omission in question constituted a crime

---

serving with or accompanying an armed force in the field). *See also id.* §818 ("General courts martial shall have jurisdiction to try any person who by the law of war is subject to trial by a military tribunal and may adjudge any punishment permitted by the law of war."). Although the U.S. authority under international law to prosecute violators is, in my view, clear, the U.S. statutory authority to prosecute is less so. *See also infra* note 81. The United States would typically not be interested in prosecuting alien violators of common Article 3 when the offenses occurred in civil wars in other countries.

[65] FEDERAL REPUBLIC OF GERMANY, FEDERAL MINISTRY OF DEFENCE, HUMANITARIAN LAW IN ARMED CONFLICTS – MANUAL, para. 1209 (1992).

[66] Canadian Forces, Law of Armed Conflict Manual (Second Draft) at 18-5–18-6 (undated).

[67] *Id.* at 18–23.

under international law at the time it was committed.[68] With regard to treaty crimes (Article 20(e)), Article 39(b) requires that the treaty in question must be applicable to the conduct of the accused under the appropriate national law of the state party to the treaty.[69] Nowhere do these provisions suggest that prosecution before an international tribunal for crimes under a treaty that does not contain provisions on universal jurisdiction clashes with the prohibition of retroactive penal measures.

One may ask how this discussion relates to common Article 3 and Protocol II. Surely, prosecution of violations of common Article 3 could be regarded as trial of crimes under general international law; prosecution of violations of Protocol II could be treated, depending on the case, as trial of either crimes under general international law or treaty crimes.

In arguing against any challenge on *ex post facto* grounds, one must emphasize that common Article 3 and Additional Protocol II are treaty obligations binding on Rwanda, that they clearly proscribe certain acts, and that those acts are also prohibited by the criminal law of Rwanda, albeit in different terms. As was already explained in the preceding section, common Article 3 and Protocol II impose important prohibitions on the behavior of participants in noninternational armed conflicts, be they governments, other authorities and groups, or individuals. The fact that these proscribed acts are considered nongrave rather than grave breaches concerns questions of discretionary versus obligatory prosecution or extradition, and for some commentators, universal jurisdiction, but not criminality. Jurisdiction over such acts can be established in other ways, for example, by national law or, exceptionally, by Security Council resolutions adopted under chapter VII.

The egregious acts listed in Article 4 of the Rwanda Statute, such as murder, the taking of hostages, pillage, degrading treatment and rape, constitute offenses under both international law and the national law of the perpetrators. Therefore, no person who has committed such acts, in Rwanda or elsewhere, could claim in good faith that he/she did not understand that the acts were prohibited. And the principle *nullum crimen* is designed to protect a person only from being punished for an act that he or she reasonably believed to be lawful when committed.

It is true that neither common Article 3 nor Additional Protocol II says anything about penalties. However, those provisions of the Geneva Conventions whose violation constitutes grave breaches also say nothing about penalties, and they incontestably establish a basis for the perperators' individual criminal responsibility, and even for universal

---

[68] Report of the International Law Commission on the work of its forty-sixth session, *supra* note 16, at 112–13.
[69] *Id*. at 113–14.

jurisdiction. The Geneva Conventions define offenses but leave it to the contracting states to determine penal sanctions. Persons prosecuted for violations of the Geneva Conventions cannot argue that they are being subjected to retroactive penal sanctions if the penalties do not exceed those previously established by their national states.[70] Although Rwandan law allows for capital punishment, the penalty imposed by the International Tribunal is limited to imprisonment. Article 23 of the Rwanda Statute states that, in determining the terms of imprisonment, the trial chambers shall have recourse to the general practice regarding prison sentences in the courts of Rwanda.

It follows, therefore, that the principal requirements of Article 15(1) of the International Covenant on Civil and Political Rights[71] prohibiting *ex post facto* penal measures are satisfied: the acts were previously prohibited under both international and national law; and the penalty that is authorized under the Rwanda Statute does not exceed the one provided for under national law and is, in fact, lighter.

The fact that some trials would be the subject of international, rather than national, jurisdiction concerns procedure rather than a fundamental principle of justice. As the post-World War II United Nations War Crimes Commission concluded, "a violation of the laws of war constitutes both an international and a national crime, and is therefore justiciable both in a national and international court."[72] The fact that offenses *ex jure gentium* that normally would be enforced by national courts applying domestic law – such as violations of the Geneva Conventions – would be enforced by an international tribunal directly vis-à-vis individuals, in my view, does not raise *ex post facto* problems.

Article 15(2) of the Political Covenant is particularly pertinent. It provides that the article shall not "prejudice the trial and punishment of any person for any act or omission which, at the time when it was committed, was criminal according to the general principles of law recognized by the community of nations." The legislative history of this provision suggests that the goal was to "confirm and strengthen" the principles of Nuremberg and Tokyo and to "ensure that if in the future crimes should be perpetrated similar to those punished at Nürnberg, they would be punished in accordance with the same principles."[73] There is no doubt that the ethnic killings in Rwanda were criminal according to the general principles of law recognized by the community of nations. Murder is murder all over the world.

---

[70] *See* Meron, *supra* note 5, at 127.
[71] *Opened for signature* Dec. 16, 1966, 999 UNTS 171.
[72] United Nations War Crimes Commission, *supra* note 54, at 232.
[73] Marc J. Bossuyt, Guide to the "Travaux Préparatoires" of the International Covenant on Civil and Political Rights 331–32 (1987).

The authority of the Nuremberg Tribunals can be invoked here. As the U.S. Tribunal established under Control Council Law No. 10 stated in the *Ohlendorf* trial, in the context of crimes against humanity, "Murder, torture, enslavement, and similar crimes which heretofore were enjoined only by the respective nations now fall within the prescription of the family of nations. Thus murder becomes no less murder because directed against a whole race instead of a single person."[74] Of course, the recognition that certain types of conduct are and have been criminal according to the principles of both national law and international law, and are thus crimes *ex jure gentium*, serves not only to answer potential *ex post facto* challenges but also to support the principle of universal jurisdiction, the right of third states to prosecute those who commit international offenses.

The International Military Tribunal (IMT) emphasized that, long before the fourth Hague Convention was adopted, many of the prohibitions in the Convention had been enforced by military tribunals in the trial and punishment of individuals accused of violating the rules of land warfare stated in the Convention.

> [Y]et the Hague Convention nowhere designates such practices as criminal, nor is any sentence prescribed, nor any mention made of a court to try and punish offenders.... The law of war is to be found not only in treaties, but in the customs and practices of states which gradually obtained universal recognition, and from the general principles of justice applied by jurists and practiced by military courts.[75]

Elsewhere the Tribunal, in referring to war crimes mentioned in Article 6(b) of its Charter, underscored with regard to certain provisions of the Hague and Geneva Conventions that the fact that their breach "constituted crimes for which the guilty individuals were punishable is too well settled to admit of argument."[76]

Or, as the Military Tribunal under Control Council Law No. 10 stated in the *High Command Case*, the Geneva Convention and the Hague Convention "were binding insofar as they were in substance an expression of international law as accepted by the civilized nations of the world."[77] The Tribunal emphasized that

> [i]t is not essential that a crime be specifically defined and charged in accordance with a particular ordinance, statute, or treaty if it is made a crime by international convention, recognized customs and usages of war, or the general

---

[74] 4 TRIALS, *supra* note 48, at 497 (1949). As Judge B. V. A. Röling put it, "The crime against humanity is new, not in the sense that those acts were formerly not criminal.... The newness is not the newness of the crime, but rather the newness of the competence to try it." B. V. A. Röling, *The Law of War and the National Jurisdiction Since 1945*, 100 RECUEIL DES COURS 325, 345–46 (1960 II).

[75] TRIAL DOCUMENTS, *supra* note 49, at 220–21.

[76] *Id*. at 253.   [77] 11 TRIALS, *supra* note 48, at 534.

principles of criminal justice common to civilized nations generally. If the acts charged were in fact crimes under international law when committed, they cannot be said to be *ex post facto* acts or retroactive pronouncements.[78]

In the *RuSHA* case, the Tribunal added that the acts of which the defendants were accused were in violation "of the laws and customs of war, of the general principles of criminal law as derived from the criminal laws of all civilized nations, of the internal penal laws of the countries in which such crimes were committed."[79] Can anyone doubt that the atrocities in Rwanda were, in the language of Article 15(2) of the Political Covenant, "criminal according to the general principles of law recognized by civilized nations"?

Challenges to Article 4 of the Rwanda Statute based on its allegedly *ex post facto* character must fail. Of course, the language of common Article 3 and the relevant provisions of Protocol II is clearly prohibitory; it addresses fundamental offenses such as murder and torture, which are prohibited in all states. The Geneva Conventions have been universally ratified and are largely declaratory of customary law. The latter is true, on the authority of the International Court of Justice, of common Article 3. Protocol II has also been ratified by a large number of states. The substantive international offenses covered by common Article 3 and Protocol II may even overlap with crimes against humanity. Their criminality cannot be questioned. Article 4 of the Rwanda Statute does not try to create new categories of grave breaches. It uses the different, and perhaps broader, term "serious violations," which obviously are matters of international concern. The meshing of the criminality of the acts prohibited under international law with their punishability under the laws of Rwanda suggests that the Statute respects the prohibition of retroactive legal measures.

Common Article 3 and Article 4 of Additional Protocol II cover areas also addressed by human rights law, in some cases even by peremptory norms. The Statute thus enhances the prospects for treating egregious violations of human rights law – not only of international humanitarian law – as offenses under international law.

NONGRAVE BREACHES AND UNIVERSAL JURISDICTION

In establishing the law for the Tribunal, how does the Rwanda Statute relate to a right of third states – i.e., states that have no territorial or nationality (active or passive) or "protective principle" links with the

---

[78] United States v. List, *id*. at 759, 1239 ("*The Hostage Case*").   [79] 4 *id*. at 597, 618.

offender or the victim – to prosecute those who commit violations in internal armed conflicts? I refer here to a principle already briefly mentioned, that of universal jurisdiction. It is worth recalling that following World War II, it was not the various international tribunals and courts of the occupying powers in Germany, but primarily the national courts of various Allied states that tried the greater number of persons for war crimes and crimes against humanity[80] – although such trials were not required by international law, and (outside of the Nuremberg Charter) the offenses were not even characterized as crimes by any general international treaty in force at the time.

The right of states to punish perpetrators of violations committed outside their territory, while admittedly broad, is not unlimited and must conform to accepted jurisdictional principles recognized by international law, as well as to national constitutions and other laws.[81] Even states committed in principle to territorial criminal jurisdiction may and do provide by statute for prosecutions regarding particular categories of offenses committed outside their territories. Often the acts concerned are recognized as criminal by international treaties, and less frequently by customary law, and sometimes by both. Obviously, universal jurisdiction over international offenses can be exercised only in those states that have the necessary national laws.

It is now widely accepted that crimes against humanity (Article 3 of the Rwanda Statute) are subject to universal jurisdiction.[82] And it is increasingly recognized by leading commentators that the crime of genocide[83]

---

[80] 15 UNITED NATIONS WAR CRIMES COMMISSION, LAW REPORTS OF TRIALS OF WAR CRIMINALS 28–48 (1949).

[81] *See* RESTATEMENT (THIRD) OF THE FOREIGN RELATIONS LAW OF THE UNITED STATES §402 (1987) [hereinafter RESTATEMENT]. *See also* Richard R. Baxter, *The Municipal and International Law Basis of Jurisdiction over War Crimes*, 28 BRIT. Y.B. INT'L L. 382, 391 (1951).

The U.S. Constitution grants Congress the power to define and punish offenses against the law of nations and permits it to make acts committed abroad crimes under U.S. law when this is permitted by international law. Andreas F. Lowenfeld, *U.S. Law Enforcement Abroad: The Constitution and International Law*, 83 AJIL 880, 881–82 (1989). *See also supra* note 64 and *infra* note 121.

[82] Dinstein, *supra* note 44, at 211–12; Baxter, *supra* note 81; 1 OPPENHEIM'S INTERNATIONAL LAW 998 (Robert Jennings & Arthur Watts eds., 9th ed. 1992); Diane F. Orentlicher, *Settling Accounts: The Duty to Prosecute Human Rights Violations of a Prior Regime*, 100 YALE L.J. 2537, 2555, 2593–94 & n. 91 (1991); M. CHERIF BASSIOUNI, CRIMES AGAINST HUMANITY IN INTERNATIONAL CRIMINAL LAW 510–27 (1992). *See also* Judgment of Oct. 6, 1983 (*In re* Barbie), Cass. crim., 1983 Gazette du Palais, Jur. 710.

In its comments on the establishment of an international criminal court, the United States emphasized that states have a continuing responsibility to prosecute those who commit crimes against humanity. UN Doc.A/AC.244/1/Add.2, para. 23 (1995) [hereinafter U.S. Comments].

[83] RESTATEMENT, *supra* note 81, §404. Reporters' Note 1 states that "[u]niversal jurisdiction to punish genocide is widely accepted as a principle of customary law." *See also* A. R. Carnegie, *Jurisdiction over Violations of the Laws and Customs of War*, 39 BRIT. Y.B. INT'L

(despite the absence of a provision on universal jurisdiction in the Genocide Convention) may also be cause for prosecution by any state.[84] Is this also true, however, of violations of common Article 3 and Additional Protocol II to the Geneva Conventions (Article 4 of the Rwanda Statute)? Possible challenges to this basis for the prosecution of offenders before the courts of third states, and conceivably even before the Hague criminal Tribunals, would presumably focus on the fact that violations of these provisions fall outside the grave breaches provisions of the Geneva Conventions.

Just because the Geneva Conventions created the obligation of *aut dedere aut judicare* only with regard to grave breaches does not mean that other breaches of the Geneva Conventions may not be punished by any state party to the Conventions. Indeed, Article 129(3) of the Third Geneva Convention provides that each state party "shall take measures necessary for the suppression of all acts contrary to the provisions of the present Convention other than the grave breaches." Identical provisions are contained in the other 1949 Geneva Conventions. As the *Commentary* to the Third Convention states, "The Contracting Parties ... should at least insert in their legislation a general clause providing for the punishment of other breaches."[85] Even if there is no clear obligation to punish or extradite authors of violations of the Geneva Conventions that are not encompassed by the grave breaches provisions, such as common Article 3, all states have the right to punish those guilty of such breaches. In this sense, nongrave breaches may fall within universal jurisdiction. Moreover, in the *Nicaragua*[86] case, the International Court of Justice recognized the applicability of common Article 1 of the Conventions to

---

L. 402, 424 (1963); Jordan J. Paust, *Congress and Genocide: They're Not Going to Get Away with It*, 11 MICH. J. INT'L L. 90, 92 & n.2 (1989).

In his separate opinion in the *Genocide* case before the International Court of Justice, Judge *ad hoc* Lauterpacht stated that the description of genocide as a crime under international law in Article 1 of the Convention was intended "to permit parties, within the domestic legislation that they adopt, to assume universal jurisdiction over the crime of genocide – that is to say, even when the acts have been committed outside their respective territories by persons who are not their nationals." Application of the Convention on the Prevention and Punishment of the Crime of Genocide, Provisional Measures, 1993 ICJ REP. 325, 443, para. 110 (Order of Sept. 13).

[84] The ILC's Statute for an International Criminal Court allows any state party to the Genocide Convention to lodge a complaint with the Prosecutor alleging that a crime of genocide has been committed (Art. 25(1)). The court will have an inherent, or compulsory, jurisdiction over the crime of genocide (Art. 21(1)(a)). Although addressing international, not national, jurisdiction, these provisions appear to reflect the principle of universal concern for the punishment of the crime of genocide.

[85] COMMENTARY ON THE GENEVA CONVENTIONS OF 12 AUGUST 1949: [No. III] GENEVA CONVENTION RELATIVE TO THE TREATMENT OF PRISONERS OF WAR 624 (Jean de Preux ed., 1960).

[86] Military and Paramilitary Activities in and against Nicaragua, *supra* note 35.

noninternational armed conflicts addressed by common Article 3.[87] The command of Article 1 that all the contracting parties must respect and ensure respect[88] may, of course, entail resort to penal measures to suppress violations.

One finds some apparent confusion in the literature with regard to the relationship of the Geneva Conventions to universal jurisdiction. In denying the applicability of universal jurisdiction to nongrave breaches of the Geneva Conventions, some commentators assume that universal jurisdiction requires recognition not only of the right, but also of the duty, to prosecute perpetrators of international offenses. I dissent. There is no reason why universal jurisdiction should not also be acknowledged in cases where the duty to prosecute or to extradite is unclear, but the right to prosecute when offenses are committed by aliens in foreign countries is recognized. Indeed, the true meaning of universal jurisdiction is that international law *permits* any state to apply its laws to certain offenses even in the absence of territorial, nationality or other accepted contacts with the offender or the victim. These are the offenses that are recognized by the community of nations as of universal concern, and as subject to universal condemnation.[89] Although Judge Röling was critical of the concept of universal jurisdiction, he agreed that "[t]he distinction between 'grave' and 'other' violations might find its perfect explanation in the *obligation* to prosecute grave violators and the *right* to prosecute those who have committed other breaches."[90] Röling argued, however,

---

[87] 1986 ICJ Rep. at 114.

[88] On Article 1, see Luigi Condorelli & Laurence Boisson de Chazournes, *Quelques remarques à propos de l'obligation des Etats de "respecter et faire respecter" le droit international humanitaire "en toutes circonstances," in* STUDIES AND ESSAYS ON INTERNATIONAL HUMANITARIAN LAW AND RED CROSS PRINCIPLES IN HONOUR OF JEAN PICTET 17 (Christophe Swinarski ed., 1984). *See also* Protocol I, *supra* note 2, Arts. 1(1) and 89. Article 89 refers to the broader category of "serious violations" rather than to grave breaches, and appears to leave to each state the choice of means for complying with its obligations to act in situations of serious violations of the Conventions and the Protocol.

[89] RESTATEMENT, *supra* note 81, §404.

[90] Röling, *supra* note 74, at 342. *Accord* HOWARD S. LEVIE, TERRORISM IN WAR: THE LAW OF WAR CRIMES 192–93 (1993). Solf and Cummings observe that breaches of the Geneva Conventions are distinguishable from grave breaches by not being made subject to extradition, but they remain crimes under customary law and the perpetrators may be punished. Waldemar A. Solf & Edward R. Cummings, *A Survey of Penal Sanctions under Protocol I to the Geneva Conventions of August 12, 1949*, 9 CASE W. RES. J. INT'L L. 205, 217 (1977). Draper points out that

> [t]he Conventions' system of repression of breaches seems to assume that non-grave breaches are to be treated as war crimes for whose suppression States have a duty to take all measures necessary. Beyond that obligation, it is left to individual States to decide the mode of suppression. This might be by way of penal proceedings, judicial or disciplinary, or of administrative action.

Draper, *supra* note 43, at 45.

that the Geneva Conventions obtain only between belligerents,[91] a view
that was debatable at the time it was expressed and that is clearly unacceptable today.

As regards the national state of the perpetrators of nongrave breaches,
its obligations go further. Given the purposes and objects of the Geneva
Conventions and the normative content of their provisions, any state that
does not have the necessary laws in place, or is otherwise unwilling to
prosecute and punish violators of clauses other than the grave breaches
provisions that are significant and have a clear penal character, calls into
serious question its good faith compliance with its treaty obligations.

I would not like to suggest that all violations of the Geneva Conventions
must thus be treated as offenses. Some provisions may address administrative matters without any penal significance. The Conventions state
many different kinds of obligations that bear on core humanitarian values
in quite different degrees. Some of these are technical or administrative
and would not seem an appropriate predicate for criminal proceedings.
For example, would a third state have the right to prosecute a foreign
army officer for failure to comply with Article 94 of the Third Geneva
Convention, which requires notification on recapture of an escaped prisoner of war? Or with Article 96, which requires that a record of disciplinary punishments be kept by the camp commander? I think not. Of course,
third states will have no interest in such breaches and usually no evidence
to prosecute the offenders. These technical breaches are not recognized by
the community of nations as of universal concern and as subject to general
condemnation.

Suppose, however, that a third state prosecuted a violator of the prohibition of torture under common Article 3 or the prohibition of rape under
Article 27 (of the Fourth Geneva Convention), neither of which is design-
ated as a grave breach. No one can doubt the categorical character of the
proscriptions stated in these articles. The identical prohibition of torture,
which is widely regarded as a *jus cogens* norm of general international
law, is defined as a grave breach for international armed conflicts. Even as
regards the "peacetime" commission of torture, third states, such as the
United States under the Alien Tort Claims Act, have occasionally exercised civil jurisdiction over the alleged torturer (in the case of suits by
aliens) without any protest by the defendant's national state.

Possibly, some governments will protest foreign prosecutions based on
activity that may reflect their state policy. And probably, legal advisers of
many foreign ministries will discourage the justice departments of their
countries from prosecuting foreign officers for their conduct during a civil
war in their own country. If protests by the national state of the accused

---

[91] Röling, *supra* note 74, at 359.

are rejected, would that state prevail in an international action against the prosecuting state alleging violation of accepted jurisdictional principles delineating the competence of states to punish acts committed outside their territory? Would the prosecuting state incur international responsibility for the prosecution? If the activity at the core of the prosecution is a significant international offense clearly giving rise to international concern, such as murder in violation of common Article 3, I believe that the answer to both questions should be, and probably would be, in the negative.

In situations not clearly regulated by treaties, difficulties could arise between the custodial state and the state of nationality of the offender when the latter, in good faith, asserts its readiness to prosecute and requests the former to desist from prosecution and to deliver the person to it. The possibility that both states would exercise jurisdiction must be subject to the *non bis in idem* principle. Given states' traditional lack of interest in prosecuting those who have committed international offenses in internal conflicts, the likelihood that two states will compete *bona fide* for the exercise of criminal jurisdiction is quite remote. It may be noted that the grave breaches provisions of the Geneva Conventions do not clearly address the priority of jurisdiction. In any event, the Conventions do not require the state ready to prosecute (the custodial state) to extradite the offender to a state party requesting extradition as an alternative to proceeding with the prosecution.

Geneva Additional Protocol I did not contribute to clarifying the criminal system of repression of violations of international humanitarian law. The Protocol uses such terms as "grave breaches," "breaches," "violations" and even "serious violations" of the "Conventions or of this Protocol."[92] Violations of the Protocol that are not defined as grave breaches have consequences similar to those resulting from violations other than grave breaches of the Geneva Conventions and may, in many cases, be prosecuted as war crimes by third states.[93]

---

[92] Protocol I, *supra* note 2, Art. 90(2) (c)(i).

[93] INTERNATIONAL COMMITTEE OF THE RED CROSS, COMMENTARY ON THE ADDITIONAL PROTOCOLS OF 8 JUNE 1977 TO THE GENEVA CONVENTIONS OF 12 AUGUST 1949, at 1033 (Yves Sandoz, Christopher Swinarski & Bruno Zimmermann eds., 1987). States parties may, of course, "suppress any act or omission contrary to the provisions of these instruments [the Geneva Conventions and Protocol I]; furthermore they must impose penal sanctions on conduct defined by these same instruments as 'grave breaches'." *Id. See also id.* at 1012. The *Commentary* recognizes that, although the punishment of other than grave breaches is the responsibility of the power to which the perpetrators belong, "this does not detract from the right of States under customary law, as reaffirmed in the writings of a number of publicists, to punish serious violations of the laws of war under the principle of universal jurisdiction." *Id.* at 1011. *Contra* Erich Kussbach, *The International Humanitarian Fact-Finding Commission,* 43 INT'L & COMP. L.Q. 174, 177 (1994) (who believes that only grave breaches of Protocol I involve individual criminal responsibility and that serious violations implicate state

WAR CRIMES AND UNIVERSAL JURISDICTION

Those concerned about the recognition of the violations of common Article 3 and Protocol II as international offenses should remember that, until fairly recently, questions were raised even about universal jurisdiction over war crimes at customary international law, which is now largely taken for granted.[94] As important a scholar as Draper wrote in 1976 of the customary law right of a belligerent to try those charged with war crimes who fall into its hands; he therefore raised the question whether such jurisdiction is genuinely universal, on an analogy with jurisdiction over piracy.[95] From that perspective, which considers trial of captured war criminals as a manifestation of the principle of self-help, the Nuremberg process represented an expanded protection of the interests of co-belligerents.[96] Hersch Lauterpacht opened the door to a truly universal jurisdiction over war crimes by arguing that, in trying enemy soldiers for war crimes, the state is enforcing not only its national law but also the law of nations: "War criminals are punished, fundamentally, for breaches of international law. They become criminals according to the municipal law of the belligerent only if their action ... is contrary to international law."[97]

Richard Baxter suggested that

> one of the intermediate stages on the way to a true international penal jurisdiction may be the recognition that any state, including a neutral, has jurisdiction to try war crimes. By what state prosecution of a particular offence will actually be undertaken would then be determined, as it is now between allied or associated belligerents, by the convenience of the forum. If a neutral state should, by reason of the availability of the accused, witnesses, and evidence

responsibility only). Mr. Di Bernardi (Italy) stated that national legislation which went beyond the grave breaches provisions could not be applied to armed forces of other states. 6 Diplomatic Conference on the Reaffirmation and Development of International Humanitarian Law Applicable in Armed Conflicts, Geneva (1974–1977), Official Records, Doc. CDDH/SR.44 (May 30, 1977), para. 76. A more persuasive view was expressed by Mr. Ullrich (German Democratic Republic), who stated that

> the definition of grave breaches within the system of the Conventions and Protocol was a specific form of international co-operation in the prosecution of war crimes, but that it did not determine or limit the scope of war crimes. There were many other war crimes which were extremely grave violations of international law.

Id., para. 90.

[94] Restatement, *supra* note 81, §404; Oppenheim's International Law, *supra* note 82, at 470.

[95] Draper, *supra* note 43, at 21. *Compare* G. Brand, *The War Crimes Trials and the Laws of War*, 26 Brit. Y.B. Int'l L. 414, 416 (1949).

[96] Röling, *supra* note 74, at 359–60. *See also* United Nations War Crimes Commission, *supra* note 54, at 30.

[97] Lauterpacht, *supra* note 52, at 64.

be the most convenient *locus* in which to try a war crime, there is no reason why that state should not perform that function.[98]

The laws and usages of war are, of course, universal and war crimes are crimes against the *jus gentium*.[99] The British *Report of the War Crimes Inquiry* states that it is a generally recognized principle of international law that belligerent *and neutral states* have a right to exercise jurisdiction in respect of war crimes since they are crimes *ex jure gentium*.[100] The British War Crimes Act 1991 allows proceedings to be brought against any British citizen or resident of the United Kingdom, irrespective of his or her nationality at the time of its commission, for an alleged World War II offense (murder, manslaughter or culpable homicide) that constituted a violation of the laws and customs of war.[101] Clearly, the object of the British legislation was to deal with suspected war criminals who had settled in the United Kingdom. It would be altogether artificial to regard the British legislation as based on the principle of passive nationality, rather than on the right of all states to prosecute serious violations of the law of nations. As the commission suggested:

> War crimes, or grave breaches of the 1949 Geneva Conventions, wherever in the world they are committed, are already triable in the United Kingdom under the Geneva Conventions Act 1957.... Parliament did not demur from the proposition that war crimes are offences sufficiently serious for the British courts to be given jurisdiction over them, whatsoever the nationality of the person committing them and wheresoever they were committed.[102]

Contemporary international law would allow the United Kingdom to go further and prosecute even those simply present in the country, as was done by Canada in 1987, without encountering any objections from other states. The Canadian legislation provides for jurisdiction over acts that constitute war crimes and crimes against humanity under either customary or conventional international law in force at the time of their commission when the alleged offender is present in Canada, and Canada, in conformity with international law, can exercise jurisdiction.[103] The Austrian Military Manual clearly recognizes the principle of universality

---

[98] Baxter, *supra* note 81, at 392 (footnotes omitted). Frits Kalshoven agrees that, in "customary international law, jurisdiction over war criminals is universal," but points out that, in practice, it is limited to the belligerent parties. FRITS KALSHOVEN, THE LAW OF WARFARE 119 (1973).

[99] 14 UNITED NATIONS WAR CRIMES COMMISSION, *supra* note 80, at 15.

[100] THOMAS HETHERINGTON & WILLIAM CHALMERS, WAR CRIMES: REPORT OF THE WAR CRIMES INQUIRY, 1989, CMND 744, at 45.

[101] For other states' war crimes legislation, see *id.* at 65–74.

[102] *Id.* at 60.

[103] *Id.* at 72–73. *See also* L. C. Green, *The German Federal Republic and the Exercise of Criminal Jurisdiction*, 43 U. TORONTO L.J. 207, 208 (1993). The Canadian law, in its most pertinent part, reads as follows:

of jurisdiction over war crimes: "If a soldier breaches the laws of war, although he can recognize the illegality of his own action, his own State, the enemy State and also a neutral State can punish him for that action."[104]

Universal jurisdiction over war crimes means that all states have the right under international law to exercise criminal jurisdiction over the offenders. Most states do not have the necessary resources or interest to prosecute offenders when the state itself was not involved in the situation in question. Many states also do not have national laws in place that allow them to prosecute offenders. The United States appears to be among these states.[105] It does have, however, ample authority under both the U.S. Constitution[106] and international law[107] to adopt the necessary legislation. Whether or not the United States, in concrete situations that may arise, prosecutes offenders involved in foreign conflicts, it should, as a world leader, have such legislation in place.

WAR CRIMES AND INTERNAL CONFLICTS

The Rwanda Statute contains no provisions paralleling Article 3 of the Yugoslavia Statute, which grants the Tribunal jurisdiction over violations

> every person who, either before or after the coming into force of this subsection, commits an act or omission outside Canada that constitutes a war crime or a crime against humanity and that, if committed in Canada, would constitute an offence against the laws of Canada in force at the time of the act or omission shall be deemed to commit that act or omission in Canada at that time if,
> ...
> (b) at the time of the act or omission, Canada could, in conformity with international law, exercise jurisdiction over the person with respect to the act or omission on the basis of the person's presence in Canada, and subsequent to the time of the act or omission the person is present in Canada.

[1987] 1 R.S.C. ch. 37.

Arnold Fradkin, who served as lead counsel for the prosecution in several Canadian war crimes cases, made this comment on the Canadian legislation:

> A second subsection provides extraterritorial jurisdiction on the basis of the person's presence in Canada where, at the time of the crime, Canada could have, in conformity with international law, exercised jurisdiction over the person with respect to the crime committed. This expresses what is known in international law as the "universal jurisdiction" concept. Certain crimes are committed not against a particular state but against the international community, and therefore any state in which the offender is located has the right to try the offender.... War crimes are crimes against humanity and should be subsumed under that same principle of universal jurisdiction.

Holocaust and Human Rights Law: The Fifth International Conference, 12 B.C. THIRD WORLD L.J. 37, 48 (1992) (footnotes omitted).

---

[104] BUNDESMINISTERIUM FÜR LANDESVERTEIDIGUNG, TRUPPENFÜHRUNG, para. 52 (1965) (my translation).
[105] U.S. DEP'T OF THE ARMY, *supra* note 62, paras. 506–07.
[106] *Supra* note 81.   [107] *Supra* note 83.

of the fourth Hague Convention and annexed Regulations. This omission reflects the accepted wisdom, which unfortunately denies war crimes a place in internal conflicts. War crimes under the "Hague law," i.e., those perpetrated in the conduct of hostilities, should also be punishable when committed in noninternational armed conflicts. This is particularly important with regard to such terrible and nondiscriminating weapons as poison gas and land mines, which have been used in internal conflicts. Despite all the obstacles, international law prohibitions that apply to international wars are gradually being extended to noninternational armed conflicts.

The ILC decided to make Article 22 of its Draft Code of Crimes against the Peace and Security of Mankind, entitled "Exceptionally serious war crimes," applicable to both international and internal armed conflicts.[108] This position is confirmed by the Commission's statute for an international criminal court. Article 22 of the statute lists serious violations of the laws and customs applicable in armed conflict among those crimes within the jurisdiction of the court. The commentary explains that this language reflects not only the Yugoslavia Statute (which in Article 3 speaks of violations of the laws or customs of war), but also Article 22 of the draft code, which applies to noninternational armed conflicts as well. Thus, the proposed court's subject matter jurisdiction would arguably include war crimes even when committed in civil wars.

Experience has shown that cultural property can be extensively destroyed in noninternational armed conflicts. The applicability of parts of the (Hague) Convention for the Protection of Cultural Property in the Event of Armed Conflict,[109] which is primarily addressed to international wars, to noninternational armed conflicts is therefore useful.[110] The Convention also contains a penal clause obligating states parties, within their ordinary criminal jurisdiction, to prosecute and impose penal or disciplinary sanctions on persons of whatever nationality who commit breaches of the Convention;[111] logically, this clause must cover breaches of obligations pertaining to noninternational armed conflicts.

The extension of prohibitions on the use of gas to domestic conflicts has already been achieved through recent international treaties. Although the 1925 (Geneva) Protocol for the Prohibition of the Use in War of Asphyxiating, Poisonous or other Gases, and of Bacteriological Methods of

---

[108] Report of the International Law Commission on the work of its forty-third session, [1991] 2 Y.B. Int'l L. Comm'n, pt. 2, at 104–05, UN Doc. A/CN.4/SER.A/1991/Add.1 (Pt. 2).

[109] May 14, 1954, 249 UNTS 240.

[110] *Id.*, Article 19(1) provides: "In the event of an armed conflict not of an international character occurring within the territory of one of the High Contracting Parties, each party to the conflict shall be bound to apply, as a minimum, the provisions of the present Convention which relate to respect for cultural property."

[111] *Id.*, Art. 28.

Warfare[112] was arguably addressed to international wars only, later treaties on this subject clearly were not so limited. The Convention on the Prohibition of the Development, Production and Stockpiling of Bacteriological (Biological) and Toxin Weapons and on Their Destruction – a 1972 arms control treaty – obligates the parties "in any circumstances."[113] Similarly, the Convention on the Prohibition of the Development, Production, Stockpiling and Use of Chemical Weapons and on Their Destruction, of January 13, 1993 (which concerns both arms control and use), provides that the obligations of states under the Convention shall apply "under any circumstances," including noninternational armed conflicts and even civil strife.[114] Article VII of the Convention contains provisions requiring each state party to prohibit natural and legal persons anywhere in its territory or subject to its jurisdiction from undertaking any activity prohibited to a state party under the Convention and to penalize violators.[115]

The most recent development in this field has been a proposal to extend the international prohibitions on the use of land mines to internal conflicts.[116] This proposal holds great humanitarian promise because of the catastrophic dimensions of the use of mines in internal conflicts. The Group of Governmental Experts to Prepare the Review Conference of the States Parties to the Convention on Prohibitions or Restrictions on the Use of Certain Conventional Weapons Which May Be Deemed to be Excessively Injurious or to Have Indiscriminate Effects is seriously considering expanding the Protocol on Prohibitions or Restrictions on

---

[112] June 17, 1925, 26 UST 571, 94 LNTS 65.

[113] Apr. 10, 1972, Art. 1, 26 UST 583, 1015 UNTS 163.

[114] Art. 1(1), 32 ILM 800 (1993). The Department of State's Article-by-Article Analysis of the Convention, annexed to the President's Letter of Transmittal to the Senate, points out that

> the prohibition on the use of chemical weapons extends beyond solely their use in international armed conflicts, i.e. chemical weapons may not be used in any type of situation, including purely domestic conflicts, civil wars or state-sponsored terrorism. As such, this article closes a loophole in the Geneva Protocol of 1925, which covered only uses in war, i.e. international armed conflicts. Note that the phrase "never under any circumstances" reflects a similar phrase in Article I of the Biological Weapons Convention.

S. TREATY DOC. No. 21, 103d Cong., 1st Sess. 4 (1993). A recent commentary notes that the words "undertakes never under any circumstances" have a universal dimension, extend to all activities of state parties everywhere, and are independent of the character of the conflict, whether it is international armed conflict, noninternational armed conflict, or civil strife. WALTER KRUTZSCH & RALF TRAPP, A COMMENTARY ON THE CHEMICAL WEAPONS CONVENTION 12–13 (1994).

[115] KRUTZSCH & TRAPP, *supra* note 114, at 109–15; S. TREATY DOC. No. 21, *supra* note 114, at 40–41.

[116] Chairman's Rolling Text, *in* Final Report of the Group of Governmental Experts to Prepare the Review Conference of the States Parties to the Convention on Prohibitions or Restrictions on the Use of Certain Conventional Weapons Which May Be Deemed to Be Excessively Injurious or to Have Indiscriminate Effects, Doc. CCW/CONF.I/GE/23, Ann. 1 (1995) [hereinafter Final Report]. *See generally* THE ARMS PROJECT OF HUMAN RIGHTS WATCH & PHYSICIANS FOR HUMAN RIGHTS, LANDMINES: A DEADLY LEGACY (1993).

the Use of Mines, Booby-Traps and Other Devices (Protocol II) to include noninternational armed conflicts; the experts are also considering applying the provisions on grave breaches of the Geneva Conventions to the amended Protocol. The revision of Article 1, which concerns material scope of application, contains two possible versions: a broader "Alternative A," proposed by Denmark, which would make the Protocol applicable "in all circumstances including armed conflict and times of peace"; and a narrower "Alternative B," based on a proposal of India, which would make it applicable to "situations referred to in Articles 2 and 3 and common to the Geneva Conventions of 12th August 1949" (international and noninternational armed conflicts covered by the Geneva Conventions), but not to the situations excluded from Additional Protocol II under its Article 1(2).

Alternative A has the advantage of avoiding the need to engage in controversies over the characterization of conflicts.[117] The adoption of either version would represent an extremely important step toward remedying an unacceptable lacuna in existing treaty law: that the use of land mines causing incalculable damage to the population of countries involved in noninternational armed conflicts has not been prohibited by the law of war treaties. According to a number of proposals, these explicit prohibitions would be accompanied by the clear criminalization of violations.[118]

On May 3, 1996, an amendment was adopted providing for the applicability of Protocol II also to situations referred to in common Article 3 to the Geneva Conventions.

---

[117] Making Protocol II applicable in peacetime offers additional advantages. A key proposal accepted in principle by most of the delegations at the experts' meetings would require that long-lived antipersonnel land mines be placed in marked and monitored areas protected to exclude civilians. Given the number of permanent, so-called barrier mine fields emplaced throughout the world, such a marking and monitoring requirement should apply at all times. Moreover, the proposal of the Netherlands to amend Protocol II to restrict the transfer of mines (Art. 6 *ter*) would make no sense if limited to times of armed conflict.

[118] The Western "Alternative C" of Appendix I, Final Report, *supra* note 116, concerning compliance provides, in Article 12(4), as follows:

The provisions of the 1949 Geneva Conventions relating to measures for the repression of breaches and grave breaches shall apply to breaches and grave breaches of this Protocol during armed conflict. Each party to a conflict shall take all appropriate measures to prevent and suppress breaches of this Protocol. Any act or omission occurring during armed conflict in violation of this Protocol, if committed wilfully or wantonly and causing death or serious injury to the civilian population shall be treated as a grave breach. A party to the conflict which violates the provisions of this Protocol shall, if the case demands, be liable to pay compensation, and shall be responsible for all acts committed by persons forming part of its armed forces. States parties and parties to a conflict shall require that commanders ensure that members of the armed forces under their command are aware of, and comply with, their obligations under this Protocol.

Another area that merits urgent attention is to extend to noninternational armed conflicts the international law prohibitions on environmental damage that are applicable to international wars.

CONCLUSION

Once internal atrocities are recognized as international crimes and thus as matters of major international concern, the right of third states to prosecute violators must be accepted. Typically, these would be offenses of such significance that the international community would have an important interest in prosecuting the violators, especially when the criminal justice systems of the state where the offenses were committed and/or the state of nationality have failed to act. Many serious violations of common Article 3 and Geneva Protocol II, as well as other significant norms of the Geneva Conventions, though not explicitly listed as grave breaches, are of universal concern and subject to universal condemnation. These are crimes *jure gentium* and therefore all states have the right to try the perpetrators. This right can be seen as an analogue, *mutatis mutandis*, of the prerogative of all states to invoke obligations *erga omnes* against states that violate the basic rights of the human person.[119]

The ad hoc Tribunals for Yugoslavia and Rwanda have concurrent jurisdiction with national courts, but have primacy over them. These international tribunals may request that national courts defer to their competence, subject to the principle of *non bis in idem*. Otherwise, the establishment of the ad hoc international criminal Tribunals for Yugoslavia and Rwanda does not affect the right or duty of states, as the case may be, to prosecute those who violate international humanitarian law.[120]

---

[119] Barcelona Traction, Light & Power Co., Ltd. (Belg. v. Spain) (New Application), 1970 ICJ Rep. 3, 32 (Feb. 5).

[120] Yugoslavia Statute, *supra* note 8, Arts. 9–10; Rwanda Statute, *supra* note 7, Arts. 8–9; International Tribunal for the Prosecution of Persons Responsible for Serious Violations of International Humanitarian Law Committed in the Territory of the Former Yugoslavia Since 1991 [Yugoslavia Tribunal], Rules of Procedure and Evidence, UN Doc. IT/32/Rev. 3 (Jan. 30, 1995); Yugoslavia Tribunal, Application [by the Prosecutor] for Deferral by the Federal Republic of Germany in the Matter of Dusco Tadić, Case No. 1 of 1994 (Nov. 8, 1994); Decision of the Trial Chamber in Case No. 1 of 1994, IT-94-1-D (Nov. 8, 1994); Yugoslavia Tribunal, Application by the Prosecutor for a Formal Request for Deferral by the Government of Bosnia and Herzegovina of Its Investigations and Criminal Proceedings in Respect of Radovan Karadzić, Ratko Mladić and Mico Stanisić (Apr. 21, 1995), Decision by the Trial Chamber in Case No. IT-95-5-D (May 16, 1995); and, concerning the Lasva River Valley Investigation, Decision by the Trial Chamber in Case No. IT-95-6-D (May 11, 1995).

Regarding the relations between national courts and the proposed international criminal court, see Report of the International Law Commission on the work of its forty-sixth session, *supra* note 16, at 129–38, Arts. 51–58.

The United States expressed the concern that the statute adopted by the ILC does not adequately reflect the principle that the jurisdiction of the proposed international tribunal should be complementary to the national criminal justice systems. U.S. Comments, *supra* note 82, paras. 6–14. The United States proposed that the state of nationality, or any other state actively exercising jurisdiction, should have preemptive rights of jurisdiction in relation to the proposed international tribunal. *Id.*, para. 68.

The extension of the concept of international criminality to violations of common Article 3 and Protocol II should not lead to the conclusion that the distinction between "common law crimes" or other crimes under municipal law and offenses under international law would be eliminated. It simply means that certain egregious crimes, such as murder, that in certain circumstances were considered as war crimes in international wars will now be treated as international offenses in situations of non-international armed conflict as well.

The impact of the explicit extension of the concept of criminality to common Article 3 and Additional Protocol II in the Rwanda Statute will depend on the achievements of the Rwanda Tribunal and, even more, on whether the normative pronouncement of the Security Council will be reiterated and confirmed, first and foremost by national laws and national courts. The normative contribution made by the Statute for Rwanda must not remain isolated. It should be clear, however, that, given the present system of international organization, even one such pronouncement by the Security Council substantially influences the shaping of international law.

It is not surprising that, on a subject of such great humanitarian importance, the practice of states lags behind *opinio juris,* and general principles of law play an important role. Nevertheless, slowly but unmistakably, the practice of states is evolving. The Belgian law entitled Crimes de droit international (1993) thus provides for the criminal jurisdiction of Belgian courts over certain breaches not only of the Geneva Conventions and Protocol I, but also of Protocol II, regardless of the nationality of the victim or perpetrator or of where the offense was committed.[121] On the basis of this law, which also established a scale of penalties, the Brussels prosecutor's office, on May 29, 1995, issued several international arrest warrants against persons involved in the atrocities in Rwanda. Providing a perfect, but also rare, example of universal jurisdiction over perpetrators of atrocities committed in internal conflicts in foreign countries, one of the three warrants was issued against a Rwandan responsible for massacres of other Rwandans in Rwanda.[122] Without doubt, the law applicable to noninternational armed conflicts will be quite different from now on.

---

[121] Loi de 16 juin 1993 relative à la répression des infractions graves aux conventions internationales de Genève du 12 août 1949 et aux protocoles I et II du 8 juin 1977, additionnels à ces conventions, Moniteur Belge, Aug. 5, 1993; ERIC DAVID, PRINCIPES DE DROIT DES CONFLITS ARMÉS 556 (1994).

[122] Other warrants involved the killing of Belgian peacekeepers, among others. Parquet de Bruxelles, Crimes de guerre au Rwanda, Press Communiqué No. 30.99.3959/94 (May 30, 1995) (in the author's files).

XIV

The Continuing Role of Custom in the Formation of International Humanitarian Law*

Two recent events demonstrate the renewed vitality of customary law in the development of the law of war (international humanitarian law): first, the *Tadić* decision of the Appeals Chamber of the International Tribunal for the Prosecution of Persons Responsible for Serious Violations of International Humanitarian Law Committed in the Territory of Former Yugoslavia since 1991;[1] and, second, the decision of the International Committee of the Red Cross (ICRC) to embark on a study of customary international law.

I

In its Decision on the Defence Motion for Interlocutory Appeal on Jurisdiction, of October 2, 1995, the appeals chamber of the Hague Tribunal decided that the Tribunal has subject matter jurisdiction over the *Tadić* case. The Tribunal's important contribution to the evolution of customary law presents a number of methodological questions that I would like to explore.

In a recent Editorial in this *Journal*, Judge George Aldrich discussed the jurisdictional aspects of the *Tadić* decision.[2] While questioning the Tribunal's decision not to determine whether the armed conflicts involved in that case were international or noninternational (I agree with Judge Aldrich that the Tribunal could have found the conflicts to be of an international character), Aldrich pointed to one advantage resulting from that approach: finding that the conflicts were international would

* I have assisted the Prosecutor, Justice Richard Goldstone, in the jurisdictional aspects of the *Tadić* case, but the views expressed here are mine only. I wish to express gratitude for their comments to George H. Aldrich, Louise Doswald-Beck, Andreas F. Lowenfeld, John H. McNeill, Benedict Kingsbury, W. Michael Reisman and Oscar Schachter.
[1] Prosecutor v. Tadić, Case No. IT–94–1–AR72, Appeal on Jurisdiction (Oct. 2, 1995), *reprinted in* 35 ILM 32 (1996) [hereinafter *Tadić*].
[2] George Aldrich, *Jurisdiction of the International Criminal Tribunal for the Former Yugoslavia*, 90 AJIL 64 (1996).

have deprived the Tribunal of the opportunity to affirm that serious violations of international humanitarian law committed in internal wars are international crimes[3] under customary law. The clarification of customary law on this subject is the most important normative contribution of the decision.

The appeals decision in the *Tadić* case is the linear successor to the three previous major decisions of international tribunals that focused explicitly on the means of creating customary international humanitarian law. In each case – the judgment of the International Military Tribunal in the *Trial of Major War Criminals*,[4] the judgment in *United States v. von Leeb* ("The High Command Case"),[5] and the decision of the International Court of Justice in the *Nicaragua* case[6] with regard to common Articles 1 and 3 of the Geneva Conventions – as in *Tadić*, the courts looked primarily to the *opinio juris* rather than the practice of states in reaching their conclusions.

There were different reasons for the need to apply customary law in these cases. In the two Nuremberg decisions, Hague Convention No. IV did not apply because of the general participation (*si omnes*) clause, several of the participations not being parties to the Convention. In addition, the 1929 Geneva Prisoners of War Convention was not binding on Nazi Germany vis-à-vis the Soviet Union because the latter was not a party to the Convention. In the *Nicaragua* case, the U.S. multilateral treaty reservation made it necessary to apply customary law. In the *Tadić* case, the Hague Tribunal had to resort to customary law so as to interpret and apply Article 3 of its Statute, which concerned "laws or customs of war," and to lay to rest *ex post facto* challenges to its subject matter jurisdiction.

In the Nuremberg jurisprudence, the tribunals paid little attention to the process or rationale by which various provisions of humanitarian conventions were transformed into customary law. In contrast, the Hague Tribunal in *Tadić* engaged in a detailed and focused examination of the formation of customary law. Like the Nuremberg courts, however, it relied on such verbal evidence as statements, resolutions and declarations rather than battlefield or operational practice, which it largely ignored. The Tribunal formally adhered to the traditional twin requirements (practice and *opinio juris*) for the formation of customary international law. Yet in effect it weighed statements both as evidence of practice and as articulation of *opinio juris*, which in the formation of humanitarian and human rights law is cardinal. What the Tribunal did, without explicit

---

[3] *Id*. at 69.

[4] Trial of German Major War Criminals, 1946, Cmd. 6964, Misc. No. 12, at 65.

[5] 11 Trials of War Criminals Before the Nuernberg Military Tribunals Under Control Council Law No. 10, at 462, 533–35 (1948).

[6] Military and Paramilitary Activities in and against Nicaragua (Nicar. v. U.S.), Merits, 1986 ICJ Rep. 14, 114, paras. 218–20 (June 27) [hereinafter *Nicaragua*].

acknowledgment, was to come close to reliance on *opinio juris* or general principles of humanitarian law, distilled, in part, from the Geneva and Hague Conventions. Its methodology was thus akin more to that applied in the human rights field than in other areas of international law. In both human rights and humanitarian law, emphasis on *opinio juris* helps to compensate for scarcity of supporting practice. In terminology, however, the Tribunal follows the law of war tradition of speaking of custom even when this requires stretching the traditional meaning of customary law.

The Tribunal's discussion of internal armed conflicts ranges over Spain, Congo, Biafra, Nicaragua and El Salvador, Liberia, Georgia and Chechnya. It addresses the development of general customary principles applicable in internal armed conflicts, such as the protection of civilian populations, distinction or discrimination, necessity and proportionality, and proscriptions on the means and methods of warfare, including prohibited weapons. Most important, it considers extension to civil wars of rules and principles traditionally regarded as applicable only to international wars. As source material, the Tribunal invoked statements by governments and parliaments; resolutions of the League of Nations and the United Nations General Assembly; instructions by Mao Tse-tung; the Nigerian army's operational code of conduct; occasional statements by one of the warring parties (the Farabundo Martí Front for National Liberation in El Salvador); statements of the European Community, the European Union and the UN Security Council; military manuals; the Declaration of Minimum Humanitarian Standards;[7] a national judgment (of the Supreme Court of Nigeria); and, with regard to the customary law character of common Article 3, the *Nicaragua* Judgment. Although such materials may not be reliable indicators of state practice on the battlefield, the Tribunal explained why resort to them must be had:

> When attempting to ascertain State practice with a view to establishing the existence of a customary rule or a general principle, it is difficult, if not impossible, to pinpoint the actual behaviour of the troops in the field for the purpose of establishing whether they in fact comply with, or disregard, certain standards of behaviour. This examination is rendered extremely difficult by the fact that not only is access to the theatre of military operations normally refused to independent observers (often even to the ICRC) but information on the actual conduct of hostilities is withheld by the parties to the conflict; what is worse, often recourse is had to misinformation with a view to misleading the enemy as well as public opinion and foreign Governments. In appraising the formation of customary rules or general principles one should therefore be aware that, on account of the inherent nature of this subject-matter, reliance must primarily be

---

[7] *See* Asbjørn Eide, Allan Rosas & Theodor Meron, *Combating Lawlessness in Gray Zone Conflicts through Minimum Humanitarian Standards*, 89 AJIL 215, 218 (1995).

placed on such elements as official pronouncements of States, military manuals and judicial decisions.[8]

In contrast to the trial chamber's Decision on the Defence Motion on Jurisdiction of August 10, 1995, which extensively cited legal literature to buttress its conclusions, the appeals chamber refrained from any mention of doctrine.[9]

One may ask whether the Tribunal could not have made a greater effort to identify actual state practice, whether evincing respect for, or violation of, the rules. Difficult as such efforts are, they could have reinforced the Tribunal's substantive appraisals of principles and rules of customary international law. Without some significant discussion of operational practice, it may be difficult to persuade governments to accept the Tribunal's vision of some aspects of customary law.

Of course, the characteristics of armed conflict make the Tribunal's approach understandable.[10] In choosing its sources, the Hague Tribunal appears to have followed Richard Baxter's insightful conclusion that "[t]he firm statement by the State of what it considers to be the rule is far better evidence of its position than what can be pieced together from the actions of that country at different times and in a variety of contexts."[11] Such statements are not to be equated with custom *jure gentium* but are an important element in the formation of custom.

The Tribunal's discussion of denials and condemnations of the use of chemical weapons, for example, alludes to some manifestations of operational practice. These denials and condemnations may in fact serve to confirm a given customary rule, neatly fitting the *Nicaragua* Judgment's paradigm:

> In order to deduce the existence of customary rules, the Court deems it sufficient that the conduct of States should, in general, be consistent with such rules, and that instances of State conduct inconsistent with a given rule should

---

[8] *Tadić, supra* note 1, at 55, para. 99.

[9] On widespread citation of textbooks and publicists by international arbitral tribunals, see Christine Gray & Benedict Kingsbury, *Developments in Dispute Settlement: Inter-State Arbitration Since 1945*, 63 Brit. Y.B. Int'l. L. 97, 129 (1992). The International Court of Justice refrains from quoting teachings of named publicists or doctrine in its decisions. Shabtai Rosenne, The Law and Practice of the International Court of Justice 614–16 (2d ed. 1985). Dissenting and concurring decisions, however, do cite doctrine.

[10] Armed conflict is "characterized by violence and violations, by the necessity of committing acts frequently not preceded by careful deliberation, by exceptional conditions, by limited third-party access to the theatre of operations, and by the parties' conflicting factual and legal justifications for their conduct." Theodor Meron, Human Rights and Humanitarian Norms 44 (1989) (discussing lawmaking in the law of war area).

[11] Richard Baxter, *Multilateral Treaties as Evidence of Customary International Law*, 41 Brit. Y.B. Int'l L. 275, 300 (1965–66). Baxter stated that military manuals provide "telling evidence" of the practice of states. *Id.* at 282–83.

generally have been treated as breaches of that rule, not as indications of the recognition of a new rule.[12]

The Tribunal concluded that some customary rules had developed to the point where they govern internal conflicts and that they cover such areas as

> protection of civilians from hostilities, in particular from indiscriminate attacks, protection of civilian objects, in particular cultural property, protection of all those who do not (or no longer) take active part in hostilities, as well as prohibition of means of warfare proscribed in international armed conflicts and ban of certain methods of conducting hostilities.[13]

The Tribunal limited the reach of its holding to "serious violations,"[14] stating that "only a number of rules and principles governing international armed conflicts have gradually been extended to apply to internal conflicts," and that the extension does not consist of a full and mechanical transplant, but of "the general essence of those rules."[15] These caveats are important but do not make it much easier to identify those rules and principles which have already crystallized as customary law.

The difficulty is enhanced by the link between the Tribunal's conclusions on customary law and the Tribunal's Statute. The peg on which the Tribunal hung its discussion of customary law is Article 3 of its Statute, which gives the Tribunal power "to prosecute persons violating the laws and customs of war."[16] The Tribunal held that Article 3, which the Tribunal considers applicable in both international and internal armed conflicts, is the residual clause that covers

> all violations of humanitarian law not falling under Article 2 [grave breaches] or covered by Articles 4 [genocide] or 5 [crimes against humanity], more specifically: (i) violations of the Hague law on international conflicts; (ii) infringements of provisions of the Geneva Conventions other than those classified as "grave breaches" by those Conventions; (iii) violations of common Article 3 and other customary rules on internal conflicts; (iv) violations of agreements binding upon the parties to the conflict, considered *qua* treaty law, *i.e.*, agreements which have not turned into customary international law.[17]

While these conclusions are the Tribunal's interpretation of Article 3 of its Statute, one wonders whether the Tribunal should not have referred, in addition, to other violations of customary international humanitarian law.

---

[12] *Nicaragua*, 1986 ICJ REP. at 98, para. 186, *discussed in* MERON, *supra* note 10, at 59–62.
[13] *Tadić*, *supra* note 1, at 67–68, para. 127.
[14] *Id.* at 51, para. 90.   [15] *Id.* at 67, para. 126.
[16] UN Doc. S/25704, annex, at 11 (1993), *reprinted in* 32 ILM 1192 (1993), *adopted by* SC Res. 827 (May 25, 1993), *reprinted in id.* at 1203.
[17] *Tadić*, *supra* note 1, at 51, para. 89. *See also id.* at 49–50, para. 87.

The question remains, for example, whether the grave breaches of the Geneva Conventions could not have been mentioned as customary law, quite apart from their articulation in the Geneva Conventions. As Judge Aldrich stated in his Editorial:

> Only the fact that the offenses described in the 1949 Geneva Conventions as grave breaches have become part of customary international law appears to have been overlooked in this examination – or at least not mentioned – for in his separate opinion, Judge Abi-Saab, who argued for greater legal coherence, asserts that the Tribunal has found that grave breaches "are subsumed in the 'serious violations of the laws or customs of war.' "[18]

The Tribunal's discussion of the process leading to the recognition that violations of international humanitarian law involve individual criminal responsibility is rather brief. One regrets that the Tribunal did not use the opportunity to elaborate this evolution fully. The Tribunal cited in this regard the Nuremberg jurisprudence, military manuals, prosecutions before Nigerian courts, the criminal code of Yugoslavia, agreements concluded between the parties to the conflict in the former Yugoslavia, and Security Council resolutions on Somalia, which it described as "[o]f great relevance to the formation of *opinio juris*."[19]

On crimes against humanity, the Tribunal accepted that "[i]t is by now a settled rule of customary international law that crimes against humanity do not require a connection to international armed conflict. Indeed, as the Prosecutor points out, customary international law may not require a connection between crimes against humanity and any conflict at all."[20] The Tribunal correctly noted that, by insisting that crimes against humanity be committed in either internal or international armed conflicts, the Security Council may have defined the crime in Article 5 of the Yugoslavia Statute more narrowly than necessary under customary international law.[21] In contrast to Article 5 of the Yugoslavia Statute, Article 3 of the Rwanda Statute[22] makes no allusion to armed conflicts, supporting the view that crimes against humanity (like genocide) can be committed in peacetime. The Tribunal's affirmation[23] that crimes against humanity can be committed in peacetime is of major importance.

---

[18] Aldrich, *supra* note 2, at 68. [19] *Tadić, supra* note 1, at 70, para. 133.

[20] *Id*. at 73, para. 141. [21] *Id*.

[22] For the Statute of the Rwanda Tribunal, see SC Res. 955, annex (Nov. 8, 1994), *reprinted in* 33 ILM 1602 (1994).

[23] On the nexus between crimes against humanity and armed conflict, see Theodor Meron, *International Criminalization of Internal Atrocities*, 89 AJIL 554, 557 (1995) [hereinafter *Criminalization*]; Theodor Meron, *War Crimes in Yugoslavia and the Development of International Law*, 88 AJIL 78, 85 (1994).

II

Most observers will support the rationale and goals of the discussion of customary law in *Tadić*. Most, including this writer, will believe that the Tribunal's final conclusions are legally correct. I agree that, as a matter of law, some important Hague rules already apply to noninternational armed conflicts and that, as a matter of policy, most, perhaps all Hague rules should be applicable *mutatis mutandis*.[24] The direction of the evolution is clear. However, the Tribunal's meshing of an analysis of Article 3 of its Statute with a discussion of the customary law of internal armed conflicts is troublesome. The Tribunal's conclusions on the state of customary (Hague) law applicable to noninternational armed conflicts are more carefully drawn than those interpreting Article 3 of its Statute.

Nevertheless, the Tribunal should have followed a more prudential course, focusing on specific Hague principles and rules, enumerating means and methods of warfare, listing prohibited weapons and avoiding broader conclusions. But the Tribunal wisely recognized that only some rules and principles have been extended to internal conflicts, and that this transformation has taken place in the general essence of the rules, not in the detailed regulations they may contain.

For the purpose of determining its jurisdiction under Article 3 of the Statute, however, the Tribunal appears to have been both under- and overinclusive: underinclusive, as suggested by Judge Aldrich, in excluding grave breaches even as customary law from Article 3 of its Statute. The Tribunal regarded grave breaches, as statutory and treaty provisions, as applicable only to international armed conflict; it apparently believed that the customary law content of grave breaches tracks their treaty content. While the conventional provisions on grave breaches involve the technical definition of protected persons and protected property, and the procedural obligations of prosecution or extradition, the appeals chamber should have devoted more attention to discussing the possibility that, divorced from some of their conventional and formal aspects, the core offenses listed in the grave breaches provisions may have an independent existence as a customary norm applicable also to violations of at least common Article 3. In his separate opinion, Judge Abi-Saab appeared to urge the Tribunal to favor such an approach. Whether correct or not, the appeals chamber's strict interpretation of Article 2 of its Statute (grave breaches) stands in stark contrast to its expansive interpretation of Article 3 of its Statute.

The Tribunal's approach may have been overinclusive in suggesting that Article 3 of its Statute covers all (serious) violations of international

---

[24] *See* Meron, *Criminalization, supra* note 23, at 574–77.

humanitarian law (both Geneva and Hague law), except for grave breaches of the Geneva Conventions (covered by Article 2 of the Statute), genocide (Article 4) and crimes against humanity (Article 5). A reasonable reading of the decision may suggest that the Tribunal considers that "the Hague law on international conflicts [and all] infringements of provisions of the Geneva Conventions [other than grave breaches]"[25] are applicable to both international and noninternational armed conflicts.

Despite the caveats listed by the Tribunal, some commentators will probably question what thus appears, from the interpretation of Article 3 of the Statute, to be the application through customary law of nearly the entirety of the Hague law to noninternational armed conflicts. Moreover, while I entirely agree with the Tribunal's views that violations of Article 3 common to the Geneva Conventions entail individual criminal responsibility under customary law, the Tribunal's apparent opinion that all serious breaches of the Geneva Conventions – outside common Article 3 – that are not listed as "grave breaches" and that, until recently, were considered to govern international wars only, are already applicable to noninternational armed conflicts may prove more controversial. These views of the Tribunal have far-reaching significance for both doctrine and practice. The Tribunal here reflects the constructive evolution toward the blurring of the dichotomy between international and internal armed conflicts and toward the extension to the latter, *mutatis mutandis*, of the more protective and comprehensive rules governing the former. One might have expected, therefore, a more detailed justification than that provided by the Tribunal's discussion of the comprehensiveness of international humanitarian law, statutory intent and a few explanatory statements made by members of the Security Council.

There are thus two distinct strands in the decision. One concerns the customary, especially Hague, law of noninternational armed conflicts, the other customary law in the context of the interpretation of Article 3 of the Tribunal's Statute. It is the first strand that the Tribunal may wish to favor in its future jurisprudence.

The *Tadić* decision demonstrates the renewed vitality and potential of customary international law in developing humanitarian law for internal armed conflicts. There are several ways that customary law strategies can figure and are figuring in the evolution of this law. First, rules initially stated in treaty provisions governing noninternational armed conflicts, such as common Article 3 and Additional Protocol II,[26] can be

---

[25] *Tadić, supra* note 1, at 51, para. 89. *See also id.* at 49–50, 71, paras. 87–88, 137; Aldrich, *supra* note 2, at 67–68.

[26] *Compare* Christopher Greenwood, *Customary Law Status of the 1977 Geneva Protocols, in* HUMANITARIAN LAW OF ARMED CONFLICT: CHALLENGES AHEAD: ESSAYS IN HONOUR OF FRITS KALSHOVEN 93 (Astrid J. M. Delissen & Gerard J. Tanja eds., 1991). For an important

transformed into customary law. Second, through customary law, some rules have also been recognized as norms whose violation gives rise to individual criminal responsibility. This development has obvious implications for human rights law and for future proceedings before the International Tribunal for Rwanda. The appeals chamber's decision constitutes the first judicial affirmation, which accords with the trend in modern doctrine, that violation of common Article 3 entails individual criminal responsibility under customary international law. Third, general principles first developed for international wars, such as proportionality and necessity, may be extended through customary law to civil wars. Fourth, prohibitions on certain weapons and means of warfare such as poison gas and land mines are gradually being applied to internal armed conflicts through customary law, as well as through the more visible process of treaty making.

The decision in the *Tadić* case will undoubtedly have a beneficial influence on the development of the customary law of war for noninternational armed conflict and will be taken into account in the ICRC study, to which I now turn.

III

The Meeting of the Intergovernmental Group of Experts for the Protection of War Victims held in Geneva in January 1995[27] recommended that

> the ICRC be invited to prepare, with the assistance of experts in IHL representing various geographical regions and different legal systems, and in consultation with experts from governments and international organisations, a report on customary rules of IHL applicable in international and non-international armed conflicts, and to circulate the report to States and competent international bodies.[28]

This role of the ICRC merits an explanation. The ICRC is of course neither a state nor an intergovernmental organization, but an association

discussion of the relationship of the Additional Protocols to general international law, see Georges Abi-Saab, *The 1977 Additional Protocols and General International Law: Some Preliminary Reflections, in id.* at 115. For an affirmation that common Article 3 is declaratory of customary international law, see *Nicaragua*, 1986 ICJ Rep. at 114, paras. 218–20.

[27] This meeting was convened following a request addressed to the Swiss Government by the International Conference for the Protection of War Victims, which met in Geneva in 1993. Both the International Conference and the meeting were convened by the Swiss Government in its capacity as depositary of the Geneva Conventions and their Additional Protocols.

[28] Report of the President of the Intergovernmental Group of Experts for the Protection of War Victims, 26th International Conference of the Red Cross and Red Crescent, Conf. Doc. 95/C.I/2/1, at 2 (1995).

under Swiss civil law. Thus, it is not a direct participant in the making of international law, which under the prevailing theory of sources is still reserved to states, with some allowance for the role of intergovernmental organizations. (The broader question of the extent to which nongovernmental organizations and other nongovernmental actors participate in or influence the development of international customary law is outside the scope of this Editorial.)

Yet, from the very first Red Cross Convention (1864), the ICRC took a leading role in the drafting of humanitarian law conventions for submission to diplomatic conferences. It prepared important commentaries to the four Conventions for the Protection of Victims of War of 12 August 1949 and their Additional Protocols; these commentaries have proved to be a leading source of interpretation affecting the practice of states and their *opinio juris*, and thus indirectly contribute to the formation of customary law. The ICRC has a recognized status and functions under the Conventions and the Protocols. Its present mandate includes "prep[aration of the] development" of international humanitarian law applicable in armed conflicts.[29] This language encompasses preparation of texts reflecting progressive development and/or codification. There is nothing radical, therefore, in the ICRC's undertaking what may become a restatement of customary humanitarian law.

In accepting the invitation, the ICRC presented a blueprint of a study to the Twenty-sixth International Conference of the Red Cross and Red Crescent.[30] The blueprint is quite comprehensive regarding noninternational armed conflicts, which were the principal focus of the 1993 meeting of experts. The ICRC's discussion of international armed conflicts addresses the Geneva Conventions and Additional Protocol I. Although the latter incorporates substantial Hague law, a more specific reference to the Hague law pertaining to the conduct of hostilities and means and methods of war would have been useful to avoid the impression, surely not intended, that only the Geneva law was to be considered.

Customary Hague law is of particular importance in this context because Additional Protocol I (143 parties), which codifies various Hague rules, does not always state those rules fully, comprehensively or definitively. Considerable space is left, therefore, for the development of customary Hague law outside the Protocol, as well as for clarifying through customary law norms that are already stated in the Protocol. Additionally, the hardening into custom of the norms stated in the

[29] ICRC, Statutes and Rules of Procedure of the International Red Cross Movement, Art. 5(2)(g) (1986).

[30] Report on the Follow-up to the International Conference for the Protection of War Victims, 26th International Conference of the Red Cross and Red Crescent, Commission I, Item 2, Doc. 95/C.I/2/2, at 6 (1995) [hereinafter ICRC Report].

Protocol cannot but enhance respect for its norms and thus its effectiveness.

Moreover, other law of war, Hague-type conventions have been sparsely ratified. The very important Convention on Prohibitions or Restrictions on the Use of Certain Conventional Weapons Which May Be Deemed to Be Excessively Injurious or to Have Indiscriminate Effects[31] has fifty-seven parties (Protocol I to the Convention, fifty-seven state parties; Protocol II, fifty-five state parties; Protocol III, fifty-four state parties). An amended Protocol (II) to this Convention laying down significant additional proscriptions and restrictions on the use (and transfer) of mines, and expanding the Protocol's reach to noninternational armed conflicts, is still under active consideration and may be agreed upon in the near future. A new Protocol IV on Blinding Laser Weapons was adopted by the 1995 Review Conference.[32] It will enter into force six months after twenty parties to the Conventional Weapons Convention have notified their consent to be bound. One state has already done so (Finland, on January 11, 1996).

The (Geneva) Protocol for the Prohibition of the Use in War of Asphyxiating, Poisonous or Other Gases, and of Bacteriological Methods of Warfare[33] has 145 state parties, but the recent Convention on the Prohibition of the Development, Production, Stockpiling and Use of Chemical Weapons and on Their Destruction,[34] which is applicable "under any circumstances" and will enter into effect 180 days after the deposit of the sixty-fifth instrument of ratification, has been ratified by only 47 states. Many weapons are still not regulated by treaties. The continuing importance of customary law here is obvious.

Apart from the question of direct applicability of the Geneva Conventions in domestic law, the ICRC considers that, because of the virtual universality of acceptance of the Geneva Conventions, customary law does not have much practical impact on matters governed by them.[35] In some cases, however, it may. The armed confrontation in December 1995

[31] Oct. 10, 1980, 1342 UNTS 137.

[32] Protocol IV was adopted on October 13, 1995, by the Review Conference of the States Parties to the Convention on Prohibitions or Restrictions on the Use of Certain Conventional Weapons Which May Be Deemed to Be Excessively Injurious or to Have Indiscriminate Effects. For the Protocol, see Conf. Doc. CCW/CONF.I/7 (Oct. 12, 1995). The 26th International Conference of the Red Cross and Red Crescent welcomed the general agreement achieved at the Review Conference that the Protocol's scope of application will not be limited to international armed conflicts. 26th International Conference of the Red Cross and Red Crescent, Conf. Doc. PR/95/C.I/3, Rev. 2, para. H(f). *See also The Vienna Review Conference: Success on Blinding Laser Weapons But Deadlock on Landmines*, 35 INT'L REV. RED CROSS 672 (1995).

[33] *Done* June 17, 1925, 26 UST 571, 94 LNTS 65.

[34] *Done* Jan. 13, 1993, 32 ILM 800 (1993).

[35] ICRC REPORT, *supra* note 30, at 6.

between Eritrea, which is not a party to the Geneva Conventions, and Yemen, which is, involved the capture by Eritrea of a number of Yemenis, and thus the question of entitlement to POW status. The importance of the Geneva Conventions as customary law in this case is clear.

While the rules stated in the Geneva Conventions would naturally apply between the parties, whether or not they are declaratory of customary law, the identification of customary law is essential for reaching nonparties, for example, the United Nations, and, in various mixed conflicts, nonstate actors, including insurgents. In addition, the Geneva Conventions contain only one article, common Article 3, that concerns noninternational armed conflicts. Thus, despite the virtually universal ratification of the Conventions (186 state parties), there is ample space for the development of customary law alongside the Conventions, *ratione personae* and *ratione materiae*,[36] in the area of noninternational armed conflicts.

Two additional statements of the International Court of Justice in the *Nicaragua* case are pertinent here: first, that, "even if two norms belonging to two sources of international law appear identical in content, and even if the States in question are bound by these rules both on the level of treaty-law and on that of customary international law, these norms retain a separate existence"; and second, that "[r]ules which are identical in treaty law and in customary international law are also distinguishable by reference to the methods of interpretation and application."[37] Obviously, the Vienna Convention's rules on treaty interpretation do not apply to customary law outside the treaty context. The Court's cryptic reference to interpretation is not very helpful. One thing is clear, however, and that is the potential importance of interpretive practice by state parties: subsequent practice in the application of the treaty may establish the agreement of the parties concerning its interpretation.[38] That new interpretation may in itself affect customary law. Through its commentaries on the Geneva Conventions and the Protocols, the ICRC influences state practice and thus, indirectly, the development of customary law.

The fewer the number of parties to law of war treaties, the greater the space left for the development of customary law. Additional Protocol II

---

[36] Lawmaking thus has a number of distinct, but interrelated, aspects. For example, state parties may, through their practice, interpretations, etc., create additional layers of treaty norms, elaborating on or supplementing their conventional obligations, without affecting customary law. Perhaps with some nonparty involvement, they may create additional or interstitial norms that become accepted as customary law for all states. State parties and other states may also bring about the maturation into customary law of the norms stated in a convention, thus resulting in extending to all states (*ratione personae*) what was first *lex scripta*.

[37] *Nicaragua*, 1986 ICJ Rep. at 95, para. 178.

[38] Vienna Convention on the Law of Treaties, *opened for signature* May 23, 1969, Art. 31(3)(*b*), 1155 UNTS 331.

contains a large number of Geneva-type rules pertaining to non-international armed conflicts but only a few Hague-type provisions. While a significant core of the Protocol reflects customary law, with 134 state parties, considerable space remains for the development of customary law.

In the context of international criminal tribunals, as we have already seen, the identification of customary law plays an important role in the interpretation and application of jurisdictional provisions of their statutes. In addition, customary law provides a yardstick for assessing whether or not the material offenses stated in the statutes of international criminal tribunals are *ex post facto*.

The significance of developing humanitarian law through customary law is enhanced by the meager prospects for the satisfactory development of the law of war through orderly treaty making.[39] Customary law is thus a major vehicle for alignment, adjustment and even reform of the law. In many other fields of international law, treaty making is faster than the evolution of customary law. In international humanitarian law, change through the formation of custom might be faster, but less precise in content, than the adjustment of law through treaty making. It is all the more necessary, in view of the critical role of customary law, that its currency not be devalued by facile assumptions and sweeping generalizations. The test for the advancement of humanitarian norms lies in their acceptability.

Echoing the so-called Baxter paradox,[40] the ICRC states that, because state parties act either in conformity with or in violation of their obligations under the Geneva Conventions, the significance of the parties' behavior for the development of customary international law remains theoretically unclear.[41] Despite the analytical importance of the Baxter paradox, as well as certain theoretical difficulties discussed elsewhere, I believe that parties to international treaties, including the Geneva Conventions, continue to play a role both in the formation of customary law pertaining to matters regulated by the Conventions and in the development of additional and interstitial norms.[42]

---

[39] Meron, *Criminalization, supra* note 23, at 555.

[40] Richard R. Baxter, *Treaties and Custom*, 129 Recueil des Cours 27, 64 (1970 I), where Baxter defines the paradox as follows: "[A]s the number of parties to a treaty increases, it becomes more difficult to demonstrate what is the state of customary international law dehors the treaty." He explains further: "As the express acceptance of the treaty increases, the number of states not parties whose practice is relevant diminishes. There will be less scope for the development of international law dehors the treaty...." *Id.* at 73. For a discussion of the Baxter paradox, see generally Meron, *supra* note 10, at 50–51.

[41] ICRC Report, *supra* note 30, at 6.

[42] For excellent discussions of formation of customary law and the relationship between treaty and custom, see Oscar Schachter, International Law in Theory and Practice 70–76, 335–42 (1991). On the role of custom in the formation of human rights law, see

With regard to Additional Protocol I, which has been ratified by fewer states (143 state parties) than have ratified the Geneva Conventions, the ICRC, reacting to the problems posed by the Baxter paradox, states (in the original French version of the blueprint) that customary international humanitarian law certainly cannot be determined only on the basis of the behavior of the fifty-three states that are not yet bound by Additional Protocol I.[43] Indeed, the actions of both nonparties and parties influence the creation of customary international law with regard to the broad range of subjects addressed by Protocol I. The practice of such nonparties as the United States, the United Kingdom and France during the second Persian Gulf war, for example, had a significant and, on the whole, constructive impact on the development of customary law relating to Protocol I.[44]

The ICRC recognizes that the evolution of customary law has not been halted by Protocol I and, moreover, that customary law is "strongly influenced ... by the behaviour of States vis-à-vis this treaty."[45] Indeed, all states, though in varying degrees and not only parties to the Protocol, contribute through their behavior to the development of customary law. In some cases, even some nonstate actors, especially the ICRC itself, and the United Nations may contribute.

As for noninternational armed conflicts, the ICRC correctly states that customary rules were codified only in part in common Article 3 and Additional Protocol II, and that with regard to the conduct of hostilities – the Hague law – the treaty rules are rudimentary and incomplete. A particularly important issue for the ICRC study to consider is the extent to which proscriptions of methods and means of combat governing international armed conflicts also apply to noninternational armed conflicts. Equally deserving of consideration in this respect are such customary law principles as command responsibility and proportionality.

In the context of both international and civil wars, the ICRC provides a useful list of types of relevant practice and their acceptance as law. This list, which will inform the ICRC study, includes

> not only the conduct of belligerents, but also the instructions they issue, their legislation, and statements made by their leaders; the reaction of other States at the diplomatic level, within international forums, or in public statements;

RESTATEMENT (THIRD) OF THE FOREIGN RELATIONS LAW OF THE UNITED STATES §702 (1987). For a different approach, see Bruno Simma & Philip Alston, *The Sources of Human Rights Law: Custom, Jus Cogens, and General Principles*, 12 AUSTL. Y.B. INT'L L. 82 (1992).

[43] ICRC REPORT, *supra* note 30, at 7.
[44] Theodor Meron, *The Time Has Come for the United States to Ratify Geneva Protocol I*, 88 AJIL 678, 681–82 (1994).
[45] ICRC REPORT, *supra* note 30, at 7.

military manuals; general declarations on law, including resolutions of international organizations; and, lastly, national or international court decisions.[46]

The ICRC's list omits any mention of the influence of the ICRC itself through its comments on various conflicts and events, and other interpretations such as commentaries on the Conventions and the Protocols. To a considerable extent, these interpretations affect the practice of states and their *opinio juris*, and thus the evolution of customary law. Although the ICRC's list is largely based on what states say – and in international humanitarian law this element is particularly important – not on what they do on the battlefield, fortunately the blueprint does mention the conduct of belligerents. Comprehensive research into the conduct of recent conflicts, including the two Persian Gulf wars and the Falklands/Malvinas war, could lead to significant lessons on the operational practice of belligerents.

Physical, operational acts on the battlefield have weight in this regard, but equally, or even more so, do denials, objections and challenges to those operational acts. To determine *opinio juris* or acceptance as law in this field, it is necessary to look at *both* physical behavior and statements.

Finally, distancing itself in effect from the emphasis placed by the *North Sea Continental Shelf Cases* on states whose interests are specially affected,[47] the ICRC emphasizes that account should be taken of all forms of state practice, "so as to permit all States – and not only those embroiled in armed conflict – to contribute to the formation of customary rules."[48] I agree. The behavior of belligerents is just one element, though a key one, in the formation and assessment of customary law.

A broader question, however, concerns the degree of weight to be assigned to the practice of various states in the formation of the international customary law of war. I find it difficult to accept the view, sometimes advanced, that all states, whatever their geographical situation, military power and interests, inter alia, have an equal role in this regard. Belligerency is only one factor here. The practice and opinion of Switzerland, for example, as a neutral state, surely have more to teach us about assessment of customary neutrality law than the practice of states that are not committed to the policy of neutrality and have not engaged in pertinent national practice. The practice of "specially affected states" – such as nuclear powers, other major military powers, and occupying and occupied states – which have a track record of statements, practice and policy, remains particularly telling. I do not mean to denigrate state equality, but simply to recognize the greater involvement of some states in the

---

[46] ICRC REPORT, *supra* note 30, at 7–8.
[47] North Sea Continental Shelf (FRG v. Den.; FRG v. Neth.), 1969 ICJ REP. 3, 42 (Feb. 29).
[48] ICRC REPORT, *supra* note 30, at 8.

development of the law of war, not only through operational practice but through policies expressed, for example, in military manuals.

I am confident that the ICRC study will result in a broadly acceptable restatement of customary humanitarian law. It could thus become an important vehicle for strengthening the normative structure of international humanitarian law, especially for noninternational armed conflicts.

XV

Answering for War Crimes
Lessons from the Balkans

In the fall of 1997 the judges of the International Criminal Tribunal for the former Yugoslavia will complete their four-year terms. If top and mid-level leaders indicted by the tribunal have not been arrested and delivered to The Hague by then, Antonio Cassese, the tribunal's president, has threatened to propose that the Security Council terminate the tribunal's mandate.[1] Cassese's warning echoes similar calls for top-level arrests from former chief prosecutor Richard Goldstone, justice of the South African Constitutional Court, and Louise Arbour, his successor from the Ontario Court of Appeals. Their frustration underscores the need for a careful evaluation of the tribunal's record and prospects.

The U.N. Security Council established the tribunal on May 25, 1993, when it adopted the Statute of the International Tribunal proposed by Secretary-General Boutros Boutros-Ghali. The council created the tribunal in response to the deliberate, systematic, and outrageous violations of human rights and humanitarian norms committed in the territory of the former Yugoslavia. Atrocities committed include summary executions, torture, rape, arbitrary mass internment, deportation and displacement, hostage-taking, inhuman treatment of prisoners, indiscriminate shelling of cities, and unwarranted destruction of private property. Of the 74 persons indicted for such atrocities, one has pleaded guilty and been sentenced to ten years imprisonment, five are currently in custody awaiting trial, and one – Dusan Tadić, a Bosnian Serb accused of committing abuses against Muslims in the Omarska concentration camp in Bosnia – is now standing trial. None of the seven, however, are top political or military leaders who gave the key orders. The absence of such leaders among those in custody has led Cassese to assert that the General Framework Agreement for Peace in Bosnia and Herzegovina reached at Dayton in November 1995 "is becoming an exercise in hypocrisy."

The tribunal's original purpose was to assign guilt for war crimes to the individual perpetrators and the leaders responsible, rather than allowing

---

[1] The tribunals for Rwanda and the former Yugoslavia share two organs: the prosecution and the appeals chamber. These organs will continue to exist even after the tribunal for the former Yugoslavia completes its business. The Security Council may thus have to amend the tribunals' statutes accordingly.

blame to fall on entire groups and nations. Its founders hoped that the tribunal could thus defuse ethnic tensions and assist in peacemaking. They also hoped that enforcing accountability would deter violations of international humanitarian law in Yugoslavia and elsewhere. Because the Hague tribunal was established while the war was still raging – in contrast to the Nuremberg war crimes trials, which began only after World War II had been fought and won – there was even a chance that it would have a deterrent effect for the remainder of the conflict. Conversely, failure to establish the tribunal would have eroded the values of Nuremberg and perpetuated worldwide the perception that even the most egregious crimes against humanity could go unpunished.

PAPER TIGER?

International or even national prosecutions for war crimes have rarely been the preferred option. Despite the bitter history of recent conflicts in South Africa and El Salvador, in both cases negotiations led to the establishment of truth commissions, not tribunals, as the principal institutions for addressing past injustices. Leaders in those countries understood that the people had to learn to coexist, and thus opted to pursue the process of reconciliation by combining efforts to set the historical record straight with pardons or amnesties for many perpetrators of atrocities. In the former Yugoslavia, the prospects for reunification and reconciliation were poor from the beginning. With the tremendous scale of atrocities, the hatred and suspicion between both the different communities in Bosnia-Herzegovina and their neighbors in the territory of the former Yugoslavia, and irresponsible leaders thriving on extreme nationalism and violence, international prosecution for war crimes appeared to be the only option.

From its inception, the tribunal has been plagued by the lack of cooperation from Serbian leaders in Belgrade, Bosnian Serb leaders in Pale, and Croatian leaders in Zagreb. In contrast to Nuremberg, where the allies had unlimited police power on the ground, the tribunal has had to depend on the readiness of the Security Council and the international community to exert pressure for full compliance on reluctant parties. When that pressure has been in short supply, the tribunal has encountered setback after setback. Suspects have been sheltered and protected. Access to sites where atrocities were committed has been obstructed, hindering the collection of perishable evidence. Witnesses, even victims, have withheld their testimony from the tribunal's investigators. That no witness for the prosecution in the Dusan Tadić case still lives in an area under the control of Pale or Belgrade speaks to the ever-present fear of reprisal among those who might testify.

Cooperation has been equally scarce at the governmental level. Republika Srpska, the Serb-majority entity in Bosnia, has failed to execute any of the scores of arrest warrants it has been sent. The Federal Republic of Yugoslavia's record has been almost as dismal; it has not arrested any of the indictees on its territory. Croatia has detained one, but has so far failed to deliver him up to The Hague. Zagreb's limited cooperation with the tribunal, to which it committed in the Dayton agreements, has been a small price to pay for Croatia's growing international legitimacy (it was recently admitted to the Council of Europe, often seen as a way station en route to the European Union).

Failure to obtain custody of a significant number of those indicted has encouraged suggestions that the tribunal resort to *in absentia* trials. Tempting as they may be, such trials would challenge the generally accepted interpretation of the tribunal's statute, raise concerns regarding due process of law, and be inherently vulnerable to error and abuse – thus risking the tribunal's credibility, its most precious asset. Recognizing those dangers, the tribunal has wisely resisted the temptation.

But without *in absentia* trials, the tribunal is left with few options. The international community has given the tribunal strong rhetorical support, but little aid in enforcement. In addition, the tribunal has faced budgetary difficulties. Were it not for favorable public opinion, government and U.N. backing for both the tribunal and its budget would be even weaker. Antonio Cassese and Richard Goldstone have consequently devoted much of their time to mobilizing public opinion behind the tribunal and its mission. Goldstone's successor, chief prosecutor Arbour, will probably find it necessary to do the same.

WORDS, WORDS, WORDS

The Dayton agreements contained fairly robust language concerning compliance with the tribunal's orders, including the surrender of those indicted. Enforcement was another matter. Two possibilities were considered. The first was a diplomatic approach. In resolution 1022 of November 22, 1995, the Security Council suspended sanctions against the Federal Republic of Yugoslavia and Republika Srpska, but provided for the reinstitution of those sanctions within five days of receiving a report that either government was significantly failing to meet obligations under the Dayton agreements, one of which is cooperation with the tribunal. Either of two officials could issue such a report: the commander of the NATO Implementation Force (IFOR) or Swedish diplomat Carl Bildt, whose responsibilities as High Representative under the Dayton agreements include co-ordinating the implementation of civilian aspects of the settlement. Since Croatia had never been subject to sanctions, this option did not apply to it. As powerful a tool as the ability to automatically reinstate sanctions might have proved to be, the Security Council recently rescinded Resolution 1022 to reward Serbian President Slobodan Milošević for holding elections, an essential step in the peace process.

When the Presidency of Bosnia-Herzegovina and a steering board of foreign diplomats met in Paris last November, the parties confirmed their obligation to surrender indicted persons "without delay," while Western leaders spoke of linkage to economic aid and even new sanctions. Such statements, which are periodically issued but rarely meant, amount to nothing more than collective hypocrisy.

The second option considered was military force. But while the Dayton agreements granted IFOR sufficient powers, its leadership, spearheaded by the United States, chose to hide behind a transparent fiction. Under bizarre operating procedures, IFOR troops are allowed to arrest indicted war criminals they encounter, but cannot seek them out. As long as the international community had no effective power on the ground, the military's reluctance to attempt arrests was perfectly understandable. But given the military muscle IFOR now possesses, it is a disgrace that the principal indictees have not been detained, let alone delivered up to The Hague, and can instead thumb their noses at the international community by continuing to appear in public places. I believe that they could have been captured without serious casualties, especially with help from the intelligence community. The risk was worth taking.

The Clinton administration appears to have been split over the more aggressive use of IFOR, but the cautious view that no lives should be risked prevailed, as could have been expected in an election year. Perhaps after the elections there will be a greater readiness to seek out and arrest the principal culprits, but this must be done before time runs out for both IFOR and the tribunal.

Because the Dayton agreements have reversed neither the effective partition of Bosnia and Herzegovina nor the Serbs' control over the territory they held at the end of the war, the Bosnian Serbs' wartime leaders, Radovan Karadžić and General Ratko Mladić, will continue to be sheltered by Pale. For the time being, a realistic assessment of the future of the Hague tribunal's workload should thus be based on the trials of Tadić and the six others now in custody. Those six include three Muslims and one Croat who were staff members at the Celibici camp and will be tried jointly for alleged abuses committed against Bosnian Serbs; a Bosnian Croat who has pleaded guilty to crimes against humanity committed while serving in the Bosnian Serb army (he participated in summary executions of hundreds of unarmed Muslim civilian men in July 1995) and was sentenced on November 29, 1996, to ten years imprisonment, which he may appeal; and Croatian General Tihofil Blaskić, who was indicted for ethnic cleansing in the Lasva Valley in central Bosnia – and was nevertheless arrogantly promoted by Croatian President Franjo Tudjman, only later to be "persuaded" to surrender to the tribunal after a rare instance of strong international pressure.

Since Serbs committed more atrocities than any other party, and since the lack of cooperation from Belgrade and Pale has made it more difficult to prepare indictments in cases where Serbs themselves were the victims, justice required that any indictments of Serbs be prepared and launched without waiting for parallel indictments of Croats and Muslims. Nevertheless, the fact that the tribunal's list of indictees was for a long time composed solely of Serbs exacerbated the Serbs' siege mentality and fueled their complaint that they were the only target.

Whatever their ethnicity, the number of people in custody is not conclusive evidence of success or failure. But numbers, along with the seniority and responsibility of individual defendants, could provide critical momentum that the tribunal may never gain. If IFOR could not carry out arrests with the tremendous firepower of its 60,000 troops in Bosnia, surely no arrests will be attempted as the NATO force dwindles and ultimately withdraws.

QUALIFIED SUCCESS

The great hope of tribunal advocates was that the individualization and decollectivization of guilt – placing responsibility on the leaders and the perpetrators of atrocities, rather than on whole communities – would help bring about peace and reconciliation. The tribunal's critics argued that it would obstruct peace negotiations. How, they protested, could those who make decisions at the negotiating table be expected to agree to provisions that might endanger their leadership and bring them to justice? The irony is that both sides were proved wrong. Because of the international community's reluctance or inability to enforce indictments, the tribunal has had no major impact, positive or negative, on national reconciliation.

It may, however, have had some positive impact on the broader peace process. One important result of the indictments, and of the Dayton agreements, was to establish a record of Karadžić's culpability in atrocities committed against Bosnian Muslims, and thus exclude him from direct participation in the political process. Whether that is a significant and lasting achievement depends on both the degree of his influence behind the scenes and his continued exclusion after the withdrawal of IFOR and its successor force. At the very least, Karadžić's absence from Dayton allowed Milošević to accept aspects of the agreement, including the lack of an amnesty clause, that Karadžić would likely have rejected.

Another of the tribunal's objectives was deterrence of continued and future violations of the law. There is some anecdotal, unconvincing material suggesting that the indictment of Serbs from the Krajina region of Croatia put an end to their rocket attacks on Zagreb. But the gravest atrocity, the Serb massacre of thousands of Muslims living in and around Srebrenica, happened in July 1995, when the tribunal was fully operational and Karadžić and Mladić had both been indicted.

Paradoxically, while the goals specific to Yugoslavia have not been fulfilled, the tribunal has had significant success in strengthening international law, an achievement that must be considered in any cost-benefit analysis. Without the establishment of the tribunal and the example of the Tadić trial, the perception that even the most egregious violations of international humanitarian law can be committed with impunity would have been confirmed. In the Tadić case alone, the tribunal has advanced the state of the law governing international and internal armed conflicts, especially as it pertains to the conduct of hostilities and crimes against humanity. It has also affirmed the customary, unwritten law that binds all states to international standards of behavior. Likewise, the appeals chamber's rulings on jurisdictional issues in the Tadić case have been the first judicial affirmation of international criminality and individual responsibility for violations of international humanitarian law since Nuremberg. Both the statute and the indictments also confirmed the international criminalization of rape. The tribunal has generated an unprecedented interest in humanitarian law and in punishing those who violate it. War crimes have entered the mainstream of political debate and U.N. decision-making.

In terms of pursuing justice within the former Yugoslavia, those indicted by the tribunal are now branded with a mark of Cain that serves as some measure of retribution, preventing them from traveling abroad and instilling in them the fear of arrest by an adversary or foreign government. In the absence of many actual trials and judgments, the confirmed indictments come as close as is possible to establishing a credible international record of the indicted persons' offenses, one that will discredit them until they stand trial.

Furthermore, without the Yugoslav precedent, the International Criminal Tribunal for Rwanda would not have been established to prosecute those responsible for the genocidal violence that swept that nation in 1994. The Rwanda tribunal also belies complaints about the Eurocentric nature of international concern over Yugoslavia. Beyond Rwanda, the International Criminal Tribunal for the former Yugoslavia has also triggered interest in the establishment of a permanent international criminal court, a concept now under active General Assembly consideration. On a national level, the revival of international humanitarian law has encouraged various countries to adopt statutes under the principle of universality of jurisdiction, granting competence to their national courts over violations of international humanitarian law committed in other states and enacting laws permitting the "extradition" of indicted persons to an international criminal tribunal. The evidence the prosecution has collected at The Hague could one day be used by national courts, especially as statutes of limitations do not usually apply to war crimes and crimes against humanity.

Last, and perhaps most important, the international investigation and prosecution of war crimes and crimes against humanity has proved credible and feasible. Helping to pave the way for future prosecution of such crimes, the tribunal has prepared a comprehensive set of rules of procedure and evidence, which, in the words of the tribunal, are the first code of international criminal procedure and evidence.

YUGOSLAVIA AND BEYOND

With four of the suspects in custody due to be tried jointly, and the trial of General Blaskić scheduled to begin in January, the tribunal's work is assured for at least another year. More time will be required if Zlatko Aleksovski, indicted for crimes against Muslim civilians, is delivered up for trial as ordered by a Croatian court and confirmed on October 2, 1996, by the Croatian Supreme Court. There is also the possibility of appeals, which might require another six months. Even with these tasks, the tribunal may soon approach the end of its working life. It should not be continued only to serve as a fig leaf for the impotence of the international community to enforce international law. Perhaps the realization that the tribunal's days may be numbered unless indicted leaders and perpetrators are arrested and delivered up to The Hague may yet shock the international community into action. Folding the tribunal before it has tried a substantial number of major culprits would be immensely embarrassing to both the international community and to the United States, which has given the tribunal more political, budgetary, and logistical support than any other nation. It is this embarrassment, more than anything else, that can extend the tribunal's lease on life. The tribunal should not be terminated before concluding the existing caseload and any additional cases and, where possible, more expeditiously issuing additional indictments of principal culprits.

Unless custody over indicted persons is rapidly obtained, a mechanism for trying persons arrested in the future will have to be devised. One option is to reconvene the tribunal. Another is to encourage prosecution by national courts, as all states already have the right to prosecute those accused of grave breaches of the Geneva Conventions. To facilitate both options, during the next year or two the prosecution should organize the material it has collected in such a way that states that are willing and able to resort to national prosecutions can easily access and use it. Recently, nations worldwide have been more ready to prosecute human rights and humanitarian atrocities, including Korea, where even ex-presidents have been convicted, Ethiopia, and Honduras. In South Africa, prosecutions are under way against persons who did not cooperate fully with the truth commission by coming forward, reporting the entire truth, and seeking amnesty. It is not absurd to suggest that in a few years Belgrade, Zagreb, or even Pale might have more responsible leaders and more credible criminal justice systems, and might be ready to prosecute before their courts some of those indicted by the tribunal. The prosecution could aid such efforts by preparing a report on the historical record analogous to the report of a truth commission.

Despite the difficulties the Yugoslav tribunal has encountered, it may be necessary to follow the same or a similar model in the future. But from now on, international criminal tribunals must be more effectively supported by police power. Just as there can be no national justice without a police force, there can be no effective international justice without arrests, subpoenas, investigations, and a reliable enforcement mechanism. The international community's inability to create such a mechanism, whether for ad hoc criminal tribunals or for the proposed international criminal court, threatens all efforts to create a system of international criminal justice.

XVI

Classification of Armed Conflict in the Former Yugoslavia: *Nicaragua's* Fallout*

I

In its opinion and judgment of May 7, 1997, in *Prosecutor v. Tadić*,[1] the trial chamber of the International Tribunal for the Prosecution of Persons Responsible for Serious Violations of International Humanitarian Law Committed in the Territory of Former Yugoslavia since 1991 faced the question whether the conflict in Bosnia-Herzegovina was an international armed conflict. If so, the grave breaches provisions of the Geneva Conventions for the Protection of Victims of War would become applicable, in addition to other provisions of international humanitarian law applying to such armed conflicts. In resolving that question, the majority of the trial chamber (Judges Vohrah and Stephen) sought guidance in the ruling of the International Court of Justice in the *Nicaragua* case.[2] That resort was inappropriate because the *Nicaragua* case dealt with quite a different question – whether, for legal purposes, the contras either constituted an organ of the United States Government or were acting in its behalf. If so, their acts could be attributed to the United States for purposes of state responsibility. The pending appeals of the trial chamber's decision offer the appeals chamber a unique opportunity to correct the course.

The case concerns the time period directly after the declared withdrawal of the Yugoslav National Army (JNA) from Bosnia-Herzegovina in May 1992. The Tribunal's majority acknowledged that the JNA had played a vital role in establishing, equipping, supplying, maintaining and staffing the Bosnian Serb forces (VRS), that many of the VRS troops had actually been transferred from the JNA, and that these troops had con-

---

* I am grateful to Georges Abi-Saab, George Aldrich, Benedict Kingsbury, Monroe Leigh, Michael Matheson, Detlev Vagts and Bruno Zimmermann for their helpful comments.

[1] Prosecutor v. Tadić, Opinion and Judgment, Case IT–94–1–T (May 7, 1997) [hereinafter *Tadić*], *excerpted in* 36 ILM 908 (1997), *summarized in* Michael P. Scharf, Case note, 91 AJIL 718 (1997).

[2] Military and Paramilitary Activities in and against Nicaragua (Nicar. v. U.S.), Merits, 1986 ICJ REP. 14, 62, para. 109 (June 27) [hereinafter *Nicaragua*]; *Tadić*, 36 ILM at 927, para. 585.

tinued to receive their salaries from the Government in Belgrade during this time.[3] However, even a showing of the VRS's complete dependence on the JNA for the necessities of war was not sufficient to demonstrate an international conflict, in the Tribunal's view.[4] Relying on *Nicaragua*, it also required proof that the Government in Belgrade had continued to exercise effective control over the VRS after the transfers of men and matériel on May 19, 1992.[5] I believe that an analysis of the reality on the ground shows that, for a certain time, the change that the May 19 announcement produced was largely cosmetic rather than substantial, continuing Belgrade's involvement, albeit in a more discreet manner. More important, however, my principal criticism pertains to the criteria the Tribunal applied. Although the majority relied heavily on the factual conclusion that the prosecution had not discharged its burden of proof that Belgrade had exercised effective control over the VRS forces and that they were more than mere allies, the criterion it applied – wrongly in my opinion – was whether VRS forces were de facto organs or agents of Belgrade.

The majority recognized that a state of international armed conflict existed at first, at least in part of Bosnia-Herzegovina because of the armed conflict between its forces and the JNA, but insisted that the nature of the conflict changed after May 19.[6] Unconvinced that the VRS could be considered as de facto organs or agents of the Government of the Federal Republic of Yugoslavia after that date, the majority excluded the grave breaches provisions of the Geneva Conventions from the body of norms it could enforce. As a result, the decision applied only the protections of common Article 3 and those norms of international humanitarian law that the appeals chamber had recognized as applicable in noninternational armed conflicts in its Decision on the Defence Motion for Interlocutory Appeal on Jurisdiction, of October 2, 1995.[7]

In her impressive dissent, Presiding Judge McDonald disagreed, suggesting that the majority had misapplied the *Nicaragua* test, which requires a showing of effective control only when no agency relationship has been found to impute liability to a state. She believed that the evidence proved beyond a reasonable doubt that the VRS had acted as an agent of Belgrade[8] and that the facts supported the existence of effective control.[9] During the relevant period, therefore, the armed conflict in the area specified in the indictments was international in character, the

---

[3] *Tadić*, 36 ILM at 929, paras. 592–95.   [4] *Id.* at 928, para. 588.
[5] *Id.* at 928, para. 588, and 929, para. 595.   [6] *Id.* at 922, para. 569.
[7] *Id.* at 933, para. 607.
[8] Prosecutor v. Tadić, Separate and Dissenting Opinion of Judge McDonald Regarding the Applicability of Article 2 of the Statute, Case IT–94–1–T (May 7, 1997), 36 ILM at 970, 979, para. 34.
[9] *Id.* at 974, para. 15.

victims were 'protected persons,' and the grave breaches provisions were applicable.

Judge McDonald appeared aware of the possible pitfalls *Nicaragua* had created for the *Tadić* case. The former applied imputability, a concept given wide currency by Article 8 of the International Law Commission's articles on state responsibility, in the attribution of fault and liability to a state. In contrast, the *Tadić* Tribunal's concern is the criminal responsibility of individuals: the analysis of 'responsibility [in *Tadić*, stated Judge McDonald] is *solely* for the purpose of identifying the occupying power.'[10] However, this was not an issue of (state) responsibility at all. Identifying the foreign intervenor was only relevant to characterizing the conflict. Thus, the problem in the trial chamber's approach lay not in its interpretation of *Nicaragua*, but in applying *Nicaragua* to *Tadić* at all. Obviously, the *Nicaragua* test addresses only the question of state responsibility. Conceptually, it cannot determine whether a conflict is international or internal. In practice, applying the *Nicaragua* test to the question in *Tadić* produces artificial and incongruous conclusions.

II

The difficulties confronting the Hague Tribunal on this issue were self-imposed, stemming in part from the October 1995 decision on the interlocutory appeal on jurisdiction. In that decision, the majority of the appeals chamber held that an armed conflict exists whenever there is a resort to armed force between states, protracted armed violence between governmental authorities and organized armed groups, or – and this is both welcome and realistic – such violence between armed groups within the state.[11] Rejecting the prosecution's view that foreign armed forces had

---

[10] Prosecutor v. Tadić, Separate and Dissenting Opinion of Judge McDonald Regarding the Applicability of Article 2 of the Statute, Case IT–94–1–T (May 7, 1997), 36 ILM at 977, para. 27.

[11] Prosecutor v. Tadić, Appeal on Jurisdiction, Case IT–94–1–AR72 (Oct. 2, 1995), 35 ILM 32, 54, para. 70 (1996) [hereinafter Interlocutory Appeal].

The appeals chamber regarded one of the agreements concluded between the parties to the conflict in Bosnia-Herzegovina as based on common Article 3, and thus as a reflection of the views of those parties that the conflict was of an internal character, and, furthermore, as an implicit recognition of the internal character of the conflict by the International Committee of the Red Cross (ICRC). *Id.* at 55, para. 73. It is doubtful, however, that the parties to the conflicts had a shared conception of their nature. The appeals chamber itself recognized that another agreement reflected the international aspects of the conflicts. *Id.* In his detailed discussion of the entire web of agreements, Yves Sandoz refrained from drawing any conclusions regarding the nature of the conflicts. With regard to one of the agreements, he observed that it fell under the category of 'special agreements' that could be concluded in either international or noninternational conflicts. All of the agreements were reached under great pressure of time. Obviously, the ICRC's primary concern was to encourage the max-

intervened in Bosnia-Herzegovina on a large scale, that the Statute included provisions normally considered applicable only to international armed conflicts, and that the Security Council's frequent references to grave breaches suggested that the situation as a whole should be treated as an international armed conflict, the Tribunal held that the conflicts were mixed, having both internal and international aspects.[12] The appeals chamber thus left the trial chambers to decide in each case whether a particular accused was involved in an international or a noninternational armed conflict.

The appeals chamber's expansive interpretation that 'laws or customs of war' in Article 3 of the Tribunal's Statute reach noninternational armed conflicts[13] largely avoided the worst possible consequences. However, the chamber refused to use Article 3 of its Statute (laws and customs of war) as a conduit to bring in as customary law conduct comprising grave breaches of the Geneva Conventions (grave breaches are the subject of Article 2 of the Statute; these can be regarded as customary law whose content parallels the pertinent provisions of these Conventions). The grave breaches are the principal crimes under the Conventions. Thus deprived of the core of international criminal law in cases deemed to be noninternational, the Tribunal can only raise the level of actionable violations to crimes against humanity and perhaps, in the future, genocide. Not only does this handicap the Tribunal's ability to carry out its mandate, but some commentators also criticize the resort to such heavy artillery against evil, but relatively minor, actors. Disregarding considerations of judicial economy, the appeals chamber has therefore enabled the creation of a crazy quilt of norms that would be applicable in the same conflict, depending on whether it is characterized as international or noninternational. No less, the potential for unequal and inconsistent treatment of the accused is great. Fortunately, until *Tadić*, the decisions of the trial chambers on indictments pursuant to Article 61 of the Tribunal's Rules of Procedure and Evidence found that the situations involved international armed conflicts and that the grave breaches provisions were therefore applicable,[14] avoiding potential chaos.

---

imum application of international humanitarian law. Yves Sandoz, *Réflexions sur la mise en oeuvre du droit international humanitaire et sur le rôle du Comité international de la Croix-Rouge en ex-Yougoslavie*, 3 Revue Suisse de Droit International et de Droit Européen 461, 466, 471 (1993).

[12] *Id.* at 56–57, paras. 74–77.

[13] Theodor Meron, *The Continuing Role of Custom in the Formation of International Humanitarian Law*, 90 AJIL 238 (1996).

[14] *See, e.g.*, Prosecutor v. Nikolić, Review of Indictment Pursuant to Rule 61, Case IT–94–2–R61, para. 30 (Oct. 20, 1995); Prosecutor v. Mrksić, Confirmation of Indictment, Case IT–95–13–I (Nov. 7, 1995); Prosecutor v. Mrksić, Review of Indictment Pursuant to Rule 61,

The appeals chamber's decision in *Tadić* was not inevitable. The majority chose to ignore the views of the United Nations Commission of Experts and the United States Government,[15] as well as the opinions of some scholars, that the fighting in the former Yugoslavia since 1991 must be seen as a whole.[16] Those favoring this approach consider the situation to be an international armed conflict, arguing that to divide it into isolated segments to exclude the application of the rules of international armed conflict would be artificial.[17] Another option, proposed by Judge Georges Abi-Saab in his separate opinion, would be for the Tribunal to include grave breaches within the customary law it recognizes as applicable even to noninternational armed conflicts.[18] In its amicus brief, the U.S. Government stated that persons covered by common Article 3 of the Geneva Conventions could be treated as persons protected by these Conventions.[19] The Tribunal's enlightened vision of such customary law as is pertinent to both international and noninternational armed conflicts certainly could have encompassed grave breaches of the Geneva Conventions. In addition, the authoritative Field Manual 27–10 of the U.S. Department of the Army has recognized these provisions as declaratory of customary law.[20]

The grave breaches provisions describe certain acts as criminal and subject the offenders to mandatory prosecution or extradition when committed against protected persons, defined in the Fourth Geneva Convention as those who find themselves in the hands of a party to the conflict of which they are not nationals. Enforcing this provision literally in the Yugoslav context, and in some other conflicts involving the disintegration of a state or political entity and the resulting struggle between peoples and ethnic groups, would be the height of legalism. Imagine, for example, that Israelis and Arabs in the area west of the Jordan River still had a Palestinian (Mandate) nationality during the 1947–1948 war. Denying

---

Case IT–95–13–R61, para. 25 (Apr. 3, 1996); Prosecutor v. Karadžić, Review of Indictments Pursuant to Rule 61, Case IT–95–5–R61, IT–95–18–R61, para. 88 (July 11, 1996).

[15] Amicus Curiae Brief Presented by the Government of the United States at 26–34, Motion Hearing, Prosecutor v. Tadić, Case IT–94–1–T (July 25, 1995) [hereinafter Amicus Brief].

[16] *See, e.g.*, James C. O'Brien, *The International Tribunal for Violations of International Humanitarian Law in the Former Yugoslavia*, 87 AJIL 639 (1993); Theodor Meron, *International Criminalization of Internal Atrocities*, 89 AJIL 554, 556 (1995); Theodor Meron, *War Crimes in Yugoslavia and the Development of International Law*, 88 AJIL 78, 80–81 (1994). For a trenchant critique of the appeals chamber's decision, see George H. Aldrich, *Jurisdiction of the International Criminal Tribunal for the Former Yugoslavia*, 90 AJIL 64, 66–67 (1996).

[17] Amicus Brief, *supra* note 15, at 28.

[18] Prosecutor v. Tadić, Separate Opinion of Judge Abi-Saab on the Defence Motion for Interlocutory Appeal on Jurisdiction, Case IT–94–1–AR72, at 5–6 (Oct. 2, 1995).

[19] Amicus Brief, *supra* note 15, at 35–36.

[20] U.S. Dep't of the Army, The Law of Land Warfare, para. 506(b) (Field Manual No. 27–10, 1956).

those captured by an adversary in that conflict the status of protected persons under the Geneva Conventions (had they been in force) because of their shared nationality would be absurd. In many contemporary conflicts, the disintegration of states and the establishment of new ones make nationality too messy a concept on which to base the application of international humanitarian law.

In light of the protective goals of the Geneva Conventions, I support an interpretation suggesting that in situations like the one in former Yugoslavia, where the fighting was pervasive and its history as a single state resulted in one nationality, the requirement of a different nationality should simply be construed as referring to persons in the hands of an adversary. Indeed, the International Committee of the Red Cross's *Commentary* to Article 4 of the Fourth Convention states that the reason for excluding a country's own nationals from the definition of protected persons was to avoid interfering in a state's relations with its nationals,[21] a concern obviously not relevant to the circumstances of the *Tadić* case, in which each ethnic group considered members of other ethnic groups as foreigners. In interpreting the law, our goal should be to avoid paralyzing the legal process as much as possible and, in the case of humanitarian conventions, to enable them to serve their protective goals.

III

The appeals chamber did not create any artificial tests for deciding whether a conflict is international and, like most scholars of international humanitarian law, probably did not even consider that the *Nicaragua* criteria of imputability for state responsibility were at all pertinent. Indeed, even a quick perusal of international law literature would establish that imputability is not a test commonly used in judging whether a foreign intervention leads to the internationalization of the conflict and the applicability of those rules of international humanitarian law that govern armed conflicts of an international character.

The *Tadić* appeals chamber's general guidance regarding the nature of the conflict was fully within the tradition of international law. First, it correctly focused on the involvement of Yugoslav and Croatian forces, finding that the intervention of the Croatian Army and the JNA in foreign states and against their governments rendered the conflict international. Second, it stated that the clashes between the Government of Bosnia-

---

[21] INTERNATIONAL COMMITTEE OF THE RED CROSS, GENEVA CONVENTION RELATIVE TO THE PROTECTION OF CIVILIAN PERSONS IN TIME OF WAR: COMMENTARY 46 (Oscar M. Uhler & Henri Coursier eds., 1958).

Herzegovina and Bosnian Serb rebel forces should be considered internal, *unless* the JNA's direct involvement could be proved, which would give these clashes international character as well.[22]

The *Nicaragua* case was 'discovered' in the review of the indictment in *Prosecutor v. Rajić*,[23] when the trial chamber asked the prosecution to present a brief on the attribution standard. The *Rajić* case concerned the conflicts between the forces of Bosnia-Herzegovina, on one side, and those of Croatia and the Croatian community in Bosnia-Herzegovina (HVO), on the other. The trial chamber pointed out that, in the interlocutory appeal on jurisdiction in *Tadić*, the appeals chamber had not established the degree of foreign state involvement needed to convert a domestic conflict into an international one.[24] The trial chamber found that the significant and continuous military intervention of the Croatian Army in support of the Bosnian Croats in fact sufficed to transform the conflict into an international one.[25] Acknowledging that this finding did not necessitate any further analysis, the Tribunal nevertheless decided to consider the prosecutor's additional argument that Croatia had exerted sufficient political and military control over the Bosnian Croats to make them agents or extensions of Croatia.[26] Invoking both the International Law Commission's provisions on imputability in Article 8 of its articles on state responsibility and the *Nicaragua* decision, the Tribunal held that the extent of the agency relationship between Croatia and the Bosnian Croats established that the conflict between the Bosnian Croats and the Government of Bosnia-Herzegovina was of an international character.[27] While residents in the applicable area were not directly or physically in the hands of Croatia, a country of which they were not nationals, they could be treated as being constructively so. Thus, these civilians were protected persons for the purposes of the application of the grave breaches provisions.[28]

Although the trial chamber did acknowledge the difference in contexts between the *Nicaragua* and *Rajić* cases since the latter did not require an inquiry into Croatia's liability for the acts of the HVO, it nevertheless disregarded this difference in ruling that the HVO forces could be considered agents of Croatia in determining the Tribunal's subject matter jurisdiction. For this purpose, the chamber found that specific operational control was not necessary and that general political and military control was sufficient.[29] Perhaps influenced by *Rajić*, the majority in *Tadić* made the state responsibility test of *Nicaragua* the gravamen of the

---

[22] Interlocutory Appeal, *supra* note 11, 35 ILM at 55, para. 72.
[23] Prosecutor v. Rajić, Review of the Indictment Pursuant to Rule 61, Case IT–95–12–R61 (Sept. 13, 1996), *summarized in* Olivia Swaak-Goldman, Case note, 91 AJIL 523 (1997).
[24] *Id.*, para. 12.   [25] *Id.*, para. 21.   [26] *Id.*, paras. 22–23.
[27] *Id.*, paras. 24–26.   [28] *Id.*, para. 37.   [29] *Id.*, paras. 25–26.

decision of May 7, 1997, which unnecessarily created an artificial picture of the situation on the ground and generated unacceptable legal consequences.

IV

The question of the character of armed conflicts does not appear in Article 8 of the International Law Commission's text on state responsibility or in its Article 15 concerning the attribution to the state of the acts of an insurrectional movement that becomes the new government of a state or results in the formation of a new state; nor is this question considered in their respective commentaries. These provisions deal with nothing more than the responsibility of states for wrongful acts. The *Nicaragua* Court's invocation of the attribution tests reflects both its respect for the work of Judge Roberto Ago, who had been the International Law Commission's Special Rapporteur on state responsibility, and Ago's desire to give practical utility and a judicial imprimatur to these important articles.

To justify resort to the *Nicaragua* test of attribution and at the same time acknowledge that, while that case concerned the responsibility of states, the case before it involved the wholly different issue of individual criminal responsibility, the *Tadić* Tribunal juxtaposed the discussion of attribution in the *Nicaragua* case with that case's conclusions on humanitarian law. Early in the Judgment, the International Court of Justice found that there was no direct U.S. intervention in combat or combat support for the contras in Nicaragua and rejected the claim that the contras were subject to United States influence to the extent that their acts were imputable to the United States. Concluding that the contras were responsible for their own acts, the ICJ stated that the United States was nonetheless responsible to Nicaragua for any unlawful acts it had committed.[30] Next, the Court reviewed the claims that the United States had violated several legal obligations vis-à-vis Nicaragua, such as the use of force and resort to unlawful intervention. The ICJ then examined the law of self-defense and, in light of the U.S. multilateral treaty reservation to the compulsory jurisdiction of the Court, the applicable customary law. Strictly in the context of the direct responsibility of the United States for its own acts and the applicable customary law, the Court held that U.S. acts against Nicaragua fell under the humanitarian law relating to international conflicts, while the relations between Nicaragua and the contras were governed by the humanitarian law applicable to conflicts of a noninternational character.[31]

---

[30] *Nicaragua*, 1986 ICJ Rep. at 61–65, paras. 105–16.   [31] *Id.* at 114, para. 219.

The ICJ's conclusion that the rules of international conflicts applied to United States-Nicaragua relations was obvious and could have been reached independently or even in the absence of any discussion of imputability. The nexus between attribution and the character of the conflict found in *Tadić* was thus never present in the ICJ's discussion. To demonstrate the dangers and artificiality of the attribution test, as applied in *Tadić*, consider a conflict in a country where practically all the fighting is done by a foreign state, but where the rebels maintain their independence from the intervening power and do not satisfy the *Nicaragua* test. Could anyone seriously question the international character of such a conflict?

V

What, then, should the appeals chamber do? Whether it regards the conflicts in the former Yugoslavia as a single international conflict, as Judge George Aldrich,[32] James O'Brien[33] and I, among others, have urged, or as a mix of international and internal conflicts, as Professor Christopher Greenwood has proposed,[34] I suggest that the appeals chamber reject the *Nicaragua* imputability test and return to the simple, commonsense and time-tested approaches of public international law. The reality, dimensions, scope and duration of a foreign military intervention, the foreign state's direct participation in the hostilities, the nature of the states and political entities involved in the conflict, their recognition by other states, the position of the United Nations Security Council, the relative involvement of local and foreign forces, and, in general, relevant strategic, factual and military considerations drive this analysis. As Professors Daillier and Pellet wrote, mentioning the former Yugoslavia, intervention by foreign states is generally the catalyst that transforms a war from civil to international.[35] Professor Dinstein agrees that intervention by a foreign state on behalf of the insurgents turns a civil war into an interstate war.[36] Specifically with regard to Yugoslavia, he writes:

> The disintegration of Yugoslavia has exposed to light a more complex situation in which a civil war between diverse ethnic, religious or linguistic groups inside the territory of a single country is converted into an inter-State war once the fragmentation into several sovereign States is effected.... [W]hen Serbia and

---

[32] *See* Aldrich, *supra* note 16.   [33] *See* O'Brien, *supra* note 16.

[34] Christopher Greenwood, *International Humanitarian Law and the* Tadić *Case*, 7 Eur. J. Int'l L. 265, 269–75 (1996).

[35] Nguyen Quoc Dinh, Patrick Daillier & Alain Pellet, Droit international public 903 (1994). *See also* Christopher Greenwood, *Scope of Application of Humanitarian Law, in* Handbook of Humanitarian Law in Armed Conflicts 39, 50 (Dieter Fleck ed., 1995).

[36] Yoram Dinstein, War, Aggression and Self-Defence 6 (2d ed. 1994).

Bosnia-Herzegovina emerged from the political ruins of Yugoslavia as independent countries, the conflict transmuted into an inter-State war by dint of the cross-border involvement of Serbian armed forces in military operations conducted by Bosnian Serbs rebelling against the Bosnian Government ....[37]

The *Tadić* trial chamber has already accepted that, before the announced withdrawal of the JNA forces from the territory of Bosnia-Herzegovina, the conflict was an international armed conflict. The facts of the situation and the rules of international humanitarian law should determine whether the JNA continued to be involved after that date and during the period pertinent to the indictments; if so, the international character of the conflict would have remained unchanged. The provisions of the Fourth Geneva Convention on termination of the application of the Convention, including Article 6, are relevant, not the legal tests of imputability and state responsibility. Finally, the appeals chamber would also be well-advised to abandon its adherence to the literal requirements of the definition of protected persons and help adapt it to the principal challenges of contemporary conflicts.

[37] Yoram Dinstein, War, Aggression and Self-Defence 6 (2d ed. 1994). *Id.* at 7.

XVII

War Crimes Law Comes of Age

The rapid and fundamental developments in the last few years on the establishment of individual criminal responsibility for serious violations of international humanitarian law have been such that it is now an appropriate time to assess their principal features.[1]

On the institutional plane, the establishment by the United Nations Security Council of the ad hoc tribunals for the former Yugoslavia and Rwanda under Chapter VII of the UN Charter was of cardinal importance. The International Tribunal for Former Yugoslavia is no longer in danger of running out of defendants. Under international pressure, Croatia arranged for the surrender of a number of indicted Croatian nationals and Bosnian Croats to the Hague Tribunal. In addition, under the umbrella of the Stabilization Force and NATO, several indicted persons have been captured *manu militari* and brought to The Hague, and several others have surrendered. Most of the indicted Bosnian Serbs, however, have yet to be arrested. The principal leaders responsible for the atrocities are still free, but they are forced to hide from international justice and their arrest remains a distinct possibility. The Security Council has recently considered establishing yet another Chapter VII ad hoc tribunal, one that would have the power to prosecute senior members of the Khmer Rouge leadership who planned or directed the commission of serious violations of international humanitarian law in Cambodia during the period 1975–1979. One of the issues before the Council regarding this proposal will be whether its powers under that chapter encompass punishing members of a defunct regime for crimes committed two decades ago.

The Hague Tribunal has issued several important decisions that clarify and give a judicial imprimatur to some rules of international humanitarian law. The international Tribunal for the prosecution of genocide and other violations of international humanitarian law in Rwanda is also functioning, despite the problems that have plagued it during its first few years.

---

[1] I have written the following articles demonstrating these developments: Theodor Meron, *The Case for War Crimes Trials in Yugoslavia*, FOREIGN AFF., Summer 1993, at 122; *From Nuremberg to The Hague*, 149 MIL. L. REV., Summer 1995, at 107; *Rape as a Crime under International Humanitarian Law*, 87 AJIL 424 (1993); *The Normative Impact of the International Tribunal for Former Yugoslavia*, 1994 ISR. Y.B. HUM. RTS. 163; *International Criminalization of Internal Atrocities*, 89 AJIL 554 (1995); *The Continuing Role of Custom in the Formation of International Humanitarian Law*, 90 AJIL 238 (1996); *Answering for War Crimes: Lessons from the Balkans*, FOREIGN AFF., Jan.–Feb. 1997, at 2.

Many of the principal indicted persons involved in the Rwandan genocide have been arrested and are in the Tribunal's custody. Like the Hague Tribunal,[2] the Arusha Tribunal has rendered an important decision concerning its jurisdiction and the Security Council's competence under Chapter VII of the UN Charter to establish it.[3] The Tribunal is currently trying several cases and should issue some judgments this year.

The work of both Tribunals demonstrates that international investigations and prosecutions of persons responsible for serious violations of international humanitarian law are possible and credible. No less, the rules of procedure and evidence each Tribunal has adopted now form the vital core of an international code of criminal procedure and evidence that will doubtless have an important impact on the rules of the future international criminal court (ICC). Creating a positive environment for the establishment of a standing international criminal court, which – despite serious hurdles – may become a reality before the end of the twentieth century, these achievements have also injected new vigor into the concept of universal jurisdiction and sparked the readiness of states to prosecute persons accused of serious violations of international humanitarian law. There is some evidence, albeit anecdotal and uncertain, that the ad hoc tribunals and the prospects for the establishment of the ICC have had some deterrent effect on violations.

As groundbreaking as these institutional developments are, the rapid growth of the normative principles of international humanitarian law equals them in significance. International humanitarian law has developed faster since the beginning of the atrocities in the former Yugoslavia than in the four-and-a-half decades since the Nuremberg Tribunals and the adoption of the Geneva Conventions for the Protection of Victims of War of August 12, 1949. Appearing in 1964, Wolfgang Friedmann's important book, *The Changing Structures of International Law*, noted that international criminal law recognized as crimes only piracy *jure gentium* and war crimes.[4] Despite the potential for a more expansive vision even in 1964,[5] the criminal aspects of international humanitarian law remained limited and the prospects for its international enforcement poor, right up to the eve of the atrocities committed in Yugoslavia.

There is, of course, a synergistic relationship among the statutes of the international criminal tribunals, the jurisprudence of the Hague Tribunal,

---

[2] Prosecutor v. Tadić, No. IT–94–1–AR72, Appeal on Jurisdiction, paras. 28–40 (Oct. 2, 1995), 35 ILM 32 (1996) [hereinafter Interlocutory Appeal].

[3] Prosecutor v. Kanyabashi, No. ICTR–96–15–T, Decision on Jurisdiction (June 18, 1997), *summarized* by Virginia Morris *in* 92 AJIL 66 (1998).

[4] WOLFGANG FRIEDMANN, THE CHANGING STRUCTURES OF INTERNATIONAL LAW 168 (1964).

[5] *See generally* Theodor Meron, *Is International Law Moving towards Criminalization?* 9 EUR. J. INT'L L. 18 (1998).

the growth of customary law, its acceptance by states, and their readiness to prosecute offenders under the principle of universality of jurisdiction. For example, the 1995 *Tadić* appeals decision of the Hague Tribunal, which confirmed the applicability of some principles of the Hague law to noninternational armed conflicts and the criminalization of violations of common Article 3 of the Geneva Conventions in such conflicts, clearly helped to create the environment for some of the developments in the Preparatory Committee on the Establishment of an International Criminal Court that I discuss below.

The Statute for Yugoslavia affirms that crimes against humanity do not require a nexus with international wars, while the Statute for Rwanda extends this conclusion to peacetime situations, as well as to the criminalization of serious violations of common Article 3 of the Geneva Conventions and Additional Protocol II.

The Statutes of both ad hoc Tribunals criminalize rape as a crime against humanity. Clarifying crimes against humanity is one of the Hague Tribunal's most important contributions. In the *Tadić* appeal, the Tribunal asserted:

> It is by now a settled rule of customary international law that crimes against humanity do not require a connection to international armed conflict. Indeed, as the Prosecutor points out, customary international law may not require a connection between crimes against humanity and any conflict at all. Thus, by requiring that crimes against humanity be committed in either internal or international armed conflict, the Security Council may have defined the crime in Article 5 more narrowly than necessary under customary international law. There is no question, however, that the definition of crimes against humanity adopted by the Security Council in Article 5 [of the Statute] comports with the principle of *nullum crimen sine lege*.[6]

Interpreting the Statute's requirement that crimes against humanity be "directed against any civilian population," the Tribunal held that the crimes must involve a course of conduct and not merely one particular act.[7] However, the Tribunal subsequently explained that, "as long as there is a link with the widespread or systematic attack against a civilian population, a single act could qualify as a crime against humanity,"[8] and a person who commits a crime against a single victim or a small number of victims could be guilty of a crime against humanity.[9]

---

[6] Interlocutory Appeal, *supra* note 2, para. 141.

[7] Prosecutor v. Tadić, No. IT–94–1–T, Decision on Form of the Indictment, para. 11 (Nov. 14, 1995).

[8] Prosecutor v. Mrksić, Radić & Šljivančanin, No. IT–95–13–R61, Review of Indictment Pursuant to Rule 61, para. 30 (Apr. 3, 1996) [hereinafter *Vukovar Hospital Decision*].

[9] *Id.*

The *Tadić* judgment reaffirmed that a "single act by a perpetrator taken within the context of a widespread or systematic attack against a civilian population entails individual criminal responsibility and an individual perpetrator need not commit numerous offences to be held liable."[10] Although crimes against humanity can be committed only against a civilian population, the Tribunal construed the term "civilian population" broadly: "the presence of those actively involved in the conflict should not prevent the characterization of a population as civilian and those actively involved in a resistance movement can qualify as victims of crimes against humanity."[11] For example, civilians or resistance fighters who had laid down their arms were considered victims of crimes against humanity in the *Vukovar Hospital Decision*.[12]

Finally, interpreting the UN Secretary-General's report on Article 5 of the Statute (crimes against humanity) disjunctively, the Tribunal held that the requirement that acts be directed against a civilian population can be fulfilled if the acts are *either* widespread or systematic.[13]

Significantly, the Tribunal found that a policy to commit crimes against humanity need not be formal, and can be inferred from the manner of the crime. Thus, evidence that "the acts occur on a widespread or systematic basis that demonstrates a policy to commit those acts, whether formalized or not,"[14] is sufficient. Even more important, the Tribunal held that this policy to commit crimes against humanity need not be a state policy. Although crimes against humanity, as crimes of a collective nature, could be committed only by states or individuals exercising state power during World War II, the Tribunal considered that customary international law has evolved "to take into account forces which, although not those of the legitimate government, have de facto control over, or are able to move freely within, defined territory,"[15] including terrorist groups or organizations.[16]

---

[10] Prosecutor v. Tadić, No. IT–94–1–T, para. 649 (May 7, 1997) [hereinafter *Tadić*].

[11] *Id.*, para. 643.

[12] *Id.* (citing *Vukovar Hospital Decision, supra* note 8, para. 32).

[13] *Id.*, para. 646. *See* UN Doc. S/25704, para. 48 (1993) [hereinafter Report of the Secretary-General].

[14] *Tadić, supra* note 10, para. 653.

[15] *Id.*, para. 654.

[16] However, I find less persuasive the Tribunal's holding that all crimes against humanity, not only persecution, require discriminatory intent. *Id.*, paras. 650, 652. The Tribunal recognized that it was departing from customary law, which did not require such intent. There was no reason for the Tribunal to regard the more restrictive Report of the Secretary-General, *supra* note 13, para. 48, as gospel. This holding unnecessarily limits the scope of crimes against humanity; a decision to follow the Nuremberg jurisprudence would have been better. Note that in the U.S. proposal on the elements of offenses under the ICC statute that was presented to the Preparatory Committee, the requirement of discrimination is limited to those crimes against humanity that involve persecution. *See* UN Doc. A/AC.249/1998/DP.11, at 7 [hereinafter U.S. Offenses Proposal]. It would have been better, I

In its decisions, the Tribunal for the former Yugoslavia has already made a significant contribution to the elucidation of some general principles of criminal law, particularly duress and superior orders,[17] and will no doubt further clarify the concept of command responsibility.

The Tribunal has also contributed to an expansive reading of customary humanitarian law.[18] Even though its jurisprudence on grave breaches of the Geneva Conventions and on the classification of the conflict as international or internal has erred on the side of legal formalism, pending appeals still offer some hope for a change.[19]

An event with enormous institutional and normative implications is the UN Diplomatic Conference of plenipotentiaries in Rome (June 15–July 17) on the establishment of an international criminal court, which as of this writing has not yet been held. The Diplomatic Conference follows four years of intensive preparatory work by the United Nations, first by an ad hoc committee (1995) and then by the Preparatory Committee on the Establishment of an International Criminal Court (1996–1998). The starting point and an important focus for the ad hoc and preparatory committees was the draft statute drawn up by the International Law Commission in a remarkably short time and completed in 1994, under the leadership of Professor James Crawford as chairman of the Commission's working group.

The Preparatory Committee[20] made significant contributions that confirm and further accelerate the radical changes taking place in international humanitarian law. It gave unprecedented attention to the clarification and drafting of general principles of criminal law, including nonretroactivity, age of responsibility, statute of limitations, *actus reus*,

---

believe, to regard inhumane acts against a civilian population, such as murder, extermination, enslavement and deportation, as crimes against humanity and to require discrimination only for persecution on political, racial and religious grounds, as at Nuremberg. I hasten to add that, although I criticize some decisions of the Hague Tribunal on this point and a few others, I believe that the Tribunal and its judges, prosecutors and registrars have been very successful overall. The solid foundation they have built will allow the international community to proceed toward the establishment of a standing international criminal court.

[17] *See* Prosecutor v. Erdemović, No. IT–96–22–A, Appeals Judgment (Oct. 7, 1997).

[18] *See* Interlocutory Appeal, *supra* note 2.

[19] *See* Theodor Meron, *Classification of Armed Conflict in the Former Yugoslavia*: Nicaragua's *Fallout*, 92 AJIL 236 (1998).

[20] See the following reports by Christopher Keith Hall: *The First Two Sessions of the UN Preparatory Committee on the Establishment of an International Criminal Court*, 91 AJIL 177 (1997); *The Third and Fourth Sessions of the UN Preparatory Committee on the Establishment of an International Criminal Court*, 92 AJIL 124 (1998); *The Fifth Session of the UN Preparatory Committee on the Establishment of an International Criminal Court, id*, at 331; *The Sixth Session of the UN Preparatory Committee on the Establishment of an International Criminal Court, id.* at 548; *see also* Report of the Intersessional Meeting from 19 to 30 January 1998 in Zutphen, the Netherlands, Preparatory Committee on the Establishment of an International Criminal Court, UN Doc. A/AC.249/1998/L.13.

mens rea, mistake of fact or law, and various grounds for excluding criminal responsibility.

Although considerable uncertainty about the final definitions of the crimes within the court's jurisdiction remains, the evolving texts suggest that – leaving aside the controversial crime of aggression whose inclusion in the statute is still questionable – the court will have jurisdiction over genocide, crimes against humanity and war crimes, including grave breaches of the Geneva Conventions. The definition of the crime of genocide tracks the definitions in the Convention on the Prevention and Punishment of the Crime of Genocide. The section on war crimes will probably include a significant catalogue of Hague law-type provisions, as well as criminalize the use of a few kinds of weaponry, such as poison gas. Rape will probably be criminalized as a serious violation of international humanitarian law or a grave breach of the Geneva Conventions, rather than only as a crime against humanity, which carries a higher burden of proof.[21]

For noninternational armed conflicts, there is an emerging understanding of the need to criminalize internal atrocities. The statute of the international criminal court will probably establish not only that norms stated in common Article 3 set standards for individual criminal responsibility in internal conflicts, but also that rape and some violations of Hague law-type provisions are subject to individual criminal responsibility.[22] However, a small number of states still oppose the applicability of such crimes and even of crimes against humanity in noninternational armed conflicts. Finally, crimes against humanity will encompass the pertinent crimes in the Nuremberg Charter and, according to some proposals, some forms of arbitrary detention. Another proposal would include among crimes against humanity the causing of disappearances.

Following a position already made known in 1996, the United States delegation to the Preparatory Committee issued a statement urging support for the no-nexus approach for crimes against humanity. In part, this statement declared: "Contemporary international law makes it clear that no war nexus for crimes against humanity is required. The United States believes that crimes against humanity must be deterred in times of peace as well as in times of war and that the ICC Statute should reflect that principle."[23]

The United States also announced robust positions – confirming its existing policy – on the criminalization of violations of common Article 3 in noninternational armed conflicts and on some principles concerning

---

[21] *See* Theodor Meron, *Rape as a Crime under International Humanitarian Law, supra* note 1.

[22] *See* Theodor Meron, *International Criminalization of Internal Atrocities, supra* note 1.

[23] U.S. statement submitted to the Preparatory Committee on the Establishment of an International Criminal Court (Mar. 23, 1998) (on file with author).

the conduct of hostilities in such conflicts. The U.S. statement of March 23, 1998, thus asserted:

> The United States strongly believes that serious violations of the elementary customary norms reflected in common Article 3 should be the centerpiece of the ICC's subject matter jurisdiction with regard to non-international armed conflicts. Finally, the United States urges that there should be a section . . . covering other rules regarding the conduct of hostilities in non-international armed conflicts. It is good international law, and good policy, to make serious violations of at least some fundamental rules pertaining to the conduct of hostilities in non-international armed conflicts a part of the ICC jurisdiction.[24]

Like the previously discussed *Tadić* opinion, the U.S. proposal on the elements of crimes, which was submitted to the Preparatory Committee on April 2, 1998, takes the disjunctive approach, i.e., that acts directed against a civilian population must be either widespread or systematic to be characterized as crimes against humanity.[25]

---

[24] *Id.*

[25] U.S. Offenses Proposal, *supra* note 16, at 3. The interpretive Report of the Secretary-General, *supra* note 13, para. 48, states that crimes against humanity are those "committed as part of a widespread *or* systematic attack against any civilian population" (emphasis added). The report was approved by Security Council Resolution 827 (May 25, 1993), 32 ILM 1203 (1993). In the Security Council discussion of Resolution 827, Ambassador Albright stated:

> Secondly, it is understood that Article 5 applies to all acts listed in that article, when committed contrary to law during a period of armed conflict in the territory of the former Yugoslavia, as part of a widespread *or* systematic attack against any civilian population on national, political, ethnic, racial, gender, or religious grounds.

UN Doc. S/PV.3217, at 16 (1993) (emphasis added).

The disjunctive formula ("or") was vigorously endorsed by the Hague Tribunal in both the *Vukovar Hospital Decision, supra* note 8, para. 30, and in *Tadić, supra* note 10, para. 646. *See also* VIRGINIA MORRIS & MICHAEL P. SCHARF, AN INSIDER'S GUIDE TO THE INTERNATIONAL CRIMINAL TRIBUNAL FOR THE FORMER YUGOSLAVIA 79–80 (1995) (who write that crimes against humanity must be committed as part of a systematic plan or general policy, rather than as random acts of violence, without mentioning widespread acts). The Statute for the Rwanda Tribunal upgraded the word "or" to the black-letter law of Article 3 (crimes against humanity): "when committed as part of a widespread or systematic attack against any civilian population."

Neither the Nuremberg Charter nor Allied Control Council Law No. 10 referred to either widespread or systematic attacks. But the Nuremberg jurisprudence suggests that international law requires a systematic governmental organization and that more than isolated acts must be proved; they must be part of a policy. 6 LAW REPORTS OF TRIALS OF WAR CRIMINALS 80 (United Nations War Crimes Commission, 1948); 15 *id.* at 136 (1949). In the *Justice* case decided under Control Council Law No. 10, the Tribunal stated:

> We hold that crimes against humanity as defined in C.C. Law 10 must be strictly construed to exclude isolated cases of atrocity or persecution whether committed by private individuals or by governmental authority. As we construe it, that section provides for punishment of crimes committed against German nationals only where there is proof of conscious participation in systematic government organized or approved procedures amounting to atrocities and offenses of the kind specified in the act and committed against populations or amounting to persecution on political, racial, or religious grounds.

One is struck by three aspects of the scope of crimes under international humanitarian law as it has emerged from the work of the Preparatory Committee. First, many participating governments appear ready to accept an expansive conception of customary international law without much supporting practice. Second is an increasing readiness to recognize that some rules of international humanitarian law once considered to involve only the responsibility of states may also be a basis for individual criminal responsibility. There are lessons to be learned here about the impact of public opinion on the formation of *opinio juris* and customary law. The International Committee of the Red Cross's study of customary rules of international humanitarian law, now in progress, will further reinforce these developments. It remains to be seen, however, whether the greater openness to customary law apparent during the various meetings of the Preparatory Committee will also materialize when the treaty establishing the future international criminal court is opened for signature and, especially, ratification. Third, the probable inclusion in the ICC statute of common Article 3 and crimes against humanity, the latter divorced from a war nexus, connotes a certain blurring of international humanitarian law with human rights law and thus an incremental criminalization of serious violations of human rights. It goes without saying that the type of offenses encompassed by common Article 3 and crimes against humanity are virtually indistinguishable from ordinary human rights violations, except, as regards crimes against humanity, for their systematic or policy basis. Significantly, one of the drafts concerning the qualifications of ICC judges requires competence not only in international criminal law and international humanitarian law, but also in human rights law. Although important human rights conventions, such as the Convention against Torture and Other Cruel, Inhuman or Degrading Treatment or Punishment, have established a system both of universal jurisdiction over certain crimes and of international cooperation and judicial assistance between states parties, we are now witnessing a process whereby some serious violations of human rights are being subjected, additionally, to the jurisdiction of international criminal courts.

---

3 Trial of War Criminals before the Nuernberg Tribunals 982 (1951). *See also* the Altstötter case, 6 Law Reports of Trials of War Criminals, *supra*, at 40; and Egon Schwelb, *Crimes against Humanity*, 23 Brit. Y.B. Int'l L. 178, 191 (1946).

The summaries prepared by the staff of the UN War Crimes Commission, in pointing out that war crimes could overlap with crimes against humanity, stated that crimes committed in "a widespread, systematic manner" may also constitute crimes against humanity. 15 Law Reports of Trials of War Criminals 134. This expression, which does not clarify the relationship between "widespread" and "systematic," does not appear in the cases. This summary may have triggered the pertinent language in the 1993 Report of the UN Secretary-General, *supra* note 13.

Another important development is the growing recognition that the elevation of many principles of international humanitarian law from the rhetorical to the normative, and from the merely normative to the effectively criminalized, creates a real need for the crimes within the ICC's jurisdiction to be defined with the clarity, precision and specificity required for criminal law in accordance with the principle of legality (*nullum crimen sine lege*). The proposal on the elements of offenses submitted by the United States to the Preparatory Committee is a step in that direction.[26]

These developments could not have taken place without a powerful new coalition driving further criminalization of international humanitarian law. Much like the earlier coalition that stimulated the development of both a corpus of international human rights law and the mechanisms involved in its enforcement, this new coalition includes scholars that promote and develop legal concepts and give them theoretical credibility, NGOs that provide public and political support and means of pressure, and various governments that spearhead lawmaking efforts in the United Nations.

These institutional and normative developments will surely generate further growth of universal jurisdiction. Although the offenses subject to the jurisdiction of international criminal tribunals should not be conflated with those subject to national jurisdiction under the universality principle, there is a clear synergy between the two. The list of crimes that has emerged from the Preparatory Committee will inevitably influence national laws governing crimes subject to universal jurisdiction. For this reason, the broader significance of the international criminal court's statute exceeds its immediate goals. Although the ICC will never be able to try more than a small number of defendants, its institutional importance lies in denying immunity to those responsible for serious violations of international humanitarian law, in fostering real deterrence of major violations, and in providing an effective criminal jurisdiction when state prosecutorial or judicial systems fail to investigate and prosecute in conformity with standards to be stated in the statute. It is in the stimulation of national prosecutions under the relevant principles of jurisdiction, and in the development and clarification of the applicable law, that a standing international criminal court's contribution will be particularly valuable.

---

[26] *See* U.S. Offenses Proposal, *supra* note 16.

Epilogue

The adoption of the Rome Statute of the International Criminal Court on July 17, 1998, is an event of historic importance. Although it is too early to assess the prospects of the effectiveness of the Court and many aspects of its Statute, this is not the case with regard to the statement of the crimes contained in Articles 6–8 (see Annex). These Articles, now part of treaty law, not only constitute the principal offenses that the ICC will try, but will take on a life of their own as an authoritative and largely customary statement of international humanitarian and criminal law, and may thus become a model for national laws to be enforced under the principle of universality of jurisdiction. In terms of substantive humanitarian law, these Articles are the most important part of the Statute. They will have great influence on the practice and the doctrine even before the Statute enters into effect.

Regarding the crime of genocide, Article 6 repeats verbatim Article 2 of the Convention on Prevention and Punishment of the Crime of Genocide as adopted by the U. S. General Assembly on December 9, 1948.

As a contribution to international law, Article 7, on Crimes against Humanity, is more important. It is – leaving aside the brief provision contained in Article 6(c) of the Nuremberg Charter and the statements of crimes against humanity in the Statutes of the criminal tribunals for the former Yugoslavia and for Rwanda – the first comprehensive multilateral treaty definition of crimes against humanity. It is accompanied by definitions of the principal offenses. The Articles on crimes against humanity and on war crimes are, on the whole, enlightened, credible and up to date.

The chapeau of crimes against humanity mentions no nexus to armed conflicts, either international or internal in character. The Statute thus confirms that crimes against humanity are as applicable to peacetime as they are to wartime. Crimes against humanity under the Rome Statute, as well as some of the offenses listed for non-international armed conflicts, overlap with some violations of fundamental human rights, which thus become criminalized under a multilateral treaty.

The chapeau does not require proof of discrimination against the targeted civilian population. This is a welcome and deliberate departure from the jurisprudence of the Hague Tribunal (discussed in Chapter XVII), which made all of the crimes against humanity subject to the proof of discriminatory intent. Instead, returning to the Nuremberg model, Article 7 makes discriminatory intent pertinent only to the offense of persecution (Article 7 (1) (h)).

The chapeau adheres to the disjunctive approach ("widespread or systematic attack") already followed by The Hague Tribunal. The disjunctiveness of the Statute is, however, balanced by a definition of "attack directed against any civilian population" (para. 2(a)) as a course of conduct involving the multiple commission of acts (referred to in para. 1). This definition of attack should not be regarded as raising the threshold for crimes against humanity. It has always been unlikely that acts not involving a multiple commission of attacks would be tried by the International Criminal Court as crimes against humanity in the first place. The definition of attack further recognizes that crimes against humanity can be committed not only by states but also by various organizations ("pursuant to or in furtherance of a State or organizational policy to commit such attack"). For crimes against humanity to be established, an element of intentionality must be shown ("knowledge of the attack"). This provision is not entirely clear and could benefit from further elaboration through the elements of crimes (Article 9 of the Statute).

The chapeau is then followed by the enumeration of eleven offenses, building on but significantly adding to the Nuremberg list. These offenses or some of their terms are then specifically defined. These definitions in themselves make a considerable contribution to international law.

The additions to Nuremberg are forcible transfer of population (not only deportations), imprisonment and other severe deprivations of personal liberty in violation of fundamental rules of international law, torture, rape, sexual slavery, enforced prostitution, forced pregnancy, enforced sterilization, or any form of sexual violence of comparable gravity, enforced disappearance of persons and apartheid.

The offenses defined are extermination, enslavement, deportation or forcible transfer of population, torture, forced pregnancy, persecution, apartheid, and enforced disappearance of persons. The definition of extermination includes "the intentional infliction of conditions of life, inter alia, the deprivation of access to food and medicine, calculated to bring about the destruction of part of a population" (I mention below the war crime of employing starvation as a method of warfare). The definition of enslavement includes the exercise of power attaching to ownership over persons in the course of trafficking in persons, in particular women and children. This provision further demonstrates the importance attributed by the Statute to the criminalization of offenses against women.

Deportation is usefully defined as forced displacement of the persons concerned by expulsion or other coercive acts from the area in which they are lawfully present, without grounds permitted under international law.

The definition of torture is not limited to acts committed by or at the instigation of or with the consent or acquiescence of a public official or other person acting in an official capacity, as was the case in the Convention against Torture and other Cruel, Inhuman or Degrading Treatment or Punishment, of December 10, 1984. The offense is thus not limited to governmental actors. This is a positive and important development.

Forced pregnancy is defined as the unlawful confinement of a woman forcibly made pregnant, with the intent of affecting the ethnic composition of any population or carrying out other grave violations of international law.

The definition of enforced disappearance of persons elaborates on earlier definitions adopted in the United Nations. It describes such disappearance as the arrest, detention or abduction of persons by, or with the authorization, support or acquiescence of, a State or a political organization, followed by a refusal to acknowledge that deprivation of freedom or to give information on the fate or whereabouts of those persons, with the intention of removing them from the protection of the law for a prolonged period of time.

Article 8 on war crimes contains, first, a section (a) tracking grave breaches of the Geneva Conventions, i.e., acts against persons or property protected by those conventions, then a section (b) on other serious violations of laws and customs applicable in international armed conflict, and several sections on non-international armed conflicts.

Section (b) is a very important and rather comprehensive statement of offenses which draws on the Hague Law and Additional Protocol I to the Geneva Conventions, and thus goes beyond the grave breaches provisions of the Geneva Conventions. The innovations include criminalization of various acts against U.N. peace-keepers and humanitarian organizations, their flags, emblems and assets, the criminalization of transfer, directly or indirectly, by the occupying power of parts of its own civilian population into the territory it occupies (which, except for the addition of the words "directly or indirectly," is a grave breach of Protocol I, but not of the Fourth Geneva Convention), committing rape, sexual slavery, enforced prostitution, forced pregnancy, enforced sterilization, or any other form of sexual violence also constituting a grave breach of the Geneva Conventions, conscripting or enlisting children under the age of fifteen years into the national armed forces or using them to participate actively in the hostilities, and intentionally using starvation of civilians as a method of warfare by depriving them of objects indispensable for their survival, including wilfully impeding relief supplies as provided for under the Geneva Conventions. One provision (para. 2 (b) iv)) concerns collateral damage or proportionality. It requires, for the criminalization of an attack launched in the knowledge that such attack will cause an excessive damage to civilians or to the natural environment, that the attack be "*clearly* excessive in relation to the concrete and direct *overall* military advantage anticipated." The words which I italicized indicate departure from Protocol I language and constitute a certain clarification of the Protocol's principle of proportionality.

The list of prohibited weapons is limited to poison or poisonous weapons (Article 23(a) of the Regulations annexed to the Hague Convention (IV) Respecting the Laws and Customs of War on Land), asphyxiating, poisonous or other gases, and all analogous liquids, materials or devices (1925 Geneva Protocol), and bullets which expand or flatten easily in the human body (1899 Hague Declaration 3 concerning expanding bullets). Additional weapons can be included in an annex to the Statute by a future amendment. Specific references to bacteriological (biological) agents or toxins for hostile purposes or in armed conflict and to chemical weapons as defined and prohibited by the 1993 Convention on the Prohibition of the Development, Production, Stockpiling and Use of Chemical Weapons and on their Destruction have been regrettably deleted. It is to be hoped that the International Criminal Court will be able to interpret the offenses concerning poison, gases, and analogous materials so as to include some of the deleted elements.

Section (c) repeats verbatim and declares criminal serious violations of common Article 3. Drawing on Article 1(2) of Additional Protocol II, the Statute (section (d)) states that section (c) applies to armed conflicts not of an international character and thus does not apply to situations of internal disturbances and tensions, such as riots, isolated and sporadic acts of violence or other acts of a similar nature.

Section (e) contains an important and significant list (but far shorter than the list of war crimes drafted for international armed conflicts) of other serious violations of the laws and customs applicable in armed conflicts not of an international character, within the established framework of international law. The recognition that war crimes under customary law are pertinent to non-international armed conflicts represents a significant advance. The list draws on the Hague law and the additional Protocols. In addition to the inclusion of some fundamental Hague law rules as offenses for non-international armed conflicts, section (e) – drawing on additional Protocol II – criminalizes the displacement of the civilian population for reasons related to the conflict, but this is qualified by a reference to the security of the civilians or imperative military reasons.

Sexual offences – rape, sexual slavery, enforced prostitution, forced pregnancy, enforced sterilization, and any other form of sexual violence also constituting a serious violation of common Article 3 – are criminalized for non-international armed conflicts as well. Conscription or enlistment of children under the age of fifteen years into armed forces or groups or using them to participate actively in hostilities is criminalized (note that there is no mention of national armed forces for non-international armed conflicts, as in section (b)). Non-inclusion of any weapon, even poison gas, for non-international armed conflicts is unfortunate. The possibility remains, however, of considering the use of gas against any civilian population in any internal conflict – or even absent an armed conflict – as a crime against humanity.

Despite considerable pressure from some states, the Rome conference resisted attempts to raise the threshold for non-international armed conflicts to that contained in Article 1 (1) of additional Protocol II. Accepting such changes would have made these sections virtually ineffectual. Instead, section (f) repeats the already mentioned language of Article 1 (2) of Additional Protocol II and adds that paragraph (e) applies to armed conflicts that take place in the territory of a state when there is a protracted armed conflict between governmental authorities and organized armed groups, and – reflecting recent developments of the law – between such groups. The reference to protracted armed conflict was designed to give some satisfaction to those delegations that insisted on the incorporation of the higher threshold of applicability of Article 1 (1) of Additional Protocol II. Attempts to interpret protracted armed conflict as recognizing an additional high threshold of applicability should be resisted. The statement that nothing in the sections on non-international armed conflicts "shall affect the responsibility of a Government to maintain or re-establish law and order in the State or to defend the unity and territorial integrity of the State by all legitimate means" must not be interpreted as allowing any government to commit the offenses enumerated in these sections of the Statute.

The offenses stated in the Statute will be amplified by "elements of crimes" to be adopted by a two-thirds majority of the Assembly of States Parties, (Article 9). Such elements shall assist the Court in the interpretation and application of Articles 6, 7 and 8. They must be consistent with the Statute.

The definitions of crimes are now in place. It is up to the states to make them effective, punish violators and deter future crimes through both national prosecutions and prosecutions before the International Criminal Court when its Statute enters into effect.

Annex

U.N. Doc. A/CONF. 183/9 17 July 1998

Rome Statute of the International Criminal Court

Adopted by the United Nations Diplomatic Conference of Plenipotentiaries on the Establishment of an International Criminal Court on 17 July 1998.

Article 5
Crimes within the jurisdiction of the Court

1. The jurisdiction of the Court shall be limited to the most serious crimes of concern to the international community as a whole. The Court has jurisdiction in accordance with this Statute with respect to the following crimes:

    (a) The crime of genocide;
    (b) Crimes against humanity;
    (c) War crimes;
    (d) The crime of aggression.

2. The Court shall exercise jurisdiction over the crime of aggression once a provision is adopted in accordance with articles 121 and 123 defining the crime and setting out the conditions under which the Court shall exercise jurisdiction with respect to this crime. Such a provision shall be consistent with the relevant provisions of the Charter of the United Nations.

Article 6
Genocide

For the purpose of this Statute, "genocide" means any of the following acts committed with intent to destroy, in whole or in part, a national, ethnical, racial or religious group, as such:

(a) Killing members of the group;
(b) Causing serious bodily or mental harm to members of the group;

(c) Deliberately inflicting on the group conditions of life calculated to bring about its physical destruction in whole or in part;

(d) Imposing measures intended to prevent births within the group;

(e) Forcibly transferring children of the group to another group.

Article 7
Crimes against humanity

1. For the purpose of this Statute, "crime against humanity" means any of the following acts when committed as part of a widespread or systematic attack directed against any civilian population, with knowledge of the attack:

   (a) Murder;

   (b) Extermination;

   (c) Enslavement;

   (d) Deportation or forcible transfer of population;

   (e) Imprisonment or other severe deprivation of physical liberty in violation of fundamental rules of international law;

   (f) Torture;

   (g) Rape, sexual slavery, enforced prostitution, forced pregnancy, enforced sterilization, or any other form of sexual violence of comparable gravity;

   (h) Persecution against any identifiable group or collectivity on political, racial, national, ethnic, cultural, religious, gender as defined in paragraph 3, or other grounds that are universally recognized as impermissible under international law, in connection with any act referred to in this paragraph or any crime within the jurisdiction of the Court;

   (i) Enforced disappearance of persons;

   (j) The crime of apartheid;

   (k) Other inhumane acts of a similar character intentionally causing great suffering, or serious injury to body or to mental or physical health.

2. For the purpose of paragraph 1:

   (a) "Attack directed against any civilian population" means a course of conduct involving the multiple commission of acts referred to in paragraph 1 against any civilian population, pursuant to or in furtherance of a State or organizational policy to commit such attack;

(b) "Extermination" includes the intentional infliction of conditions of life, inter alia the deprivation of access to food and medicine, calculated to bring about the destruction of part of a population;

(c) "Enslavement" means the exercise of any or all of the powers attaching to the right of ownership over a person and includes the exercise of such power in the course of trafficking in persons, in particular women and children;

(d) "Deportation or forcible transfer of population" means forced displacement of the persons concerned by expulsion or other coercive acts from the area in which they are lawfully present, without grounds permitted under international law;

(e) "Torture" means the intentional infliction of severe pain or suffering, whether physical or mental, upon a person in the custody or under the control of the accused; except that torture shall not include pain or suffering arising only from, inherent in or incidental to, lawful sanctions;

(f) "Forced pregnancy" means the unlawful confinement, of a woman forcibly made pregnant, with the intent of affecting the ethnic composition of any population or carrying out other grave violations of international law. This definition shall not in any way be interpreted as affecting national laws relating to pregnancy;

(g) "Persecution" means the intentional and severe deprivation of fundamental rights contrary to international law by reason of the identity of the group or collectivity;

(h) "The crime of apartheid" means inhumane acts of a character similar to those referred to in paragraph 1, committed in the context of an institutionalized regime of systematic oppression and domination by one racial group over any other racial group or groups and committed with the intention of maintaining that regime;

(i) "Enforced disappearance of persons" means the arrest, detention or abduction of persons by, or with the authorization, support or acquiescence of, a State or a political organization, followed by a refusal to acknowledge that deprivation of freedom or to give information on the fate or whereabouts of those persons, with the intention of removing them from the protection of the law for a prolonged period of time.

3. For the purpose of this Statute, it is understood that the term "gender" refers to the two sexes, male and female, within the context of society. The term "gender" does not indicate any meaning different from the above.

Article 8
War crimes

1. The Court shall have jurisdiction in respect of war crimes in particular when committed as a part of a plan or policy or as part of a large-scale commission of such crimes.
2. For the purpose of this Statute, "war crimes" means:
   (a) Grave breaches of the Geneva Conventions of 12 August 1949, namely, any of the following acts against persons or property protected under the provisions of the relevant Geneva Convention:

      (i) Wilful killing;
      (ii) Torture or inhuman treatment, including biological experiments;
      (iii) Wilfully causing great suffering, or serious injury to body or health;
      (iv) Extensive destruction and appropriation of property, not justified by military necessity and carried out unlawfully and wantonly;
      (v) Compelling a prisoner of war or other protected person to serve in the forces of a hostile Power;
      (vi) Wilfully depriving a prisoner of war or other protected person of the rights of fair and regular trial;
      (vii) Unlawful deportation or transfer or unlawful confinement;
      (viii) Taking of hostages.

   (b) Other serious violations of the laws and customs applicable in international armed conflict, within the established framework of international law, namely, any of the following acts:

      (i) Intentionally directing attacks against the civilian population as such or against individual civilians not taking direct part in hostilities;
      (ii) Intentionally directing attacks against civilian objects, that is, objects which are not military objectives;
      (iii) Intentionally directing attacks against personnel, installations, material, units or vehicles involved in a humanitarian assistance or peacekeeping mission in accordance with the Charter of the United Nations, as long as they are entitled to the protection given to civilians or civilian objects under the international law of armed conflict;
      (iv) Intentionally launching an attack in the knowledge that such attack will cause incidental loss of life or injury to civilians or

damage to civilian objects or widespread, long-term and severe damage to the natural environment which would be clearly excessive in relation to the concrete and direct overall military advantage anticipated;

(v) Attacking or bombarding, by whatever means, towns, villages, dwellings or buildings which are undefended and which are not military objectives;

(vi) Killing or wounding a combatant who, having laid down his arms or having no longer means of defence, has surrendered at discretion;

(vii) Making improper use of a flag of truce, of the flag or of the military insignia and uniform of the enemy or of the United Nations, as well as of the distinctive emblems of the Geneva Conventions, resulting in death or serious personal injury;

(viii) The transfer, directly or indirectly, by the Occupying Power of parts of its own civilian population into the territory it occupies, or the deportation or transfer of all or parts of the population of the occupied territory within or outside this territory;

(ix) Intentionally directing attacks against buildings dedicated to religion, education, art, science or charitable purposes, historic monuments, hospitals and places where the sick and wounded are collected, provided they are not military objectives;

(x) Subjecting persons who are in the power of an adverse party to physical mutilation or to medical or scientific experiments of any kind which are neither justified by the medical, dental or hospital treatment of the person concerned nor carried out in his or her interest, and which cause death to or seriously endanger the health of such person or persons;

(xi) Killing or wounding treacherously individuals belonging to the hostile nation or army;

(xii) Declaring that no quarter will be given;

(xiii) Destroying or seizing the enemy's property unless such destruction or seizure be imperatively demanded by the necessities of war;

(xiv) Declaring abolished, suspended or inadmissible in a court of law the rights and actions of the nationals of the hostile party;

(xv) Compelling the nationals of the hostile party to take part in the operations of war directed against their own country, even if they were in the belligerent's service before the commencement of the war;

   (xvi) Pillaging a town or place, even when taken by assault;

  (xxiii) Employing poison or poisoned weapons;

 (xviii) Employing asphyxiating, poisonous or other gases, and all analogous liquids, materials or devices;

  (xix) Employing bullets which expand or flatten easily in the human body, such as bullets with a hard envelope which does not entirely cover the core or is pierced with incisions;

  (xx) Employing weapons, projectiles and material and methods of warfare which are of a nature to cause superfluous injury or unnecessary suffering or which are inherently indiscriminate in violation of the international law of armed conflict, provided that such weapons, projectiles and material and methods of warfare are the subject of a comprehensive prohibition and are included in an annex to this Statute, by an amendment in accordance with the relevant provisions set forth in articles 121 and 123;

  (xxi) Committing outrages upon personal dignity, in particular humiliating and degrading treatment;

  (xxii) Committing rape, sexual slavery, enforced prostitution, forced pregnancy, as defined in article 7, paragraph 2 (f), enforced sterilization, or any other form of sexual violence also constituting a grave breach of the Geneva Conventions;

 (xxiii) Intentionally directing attacks against buildings, material, medical units and transport, and personnel using the distinctive emblems of the Geneva Conventions in conformity with international law;

  (xxv) Intentionally using starvation of civilians as a method of warfare by depriving them of objects indispensable to their survival, including wilfully impeding relief supplies as provided for under the Geneva Conventions;

 (xxvi) Conscripting or enlisting children under the age of fifteen years into the national armed forces or using them to participate actively in hostilities.

(c) In the case of an armed conflict not of an international character, serious violations of article 3 common to the four Geneva Conventions of 12 August 1949, namely, any of the following acts committed against persons taking no active part in the hostilities, including members of armed forces who have laid down their arms and those placed hors de combat by sickness, wounds, detention or any other cause:

  (i) Violence to life and person, in particular murder of all kinds, mutilation, cruel treatment and torture;

    (ii) Committing outrages upon personal dignity, in particular humiliating and degrading treatment;

   (iii) Taking of hostages;

   (iv) The passing of sentences and the carrying out of executions without previous judgement pronounced by a regularly constituted court, affording all judicial guarantees which are generally recognized as indispensable.

(d) Paragraph 2 (c) applies to armed conflicts not of an international character and thus does not apply to situations of internal disturbances and tensions, such as riots, isolated and sporadic acts of violence or other acts of a similar nature.

(e) Other serious violations of the laws and customs applicable in armed conflicts not of an international character, within the established framework of international law, namely, any of the following acts:

    (i) Intentionally directing attacks against the civilian population as such or against individual civilians not taking direct part in hostilities;

   (ii) Intentionally directing attacks against buildings, material, medical units and transport, and personnel using the distinctive emblems of the Geneva Conventions in conformity with international law;

  (iii) Intentionally directing attacks against personnel, installations, material, units or vehicles involved in a humanitarian assistance or peacekeeping mission in accordance with the Charter of the United Nations, as long as they are entitled to the protection given to civilians or civilian objects under the law of armed conflict;

  (iv) Intentionally directing attacks against buildings dedicated to religion, education, art, science or charitable purposes, historic monuments, hospitals and places where the sick and wounded are collected, provided they are not military objectives;

   (v) Pillaging a town or place, even when taken by assault;

  (vi) Committing rape, sexual slavery, enforced prostitution, forced pregnancy, as defined in article 7, paragraph 2 (f), enforced sterilization, and any other form of sexual violence also constituting a serious violation of article 3 common to the four Geneva Conventions;

  (vii) Conscripting or enlisting children under the age of fifteen years into armed forces or groups or using them to participate actively in hostilities;

(viii) Ordering the displacement of the civilian population for reasons related to the conflict, unless the security of the civilians involved or imperative military reasons so demand;

(ix) Killing or wounding treacherously a combatant adversary;

(x) Declaring that no quarter will be given;

(xi) Subjecting persons who are in the power of another party to the conflict to physical mutilation or to medical or scientific experiments of any kind which are neither justified by the medical, dental or hospital treatment of the person concerned nor carried out in his or her interest, and which cause death to or seriously endanger the health of such person or persons;

(xii) Destroying or seizing the property of an adversary unless such destruction or seizure be imperatively demanded by the necessities of the conflict;

(f) Paragraph 2 (e) applies to armed conflicts not of an international character and thus does not apply to situations of internal disturbances and tensions, such as riots, isolated and sporadic acts of violence or other acts of a similar nature. It applies to armed conflicts that take place in the territory of a State when there is protracted armed conflict between governmental authorities and organized armed groups or between such groups.

3. Nothing in paragraphs 2 (c) and (d) shall affect the responsibility of a Government to maintain or re-establish law and order in the State or to defend the unity and territorial integrity of the State, by all legitimate means.

Index